Making Modern Mothers

The publisher gratefully acknowledges the generous contribution to this book provided by the General Endowment Fund of the University of California Press Associates.

Making Modern Mothers

Ethics and Family Planning in Urban Greece

HEATHER PAXSON

University of California Press

BERKELEY   LOS ANGELES   LONDON

University of California Press
Berkeley and Los Angeles, California

University of California Press, Ltd.
London, England

© 2004 by the Regents of the University of California

Library of Congress Cataloging-in-Publication Data

Paxson, Heather, 1968–
    Making modern mothers : ethics and family planning in urban Greece
/ Heather Paxson.
        p.   cm.
Includes bibliographical references and index.
    ISBN 0-520-22371-3 (cloth : alk. paper) —
ISBN 0-520-23820-6 (pbk. : alk. paper)
    1. Feminist anthropology–Greece–Athens.   2.
Women–Greece–Athens–Social conditions.   3.
Motherhood–Greece–Athens.   4. Birth control–Greece–Athens–Public
opinion.   5. Public opinion–Greece–Athens.   6. Athens (Greece)–
Social life and customs.   I. Title.
GN585.G85 P39   2003
305.42'09495'12—dc21   2003005046

Manufactured in the United States of America

11   10   09   08   07   06   05   04
10   9   8   7   6   5   4   3   2   1

The paper used in this publication is both acid-free and totally chlorine-
free (TCF). It meets the minimum requirements of ANSI/NISO Z39.48–1992
(R 1997) (Permanence of Paper).

Contents

Illustrations

Acknowledgments

The better part of my adult life has been taken up with the questions, thoughts, and conversations that have culminated in this book. Just as my field notebooks are littered with the scraps of letters to faraway friends, this manuscript contains for me memories of people I love and many more I wish I had come to know better. Their contributions to this book have been fundamental.

Upon my arrival in Athens, the unflappable staff and committed language instructors at the Athens Centre served as my welcoming committee. Eleni, Frosso, and Koralia exercised my Greek and validated my research plans; Dora Papaïoannou became a friend and confidant. Caroline Littell followed my life in Athens from that excruciatingly jet-lagged first week to the bittersweet end nearly two and a half years later, and she graciously lent me her flat when I returned during the scorching summer of 1998.

Many kind folk took time out from their busy schedules to guide me in Athens. I am especially indebted to the generosity and interest of Fotini Dimitiadou, Tasso Gaitani, George Kindis, Eftyhia Leontidou, Merope Michaeleli, Eleni Pambouki, and Haris Symeonidou. David Turner schooled me on Orthodox thought and practice. Chloe Dondos and Eurydice Spiropoulou helped me transcribe and translate interview tapes, often adding their own insightful commentary in parentheses. Dimitra Gefou-Madianou introduced me to the Department of Anthropology at Panteion University. With Marina Iossifides I enjoyed helpful expatriate anthropological conversations. Joanna Skilogianis, conducting related research toward her doctorate at Case Western University, was a source of support and inspiration. Nia Georges, Peter Loizos, and Ritsa Veltsai have been valuable interlocutors at various stages. I especially thank Michael Herzfeld for the generous help and encouragement he has provided me over the years since

I first met him in Athens, and for his meticulous reading of a draft of this volume.

Kathy Hall, my Pangrati flatmate, traveled with me to various islands and introduced me to the British School at Athens, which became my second base of operations. I am grateful to Guy Sanders, Ian Whitbread, and Penny Wilson for making me feel welcome in the library and beyond. I thank my friends at the BSA who shared with me a unique intellectual and social community: Roger Doonan, Louise Joyner, Seamus O'Buchala, Jonathan Tomlinson, Charles Watkinson, and Ruth Westgate. Michael Boyd kept me company into the wee hours of the morning as each of us encouraged the other's ethnographic and archaeological translations and interpretations. Katherine Alexander shared with me her memories and offered gentle advice. After breezing in and out of our lives in Athens, Wendy Walker rematerialized as my neighbor in New York City, where her convivial dinner parties saved me from my own writing.

My fieldwork was framed by reading, writing, and reflection in Palo Alto and San Francisco, California. The questions I took to the field, and the ways I came to make sense of my data back "home," crystallized under the astute guidance of my sympathetic and conscientious advisor, Jane F. Collier. At Stanford, Eva Prionas taught me Greek verbs and prepared me for living in Athens. Carol Delaney's "Creation and Procreation" course and Sylvia Yanagisako's "Gender and Kinship" seminar propelled much of my proposal writing; Carol and Sylvia also provided a useful critique of my dissertation. Many others have contributed to my thinking and phrasing since then, and their words are buried as deeply as layered archaeological fragments within this book. I thank for their collegial commentary and support Vincanne Adams, Katerina Akassoglu, Genevieve Bell, Amy Borovoy, George Collier, Sarah Franklin, Helen Gremillion, Sherine Hamdy, Aída Hernández Castillo, Marcia Inhorn, Gwynne Jenkins, Carina Johnson, Lynda Lane, Julia Olson, Michele Rivkin-Fish, Stacy Leigh Pigg, Sheila Ruth, Nikolai Ssorin-Chaikov, Mukund Subramanian, and Sue Visakowitz. The wisdom of Gail Kligman, Lynn Morgan, and Soheir Morsy, serving as discussants on conference panels in which I presented pieces of this research, has stuck with me and, I hope, sunk into subsequent writing. I am also beholden to the engagement and enthusiasm of my students in "Gender/Body/Ethics" and "Techniques of Gender," graduate seminars I taught at New York University while making revisions.

Marcy Dermansky, Erika Flesher, and Kamala Jain have moved in and out of my orbit over the past decade and more. Our shared stories of writing and relationships, our traded tips on juggling personal and professional lives, are not entirely dissimilar to the stories of Athenian women gathered in this book. I am grateful for these friends as I begin to imagine—one way or another—my own potential encounter with modern motherhood.

In 1975, my parents, Thomas and Judith Paxson, decided I would learn more with them living in Greece for three months than attending the final quarter of first grade. They bought me a Greek alphabet book, handed me books of classical mythology, and dragged me around innumerable archaeological sites. At age six I planned to become a classical archaeologist when I grew up; eighteen years later I returned to Greece, although to conduct ethnographic research. My parents were there again, visiting and lending me money when my grant expired before my list of research questions. Later, my father trained his exceedingly careful, professional eyes on the more philosophical portions of this manuscript. I cannot thank them enough. I am grateful too to my sisters, Jessica Paxson Joseph and Laura Paxson, for continuing to look out for me from afar. And I thank Mary and Gisbert Helmreich for making me feel at home.

At nearly every step of this project, from initial grant proposal writing to revising the final sentences of this manuscript, Stefan Helmreich has been at my side. For all he does to sustain me, I am ever thankful.

At the University of California Press, I thank my editor, Naomi Schneider, for her confidence that this book would eventually come into being. Jacqueline Volin and Bonita Hurd helped make it happen. Financial support for my fieldwork was provided by the National Science Foundation (SBR-9312633), the Department of Anthropology at Stanford University, and the Stanford University Center for European Studies. Dissertation writing was supported by the Foundation for Hellenic Studies, the Institute for International Studies at Stanford University, and a Mellon Dissertation Writeup Grant administered by the Stanford Department of Anthropology. I am grateful to the Modern Greek Studies Association for awarding my dissertation second place in its Biennial Dissertation Prize Competition (1998).

Epigraphs to chapter 2 are reproduced with permission:

Excerpt from *Children of Byzantium*, by Katherine Alexander, is reprinted with the permission of Cormorant Books and Katherine Alexander.

Excerpt from *God's Snake*, copyright © 1986 by Irini Spanidou, is reprinted with the permission of The Wylie Agency, Inc.

A Note on Transliteration

There is no consensus among scholars as to how modern Greek should be transliterated into English. I tried here to present words so that non-Greek speakers will be able more or less to pronounce them, and Greek speakers will be able to recognize them. Because the meaning and sound of some Greek words and prefixes will be already familiar to non-Greek speakers, my transliteration is not entirely consistent. I tried on occasion to preserve the familiar English spellings of borrowed prefixes: thus *polýteknes* (having many children), rather than *políteknes*. When quoting from English sources, I kept Greek transliterations as originally published: hence *both* Mestheneos and Mesteneos. Generally speaking, I used *dh* for δ (pronounced like the *th* in *the*) and *ks* for ξ, while χ became either *h* or *ch*, depending on which seemed more appropriate. Similarly, γ may be *y* or *g* or *gh*. The accent mark indicates emphasis. Personal and place-names are not made to conform to my transliteration system.

Prologue

VARNAVA SQUARE

Varnava Square is tucked into the narrow streets folded behind the Panathenaic stadium, which was carved out of white marble to host the first modern olympiad in 1896. Surrounding a cement fountain at its center, the square is lined with trees and wooden benches facing the automobile, bus, and moped traffic circulating perilously a few feet away. For more than two years in the middle 1990s, I lived a block and a half up the hill from here, in the residential area of Pangrati, which flanks the northeast side of the city's largest cemetery. A snack shop, a recently upscaled souvlaki joint, an ouzo bar, a pizza place, and a restaurant serving a rich midday meal of dishes baked in olive oil stand across the street but crowd their metal tables and plastic chairs onto Varnava Square's uneven concrete surfaces, extending, from across the road, territories invisibly mapped out. After the early morning crowd of coffee drinkers thins on a typical spring weekday, the square warms in relative quiet as the sun rises in a cloudless sky. Middle-aged women push baby strollers. Seriously silent men sit and smoke, drinking syrupy coffee. Black-clad widows huddle together on the street-view benches, trading gossip.

At midday, high school kids pass through on their way home for lunch. Some hang back to loiter in the square, looking tough in their big clompy boots, denim jackets, long hair, and self-assured poise—girls and boys alike. They queue at Yianni's *períptero* (kiosk) to use the rotary telephone, flipping pages of the latest teen magazines as they wait. Eighteen hours a day, one can purchase newspapers, political and pornographic magazines, cartons of juice and milk, five-hundred-milliliter cans of imported beer, cigarettes, packaged cookies, ice cream bars (in summer), toilet paper, tampons, aspirin, bus tickets, phone cards, and condoms from the *períptero*, this monument to Greek entrepreneurship.

In a few more hours, the younger kids take Varnava's center stage. Boys kick around a soccer ball; girls race about or chat happily in clusters. Kids, young kids, stay outside, seemingly unsupervised, long after dark. Occasionally some adult will call out for them to calm down. No one listens. The adult seems not to expect to be heard. In the afternoon (in Greece at this time of year, from 6 P.M., following siesta, until dusk or around half past eight), it is not uncommon to see a proud father taking over stroller duty or swinging a squealing child up in the air. Returning to Athens as an adult, I remembered that, when I first visited in 1975 as a six-year-old, I cultivated the habit when riding trolleys of cradling my chin in the palms of my hands: I had to protect my cheeks from the pinching fingers of enthusiastic women. At night, groups of friends and multigenerational families come to eat their evening meal in the open air and feed food scraps to the scrawny cats milling about under the tables. The adult world is inclusive of children, if not strictly family oriented. People talk and laugh aloud. Resinated wine stands in glass carafes on most tables. It is late now, nearing midnight. Children run out into the street. They torment the cats. No one complains.

1 Realizing Nature

Phoebe and I were sitting in the shade of a patio umbrella in the courtyard of the Athens school where she worked as an administrative assistant. Carefully sipping her iced coffee so as not to spill it on her immaculate linen blouse, Phoebe said to me:

> I believe that with having a child comes as well the fulfillment of the woman. You are completed as a woman. Now, to tell the truth, beyond all these things—you know, with the feminist movements and all that—you can't change your nature. The nature of a woman is to have children. We can't change this at all. The woman is completed having a child.[1]

With these words, Phoebe explained her passing comment to me that she "of course" would like to have children. She had never had a child during eight years of marriage because she and her former husband "couldn't communicate. I thought about what a problem it would be if we tried to raise a child together," she told me, "and so I decided not to have a child, consciously." Prior to working at the language school, Phoebe had held a variety of office jobs and for a short time owned a clothing boutique on Varnava Square in Pangrati. I had come to know Phoebe as an energetic forty-year-old woman who dressed fashionably, spoke fluent French and serviceable English, enjoyed her work, and had a wide circle of friends. Early on in my stay in Athens, I was intrigued that Phoebe, while asserting that women are *incomplete* if they do not become mothers, also believed she had acted responsibly in deciding not to bring a child into a troubled marriage.

Phoebe is not alone. Visitors to Greece—especially North Americans like myself—immediately impressed by the way Greek adults treat children with affection and regard, are surprised to learn that their country has one of the lowest birthrates in Europe. During the 1990s, Greek women of reproductive age had on average fewer than 1.4 children (compared with 2 in the United States). Athenians frequently draw negative comparisons between their country and the relatively burgeoning population of Greece's political foe and eastern neighbor, Turkey. Pronatalist nationalist rhetoric decrying Greece's "underfertility" is legion, voiced by official state sources, Greek Orthodox priests, and popular media. Yet while the praises of full-time motherhood and large families are frequently sung, Greek women are having, or expect to have, fewer children than they or anyone else would like.

Athenian women of Phoebe's generation were raised by parents who grew up in village or neighborhood communities where social personhood was established through active domestic, consanguineous, and spiritual kin relationships. Many, like Phoebe's mother, emigrated to the capital city from rural areas during or after World War II. According to popular and ethnographic accounts, women were awarded adult standing upon bringing forth their firstborn child, while spinsters, nuns, and other women who never birthed were considered social anomalies.[2] In this sense motherhood is said to have represented the purpose of a woman's life. Sitting together during her coffee break at work, Phoebe and I talked about how many things have changed over the last half century. Having owned a women's clothing boutique, Phoebe is aware of how mass media and tourism are continuously "modernizing" (modernízoun) Athenian standards for fashion and figures. The government, having eased previous restrictions on contraceptive access, established family planning clinics in select state hospitals. Phoebe told me that Harlequin romance novels in Greek translation were on sale at the supermarket down the street. Bourgeois models of romantic love are encouraging women to seek men who, as husbands, can be their friends as well as domestic partners. Everyday life is increasingly secularized. Perhaps most significantly, women have entered the waged workforce in significant numbers while the Greek economy has suffered under a devalued drachma and inflationary prices. More and more women, like Phoebe, watch their prime reproductive years pass while feeling they are unable to have a child: they cannot afford it without working, and for many women, earning an income has become important to their sense of self in ways that complicate their domestic relationships. How, in this context, was I to understand Phoebe's contention that her childlessness leaves her incomplete as a woman?

Thinking back to my earliest ethnographic encounter from the previous year added another wrinkle to Phoebe's idealized, seemingly elusive image of Greek motherhood. On a foggy June day in 1992, leaving Stanford University at the end of my second year of graduate school to study modern Greek and conduct preliminary research, I waited impatiently at the San Francisco airport to board a plane for Athens. Having previously visited as a tourist, I happily anticipated living in a residential neighborhood of the city, and I determined to distinguish myself from the sun-sea-sex-shopping set of tourists that flock each summer to experience the romance of Greece. Timidly, I shared these thoughts with a friendly looking woman seated beside me, who turned out to be a thirty-one-year-old Athenian academic taking a leave of absence from a California university to look after her ailing mother back home. Her first words on the subject of my proposed research—delivered in a tone intended both to stun and inform me—were: "Oh, we love abortion. Did you know?"

Since the 1980s, more pregnancies in Greece have resulted in abortion than in live birth, giving Greece what is purportedly the highest abortion rate in the European Union. Greek politicians, demographers, physicians, psychologists, and family planners have been puzzled by the seeming paradox of a child-centered society with low fertility—and moreover, by the fact that this dwindling fertility coexists with the lowest rate of oral contraceptive use in the European Union.[3] Taking United States and western European case studies as standards for comparison, Athenian professionals tend to make sense of a simultaneous appreciation of motherhood and the prevalence of abortion in Greece by arguing that reliance on abortion results from the tenacity of tradition. But where such professionals view cultural tradition as a static force impeding people's acceptance of biomedical lessons about the body and use of modern contraceptives, I see Athenians as being in the thick of ideational change, as morally and socially reevaluating their own and others' ideas about sexual and reproductive agency. In other words, if Athenians are not drastically changing their fertility control practices, I found that the ways they *think* about these practices are certainly shifting.

My first clue came from Phoebe, who, while detailing how things today were not what they were in the past, at the same time called on "nature" to forward her claim about motherhood: "The nature of a woman is to have children." What *is* this nature, I began to wonder, which Phoebe believes "we can't change," and yet which her own life experiences appear to challenge? She could be referring to biology, implying that having a uterus suggests that, since women make babies, all women *should* do so as a fact of life. Alternatively, might she be thinking of cosmological associations between divine creation and female procreation represented in Greek Orthodox iconography, implying that it is women's natural calling by God to give birth, just as Mary did? Or might her reference to nature point somewhere else altogether?

Through ethnographic fieldwork conducted in Athens primarily between 1993 and 1995, I have come to see urban Greeks—professionals and lay persons alike—redefining the nature that women should appropriately control or channel in order to have children and thus be "completed" as women. These transformations gradually became visible to me as I continued to meet middle-class women—single, married, divorced, with and without children—who echoed Phoebe's assurance that motherhood completes a woman. A couple of weeks after that early conversation, I met Niki Stavropoulou and her mother, Maria Stavropoulou (not their real names; here, as elsewhere, I use pseudonyms). Affirming her seventy-year-old mother's announcement that "all women want to become mothers," thirty-five-year-old Niki explained that, while often "there are economic problems so they decide not to do it, I believe that all women want to become mothers. How can I tell you? It completes them [tis oloklíróni]." This time, I was prepared. I pressed Niki, who was married and childless, asking, "But you are a woman now, you don't feel complete?"

> No, I do not feel complete, how do you say? Full [yemáti]. Simply, the child is a mission [proörismós], a goal [skopós]. That you have formed a new life. Apart from whether or not you will face problems—and how you will face these problems. I consider that this is the goal of the woman. [But] not only this; it's not the only thing, of course.

Talking with Daphne, an unmarried high school teacher and active feminist in her early thirties, helped me to recognize the significance of Niki's concluding sentence. Daphne pointed out that, while most middle-class Athenian women today wish to become mothers, and view motherhood as crucial to their self-regard as women, they talk about having children as a complicated goal, in explicit contrast to the single-minded purpose that motherhood purportedly posed for their mothers and grandmothers:

> For my mother's generation, I can say that becoming a mother was the purpose of a woman's life. But for the women my age or maybe younger—the modern woman, let's say—they work and they have a social life and they are involved with different activities. Maternity is something that could make you a whole woman. You complete the purpose of life. And I think especially here in Athens, in the cities, they accept you if you don't have a child; but they admire you more, they accept you more, if you are a working woman and you have your husband, your family, your house, and your children.

I came to discern a subtle yet crucial distinction between viewing mother-hood as that which invariably gives purpose to a woman's life—a view that Athenians now relegate to past generations or cultural tradition—and the modern woman's attitude that motherhood is a virtuous goal that she works to achieve. Significantly, this suggests that women are obligated to realize through their actions the nature that Phoebe claims "we can't change."

What does it mean, then, to suggest there is nothing we can do to change the maternal nature of a woman, and yet that "the woman is com-pleted" by doing what she needs to do to achieve motherhood? This seems, on the surface, to be a paradox, a contradiction. I argue here, however, that, for Greeks, human nature is not fixed but rather is realized through so-cially recognized activity. This affects how nature is called on in the forma-tion of women's identity. Indeed, this has implications for the relationship between nature and gender more generally—something suggested by the fact that the Greek language does not differentiate between sex—as a bio-logical given—and gender, the cultural elaboration of roles and values as-sociated with persons who are biologically sexed. Greek notions of a so-cially realized nature deeply affect how Athenians experience their bodies, their selves, and their persons as gendered.

How can we understand this? And how can we understand what it takes for women to realize their natures in a world characterized by changing social, economic, and political contexts? I explore such questions here through the lens of fertility control: contraception, abortion, in vitro fertil-ization, and other means of assisted conception. Practices of fertility con-trol lie at the heart of anxiety about falling birthrates in a climate of na-tionalist pronatalism, and they bring into focus the conjoined notion that motherhood completes a woman and imperative that a woman take re-sponsibility for being a good mother.

The present work, then, contributes, and is indebted, to what has be-come a commonplace understanding in anthropological and feminist schol-arship: conception, pregnancy, birth, and other aspects of human reproduc-tion are not immutable events given in nature but are understood through culturally specific meanings of gender, kinship, and procreation, and are re-alized through power-laden social relationships.[4] With this anthropological edict in mind, I explore how a local notion of realized nature in urban Greece is transforming as it accommodates imported technologies for con-traception and conception. We might inquire, for instance, into the *sub-stance* of the nature Phoebe sought to control to avoid becoming pregnant throughout eight years of marriage ("fortunately," she told me, she has had no "unpleasant surprises," that is, inopportune pregnancies). Did she work to regulate the "nature" of her *sexuality* (abstaining during her fertile days) or the "nature" of her *fertility* (by taking oral contraceptives or having an intrauterine device)? How might this affect Phoebe's sense of herself as a woman and potential mother? In short, this book tracks changes in the substance and meaning of the nature that Athenians call on to morally legitimate their actions.

In the United States and Britain, as anthropologists have noted, the ideology of women's reproductive choice, as well as contemporary fertility and reproductive technologies, is making the fact of gender's social construction ever more explicit (Ginsburg 1990; Strathern 1992a,b; Franklin 1993, 1997; Rapp 1999; Becker 2000). Understanding what is being made explicit, how, and what people do with such knowledge calls for cross-cultural comparison. In listening to personal, medical, academic, and political conversations among Athenians about contraception, abortion, and in vitro fertilization, we witness culturally distinctive negotiations of gender, family, nature, and citizenship. In an urban context of expanding market capitalism, bourgeois sensibilities, and European integration, these negotiations are carried out in a self-conscious idiom contrasting past and present, "traditional" and "modern," ways of thinking and doing. I explore the significance and repercussions of Greek notions of achieved motherhood and realized nature through the bifocal lens of cultural studies of modernity and feminist anthropology.

MAKING MODERN MOTHERS

During the 1980s, as Greece became incorporated into the European Economic Community, and as women were beginning to approach mothering as a project to be scheduled into their busy lives, women's increased public mobility in Greek cities was tempered by the designation of domestic duties as women's "proper" activities.[5] The non-wage-working woman, the stay-at-home mom, became a symbol of upward social mobility (Stamiris 1986, 104), although even she approached mothering less as an identity than as a project to raise successful children ready to compete in school examinations and in the marketplace. Few women could afford to stay home with their children. It became clear to me that by the middle 1990s Athenian women were commonly questioning and second-guessing what they could expect of their lives in the workforce, in motherhood, in romance. Over dinner one night with a friend, conversation took a predictable turn to the topic of romantic relationships: "From my perspective," Moira declared, alluding to her divorcée status and contrasting her forty years to my twenty-five, "it's more difficult for women today. Now that we [women] have the freedom to live on our own, more educational and occupational opportunities, the possibility to make independent choices—now we don't know what we want. No one knows how to live in today's society."

Attuned to such pleas a decade earlier, the Athenian social psychologist Mariella Doumanis, in her *Mothering in Greece: From Collectivism to Individualism* (1983), laments a loss of respect for women's efforts in householding and raising children, which was brought about by what she describes as a transition from a traditional agriculture-based society to a modern market-driven one. She writes, "As the traditional family group gave way to the sum of individuals we now call a family, the mother lost her traditional position as manager of the most sacred of institutions to become an attendant to the needs of each separate member of her family. Additionally, the modern way of life reinforced certain skills and attitudes that lead people, including mothers, into acting with no regard to relevance" (1983, 107). At the seminar "Birth and the Future," designed to educate obstetricians and midwives about the "psycho-social elements of birth and infancy," I met a psychologist who had studied with Doumanis and who expressed distress that "today motherhood does not seem to be lived as a fun experience. Women feel a lot of pressure regarding everything. They feel they have to perform as experts, and they feel they have to rely only on their own. They don't so easily ask other women to help them, to guide them. Mothering is not shared."[6] Women's domestic networks, stretched thin by urban migration and foreign emigration, have been partially replaced by expensive household appliances, how-to books like Aleka Sikaki-Douka's *Childbirth Is Love*, and periodicals such as *Parents: The Magazine for Those Who Create Life*.[7] If mothering is no longer shared, it is increasingly partitioned into a set of activities serviced by products and organized by the logic of consumption. By the late 1990s, it was not the stay-at-home mom who represented Athenian affluence but the career mom who employed an immigrant live-in nanny to raise her children.

Seeing urban women in the early 1980s "trying to meet all at once the requirements of the 'proper woman' as advertised by the mass media (mother, housewife, socialite, glamour girl, all in one)," Doumanis romanticizes the "old days," when women apparently knew and carried out clearly determined roles as mothers, as wives, as daughters and daughters-in-law (1983, 13). Modern women, she argues, face new insecurities and are compelled to seek out recognition in all areas of life, even as mothers. I too found that maternal behavior, apparently once taken for granted as a woman's destiny, is now being held up for approval and recognition. A woman's maternal nature, as Phoebe put it, must be proved. Personal choice or will is replacing fate or custom as the leading agent in Athenian women's reproductive narratives and also in the social analyses of Athenian academics and politicians. But contrary to Doumanis, I do not view recent changes as a replacement of old ways by new ones. Rather, I hear in Athenian women's life narratives attempts to make sense of continuous, inconsistent cultural change. One woman commented to me, "Things are a little muddled in the Greek family." If these days it is increasingly difficult for Athenian women to discern how to act as good mothers, wives, daughters, and daughters-in-law—and yet be "true" to themselves—this is not just a matter of having to address additional worries; rather, it signals a sense that women's very selves are changing.

More than in cataloging changes or continuities in what people are doing, I am interested in understanding social change at the level of how they think about themselves in relation to what they do. Wanting to reconcile transformations in people's practices over the past decades with their sense of what they do and why they do it, I describe the ongoing adoption and adaptation of newly modern subjectivities in urban Greece. Here my project is inspired by the work of Jane Collier (1986, 1997). Rather than follow Doumanis in casting modernity as the absence of tradition and vice versa, Collier draws on fieldwork spanning three decades in rural Andalusia to locate a political-economic distinction between traditional and modern subtraditions of the Enlightenment. In the 1960s, the Spanish villagers she visited voiced a traditional subjectivity concerned with upholding externally imposed social conventions; this makes sense, Collier argues, in agricultural settings where status and wealth are largely inherited. In the 1980s, villagers who were now engaged in waged labor and operating within a system of achieved status felt compelled to verbalize their inner thoughts and to realize personal desires. Refuting the view that modernity entails a proliferation of opportunities from which people must choose (cf. Giddens 1991), Collier concludes that it is not what people do but whether they see themselves as acting out their inner desires that represents the most significant determinant of modern subjectivity.

I too show how Greek women have acted, quite variously, in ways that make sense under different material and social circumstances. But unlike Collier and Doumanis—in part because I conducted fieldwork only in the 1990s—I do not describe the replacement of "older" beliefs and practices with a "newer" model so much as describe how Athenians understand their contemporary social world in reference to a selectively recollected past (Williams 1977, 115) or to a constellation of invented traditions. Modernity, in any case, never signals a clean break with the past. Attention to how people understand why they do what they do—attention to subjectivity—has also led me to conclude that if middle-class Athenian women feel whole in their womanhood only after birthing a child, or feel that without a child they are incomplete in their gender, this is *not* strictly a matter of reproducing as tradition the beliefs their mothers held. This is not a story of cultural survivalism. To view motherhood as an achievement is to impose new value judgments on how women go about becoming and being mothers. When motherhood is talked about as a personal achievement, it cannot be consistently taken for granted as an essential aspect of womanhood. And when motherhood is no longer taken for granted as part of female adulthood, the majority of Athenian women feel compelled to (at least try to) achieve motherhood in order to fully realize their womanly nature. Demonstrating to others that one is a *good* mother, a giving mother, is reorganized by new consumer demands. As spouses are renegotiating gendered household roles in the process of renegotiating work practices (Sutton 1986), they are thinking about the process of having children in newly deliberate ways.

Faye Ginsburg, tracing similar shifts in the United States to the post–World War II rearrangements of the gendered division of labor and the domestic and public spheres, writes, "As motherhood is being reframed as an achievement (rather than an ascribed status change) in the construction of female identity in American culture, so a general understanding of gender is shifting as well as the players themselves recognize (and make use of) its mutability" (1990, 72). Since modern ideals do not negate traditional virtues but indeed require and in some instances re-create what counts as tradition (Ivy 1995; Collier 1997), I intend to demonstrate how Athenians self-consciously, often wryly, make use of the tradition/modernity division to explain to themselves the contradictions they face within an historically specific instance of urban Greek modernity. Following Marilyn Strathern, I do not view change as a measure for continuity but rather try to see how each, change and continuity, "depends on the other to demonstrate its effect" (1992a, 3). The constitution of choice as a newly appropriate framework for guiding individual action simultaneously constructs fate as its historical opposition. If Greeks have never been modern, to borrow a phrase from Bruno Latour (1993), neither have they been fatalistic.

For some, the choices involved in having and raising children appear to be at odds with being a proper woman. One Athenian psychologist I interviewed went so far as to suggest that today womanhood is one thing, motherhood quite another. "Once you make the child," said Vaso Skopeta, who runs assertiveness training workshops for women, "you are not a woman anymore, you are a mother. A giving person."[8] "Good" mothers have always been giving persons in Greece, but only recently has this come into conflict with ideals for adult womanhood. Over the past couple decades—under the liberal influences of market capitalism, biomedical models of health and well-being, and policy reformulations required by the European Union and directed at gender equity—being a woman and being a mother have come to symbolize the paradoxically opposed poles of female adulthood. As modern *adults,* women are supposed to act independently, exercise reasoned decision making, and assume responsibility for their actions. But as adult *women* (which includes mothers or potential mothers), they are to subordinate their own interests to others', be swayed by emotion, and act cunningly. Some middle-class Athenian women—such as those few who seemed to rationalize to themselves as they explained to me that they employed other women to look after their children while they were "at work"—are even questioning whether it is possible today for a good woman to be a good mother, and vice versa. The ideals of gender and kinship, for women, are moving out of phase with one another. And yet, if motherhood is one thing and womanhood another, as Skopeta suggested, this strongly begs the question of why modern women, like Phoebe and Niki, continue to claim that motherhood completes a woman.

After living a couple of years in Athens, I came to read my friend Moira's uncertainty—"no one knows how to live in today's society"—as diagnostic of middle-class women's experiences in contemporary urban Greece. The freedom and choices to which she refers, the opportunities to pursue waged work and secondary education while employing fertility control (including abortion) to plan their families around such extradomestic activities, must be managed by women *responsibly.* Phoebe, further clarifying her comment that "of course" she would like to have a child, went on to muse, "[But] because our world isn't so good, too much is happening around us, you wonder, Is it right? Is it wise to bring a child into the world? What life will it have, what will it face in its life?" Freedom, as Moira and Phoebe seem acutely aware, does not mean that women can do whatever they wish—even if they know what they want. The responsibility of taking advantage of modern opportunities entails making the *right* choices. What those choices should be—what kinds of women, and mothers, should represent contemporary Greek modernity—have been subject to popular and legislative debate and constitute the subject of this book. It is here that we witness the making of modern mothers.

AN ETHICS OF GENDER

From my earliest interviews on, I saw that the question of how gender works in Athens—how people recognize and realize themselves as men and women, and how this relates to motherhood and fatherhood—requires an approach different from any anchored in Anglo-American cultural assumptions about sex, gender, and kinship. In this book, I theorize gender as a system of virtues, examining what it takes to be good (at being) women or men. My warrant is both ethnographic and theoretical. When Athenians speak of themselves and others as gendered individuals, they address the manner and extent to which their actions conform to social norms. And they describe social conformity, or custom, in ethical terms. The Greek word (both ancient and modern) for "custom" or "convention," *éthos,* provides the semantic root for *íthos,* usually translated as "moral virtue." The *Oxford Greek-English Learner's Dictionary* lists as translations for *íthos* both "morals, ethos, moral standards" and "manners and customs, ways of living."

A connection between virtuous and customary behavior was made explicit by Aristotle, for whom ethics concerned the socially orchestrated actualization of potentialities given us by nature. "None of the moral virtues," according to Aristotle, "arises in us by nature; for nothing that exists by nature can form a habit contrary to its nature. . . . Neither by nature, then, nor contrary to nature do the virtues arise in us; rather we are adapted by nature to receive them, and are made perfect by habit" (1947, 331). My introduction of Aristotelian ethics reflects my own attempts to understand what I saw in Athens, although it is true that urban Greeks read their classics in school and frequently use them to illustrate experience; more than one woman cited Plato in explaining to me about love and its multiple guises. It is appropriate here to draw on Aristotle, because the ethical system that underlies contemporary Greek cultural logic, supported by Orthodox Christian theology, is organized by an attitude that moral theorists term *naturalism.* Susan Parsons writes, "Under the influences of Aristotelian thinking, naturalism views the moral project as teleological, its *raison d'être* being to bring to fulfillment those features of our humanness which are present as potentialities within us and which constitute our uniqueness as human" (1987, 390). I understand that gender works in Greece in just such a way.

In contemporary Greece, *ánthropi* (human beings) are expected to realize gendered natures through activity appropriate to women or men, conforming to normative behavior learned through example. Writing of a Greek village, and drawing on fieldwork conducted in the 1960s, Juliet du Boulay brilliantly recognized this and describes it through the idiom of divine destiny:

> The people of Ambeli do not argue that gender characteristics are inherent in the biology of sexes; they argue from the gender characteristics themselves, with both men and women being understood to possess a "nature" and a "destiny" as a direct inheritance from their society. What I have called "destiny" is an ideal pattern that is prescribed a priori, while what I have called "nature" consists of the observed deviations from this destiny that answer to the pattern of temptation in daily life. The villagers themselves, however, do not use the terms "nature" or "destiny" but embody these concepts in images—on the one hand, of Adam and Eve, and on the other hand, of Christ and the Mother of God. (1986, 157)

According to du Boulay, both Eve and the Madonna are inevitable and therefore justifiable (to the villagers, presumably) components of the condition of womanhood. Through her appropriate action, the *moral* woman "transforms" Eve into the Mother of God; she recognizes and accepts her fallen nature but overcomes it by fulfilling her maternal destiny. In du Boulay's formulation (which calls to mind Phoebe's), the moral woman, the maternal woman, is also the true, complete woman. While the religious dictates described by du Boulay were not so audible in Athens in the 1990s, people still had to meet gendered expectations. As one young woman said to me while we were discussing reproductive decision making, "All one's actions and everything that one does, one does in the interest of what others will confirm about one's self." Lela, the thirty-four-year-old mother of a toddler son, offered this telling comment in an interview: "Boys and girls, I think, are just the same. Society is the one that makes the difference between them. We are all born the same in [the] hospital, and then we follow our own destiny."

What I think of as *gender proficiency* entails the ongoing, everyday public negotiation of moral proscriptions for being good at being a man or a woman. So although Greeks' descriptions of what constitutes femininity or masculinity might (and often do) refer to "natural" *(fisikí)* characteristics and capacities (e.g., for nurturing others or in exercising self-control), gender here is not simply mimetic of biological sex difference. Greeks do not popularly believe that biology is destiny so much as they view gender as a metaphysical category. Gender is metaphysical in that it requires the social actualization of certain virtues and relationships realized first in practice and second in the public recognition of that practice. A metaphysics of gender can be useful to think with more generally, for it avoids assuming a fixed nature on which culture merely elaborates (Yanagisako and Collier 1987; Strathern 1980, 1988; Fuss 1989; Butler 1989, 1993; Haraway 1991, 198; Moore 1993).[9] In practice, gender is a matter of moral responsibility, in Greece as elsewhere.

BEYOND HONOR AND SHAME
IN CONTEMPORARY GREECE

To students of Mediterranean and Middle Eastern ethnography, this argument will sound familiar. The well-rehearsed "honor and shame complex" that once purported to unify diverse societies of the Mediterranean into a single "culture area" depicted a cultural system in which a person's moral virtue and social repute were secured by the recognition of others that he or she had met established, strictly gendered behavioral norms (Campbell 1964; Peristiany 1966; Pitt-Rivers 1966; Abu-Lughod 1986; Gilmore 1987). According to this ideal typic model, one's honor must be recognized by public opinion because the community, and not the individual, is the custodian of social values (du Boulay 1974). Social repute depends so fully on social recognition that what is ethically important is less what one does than what people believe one does (Herzfeld 1985). In virtue-based ethical systems, moral character is built through the public recognition of proper behavior, and gossip and the threat of ridicule serve as significant forms of social control; a person of honor, one might say, is a person who does not get caught. Studies of honor and shame have been important for demonstrating how moral codes guide kin-based relations and how gender plays a determining role in wider social settings where individuals vie for status.

Most of these studies, however, sought gender relations and, hence, the foundations of moral systems primarily within domestic households, and so largely reduced femininity and masculinity to functionalist kin-based domestic duties (see also Cole 1991; Loizos and Papataxiarchis 1991b). Swayed by the local attribution of honor and shame to male and female natures, and arguably falling back on their own cultural assumptions about biological facts of life, these ethnographers' earlier analyses conflated gender with sex difference and described gender roles as fully distinct and harmoniously complementary. Codifications of honor and shame simplistically depicted society as a "seamless whole" (Coombe 1990, 224) and left little room to recognize, let alone account for, cultural change or any wider context, such as incorporation into a global economy of transient labor and diasporic migration (Jowkar 1986; Cowan 1990). Moving beyond such studies, I look at multiple, overlapping local articulations of global formations such as nationalism, biomedical models of well-being, and modernity, showing how Athenians variously make use of these in their personal narratives and professional analyses.

When people realize a gendered sense of self through ethical behavior, they take on multiple responsibilities loaded with moral and social implications that are very much subject to change. I show how middle-class Athenians are recasting the ethical system governing sexuality, procreation, and having children in light of economic, political, social, and biomedical transformations that have been building rapidly in Greece over the last decades. In thinking about how such changes have impacted the moral subjectivity of womanhood, I once again find helpful Aristotle, who was unwilling to give moral credit for involuntary acts. Aristotle describes moral virtue as a matter of choice entailing the exercise of reason. Virtue (and vice) are actualized through the means an individual chooses to reach an end. The end itself is given; it requires no deliberation and thus does not deserve to be credited with virtue. "A doctor," Aristotle points out, "does not deliberate whether he shall heal" his patient; a doctor *is* someone who heals patients—a *virtuous* doctor does so through courageous means (1947, 355). Similarly for the case of feminine gender identity in Greece today, a woman rarely deliberates over whether to become a mother (or more precisely, she is expected not to do so): motherhood completes a woman. But if motherhood is the "end" of womanhood, the choices a woman faces in realizing this—pertaining, for example, to the means of sexual and fertility control—*are* being visibly transformed and reevaluated.

In what follows, I examine how Athenians call on the moral stability of motherhood—as both social institution and daily experience (Rich 1986)—to lend equilibrium to contradictions inherent within local articulations of modern womanhood. Motherhood in Greece, with its iconic representation in the Panayía, or All Holy Mary, Mother of God, is an indisputable, absolute good. Motherhood is an idiom of morality, and such idioms, as Michael Herzfeld notes, benefit from "the semiotic illusion of invariance": the terms of what it takes to be a good mother, and the actual practices women follow to demonstrate that they are good at being women, are allowed amazingly free play under the justificatory banner of motherhood (1997a, 20). "The point to be emphasized," Herzfeld writes, "is not just that moral standing can be, and is, negotiated but that the negotiability of the identity in question is made possible by both the seeming fixity and the ac-tual lability of the terminology" (1997a, 46). Indeed, the women whose stories populate these pages claim, under specific conditions, that women having an abortion, not having an abortion, using contraception, not using contraception, having children, not having children, and employing in vitro fertilization all do so because they want to be good mothers. Under-standing gender as a system of virtues leads me to argue that mother-hood—at once an emblem of moral virtue, the validation of female adult-hood, and a metonym of the means of human generation appropriated by church and state—provides a stable signifier for the shifting terms of what it takes (according to a variety of sources) for a woman to realize and prop-erly demonstrate her womanly nature.

Thus my attention to virtue ethics as a cultural system through which gender is consolidated in Greece also follows the turn taken by feminist anthropologists to focus not on the assignation of gender roles (as in stud-ies of honor and shame) but on gendered practices. Such projects have adapted for gender Foucault's argument that modern discursive formations (psychological, medical, penal, etc.) construct various sexualities out of sexual practice. As Foucault (1990a) says about the emergence of modern understandings of sexual identity, recognized action has been grafted onto the actor so that that person "becomes" this set of actions; in this way sex-ual identity has been created out of sexual behavior. Although Foucault himself did not apply this to a discussion of gender difference, his insight has been crucial for feminism in demonstrating that sex—whether sexual activity, a biological category of difference, or the politically powerful conflation of the two—is not, after all, prior to culture. Sex cannot be an origin (e.g., for gender), for it is itself an effect of discursive and political-economic power (Moore 1993, 197; Vance 1984; Butler 1989, 1993; McNay 1992). As Teresa de Lauretis puts it, since "gender is the representation of a relation," the "representation of gender is its construction" (1987, 4–5). Anthropologists are particularly well positioned to follow up on this in-sight through our methodology of participant-observation and under-standing that, in matters of cultural expertise, no person's perspective is more authoritative than another. People represent—and thus generate—gender in the way they carry themselves, choose words and expressions, select clothing to wear, pursue occupations, and follow or transgress cul-tural prescriptions—in short, in both their deliberate and habitual move-ments in their daily lives.

Applying a practice approach (Ortner 1984; Collier and Yanagisako 1989) to gender in Greek cultural settings, Jane Cowan, echoing Aristotle and du Boulay, has written of dance as a practice through which "gender ideas and relations are *realized*—that is, comprehended and made real" (1990, 16). In his *Poetics of Manhood* (1985), Michael Herzfeld argues persuasively that, among Cretan men, masculinity does not describe a set of ideal characteristics and values that inhere in men; rather, men must demonstrate their ability to enact masculine characteristics and values, such as *eghoismós* (aggressive self-regard) and *filótimo* (social excellence). Masculinity, he concludes, depends less on "being a good man" than on "being *good at* being a man" (16). Herzfeld, Cowan, and Jill Dubisch (1995) all demonstrate that Greek claims to what I call gender proficiency (not gender identity) must be continuously proven and sustained over the course of one's life (see also Herzfeld 1986, 1991).

My work builds on this rich literature by suggesting that everyday practices constitute ethical choices, as well as by tracing partial, historical shifts in the ways urban Greeks conceive of themselves and others as virtuous—and gendered—subjects. In short, I propose applying practice theory to ethics. And because I see that claims to moral virtue hold together ideas about gender and kinship in Greece, I revise Herzfeld's formulation to explore the relationships among "being good at being a woman," "being a good woman," *and* "being a good mother." To do this, I consider virtues of femininity alongside masculinity, and expectations about mothering alongside those about fathering. And I look beyond changes in moral codes (e.g., women today are allowed comparatively free access to public spaces, and premarital sex is becoming more the norm than an exception) to acknowledge that ethical systems always involve more than agreed-upon sets of "values and rules of action that are recommended to individuals through the intermediary of various prescriptive agencies such as the family[,] . . . educational institutions, churches, and so forth" (Foucault 1990b, 25). After all, people may opt or be compelled to compromise moral codes or other norms in actual practice (Bourdieu 1977). Ethical systems always constitute a dynamic, dialectical relationship between socially approved moral norms and individual moral behavior.

The insight that, if one talks about moral conduct, one must also discuss the formation of the self as an ethical subject within specific contexts for action, was fundamental to ancient Greek ethics of any school. Modern ethics and moral theory, which are committed to normative rules that can be applied universally under objective conditions, dropped this connection. In *The Use of Pleasure*, Foucault revisits ancient Greek ethics to reestablish the link, advocating inquiry into how people act "in relation to the rules and values that are recommended to them" (1990b, 25). But in his discussion of the ethical self, Foucault once again undertheorizes the role of gender. I argue that, at least (but not exclusively) in contemporary Greece, the formation of the ethical self is at the same time the formation of the gendered self. Gender proficiency entails a kind of moral relationship with the body—one's own as well as others' bodies.

In arguing that concern for virtuous behavior and moral recognition contributes to the lived experience of gender difference, I am not setting out to describe—unlike studies of honor and shame or much of feminist moral theory (e.g., Gilligan 1982; Noddings 1984)—a feminine ethics that is essentially (by nature) or fundamentally (by social construction) different from a masculine ethics.[10] The ethics, or moral framework, I describe is a fundamental aspect of culture not segregated from economics, political economy, law, and other more recognizably "rational" social institutions. Therefore, a single ethical system based on the socially recognized realization of one's proper self applies to all persons. The philosopher Susan Parsons quips, "Morality is one, though it may be bisexual" (1987, 391). Women and men feel the burden of moral responsibility differently in Greece because gender ideology is voiced—and gender proficiency is realized—from the beginning through virtuous behavior. How one demonstrates one's virtue helps establish whether one is a man or woman, although ethical self-fashioning in Greece depends as well on one's age, social position, marital status, and with whom one is interacting. Some virtues are distinctively appropriate to *ándres* (men) or *yinékes* (women): aggressive self-regard *(eghoismós)* is a paradigmatic masculine principle (which women may strategically employ), while suffering and sacrifice are quintessential feminine virtues (which men might effectively assume). Other principles of moral virtue are shared by all persons as *ánthropi:* hospitality, self-mastery, and moderation constitute virtues for all, even if men and women are expected to demonstrate these virtues to different effect through different sorts of practices.[11] Ethics, the moral values and agreed-upon virtues of a society, is a major mechanism not only for subjectification, as Foucault demonstrates, but also for the consolidation and reproduction of social inequality, including that organized through gender.

In viewing ethics through the lens of cultural, rather than moral, relativism, I find it is not immediately troubling that the virtue ethics I describe for urban Greece reproduces gender inequalities. What Strathern says of gender, I say too of ethics: "Society is not constructed independently of gender and cannot in this sense be an explanatory context for it" (1988, 32). Furthermore, recognizing that "all societies are systems of inequality" does not only free us from having to explain the existence of inequality (trying not to fall back on natural preconditions) but further leads us to ask why social inequality, and its reproduction, "takes the qualitatively different forms it does," cross-culturally and transhistorically (Yanagisako and Collier 1987, 40). Anthropological investigation illuminates how the nature of *ánthropos* is never fixed, but is instead realized through historically contingent, socially recognized activity. Understanding gender as a system of virtues can better attune us to the ways agency and inequality are formulated, inhabited, and transformed in a fashion that does not require us to work within the essentialisms of either biological determinism or cultural constructivism.

In their introduction to *Naturalizing Power* (1995), Yanagisako and Delaney argue that nature legitimates power precisely through nature's assumed durability. But in Greece, because gendered nature encompasses character traits and moral dispositions as well as biology, the nature that is actualized as gender difference through virtuous behavior is not taken to be immutable—if it were, people would not be pressed to *do* anything with it. This marks a significant divergence from the nature Yanagisako and Delaney describe as a fixed substrate on which social identity is built and based (see also Strathern 1988). Motherhood completes a woman in Greece not because it actualizes some essentially female biological capacity but because, by demonstrating they can be good mothers, women assert their proficiency at being good *at being* women and at being *good* women—and they fulfill their part of a unwritten contract of social reproduction.

Although the nature at the heart of gendered formations that are organized around the realization of virtues (rather than the elaboration of biology) is more malleable and changeable, it is, however, no less a tool for legitimating power. Childless women in Greece can be treated as second-class citizens because, in failing to produce children, they may be regarded as individuals who have not lived up to a *social* duty. Here, a childless woman is not regarded as unnatural so much as morally irresponsible; less drastically, she is denied the social credit and support that other women, as mothers, receive. The psychologist Vaso Skopeta explained it this way: The childless woman "is incomplete. She hasn't completed her compassion circle—it's not a biological circle—but she is not complete." A woman's "compassion circle" encompasses her relationships with her parents, in-laws, siblings, children, friends, spouse, even coworkers, as well as with any potential children, for these relationships are all contingent. Skopeta's circle metaphor nicely captures the extent to which gendered identities in Greece may be viewed as consonant with biological nature but not determined by it.

A view of these dynamics as embedded in a system of virtues allows us to understand how nature can underwrite a variety of socially acceptable goals yet also provide people with legitimate excuses for not reaching these goals. There is room for some degree of self-fashioning within virtue-based ethical systems. This opens up possibilities for social change and political intervention. In pointing out such possibilities, my work engages the emancipatory projects of ethical feminism (McNay 1992; Cornell 1995; Gatens 1996; Parsons 2002) and radical humanism (Weeks 1995) aimed at propelling Western societies toward social egalitarianism. I reject the common criticism of a recent "turn to ethics" in literary and cultural studies as being apolitical (Garber et al. 2000). As ethics is inextricable from historical context, it cannot be untethered from political control or, for that matter, political struggle.[12]

I hope this book on contemporary urban Greece will be relevant to political and ethical discussion elsewhere by means of comparative analysis. In Greece, moral conflict is waged between alternative systems of virtue, directing attention to conceptions of self and body that are clearly gendered. In societies such as that of the United States, in contrast, ethical debates are generally carried out in the vocabulary of rules of conduct; this abstracts ethics from social relations and thus directs attention away from the lived self. Feminist psychologists and philosophers have suggested that moral thinking in Western settings is influenced by the gender of the moral agent, and they have stressed the need for moral theory to take gender into account (for reviews of this literature, see Parsons 1987; Jaggar 2000). My ethnographic data from Athens suggests a complementary thesis: that people's experiences as gendered beings are embedded in moral principles, and thus gender theory should take into account historically and culturally contingent ethical systems.[13] Viewing gender as a system of virtues also addresses people's motivations in acting as they do, a point often neglected by performance studies (see also Mahmood 2001). Does it not matter *why* people are compelled to perform in certain specific—and gendered—ways? Attention to how one forms oneself as an ethical subject can be instructive. People probably follow convention because they believe doing so is morally appropriate (Collier 1997); from this they not only gain prestige from their peers but also cultivate a sense of self-worth from feeling they "did the right thing." Conversely, they may doubt their self-worth if in retrospect they believe they made an inappropriate decision or in the end compromised too much. Debates about what constitutes moral conduct for women, and how their approaches to having children and regulating fertility enter into this, form the basis of this book and open an essential window on the changes unfolding in Athens today.

NAVIGATING TRADITION AND MODERNITY

When Athenians speak of a "traditional past" as distinct from a "modern present," or when they call out aspects of traditionalism that continue to flourish today, the terms appear saturated with self-orientalizing and self-occidentalizing images (Papagaroufali and Georges 1993). Indeed, I use the word *tradition* as a proxy for elements of local culture that insiders deem characteristic of Greece's "Eastern past," inclusive of Byzantine Christianity and Ottoman occupation. Because many of the old ways are traced to the Ottoman period and are today associated with rural peasants, those who display aspects of traditionalism run the risk of being pejoratively labeled "backward" *(íne lígho píso)* or "a little Eastern" *(lígho anatolítis)*, in the everyday parlance of middle-class Athenians. In comparison, *modernity* stands for local idioms that invoke Greece's "Western," or "European," destiny (Friedl 1962), and "modern" individuals are said to be relatively "mature" *(orimós)* in the global (or at least hemispherical) context of a family of nations over which such paternalistic powers as the United States and, increasingly, Germany preside. But at the same time, tradition is what makes Greece distinctively Greek and is therefore to be preserved and valued, if contained and deployed selectively. This sort of tension between political appeals to modernity and claims to cultural tradition was being felt by member states in the European Union at the end of the century, especially as presses were being set to mint a new, unified currency. A Greek representative on the Council of Europe said to me in a 1994 interview, "The conception throughout the European community is that the small places should keep their culture and their identity, but [should] feel European at the same time. And this is difficult to reconcile, but it is a goal for the future."

While this tension is by no means particular to Greece, there is a specificity to modern Greek claims to cultural tradition that must not be elided. Recalling that "the traditional/modern dichotomy is itself a product of modernity" (Collier 1997, 10; see also Dirks 1990) brings into focus how, in political speeches and everyday lives, Greeks can take umbrage at foreign doubts over their European status one moment and refer to a Europe quite distinct from Greece the next (Herzfeld 1992, 1987, 1997a; Sutton 1994, 1997). The difference is not merely one of political strategy but also entails a more profound indeterminacy in how contemporary Greeks cast themselves as subjects, or view themselves as individuals and groups in their own society and in the wider world. To understand the ambivalence with which many Greeks view the contemporary cultural and commercial symbols of continued foreign influence, it is instructive to hold in mind the nation's modern history. This history, beginning with Greece's emergence as a nation-state, reveals the fundamental role of international powers in shaping (and continuously reshaping) Greece as a democratic Balkan country and, later, a strategic NATO member. It also illuminates how dualistic stereotypes coexist as an "instrument and an effect of the peculiar circumstances under which Greece became an independent, modern nation-state" (Herzfeld 1992, 41, 1997a). Moreover, it accounts for the diversity of the "tradition" found for sale to locals and foreigners alike: plastic models of the classical Parthenon clutter the same shelves as faux-aged, painted Orthodox icons, both competing for attention with shiny, blue glass beads (ubiquitous too in Turkey and throughout the Middle East) to ward off the evil eye.

The Greek War of Independence in the 1820s, following four hundred years of rule by the Ottoman Empire, was instigated and largely financed by a Greek intelligentsia who, in German and British universities, picked up and adopted ancient ideals of Greek democracy distilled in Enlightenment philosophy (St. Clair 1972; Clogg 1992). The founding fathers of the modern nation-state that was forged in 1830 abruptly overlaid Byzantine cultural patterns—centered on the extended family—with liberal political institutions and Western legal codes based on individual rights (Pollis 1992)—and they did this under the watchful eye of the Great Powers of Russia, Britain, and France (Herzfeld 1987; Clogg 1992). The Greek Orthodox Church joined in the struggle for self-determination and national independence from the Ottoman Empire, and church and state today remain fraternal institutions (Pollis 1992; Dubisch 1995, 164–74). During the 1993 prime ministerial elections, a volunteer stationed in Pangrati Square, campaigning for the populist Pan-Hellenic Socialist Party, asserted to me, "The church is the state, for me." In forging the nation-state, "although names, concepts, and institutions were imported and imposed, and although conceptual and legal separations of state and society, private and public, honesty and virtue were inevitably introduced," Constantine Tsoucalas writes, "prevalent values, real practices and normative codes remained embedded in the traditional complexity of social relations" (1991, 11). The result, he adds, has been "cultural schizophrenia."

Since then, Europeans and North Americans have continuously reminded Greeks of their multiple personalities. Political pundits, journalists, and intellectuals have delighted in celebrating Greece's ancient past as the political and philosophical ancestor to the Enlightenment while simultaneously denigrating the modern Greek nation-state as ever-modernizing, held back by the lingering Eastern influence of Ottoman rule deemed responsible for visibly threading the fabric of everyday life with such "irrational" practices as patronage and clientelism (e.g., "Special Report on Greece," *The Economist* [22 May 1993]; Michas 1999). But again, the issue is not the degree to which Greeks and their social institutions are rational or modern but rather what kind of modernity they represent. When moral standards have centered not on the individual but on the community, this has set the stage for prescriptive civic morality, in which the morality of the individual consists in fulfilling the duties of one's social position.[14] Politically, this resulted in the adoption of legal positivism, according to which an individual's rights are to be given by the state, rather than seen to inhere naturally in individuals. Consequently, according to the political scientist Adamantia Pollis (1992, 174), "whereas tensions between the rights of the individual, the autonomy of civil society, and the claims of the state have been among the central concerns of western thought, in Greece the individual and his or her rights have been subordinated to the prior claims of the state owing to the transposition of traditional local Greek communalism to the nation—the *éthnos.*" Greeks view their state as the embodiment of the *éthnos,* and the state demands the exclusive loyalty of its citizens.

Trading on the discursive tensions of Greece's marginal European status, partisan politicians work both to rally patriotic support by upholding elements of Greek tradition and to appeal to the upwardly mobile electorate's aspirations for a more European modernity. So visibly is Greece caught between the constructed categories of East and West, tradition and modernity, that these are made the subject of everyday conversation and political contestation. In the 1970s, Andreas Papandreou, abandoning his position as chair of the Department of Economics at the University of California, Berkeley, returned to Athens to establish the Pan-Hellenic Socialist Party (PASOK) in response to what the left viewed as the right's selling out to Western corporate interests. The leader of the New Democracy Party, Constantine Karamanlis, propelled Greece into the European Economic Community in the late 1970s under the slogan "Greece belongs to the West"; the rival PASOK party has held contrarily that "Greece belongs to the Greeks." Most often, PASOK has represented the centripetal forces of Greek political culture; the New Democracy Party the centrifugal. Greece became a full member of the European Economic Community in the early 1980s, and by the mid-1990s Greece's European status at home was not so much a national question as a moral challenge posed to individuals.

ETHICS AND ORTHODOXY

Although Athenians by and large profess they are not very religious, either personally or as a people, the national religion represents perhaps the most revered, and dynamic, aspect of Byzantine tradition today. Orthodoxy is not revealed by weekly church attendance but permeates the everyday lives of practitioners in ways that are gendered and visible at two levels: the clearly ritual (weddings, baptisms, saints' days, and religious holidays) and the taken for granted (Panourgia 1995, 98; Dubisch 1995; du Boulay 1974; Just 1988; Hart 1992; Stewart 1991; Seremetakis 1991). As Dubisch suggests, Orthodox belief and practice is best viewed less as "a set of acts one performs, not only inevitably, but almost naturally (part of what Bourdieu has termed *habitus*)" (reference omitted; Dubisch 1995, 58). This can easily be sensed by an outsider riding a trolley as it passes a church: a good number of passengers will absentmindedly cross themselves without so much as a glance at the church, without missing a beat in conversation. For these believers, crossing oneself is as much a part of trolley riding as of Orthodox faith. In this sense Greek Orthodoxy, even among self-proclaimed agnostics, constitutes what Carol Delaney calls an "embracing context" as Orthodox belief and Greek cultural traditions have been mutually implicated in national identity formation (1991, 283). That the identity card which citizens were until recently required to carry listed one's religion as a personal vital statistic signifies the centrality of religion for Greek cultural and even political identity (see Pollis 1992, 182).[15]

Athenians frequently explained to me the role of the church in their everyday lives by contrasting it with Roman Catholicism; as one woman asserted, "We have no pope!" Another, talking about means of preventing pregnancy, told me, "The pope is strict. He only allows one or two things [i.e., the rhythm method and abstinence]. The Orthodox Church, they don't say anything. You must write this." In numerous interviews, the patriarch of Constantinople has condoned the use of prophylactics to prevent the spread of HIV, even addressing the European Union on this topic. On national television in 1993, Bartholomew of Constantinople confirmed that it was not up to priests to legislate what goes on in people's bedrooms. The church trusts people to make peace with their own sin, which is, according to Orthodox theology, inevitable to the human condition and therefore not translated into personal guilt.

Many points of theological difference distinguish Orthodoxy from Catholicism, marking the Eastern and Western routes that early Christianity took with regard to sin, morality, and how ethical questions are deliberated (Ware 1963; Meyendorff 1974). The place of self is located differently in these religious traditions, with post-Enlightenment Catholicism stressing the interiority of the self to be revealed through confession, and Byzantine Orthodoxy viewing the self as inherently relational to others. While ritual confession is an Orthodox sacrament, it does not play a punitive role in everyday religious practice; this is a key point in considering ethics. Because people conceive of selves in relation to others and are held morally responsible for acting in the collective interest, standards are internalized and moral authority is diffused.

In viewing the formation of the ethical self as a key site where people imagine contrasting subjectivities, name them "traditional" or "modern," and play them off one another, I draw a distinction between a Greek virtue-based ethics underwritten by Orthodox theology, and the ethic of liberalism based on epistemic objectivity. In the language of moral philosophy, Orthodox ethics is concomitant with the "external standard" and is based on the belief that we are who we are over time: morality is judged on the basis of one's character, on what the agent has done in the past and will likely do in the future. According to this characterological ethical orientation, compliance with socially and morally appropriate behavior is conceived not as a single act but as an established pattern of living. A single act can be out of character, but an established pattern of living *is* one's character. In practice, the privileging of appearance over what Enlightenment subjects would call authenticity often allows morally ambiguous behavior to go unchecked. Normative ethics, characteristic of Enlightenment moral theory in presupposing the autonomy of the will, tries to assess the rightness or wrongness of each discrete act without regard to the character of the agent, which is supposedly irrelevant in the determination of morality. Moral compliance is expected, but each act should also be accompanied by a personal justificatory narrative to demonstrate the rational control of choice. In the secularizing views of urban Greeks are revealed emerging tensions between, on the one hand, the traditional privileging of outer act over inner state, and on the other, the modern need to reveal one's inner motives and intentions. The convergence of these ethical systems largely constitutes what James Faubion terms "the Greek modern" (1993).

In suggesting that Greek notions of individualism and ethics are or have been somehow, at some level, different from Enlightenment ideals, I run the risk of being accused of orientalizing, of suggesting that Greeks are or have been in this sense more Eastern than Western. Observation of what Dubisch has dubbed "the issue of outer act versus inner state" has preoccupied anthropologists from the students of honor and shame onward (1995, 224), because the possibility that inner state is incidental to morality negates the fundamental assumptions of Enlightenment thought and modern morality. But in pointing out where Greeks "fail" to live up to Enlightenment ideals, I do not suggest that they cannot live up to them because they are too traditional, but rather that Enlightenment ideals are *themselves* contradictory and therefore unrealizable.[16] Here my insistence on Greece's "other," or "alternative," modernity (cf. Rabinow 1989; Gilroy 1993; Faubion 1993; Appadurai 1996; Ong 1996; Piot 1999; Rofel 1999) is meant as critique of my own culture. That social life entails some degree of emotional and social dependency on others has, for example, been demonstrated by North American feminist philosophers (Kittay 1999). Owing to Greece's ambiguous historical and cultural positioning with respect to the West, anthropologists have long pointed out that it presents an especially illuminating site at which to query aspects of modernity (Herzfeld 1987, 1997a, 1992; Faubion 1993; Sutton 1994; Panourgia 1995; Georges 1996b; Gefou-Madianou 1999). My project joins others in trying to rethink totalizing visions of what modernity has been and continues to be.

At the same time, Athenians frequently tried to clarify for me (and often for themselves, it seemed) what was distinctly Greek in comparison with the outside world. In the course of interviews, I was often asked, "Is it also like this in America?" I realized that I, a young, single woman working toward my doctorate degree, was widely perceived by the people I interviewed as representative of unquestionably modern culture; I stood for what many Athenians feel they have become or are becoming (see also Collier 1997). I came to expect such comparisons and often reassured Athenians that issues were confusing too for young women in America, and that I was curious to learn how the terms of our confusion might converge or diverge. In this sense too, my ethnography of urban Greece is, implicitly and by default, a comparative study. Throughout the book, my personal as well as analytic understanding of European-American personhood and cultural engagement serves as the ground against which I bring into focus urban Greek meanings and practices. This further reinforces my claim that the conflicted state of contemporary Greek civil society is a product of modernity *even as* it (apparently) fails to conform to the normative standards set by liberal political ideals.

FIELD SITE AND RESEARCH METHODS

Seeking to understand "the cultural meanings people realize through their practice of social relationships" (Yanagisako and Collier 1987, 40), I explored reproduction in a number of ethnographic contexts. After conducting preliminary fieldwork and studying Greek during the summer of 1992, I returned to Athens in the spring of 1993, staying through the summer of 1995. I interviewed gynecologists, midwives, psychologists, pharmacists, a European Union politician, family planning counselors, state-employed demographers, feminist activists, and a biologist who works in an in vitro fertilization clinic. To learn how imported family planning ideology is tailored and translated for an Athenian audience, I attended professional conferences where gynecologists debated clinical approaches to family planning, as well as two public symposia organized by the privately funded Family Planning Association of Greece to discuss the social and national impact of family planning. I studied brochures from the Family Planning Association and the Ministry of Health and Welfare; I pored over transcripts of the 1986 parliamentary debates over legalizing abortion. I sifted through pages and pages of legislation pertaining to family law, family planning, equality provisions for women, and family leave policy. I compiled demographic statistics and reviewed Greek psychological, sociological, and medical studies of abortion, contraception, and adolescent pregnancy. I also collected and read newspaper articles and magazine advertisements for popular representations of gender and sexuality. My first stage of research thus investigated the institutional framework within which reproductive practices unfold. This allowed me to understand the material conditions to which individuals would refer, or about which they might query me, in the course of personal interviews. And, since most professionals in Athens speak at least one foreign language, I was able to conduct several of my early interviews in English or a mixture of English and Greek, itself an interesting symptom of the hybrid reality urban Greeks now inhabit.

The second, overlapping phase of my research involved speaking with Athenians about their personal experiences of reproductive events and fertility control practices and collecting their opinions on everyday life in Athens. I found my first interviewees at the private school where I took several courses in modern Greek. Many of my classmates were foreign women who had partnered up with Greek men and entered extended Greek families. In 1992 I attended the Orthodox wedding of one of my instructors. Another teacher, Moira, became a supportive friend and imparted insightful cultural critique over many a bottle of Greek wine. A classmate referred me to her gynecologist, a feminist activist who became for me a key interlocutor. At the close of each open-ended interview conducted, I solicited additional names of people who might be willing and able to talk with me, gathering many telephone numbers in this way. (I cannot resist noting that obtaining a telephone number was only the beginning of gaining an interview. My telephone performed mysteriously. It never worked properly when it rained following a drought—dust on the aerial lines turned to mud and became caked, somehow preventing calls from going through. Meanwhile, heavily charged electric phone wires stuck out from my apartment's wall and required continuous maintenance with electrical tape. More than once, electric shock threw me to the marble floor as I attempted to rewire the telephone.) I loved living in Athens. This city had been for me the subject of countless childhood fantasies. At moments of disorientation and self-doubt, I could, when walking along, catch a glimpse of the Parthenon glittering atop its Acropolis, and a wave of self-assurance would wash over me. First brought to Greece as a six-year-old child by philhellene parents, I was not immune to classical romanticism. After a year, Athens came to be my home. Through circuitous chains of personal introductions, I gradually met people to interview.

In the end, tape recorder running, I formally interviewed thirty-eight women, some over the course of multiple meetings, about their reproductive histories, experiences with contraception, attitudes toward Greek family dynamics, hopes and hesitations about having children, opinions about abortion and state family policies, and the changing texture of everyday life in Athens.[17] On one occasion I interviewed a mother and daughter together; I also conducted joint interviews with three friends in their late twenties and another pair in their midtwenties. I found group interviews helpful because they let me hear people's critical as well as collaborative interactions, and because friends and family members often were more insistent than I in pushing interviewees to clarify their positions. Through the people I spoke with, I was introduced to a wide spectrum of middle-class Athenian lives.

The category of class in Greece is irreducible to a single element, be it economic or occupational security, education, or urban or cosmopolitan sensibility: all these play a role in consolidating class dispositions. It is tempting to offer a negative definition for the Athenian middle-classes, excluding from one end the trace elements of aristocracy, international businesspeople, and a foreign-educated intelligentsia (see Faubion 1993), and from the other end, the largely refugee population of the urban under- and working classes (see Hirschon 1989), who increasingly include migrant domestic workers and nannies (Lazaridis 2000). The middle-class women I interviewed are small-business owners, civil servants, and schoolteachers. Only two are, or have been, full-time homemakers. Many hold down two paying jobs. Because I interviewed a few physicians and psychologists both professionally and then on separate occasions personally, as women and (at times) mothers, my cross section of middle-class life is somewhat skewed toward the upper end, encompassing what Thomas Malaby has called Greece's "professional class" (2001, 5). But when it comes to values expressed regarding motherhood and having children, I discerned little systematic disagreement between wealthy professionals and bank tellers who have not studied beyond *gymnásio* (similar to British O levels, or about the tenth grade in the United States). Most of the thirty-eight women graduated from high school; nineteen earned college degrees and eleven of these earned or are working toward advanced degrees in Greece or abroad—a college degree in Athens is coming to represent what it does in the urban United States: a necessity for middle-class life, or what a high school degree meant twenty years ago.

The women I interviewed ranged in age from twenty to over seventy. They maintain close ties to their family village and count on yearly supplies of olives and oil from family lands. On Fridays they buy vegetables, fruit, and flowers fresh at the people's market *(laïkí aghorá)*, the weekly takeover of Archimidous Street by scores of farmers' stalls. They spend Easter week and the month of August in mountain villages or coastal towns. They are single, married, divorced. Unless otherwise indicated, I use pseudonyms. I give surnames to people I interviewed in their professional capacity. When I discuss the women I interviewed both professionally and personally, their personal stories appear under first-name pseudonyms different from their professional pseudonyms. Unless otherwise noted, interviews were conducted in Greek. I employed two bilingual students to help me transcribe and, on occasion, translate my interview tapes. The final translations are mine, and I take full responsibility for them.

With the exception of persons professionally engaged in reproductive issues (gynecologists, demographers, a theologian who had worked with the Ministry of Education and Religion, etc.), throughout this study I give voice primarily to women's experiences and perceptions. My strategy here is similar to Rayna Rapp's "women-centered" approach employed in her exemplary study (1999) of amniocentesis in New York City (see also Inhorn 1994).[18] "Because pregnancy and motherhood are culturally marked as such totalizing female responsibilities in the contemporary United

States," Rapp explains, "women's decisions surrounding prenatal testing take on a weight they might not have if the burdens were more widely and socially distributed" (308). Similarly in Greece, sexual restrictions, conception, pregnancy, birth limitation, child care, and now, increasingly, contraception are framed as primarily the responsibility and moral concern of women. Foregrounding women's experiences enables me to demonstrate that reproductive beliefs and practices are central to many of the most intimate and important issues facing contemporary Greece at every level of social political life: in claiming national identity, in pursuing medical care, going shopping, engaging in sexual relations, and entering into marriage and family life. In this context, the critical perspectives of women provide an especially clear vantage point from which to view a range of dynamics and contradictions constitutive of urban Greek modernity. The women I interviewed were not mere "informants" but were cultural critics themselves. My analysis often follows their lead.

Although I had intended to limit my personal interviews to the residents of a single neighborhood, I followed where my connections led me, which at times meant to outlying neighborhoods such as wealthy Kifisia and the more working-class Marousi. Still, the majority of the women I interviewed lived, as did I, in the solidly middle-class district of Pangrati, which fans out behind the Panathenaic Stadium to encompass Varnava Square and is within walking distance (for tourists if not locals) of the commercial and symbolic center of the city. The city center encompasses a triangle drawn by joining the points of Syntagma, Omonia, and Monastiraki Squares. Syntagma, the tourist center of Athens, is flanked on one side by the neoclassical Parliament building and on the other by the National Bank of Greece and a three-story, air-conditioned, marble-floored McDonald's. Parallel thoroughfares, Leofori Stadhiou and Eleftheriou Venizelou, run northwest from Syntagma to Omonia. The University of Athens sprawls midway between these two squares on Eleftheriou Venizelou, which is usually called Leoforos Panepistimiou (University Avenue). Omonia is a still-seedy although recently somewhat cleaned-up red-light district, today largely populated by Albanian refugees. Athinas, the street running south from Omonia to Monastiraki, is a major shopping destination that seems to propel one back in time. Family-owned and -operated shops sell assorted housewares, cheap clothing, salted fish, cured olives, and freshly baked bread. In 1975 the sponges were natural, from the Aegean; in 1995 they were a rainbow of pastels, 100 percent synthetic. Off Athinas shoots a small lane devoted to fabric stores. Turn right and every shop is filled with doorknobs. Turn left and you find lamps and light fixtures—in every store.

Off Monastiraki Square lies the ancient Agora, where Socrates loitered among the Athenian youths. From here a brisk twenty-minute walk takes one through the tourist area of Plaka at the base of the Acropolis, past the imposing columns of the Temple of Olympian Zeus, up behind the Pana-thenaic Stadium, and, skirting around the corner of the First Municipal Cemetery, to my old flat up the hill from Varnava Square in Pangrati. Pan-grati is one of the older residential areas in Athens proper, one that still has a neighborhood, or even village, feel to it. Many of its families have lived here for generations. Everyone addresses the white-haired man who sits in Varnava Square's *períptero* (kiosk) by his first name. Women shout across to each other from balcony to kitchen window, pitching their voices over the roar of motor scooters whizzing by below. Housing prices (for the pur-chase of flats) in Pangrati are among the most affordable in Athens.[19] In these modest apartments, a typical family (mother, father, one or maybe two children, and an optional grandparent) might live in three or four rooms. In this neighborhood I conducted the majority of my interviews, with women in their homes.

A Woman-Centered Analysis and Reproductive Agency

The stories people tell about fertility, fertility control, and questions con-cerning having children convey assumptions about what it takes to be good women and men and, thus, to be good at being women and men. But sto-ries of fertility control and having children convey wider messages, too, messages that often use women's and men's fertility to comment on the well-being or weakness of a population or nation (Pfeffer 1993, 4). Politi-cal-economic and demographic theories in the twentieth century desig-nated the birthrate as a key signifier of a nation's economic and political status in a global family of nations. In the 1960s, nations began to be ranked by intended family size, "so that intended fertility became 'a fea-ture of the national heritage in the same way as the flag, defence of the homeland, respect for the law and so forth. It now represents the number of children the nation wants'" (Borgeois-Pichat 1983, 234, quoted in Pfef-fer 1993, 23). My argument runs counter to the language of demographic transition, in which the increased consciousness among Athenians in thinking (twice) about having children self-evidently articulates with the nation's declining fertility and trend toward smaller families, providing empirical evidence of Greece's modernization.

Steeped in Malthusian ideas, demographic transition theory was devel-oped in the 1930s to account for and rationalize a decline in fertility across western Europe starting in the late nineteenth century. It upheld fertility decline as an evolutionary stage through which all nations must pass if they were to become modern industrialized societies (Pfeffer 1993, 22–24). Defined against a traditional, or agrarian, model, in which small families and a subsequent fertility decline signaled poverty and population weakness, the lower fertility of modern economies came to indicate a nation's wealth, higher standard of living, heightened rational consciousness, and maturity of its people. So clearly synonymous had the radical reduction of annual birthrates across western Europe become with social and economic modernization that such modernizing forces as urbanization and industrialization lost their explanatory power to account for the fertility decline: the fertility decline helped define this periodization in the first place (Saporiti 1989).

Rather than try to isolate one ideational or economic aspect as the primary cause of fertility decline, I find it more valuable to think in terms of a shift in the kind of agency people assume in directing their sexual and reproductive lives.[20] In following how women have pictured themselves as active subjects in regulating their fertility while working to realize their "destiny" as mothers—or in explaining why this has not happened—I talk about changes in the *kinds* of control, not in the *amount* of control, people exercise in directing their reproductive lives. Insofar as motherhood in contemporary urban Greece is ideologically portrayed as a chosen identity, a focus on kinds of reproductive agency begs the question of choice. Throughout their life courses, people face an array of reproductive choices over which they have varying control: whether or not to become a parent at all; what techniques and technologies to employ (and who will employ them); what cultural norms to follow or challenge; what social identities or roles to forge in the process of becoming a parent or being an adult without children; and how to be a good parent, including consideration of family size, economic resources, time management, and marital and other relationships. At the same time, social, economic, religious, medical, political, and other pressures impinge on the choices of everyday life. As Rayna Rapp writes, "Broad demographic, sexual, reproductive (and nonreproductive) patterns are ultimately *social* patterns, contextualized by the rationalities of class, race, ethnicity, sex, religious background, family, and reproductive history, and not simply by individual 'risks and benefits'" (1991, 385). For women and men who wish to become mothers and fathers but never will—owing to early divorce, never marrying, economic hardship, low fertility, or some physiological problem—the notion of reproductive choice can seem a cruelly unfulfilled promise.

Contrary to the tenets of modernization theory, then, I argue that women's increased consciousness or articulation of fertility control issues amid an expanded array of technological options does not increase their agency. In fact, the following chapters demonstrate how the symbolic trappings and ethical expectations of modernity translate into increasing conflict and contradiction for many women. The changes in women's reproductive agency that I track reflect people's ongoing, if at times ambivalent and partial, adoption of modern sensibilities (if not practices) and ways of positioning themselves as moral subjects.

Competing Ethics of Womanhood

Of signal importance in the anthropology of modernity has been attention to the gendered valences of rational thought and modern social institutions (Strathern 1992a; Collier 1997; Abu-Lughod 1998; Stivens 1998; Rofel 1999; Schein 1999). I have noted that, when Athenians critically evaluate their society's and personal claims to modernity, they hold themselves in an uneasy tension between orientalizing and occidentalizing stereotypes; since oriental and occidental images are symbolically coded feminine and masculine, respectively (Said 1978; Herzfeld 1986, 1997a), looking directly through the lens of gender can give us insight into local modern logic. Family size, reproductive strategies, and gendered practices figure importantly in these discussions. While many Athenians today tout contraceptive responsibility as an important measure of modern mentalities (cf. Kanaaneh 2000), there is no consensus on how such mentalities develop, or on what they actually entail. For example, an Athenian woman might view herself as a modern person, choosing for herself a future guided by relatively autonomous considerations, but on occasion employ what she considers to be traditional means (including the aid of other people) to get there.

Abortion, widely considered a common, and therefore rather unremarkable, means of birth limitation, has recently been labeled by medical professionals, politicians, and lay women as backward: from a biomedical perspective, abortion might express a woman's ignorance of effective female-controlled contraception (such as the pill or IUD). But abortion can also be justified as an effective means of achieving modern, liberated femininity insofar as it can be employed to reject the notion of motherhood as a woman's exclusive occupation, initiated "when God wills it." In addition, some middle-class Athenian women, as we shall see, strategically map the oriental/occidental division onto a political battle between Greek forms of patriarchy (marked oriental and backward) and feminism (deemed occidental and progressive) (Papagaroufali and Georges 1993). This situation defies analytical attempts at differentiating between two types of person, those who remain traditional and others who become modern. Athenians, in their inconsistent identification of what counts as traditional or modern—and in believing that they ought to act by choice yet live in a world governed by a fixity of givens—themselves reveal, often quite consciously, fissures in the supposedly totalizing ideal of Western modernity.

I expose such fissures by following how middle-class Athenians in the mid-1990s described three major, if partial and overlapping, shifts in how women's virtue and reproductive capacity are ideally related to one another as articulated through "proper" attitudes toward motherhood and fertility control. These shifts, which correspond roughly to the past three generations of women to reach reproductive age, have been precipitated by numerous factors: fluctuating economic conditions, legalized abortion and gender equity legislation, urbanization, an increase in women's waged labor, the influence of Western media, the medical modernization of childbirth and contraception, nationalist concern over a declining population growth rate, awareness of HIV and AIDS, and the introduction of in vitro fertilization and other reproductive technologies. I track such changes as material and conceptual processes through which Athenian women see themselves becoming (ever newly) modern women, and I examine the moral conflicts this creates for modern mothers and potential mothers. For purposes of abbreviation, I distinguish these shifts in terms of an *ethic of service,* an *ethic of choice,* and an *ethic of well-being.* I frame these as ethics in keeping with my view of gender as a system of virtues, and of subjectivity as realized through public recognition of appropriate action.

Ethic of Service.   When Athenians learned that I intended to write about them, many were generously forthcoming with unsolicited, often helpful advice. In addition to "Tell them about the church," another frequently offered suggestion was "Start with the war." As when Daphne spoke of her mother's generation, from a contemporary perspective "tradition" is imagined to have flourished until World War II and the subsequent Greek Civil War; this is the point of departure for many narratives of social change. I was told, for instance, that "before the war" and shortly thereafter, "the husband was the master" of the family, and women "were always under" the control of men. A woman's virtuous behavior, say in offering customary hospitality, was depicted as an extension of her husband's social excellence (Herzfeld 1985, 136). Women's primary concern in demonstrating virtue involved guarding their chastity, thus protecting the repute of the family and proving themselves to be good daughters, wives, and mothers. Women's virtue, then, has been *in service* of men: "It is the women's willingness to behave chastely, modestly, and becomingly that is a prime necessity for the maintenance of men's self-esteem" (Friedl 1967, 108). Similarly, Herzfeld writes of a Cretan woman's hospitality that "her actions in this regard are viewed as a metonymical extension of her husband's *eghoismos* as a host, as are her verbal duels in defense of her home and her marital patrigroup" (1985, 136).

Furthermore, the traditionally internalized and externally enforced regulation of female chastity codes, the conceptual equating of sex with procreation, and the notion that birthing legitimates female sexuality, all indicate that reproduction has been significant in Greek culture not only for continuing family lines but also for *making mothers*.[21] Motherhood redeemed female sexuality and accorded women adult status under what I call an ethic of service. The narratives of this generation of women (and the narratives of younger women relating the lives of their mothers and grandmothers from this era) feature tales of maternal suffering and sacrifice, and fate looms large in their (post hoc) justificatory appeals. Because premarital sex (or rather, sex before engagement) was seemingly rare, married women had babies when and as often as "God brought them." Supposedly unnecessary, abortion before the war was an exceptional occurrence, immoral in the eyes of local priests (Comninos 1988). But in the wake of World War II and the Greek Civil War, married women faced with postwar dislocation and poverty suddenly, and in large numbers, "discovered" abortion as a means of family limitation. They incorporated abortion into an ethic of service by which women were morally required first and foremost to serve their families as wives and mothers. In not having children that they could not afford to raise properly, these women demonstrated—through abortion—that they were good mothers. Abortion in this economic and ethical context did not itself pose a threat to women's virtue.

Ethic of Choice. The children of parents who came of age during the wars—just a few years older, perhaps, than the United States' baby boom generation—grew up benefiting from parental sacrifices and a gradually mending economy. Many were given educational and economic opportunities their parents never had. Some who came of age in the 1960s and 1970s participated as well in new social opportunities afforded by wage work and, more controversially, by liberation from prescriptions against nonmarital sexual relations. The 1980s brought the liberalization of legislation pertaining to women's reproductive rights and labor opportunities, as mandated by European Economic Community directives. But with increased choice and the promise of autonomy comes increased responsibility, and women who grew up in the wake of the wars describe their lives as series of compromises, contradictions, and hidden agendas. The most salient theme in these women's narratives is their awakened consciousness surrounding reproductive events and the responsibility of choice. Under an emergent ethic of choice, women's virtues of service and sacrifice are weighed against newly available virtues of self-determination and autonomy. Women I talked with described two significant shifts in reproductive practices and women's relationship to motherhood, the first occurring during the war and the second really gaining momentum in the 1970s and 1980s. The attitudes of young women in the 1990s were characterized more by an openness to talking about such issues than by any change in how they thought about issues themselves. The premise that people must actively realize their gendered natures underlies an ethical continuity between what Athenians might describe as traditional and modern moments. The analytical and cultural question, as already noted, concerns the substance and meaning of this nature.

Ethic of Well-Being.   In recent years, the increased availability of technologically advanced biomedical care has introduced a normative ethical system to the realm of reproductive decision making and to the question of gender proficiency. Interestingly, the third shift in reproductive attitudes and gendered values I describe does not correlate with the current generation of young women so much as with a certain set of professional opinions and practices. The third shift is incomplete, ongoing, and promulgated through the institutionalization of such Western ideologies and technologies as preventative health care, safe sex, female-based medical contraceptives, prenatal ultrasound imaging, and in vitro fertilization. Technology transfer entails the translation of ethical frameworks encoding instructions for the proper use of technology. Childbirth and pregnancy have been medicalized in Greece for decades (Arnold 1985; Lefkarites 1992), inculcating the idea that a good mother must be a *healthy* mother (Oaks 2001). Newly modern women are encouraged to follow an ethic of well-being, prioritizing their own mental and physical health before others' needs and expectations. And they are expected to do this by adopting a liberal understanding of rational morality that "relies on the belief that each of us is capable of transcendent consciousness" (Parsons 1987, 384). In this view, abortion has been newly coded by professionals as an aspect of Greek cultural tradition that is amoral insofar as it has been practiced without regard for the potential harm it can render to a woman's body. Nationalist government officials have picked up this medical warning, condemning women's recourse to repeat abortions for causing secondary sterility, which they hold partially accountable for Greece's plummeting birthrate. In this way state officials have been led to advocate newly modern models of womanhood that tout women's supposed autonomy and liberation, but that ultimately compound their reproductive accountability.

SCHEME OF THE BOOK

The Greek word for history, *istoría*, also means story, reminding us that the telling of history is always the telling of particular stories (Herzfeld 1987; Dubisch 1995). The stories told to me were, of course, selected by others from entire lifetimes of experiences as they saw fit to present them to an unmarried American who looked to be barely in her twenties. The following chapters are my stories, the end result of efforts to create a co-herent narrative from the data I collected in Athens and carried back with me to San Francisco and, later, to Santa Cruz and Manhattan, where this book was written. I have selected from my notes the stories that best illus-trate the making of modern mothers in urban Greece.

On the basis of my interviews with Athenian women, and drawing on the ethnographic literature of rural Greece, in chapter 2 I trace material, ideational, and ethical shifts in what Athenian women have been expected to do in order to demonstrate gender proficiency and be good mothers. Alongside this, I track changing family strategies within a secularizing context of increased labor market participation, consumerist dispositions, and medical means of fertility control. I also draw from these narratives local critiques of modernity and patriarchy that emerge from the confluence of an ethic of service and an ethic of choice for women.

In chapter 3, I relate the history of abortion and family planning as told by Greek professionals who work in medicine, psychology, and demogra-phy. Family planning was introduced to Greece as a "means of modernity" (Appadurai 1996); I demonstrate how its ideology and methodology join other development projects in encouraging modern subjects who "think for themselves" to view social conventions, morality, religion, and custom as impediments to the rational realization of personal desires and self-preservation. I critique the gender neutrality embedded in family planning ideology, and examine how women accustomed to viewing abortion in terms of an ethic of service receive family planning's attendant ethic of well-being.[22]

Chapter 4 looks at how nationalist-minded politicians, accepting the rationalizing promises of family planning, have tried to adopt family planning as a means of pronatal population policy. In critically evaluating Greek population and family policy, I draw from meetings I attended of the Athens chapter of the European Forum of Left Feminists as well as from public symposia organized by the privately funded Family Planning Association to address the "demographic problem."

I return in chapter 5 to the notion of realized nature and I take up the question of what happens to a local metaphysics of gender and kinship when it encounters the imported medical technology of in vitro fertilization. This brings me, finally, to an account of why women like Phoebe and Niki, who have made conscious, if reluctant, decisions not to have children, still insist that motherhood completes a woman.

2 Remaking Mothers

*From an Ethic of Service
to an Ethic of Choice*

"My dear Thanassi, 'innocence' is a creed like the Immaculate
Conception," said Grandpa. "You believe in one, you certainly
must believe in the other. Sex exerts its influence from the cradle
to the grave. To call sex a sin is to think life a travesty and make
hypocrisy a pleasure. I'd rather, like the ancients, believe in virtue.
Virtue is proven, not bargained for with some priest."

IRINI SPANIDOU, *God's Snake*

She had been so certain all these years that babies came into this
world or left it as a result of the will of God, and that even if a
person didn't understand why God gave babies to some women
and not to others, it was something that was never questioned. You
prayed and hoped, and then left it up to God.

KATHERINE ALEXANDER, *Children of Byzantium*

Couples consciously decide to have a child. That is, the cases when
some child comes without you wanting it or without you knowing
it have decreased. A couple these days consciously decides to have a
baby.

PHOEBE, forty-year-old administrative assistant

The word *teknopiía*—from *tékno* (child, offspring) and the verb stem *pió*
(to make or do) can be rendered in English as "the making of children." Its
sense is semantic, generalizing the specific action of "to have a child," *káno
pedhí*, to a cultural abstraction. When Greeks talk about *teknopiía*, they
refer to socially appropriate contexts and strategies for bringing a child
into the world and, at the same time, comment on how having children (or
not) affects one's life, one's relationships, and one's sense of self. *Teknopiía*
unfolds in an ethical context, one that embraces and shapes gender as a socially ascribed and institutionally reinforced category of difference as-

sumed by persons as a matter of moral responsibility. I trace transformations in this ethical frame by addressing the sources of obligations Athenian women face in being good mothers and proper women, and the ways women address themselves to such obligations.

In depicting changing ideas about *teknopiía*, Athenians frequently voice a narrative of increased "consciousness." "In the past," women told me, people "didn't think" about having children. What I, following middle-class Athenians, gloss as a "traditional" approach to procreation is eloquently expressed in the second epigraph to this chapter. In Katherine Alexander's 1987 account of a teenage Greek woman's emigration to Canada during the early part of the twentieth century, her fictional protagonist, Eleni, states that having babies is largely a matter of God's will. This humble attitude toward fertility control corresponds to a sense that motherhood constitutes the purpose of being a woman. Today, when motherhood is depicted as a goal that women must achieve, my friend Phoebe states in contrast in the third epigraph that Athenians consciously decide to have children. As an idiom of human will replaces that of God's will in women's reproductive narratives, contemporary Athenians perceive reproductive agency differently than did their mothers and grandmothers.

Soula, a thirty-nine-year-old clerk and mother of a young child, put it to me this way:

> I believe that in the past they had children, they had a lot of children, and they *just happened* without planning it, without so much consideration. Today I believe young people are *thinking hard* about it, and they have children consciously—that is, they *know why* they are having children, what a child means for them. [Emphasis added]

Not only do people today make conscious decisions about family size, they (are supposed to) act to achieve this desired outcome through premeditated fertility control. And they explicitly contrast this with an early modern ethic—what Athenians label as traditionally Greek—that demands compliance with convention without expecting individuals to question their motives for a particular act: the knowledge that one's duty is conventional is reason enough. Contemporary modern ethics, which prompted Soula's comment, takes a more inward-looking view of subjectivity and asks that people at least consider, consciously, the individual reasons behind their actions. Women should "know why" they have children, presupposing they understand "what a child means for them" personally—not just as "a woman," or even as a Greek woman. To be properly self-attentive women, modern mothers must demonstrate an authentic desire for children and actively pursue that desire in achieving motherhood. This reflects a widely perceived shift in an ethics of gender for women, what I depict as a shift from an ethic of service to an ethic of choice.

The pointedly vague "then" and "now" language with which Athenians talk about social change obscures ongoing transformations best traced over a succession of historical periods. These continue to mark the ever-shifting relationship between continuity and change linking memories of everyday life under German occupation and during civil war to the increasingly "European" present. In this chapter, I focus primarily on how Athenians talk about two shifts: the first occurred after the war era (circa the 1950s), and the second, during the late 1970s and 1980s, a period that witnessed intense national political and ideological debates, as well as Greece's entry into the European Economic Community. The history I provide as context for women's narratives is told from the perspective of those I spoke with in the middle 1990s. My intent here is to portray how middle-class Athenians engage in the invention of tradition, specifically regarding family and household relations, in order to define and justify their own reproductive decisions as well as to measure and evaluate wider cultural change in their society. In talking about ongoing reorientations of Greek modernity, I am not tracing any progressive march of modernization. The ethic of service said to have flourished before the war has not disappeared; it has been overlaid with an ethic of choice. "Old" and "new" attitudes and ethics fold in on one another, even as each is called on to explain everyday life.

"IN THE PAST": AN ETHIC OF SERVICE

Agricultural life prevailed in all but the most urban areas in the past to which Athenians today refer when they draw on collective memories of the first half of the twentieth century. These were socially conservative times. Leading up to Greece's engagement in World War II, General Ionnes Metaxas presided over a paternalistic, authoritarian dictatorship that appropriated the symbols of both classical paganism and Byzantine Christianity; borrowing from the Third Reich, Metaxas dubbed modern Greece the Third Hellenic Civilization (Clogg 1992).[1] For women during, and in the wake of, the war era, the virtue of self-control was central to an ethic of service that directed one's behavior toward family members and patriarchal institutions.

Accepting God's Will: Virtues of Self-Control and Service to Realize Feminine Nature

The moral concerns of a proper Greek woman in the past revolved around her sexuality.[2] Did she carry herself modestly? Was she chaste until marriage and then faithful to her husband? As John Campbell writes in his classic ethnography of the Sarakatsani shepherds of northern Greece, "The consequences of sensuality . . . destroy the integrity and honour of the family. Sensuality . . . threatens to undermine this institution from within. It must, therefore, be disciplined by all the strength and will of each man and woman" (1964, 326). Lela, a thirty-four-year-old Athenian native who worked for the National Electric Company, described to me the ethical codes of her mother's and grandmother's generations:

> For a woman, it was moral *[ithikí] not* to go out, even just to the corner. To have a date with a boy was immoral—to be seen just walking along the road with some man, some boy, someone of the opposite sex. This is what ethics *[íthos]* meant for women, not men. Only for women was this the ethic. The man *had* to go with a woman [sexually] by a certain age, to show his manhood.[3] The woman simply had to be guarded so that no man approached her. This was so until a few years ago. Slowly, the issue of ethics is falling away, but I think that this isn't happening in Greek society as quickly as in other countries. Especially in the countryside, because there you have fewer people and everyone knows everyone else. In Athens there are so many people that you might not even know the neighbor across from you; no one knows you, so you can do what you want.

Under the Greek ethic Lela described, the substance of the nature women must be seen to have mastery over includes, prominently, their sensuality.[4] But while women are enjoined to control their sexuality ("to be guarded"), a man is seen as not as capable (or in need) of such control (du Boulay 1974, 1986; Hirschon 1978; Cowan 1990, 201). Whereas men's sexual needs are ideologically incontestable and insatiable, women can wait. It was left to women to keep themselves out of the reach of "naturally" agitated men, who were told that prolonged abstinence could result in serious physical and mental consequences, even insanity, and so were honor bound, as Lela intimated, to attempt seduction at every opportunity (although they were equally honor bound to retreat if the object of desire were unwilling; Hirschon 1978; du Boulay 1986; Zinovieff 1991). This kind of ethical-gender ideology appears throughout the Mediterranean world; I suggest that what has been overgeneralized as the honor and shame system is helpfully viewed, at least in the Greek context, as an ethic that reflects an Aristotelian sense of nature: an innate capacity for self-actualization that is gender specific in its terms. Under the ethic of service, Greek women have been bound to actualize their natures as self-controlling. In this way women served the community by preserving the social institutions of female chastity and paternity as absolute goods that reflect a woman's moral character and serve the repute of her family.

As suggested by Irini Spanidou's fictional protagonist in the first epigraph of this chapter, Greeks themselves have widely articulated this view of human sexual nature in the terms of Orthodox Christianity. Greek Orthodoxy regards sensuality as a sin categorically relegated to original sin (Campbell 1964). Inherited by humans after the sin of Adam and Eve, sensuality is an inevitable part of the human condition and thus only partially within the reach of individual will: it is something to acknowledge and master, but not condemn. Therefore, and unlike Protestant Christianity with its attempts to suppress sensuality at every turn, Orthodoxy does not hold individuals morally culpable for the expression of sensuality, although people are expected to endeavor to control it. Because, in keeping with Aristotelian ethics, women are seen to have more choice in the matter of managing their sexual impulses, chastity is far more central to the realization of women's virtue than abstinence is to men's virtue. Just as Eve is blamed for Adam's fall, the notion of original sin places the moral burden for the eruption of sensuality in daily life primarily on women (Campbell 1964, 327).

Ethically, as Lela further pointed out, it mattered less what a woman actually did than what others assumed she did. The axiom of an ethical system based on established moral character—that a person of honor is a person who does not get caught—finds as its corollary that a person discovered in a compromising position is thereby compromised. A woman's Edenic inheritance from Eve, her "passive" sexual orientation, and her anatomy perceived as vulnerable, all seemingly opened not only her body but also her entire household to foreign penetration.[5] Thus she was kept closely tethered to the home, unable to move freely in the public world of men (du Boulay 1974; Hirschon 1978). Her very presence in the streets, unchaperoned, would lead neighbors to the inevitable conclusion that she must be a woman of the road, or prostitute.[6]

Through socially restricting men's sexual access to women (and vice versa), the symbolic and physical confinement of women has further served to limit conception and birth to the socially appropriate context of marriage. In midcentury Greece, a girl's parents would strictly chaperone her courtship, although unmarried couples who had "promised" themselves to each other were in some regions allowed to share a bed in the woman's natal home, with the bedroom door respectably left open. Prior to 1983, the Greek Civic Code stated that "only the child who had been born in marriage was calculated to be 'legitimate' and indeed comprised the foundation of the *ikoyénia* and the aim of marriage" (Koumantou 1985, 242). Orthodoxy reinforces the equation between marriage and *teknopiía* (the making of children). Until the 1980s reforms undertaken by PASOK, an Orthodox wedding was the only legally recognized means of marriage in Greece. At one point in the centuries-old Orthodox wedding liturgy, the priest likens the bride to Sarah and the groom to Abraham, an Old Testament couple whose ambiguous marriage (they were half siblings and long infertile) was eventually validated by God's willing Sarah to become pregnant. As Sarah's pregnancy was most explicitly an act of God, Orthodoxy suggests here that women are to become mothers in marriage not because they want it, but because *God* wants it. A childless marriage in Greece has hardly constituted a "real" marriage; divorce, legally available on demand by either husband or wife only since 1981, has long been condoned by church and state following a couple's failed attempt to be (procreatively) "successful" in marriage (Ware 1963). The bond of marriage, unbreakable even by death (Stewart 1991, 68), is not complete until husband and wife become, as father and mother, "one flesh" in the body of their child (cf. Schneider 1968; du Boulay 1984; Iossifides 1991, 139).[7] Orthodoxy figures *teknopiía*, the making of children, as a matter of divine service, not as a personal choice.

Symbolically, the regulation of female sexuality through monogamous marriage is important not only for conferring legitimacy but also to ensure the tracking of paternity. Under Greek law, paternity is implied by the legal marriage of the mother: whoever is married to the woman who births a child is that child's father. Recognizing the legal and symbolic significance of paternity throughout monotheistic cultures, Carol Delaney argues that, within so-called honor and shame societies, a woman's value is based "not so much on her fertility, her intrinsic nature, but on whether she is able to guarantee the security of a man's seed" (1987, 39).[8] In Greece, a woman's social value and moral virtue has thus depended on wedded motherhood, women's properly realized nature, or what du Boulay (1974, 1986) calls women's destiny.

Traditionally, women realized their womanly nature through active, recognized service to God, to men (particularly fathers and husbands), to children and households, and most evidently during World War II, to the *éthnos,* the Greek nation and people. Their greatest service was through *teknopiía,* the making of children. Pregnancy was expected of a new bride and welcomed when it occurred.[9] If pregnancy did not soon follow a wedding, a bride could be looked on with suspicion or, eventually, pity. "It is only with the birth of children, especially males," writes Marina Iossifides of a northern village, "that the new wife begins to be recognized as a member of the house, for she is now attached to her husband's *ikoyenia* [family] through the children she has borne" (1991, 140). In villages where patrilocal residence was practiced, daughters-in-law were accepted by powerful mothers-in-law *(petherádhes)* when they successfully produced a child—extra laurels were bestowed on the mother if that child proved to be a son. Muriel Dimen summarizes the kin-based foundation of an ethic of service: "Women begin as daughters, attain adulthood only as daughters-in-law, get no satisfaction until they are mothers of sons, and become powerful only when they are mothers-in-law" (1986, 64).

Still, women are not depicted here as authors of procreation, but rather as its disciplined vehicles (in other contexts, see Corea 1985; Delaney 1986, 1991; Rothman 1986; Inhorn; 1994, 1996). Artemis, a schoolteacher in her forties, recalled to me that "in the past" people regarded children as a gift of God, and procreation as a matter of God's will: "In the villages, most of the children, they just come. You know. It was okay. It doesn't matter—one, two, three. They may not have had bread for everyone, but they did it because God sent them. I speak about now about half a century ago." Especially before World War II, when knowledge and practice of biomedical care were virtually unknown in rural areas (Blum and Blum 1965; Arnold 1985), people in Greece widely understood procreation as a divine mystery in which nonhuman forces could, and often did, intervene (Stewart 1991).[10] A theory of procreation that does not expect conception or gestation to conform to the whims of human desire pushes the site of women's reproductive agency to the realm of *social* control: sexual relations, rather than biological fertility, are figured as the appropriate, effectual site of human intervention. Restrictive sexual codes organized by an ethic of service to limit sexual intercourse to the socially appropriate context of marriage or engagement serve as a major means of reproductive control. Describing the process of procreation as a divine mystery has never rendered women powerless to direct their sexuality or even fertility (McLaren 1984). Women have exercised control, for instance, by encouraging fertility through serving foods with purported aphrodisiac qualities and ingesting herbs designed to increase fertility. And birthing was certainly limited or spaced through human intervention prior to the possibility or after the fact of conception.

When people did engage in premarital (and marital) heterosexual activity, they could seek out a host of home-brewed contraceptives and abortifacients said to bring on menstruation, which have long been known to midwives and practitioners of practical medicine, *praktiká* (Blum and Blum 1965; Arnold 1985; Riddle 1992). Eleni, a feminist publisher in her sixties, proudly told me of her husband's mother who in 1904 received a midwifery diploma.[11] Eleni once overheard this *maía* (midwife) explain to Eleni's own daughters, the midwife's granddaughters, how to fashion a barrier method of contraception:

> She explained how you take a small piece of sponge—natural, of course—douse it in lemon juice, tie it to a string, and insert it into the vagina. It was effective, as effective as today's sponge. I didn't know that! I think contraception has been around since women made the connection between making love and having children. My husband's mother had three children, and I don't think she had an abortion; maybe she did. And with all her children, her *maía* was her mother.

The most widespread method of preventing pregnancy in Greece, according to my acquaintances and confirmed by national studies (Agrafiotis et al. 1990a; Symeonidou 1990; Apostolopoulou 1994; Emke-Poulopoulou 1994), has been and continues to be what is commonly referred to as "being careful." This category can include withdrawal, called *trávigma* (pulling out), as well as following one's menstrual cycle and avoiding intercourse on the more "dangerous" days (called "counting" or "paying attention"). Women do not exercise full control over these methods. Their success depends on the regularity of a woman's menstrual cycle as well as the willing cooperation and agility of her male partner—and on the tone of her relationship with this man.

Under circumstances where pregnancy was clearly unacceptable, for instance when a couple was neither married nor engaged, or was older and already had nearly grown children, men for the most part have tried to cooperate in contraceptive precautions. Writing about Tuscany, Germaine Greer (1984) suggests that men may view their prowess in the art of withdrawal as a point of honor, the distinction of an adroit lover; my sense from talking with Athenian women is that this can be said too of many Greek men (on Sicily, see Schneider and Schneider 1995).[12] Juliet du Boulay confirms that "in Greece . . . the honor of the men is in fact closely bound up with the value of not approaching a woman against her will" (1986, 156). That men are usually responsive to women's volition outside marriage is suggested by the strikingly low number of reported extramarital births: only 1.3 percent of all births before the war (and before abortion was routinely practiced),[13] 1.1 percent in 1961, and 1.2 percent the following decade (Siampos 1975, 342). Within marriage, however, conjugal relations are customarily (and, until recently, legally) a man's God-given right.[14] Du Boulay has commented that, in a Viotian village in the 1960s, it was not uncommon for men to have sex with sleeping wives tired out from a day's labor (1986, 151). A woman in her late twenties told me that her mother talked about a friend who had had five abortions "because this woman's husband 'wasn't nice.' "

Within an ethic of service, when reproductive agency was properly exercised, through social means (by regulating sexual activity), the burden of sexual and reproductive accountability was ultimately collective. "A man of God may win an individual and inward control over the condition of sensuality, but ordinary men need the help of kinsmen and the support of institutions in the unequal fight," writes Campbell (1964, 326). So, too, ordinary women were seen to require the help of kin and the support of institutions to protect their chastity before marriage. Responsibility was not solely shouldered by women. At the same time, if God gave a woman a husband who "wasn't nice," she could—and indeed, should—attempt to correct for his moral weakness with her own moral strength. Although abortion seems to have been infrequently practiced before 1950 (Comninos 1988), during the 1950s, as I discuss below, Greek wives began turning to abortion in rapidly increasing numbers.

Household-Based Economies and the Sexual Ethics of Femininity and Family

Attending to the social and economic significance of family and household within the agricultural settings of midcentury Greek life provides important context for understanding *why* Greek women's gender proficiency has been assessed in terms of self-regulated sexuality. This ground has been well covered by feminist anthropologists. Ernestine Friedl (1962, 1967) and Jane Collier (1986, 1997) have argued from a political-economic perspective that the regulation of female sexuality in ensuring paternity is important for securing paths of inheritance. I build on their work by tracing a gradual transformation in Greek approaches to *teknopiía* during the last century, and by framing women's gender proficiency as the ethical demonstration of self-control directed at the service of God, the honor of one's family, and the reproduction of patriarchy.

In early modern Greece, as in other agricultural areas of early modern Europe, dominant sexual ethics and the institution of marriage domesticated women's sexual desire, accepting only that which was heterosexual and in conformity to a "procreative ethic" (Katz 1990, 13; see also Abelove 1992). Three score years ago, when people "just had" children, the majority of the populace lived on rural properties, engaging in mostly self-sufficient economies. Athens was less an urban metropolis than a semiurban sprawl of two-story homes surrounded by cultivated gardens (Panourgia 1995; Gefou-Madianou 1992). In the outer suburbs and beyond, vegetable gardens provided the mainstays of seasonal dishes, and people pressed their own olive oil, fermented their own retsina wine, and cultured feta cheese from the milk of their goats. City dwellers regularly visited rural family homes to stock up on such staples. Large families were advantageous, expected, and for the most part, possible (see appendix 1 for total fertility rates in the twentieth century).[15] Multiple children were desired in part as insurance against high rates of infant and childhood mortality.[16] Thus the "classic Greek family," according to ethnographic accounts and the recollections of older Athenians, developed in relation to agricultural production: the reason to succeed economically was to provide the next generation with at least the same amount of land and assets; the practical reason to have children was to increase the number of hands available to work the land, tend the stock, and expand the family holdings.

In agricultural communities such as those that prevailed in Greece until the 1970s, the primary mechanism of reckoning status and transmitting wealth has been through inheritance (Friedl 1962; du Boulay 1983). A man can leave property to his children only if he knows who those children are, hence the concern for female chastity and women's marital fidelity. Patrimonial or matrimonial land, olive groves, vineyards, and sheep herds were divided among children equally by law. In most areas, daughters were handed their inheritance at marriage in the form of *rúha* (the bedding, tablecloths, embroidery, and clothing that a girl prepared for her betrothal) and dowry proper, or *príka* (often cash for an apartment in Athens if not a portion of the family property). Sons had to wait for outright ownership of their inheritance until the death of the family patriarch, although they worked on and benefited from these lands—and endeavored to expand them—throughout their adult lives. A couple rich in lands, but which had no children, was considered impoverished (Friedl 1962, 18).

The word *ikoyénia*, which can be rendered as "family" in that it refers to a unit of persons related by blood or marriage and who share affective bonds, derives from the ancient Greek *oikos*, "house," and *yeniá*, "birth" or "generation" (du Boulay 1986, 141; Iossifides 1991, 137). The family is expected to rejuvenate "the house" (and in some regions, to regenerate the patronymic [Herzfeld 1985]) through the procreation of new generations *and* by household production. "Maternity must not be seen only in relationship to children," Jill Dubisch notes, "but also in connection with the general duties regarding the maintenance of the house, which is not only the seat of family life but also a metaphor for family" (1995, 209).

In this regard my friend Katherine's experience in her position in Athenian society as Greek-Canadian, as *kséni*—a foreign woman with civilizing potential—is instructive. When she married an Athenian in the early 1960s, her mother-in-law greeted her with wary skepticism. To her *pethéra*, Katherine was a loose *kséni* who had lived alone without her family—suspicious indeed. After a year of marriage and, more significantly, after demonstrating that she was a good mother to her infant son, Katherine was eventually accepted and even loved by her in-laws. She told me:

> I think what happened was that I proved to her I was a good mother. This was the thing, you see, for a Greek woman. They think of *ksénes* as being sort of—look, you live alone, you're flibbertigibbet—I just didn't fit into their world, exactly. But then she saw that I was a good *nikokíra* [homemaker]; I looked after my son and all that. I was a good mother, and that did it for her. So the first year was hard, but then she was terrific to me.

By providing for her child *and* by keeping an orderly household, Katherine not only proved to her mother-in-law that she was a good mother, but that she was a proper Greek woman.

Life for a married woman who encountered difficulty having a child (or did not really *want* to birth a child) could be lonely and without much reward, as it was for the childless widow or the woman pushed to the fringe of society by never marrying.[17] Eleni, a widow in her sixties, explained that "for a long time there were *yerontokóres* [old maids], and they had another kind of *ikoyénia*. These were unmarried women living close with family, with brothers or some family, as a parasite. They were something in between family and servant, sister and helper."

A man, too, must marry and produce offspring in order to fulfill his adult potential; however, a Greek man marries not to become a man but to become master of his own house. Fatherhood usually follows the mandatory military service, which initiates male youths into the world of men. Marriage and kinship extend and perpetuate male worth; they do not exclusively create it. Nor have men customarily approached domestic relations as a site of affection or desire. In Nikos Kazantzakis's classic *Zorba the Greek* Zorba's new friend, our unnamed narrator, innocently asks the worldly Zorba, "Married?" " 'Aren't I a man?' he said angrily. 'Aren't I a man? I mean blind. Like everyone else before me, I fell headlong into the ditch. I married. I took the road downhill. I became head of a family, I built a house, I had children—trouble' " (1952, 13).[18] Whereas motherhood has signaled adult womanhood, fatherhood has extended a man's household and establishes dependents over which he is master; this both reinforces his manhood and compromises his autonomy.

One woman who described to me the inequities of traditional marital relations was seventy-year-old Dina, who was introduced to me by her young family friend Nia (Nia's elderly father is a longtime friend and former coworker of Dina's younger brother; Nia, a college student who lived with her father in my neighborhood, majored in social anthropology). Dina explained:

> In the really old days—I don't know if Nia knows this—the husband was the master [*kírios*], especially in villages. The woman would come home from the fields on foot whilst the husband was on horseback. He had the veto, everything had to go through him. Now of course, things are different. Before, they [wife and husband] didn't talk, they didn't exchange opinions.

A man socialized at the coffeehouse and taverna (Papataxiarchis 1991). Home was where he worked, ate, and slept with his wife. Husband and wife, brought together more likely than not through an arranged marriage, were first and foremost economic partners. The Greek word for "spouse" encodes this: *sízigos* means "under the same yoke." Civil and religious law colluded in institutionalizing patriarchal rights. Under the Greek Civil Code until 1983, women were considered the legal property of men: they were under the jurisdiction of fathers until being handed over—or, in light of certain dowry practices, sold off—to husbands (Moschou-Sakorafou 1988). Thus, while marriage constitutes a contract that establishes alliances between two families, an economic partnership of husband and wife, and the legally and religiously sanctioned setting in which to bring children into the world, within this partnership the husband-father officially had the upper hand.

Beyond the economic advantages of children for household operation and the social obligation of couples to "bring forth" children, women mentioned to me positive, emotional aspects of *teknopiía*. Maria, a seventy-year-old mother of three grown children, told me proudly in the company of her younger daughter, Niki, that, unlike many Greek women of her generation, "I wanted two girls. After I had [my older daughter], I said to her," nodding toward Niki, "when I was pregnant [with her] to become a girl so that we could keep company [kániame paréa]. With a male, I say, the boy will go outside [the house] and find a friend. The woman now, she's like sisters with [her mother], she will tell her secrets—" "They will be friends," daughter Niki interjected. "Yes," her mother continued, "that's right. Because of this I wanted her to be a girl. And I was like that with my mother." That mothers often boast that their daughter is their best friend should be considered in tandem with the popular wisdom that a spousal relationship often is not companionate (see also Hart 1992, 175).

When I asked Dina whether she has known any woman who has chosen to not have a child, she replied:

> No. I do not know even one, and nobody would tell her "Good for you." I believe that they all want to have a child. The purpose of marriage is making a child. What meaning would my own life have, now that my husband has died and I live alone, if I had no children and grandchildren? Now I see the youngsters, I see my grandchildren. My life is full with them.

This I had heard from other women. But Dina went on, leaning forward in her leather armchair: "Motherhood is something that God gave to women— to maidens, in my opinion. They are special. It is a good thing." Here, motherhood is not a divine gift to women qua woman but to women as kóri, or maiden. Hearing this, I was immediately reminded of du Boulay's argument that, through marriage and motherhood, a woman is redeemed: she is transformed from questionable maiden to proven matron, "from Eve to Madonna." For this reason, I suggest, Dina edited her statement: "motherhood is something that God gave to women—[no] to maidens." In the past, motherhood distinguished immature "maidens" from fully grown "women." Again, the primary social significance of teknopiía for women under the ethic of service was that it conferred on them adult status. Indeed, in many patrilocal areas of the country, before a bride became a mother her husband's family would refer to her generically as "bride," nífi, in lieu of her given name.[19] I came to regard the customary phrase with which pregnant women are greeted, kalí 'leftheriá, or "happy freedom," not only as a wish that a woman be freed of her pregnancy but also as a congratulation for leaving behind her childhood and entering the adult world as a validated woman.

Motherhood is emblematic of women's ethical service to the family, the community, and—as we shall see—the nation. Under conditions of character-based ethics and inherited status, motherhood marks a significant rite of passage for a woman and is the purpose of being a woman. In contrast to women's ever vulnerable sexuality in need of control, motherhood itself is regarded as indisputable, immutable, inalienable. Taken as the positive aspect of women's nature—as the divinely given but actively and appropriately social realization of women's potentiality—in the past, maternal practices were far less subject to moral scrutiny than were sexual practices.

German troops rolled into Greece in April 1941.[20] Athens itself became nearly unrecognizable. Shanty towns that sprang up around the Athens area to accommodate war refugees were soon cemented over by characterless apartment blocks. The city's neoclassical tile-roofed houses were partially replaced with five- to seven-story concrete buildings that shadowed narrow streets and turned in on themselves on a gridless nest of streets.[21] In 1951, 18 percent of the national population lived in Athens, but by 1991 this percentage had nearly doubled (NSSG 1992). Athenians today complain of pollution, congestion, filth. They voice nostalgia for the days when sidewalks were reserved for pedestrians, not parked cars, and when one could expect views of the Parthenon unobstructed by high-rises and choking smog. In the midst of postwar poverty and urban relocation and reconstruction, people began to reconsider what constituted an appropriate family size.[22] Pregnancies that once may have been joyously welcomed now posed an economic problem. People began to think more about the consequences of *teknopiía*, the making of children, and through an ethic of service they rethought ways of handling these consequences. More and more women who had been having children "as God willed" learned of and began to seek out abortions. Physicians, themselves frequently the husbands of mothers with limited access to reliable contraception, began to take over the practice of abortion from midwives (Arnold 1985; Comninos 1988).

Discovering Abortion: Enacting Reproductive Agency within an Ethic of Service

Today, Athenians commonly describe abortion as a "traditional form of birth control" that women in the 1950s frequently discovered, while already mothers, to limit the size of their families. As Maria's eldest daughter, thirty-eight-year-old Maro, told me:

> One would tell the other, one friend to her friend—someone older, married—suddenly she understands what it means to get married, what it means each time you have sex, what it means to have four children. . . . Oh so many. One right after another. You understand it happened like this.

Abortion, an intervention to control birth *following* procreation, is conceptually consistent with an understanding of reproductive agency that regards conception as not fully within the reach of human influence. As Katherine Alexander's novel *Children of Byzantium* makes painfully clear, it is also the one method through which married women could exercise unilateral control. Speaking from the first half of the twentieth century, Eleni, the Greek immigrant protagonist of Alexander's novel, quoted meditating on God's will in an epigraph to this chapter, begins to question her acceptance of "God's gift" after becoming pregnant for the sixth time in close succession. Eleni's closest friend, Matina, the wife of her husband's cousin and business partner, assures her, "We'll do something, don't worry," and suggests, too, that fault lies with Eleni's husband for not "thinking about" his young wife exhausted by frequent birthing and caring for four young children (also burying one). Eleni is shocked by her friend's innuendo. Days pass. As Eleni falls asleep each night, her head fills with visions of "year after year . . . another baby, another baby, another baby" (1987, 46). She goes with Matina to have it done (neither woman speaks the word *abortion*). Later that day, in bed after the bleeding has abated, Eleni awakes to see her husband Costa smiling down at her. He says to her, "Matina told me what happened. . . . It was God's will" (56). The following day Eleni learns from Matina that her husband was told she had an *apovolí*—an "expulsion" (more ambiguous a term than the English *miscarriage,* yet not synonymous with abortion)—"and needed to spend a few days in bed" (56). In Alexander's hindsight narrative, we see how women, fully consistent with an ethic of service, have managed reproductive affairs behind the scenes to a larger extent than men often realize. Matina deploys the traditional belief, that procreative affairs are a matter of God's will, to dissuade Costa of any suspicions he might have and to placate Eleni's pricked conscience. Alexander celebrates the ways women have interpreted God's will and used the system to their own transient advantage. But her 1980s feminist commentary is explicit: abortion, if strategic, poses for women a moral and bodily compromise. Recourse to abortion does not follow from metaphysical considerations. It is necessitated by economic want, the failure of men to "be careful," and socially compromising conditions.

In 1950, around the time that Greek women in significant numbers began seeking abortions, abortion was quietly made a criminal act. Several contributing factors explain why. First, urbanization and poverty challenged village communality and the gendered division of everyday life: without household lands to support even the most basic diet, women were beginning to enter the labor force in significant numbers. Amid Westernizing change, in criminalizing abortion, Parliament found one policy measure that would placate the socially conservative church, which was an influential party to this legislation.[23] Second, it is possible that a few politicians had recognized the demographic consequences of a decade of war and famine and viewed abortion in terms of further demographic weakening, although most studies trace this discussion to a decade or two later. Third, it is clear from the wording of the law that abortion was criminalized in an effort to secure the paternal rights of men to their heirs and to control their wives' fertility more effectively. Obtainable without the permission of their husbands, abortion offered women their only unilateral method of birth control—it thus posed a potential threat to men wishing to exercise their legal right to decide family issues, including reproductive ones. It is not surprising that politicians (during this era virtually all were men) felt patriarchy could use some legal reinforcement in postwar Greece, for many women had grown accustomed to new autonomy during the decade of war as heads of household in their husbands' absence or as political prisoners and even soldiers themselves (Fourtouni 1986; Hart 1996). Furthermore, it is worth noting that in 1950 Greece remained under the Marshall Plan, and the United States had not yet given up its designs for restructuring the Hellenic Republic in its own pre–*Roe v. Wade* democratic image.

Law No. 1492/50 stipulated: "The person who performs an abortion is punishable by imprisonment of six months if the abortion is done with the consent of the pregnant woman and imprisonment up to ten years if done without her consent." It went on to say: "The woman who induces her own abortion or accepts the illegal interruption of her pregnancy is punishable by an imprisonment of up to three years" (Comninos 1988, 208). Exceptions were allowed when the health of the pregnant woman was threatened or when pregnancy resulted from rape, incest, or the seduction of a minor age fifteen or under. No term limit of pregnancy was stipulated for cases when abortion was permitted. Furthermore, the law criminalized the transmission of information about abortion: "Any person who publishes advice or information or any advertisement relating to abortion, or in any way offer his/her services to this end can be imprisoned for up to one year" (Siampos 1975, 344). It was also illegal to advertise the contraceptives then available for purchase, such as condoms.

Although the law was strict in its wording, in practice illegality never posed a great deterrent to having an abortion. Because abortion was not something people (including politicians) much talked about publicly, many women seeking an abortion never realized it was illegal (Valaoras and Trichopoulos 1970, 288). Abortions were performed clandestinely by midwives and then, increasingly, in private doctors' offices; secrecy was welcomed by women who were concerned for their reputation. In this sense, abortion's criminalization may have placed more control in women's hands. Before legalization in 1986, only about twenty cases of illegal abortion were ever brought to court in a given year (Siampos 1975, 344), although as many as 250,000 abortions were performed annually (Comninos 1988, 210). Being illegal, however, abortion techniques were not taught to medical students. In underground spaces, physicians shared knowledge of the procedures with their colleagues because, as one gynecologist who trained in the 1960s said to me, "this is everyday practice in gynecology. It was so silly that it was not [officially] taught." Through similar word-of-mouth communications, women gradually discovered that they could seek medical help in solving the problem of an inopportune pregnancy.

As abortion became more readily available, women learned they could either accept God's gift of pregnancy or decline it, through abortion. As abortion became a standard, if underground, medical procedure, few women died from it, and this too encouraged women to rely on abortion as a surefire backup to the contraceptive methods they knew, primarily withdrawal and the rhythm method. As Eleni said to me, "I think in Greece we never had problems with safe abortions. It was illegal, but we could get the best abortion in all the world. And for a long time it was the only kind of contraception. In some ways it still is." Eleni's malapropism—abortion may be a form of birth control, but it is *not* contraception—is one I heard repeatedly and is indicative of the extent to which heterosexual women have normalized abortion as something they might expect to encounter in the course of their lives. Throughout the 1950s and 1960s, even in urban areas women were largely left in the dark about contraceptive options aside from condoms (which were not very popular) and "being careful." Since what has come to be known as family planning was not included in the medical school curriculum, doctors were not a great source of help. More cynically, several women suggested to me that the incentive of nontaxable income prompted many doctors actually to encourage women to rely on abortion as a "method of birth control" (see also Arnold 1985; Georges 1996a). One woman assured me, "When abortion was illegal, it was even easier [to get one]—there were always doctors who did it only for the money." Nadia concurred: "A doctor in Greece won't tell you we can't have an abortion. He just tells you only in the case when you have gone many months and the abortion can't happen; then he'll tell you no. But at one or two months, he pounces on you." The price of abortion in a doctor's private office has risen over recent decades in line with double-digit inflation, its relative cost remaining on a par with a new baby stroller (i.e., in 1995, this amounted to between U.S.$170 and $300; the range is great because there are no state controls in the private sector of medicine). Economic class seems not to have significantly restricted access to abortion.

Women's widespread embrace of abortion may at first glance appear to be a surprising detour away from the strong cultural association between womanhood and motherhood depicted earlier, and from the general appreciation of children portrayed in this book's prologue. And yet abortion has not (until recently, perhaps) constituted a social or moral problem in Greece. Instead, firmly situated within an ethic of service, it has been presented as a solution—howsoever fraught and imperfect a solution—to the problem of a pregnancy that occurs when a woman is not in a position to fulfill the social requisites of being a good, providing mother to a new child.

Over the last fifty years, Greek women have come to regard abortion as a necessary evil *(éna anangéo kakó)*. Continuing to draw on the ethic of service through which abortion was first accommodated in Greek society, Athenian women I spoke with agreed that a woman does not terminate a pregnancy because she chooses to have an abortion, but because she finds herself in a situation where abortion becomes an unfortunate necessity (see also Arnold 1985; Georges 1996a; Skilogianis 1997). The conditions said to compel a woman to seek an abortion—the social and economic conditions that preclude carrying a child to term and raising it—articulate with historically particular attitudes toward *teknopiía*. Beyond illegitimacy, the most frequently voiced reasons concern material conditions: can the prospective parents afford to raise a child properly and provide for it sufficiently? While a woman may feel it is a terrible thing to deny a potential child the opportunity for life, the loss is weighed against the bleak future into which this child, if born, would grow. As Lela, the electric company employee and the mother of one young son explained it:

> Of course the Greek church does not accept it, but on the other hand, I
> don't think that it has taken a negative position on it. I haven't followed
> the subject, but surely it wouldn't accept it. It is a control of the family,
> births. It is bad for you to have an abortion. But then who will bring up
> the child for you—and if your relationship is not working, is it better
> to bring up your child in an already disintegrating family? It is better
> to have an abortion than not be able to give it a good life.

While abortion is clearly deplored, it is often said to be "better than" some other consequence. At the same time, abortion can also represent the outcome of a compromise made with oneself, or something one is pressured into by family members or the fear of social stigma: What will "they" say of her or of an inopportune child? From the pull of social obligations—from the traditional ethics of femininity—arise ambivalent feelings about abortion.

During the 1960s, my friend Katherine Alexander—who fictionalized her mother's experiences with abortion and immigrant Greek family life in the novel I have quoted—became pregnant four times with two men, had two abortions, and birthed two sons. She also married. Katherine's account of her abortions, each of which she views as "completely different," highlights the ways autonomy and control, marriage and social relations, economic and personal situations, all come together to uniquely shape a woman's sometimes multiple experiences of abortion.[24] She speaks of the first time she became pregnant in passive tones, as something that "just happened": there was a charming Greek man and "a momentary lapse." At the time, she was aware of oral contraceptives but "was scared to take the pill. It was new, untried."[25] Katherine was in her midtwenties and unmarried; she was not in love. Since there would be no wedding, there was no question of having the child. When she missed her period, her only thought was "Am I or am I not" pregnant? As soon as a physician confirmed the pregnancy, she had the abortion in a private doctor's office. No questions asked, no waiting period (once the pregnancy was verified), no counseling. Although at the time abortion was illegal, from her mother's experience Katherine knew it to be a routine outpatient medical procedure and commercial transaction. This is how Katherine recalled the experience: "I just felt relieved, actually. I didn't feel anything except relief. I didn't feel pregnant. *In my mind it was a late period,* my concern was to get it done. I wasn't afraid. I wasn't upset. I felt nothing. I mean, I wasn't affected by it."

As Katherine told the story, having this abortion was not the result of a decision about whether to carry a child to term. Motherhood does not enter into the story. She described the abortion as a medical procedure she needed to continue the normal functioning of her menstrual cycle. Although Katherine seemed to approach this abortion pragmatically, and she experienced this pregnancy, her first, as a late period rather than as the gestation of a baby within her, she nonetheless felt "something" was wrong:

> But I never told anybody. Not even my best friend. Because I had felt I had done something—in a way I felt I had done something wrong. It's hard to explain. *I* didn't feel it, but you're so conditioned to feel that—you know, you don't *talk* about it. Secrecy. Because my mother was very much like that, my mother used to have abortions all the time,

and so did her friends, back in the days before they had [medical] birth
control. My mother discovered abortion after she had four kids, one
after another. I have a feeling she probably tried to abort me, but she
left it until too late. I came along quite late in her life and she probably
thought it [this pregnancy] was early menopause. Anyway, to me abortion was just something you did if you got pregnant. Women here did
it all the time. I grew up with it as an okay thing to do, as a necessary
thing to do. *Not that it was a good thing.* You did it because *it was necessary.* [Emphasis added]

The young man in question accompanied her to the doctor's office and paid
for the procedure, although to Katherine's retrospective disgust, he later
accepted her full repayment. This was clearly, to both their minds, her
problem, her responsibility. Then again, since she told no one else of her
predicament, it was a situation over which she was fully in control.

A few years later Katherine had a second abortion under very different
circumstances. She was now a married woman, a mother. Following the
birth of her second son, she missed her period a few weeks after having
what she thought was "safe" intercourse according to the rhythm method
(her ovulation, she now realizes, must have shifted following gestation).
Under economic strain her marriage was not going well. But as she said to
me, "I love babies and I still loved my husband," and, had it been up to her,
she "would have kept the child." With this pregnancy, however, she had in
stereo a "Greek chorus" of both their mothers (her mother rather forcibly
moved in with them after the wedding) who despaired of her ability to
handle another child: "She has two small ones already, she can't do it!" *Na
to ríksis,* they advised, "Toss it," using the colloquial expression for having
an abortion that signals its routinization. Her husband had the final veto.
"I wanted it [the child], but he said no, and he wouldn't even talk about it."
As a wife, mother, daughter, and daughter-in-law, Katherine was not in
control of this pregnancy; its fate was not hers to decide. Resigned, she let
her husband take her to the doctor, who proceeded immediately with the
abortion. Again, she referred to the procedure itself without a sense of
trauma: "It was only the second or third week, so it was as if he brought my
period on for me." Yet this abortion was different from the first. As a
young married woman, Katherine did not feel this abortion as a personal
necessity so much as something she was coerced into by her relatives. Because this time the loss was forced on her, and because she was now married and already a mother, she had a greater sense of the fetus as a potential child, her child. "I didn't want to think whether it was a boy or girl,"
she said softly. Now, at age sixty when we spoke, she clearly regretted not

having had the baby, who might have become her daughter: "I think I hated [my husband] at that moment." The marriage lasted only another two years.[26]

As Katherine's stories indicate, the moral frame into which abortion has been accommodated in Greece, an ethic of service, takes as its unit of reference not the autonomous, liberal individual who is ideally self-interested, but a person whose sense of self is *self-consciously* filtered through a series of allegiances, loyalties, and obligations beginning with the family. This moral frame remains salient to women in Athens today.

I discussed the question of ethics and abortion with a practicing midwife and professor of midwifery, Ourania Katsigianni.[27] Addressing the question of why, today, the overwhelming majority of women who seek abortions prefer to pay for the privacy of a doctor's office, rather than have a legal abortion paid for by national health insurance at a state hospital, Katsigianni invoked the ethic of service: "I think it's the Greek ethics. It's what other people will say about you." I asked her what kinds of things they would say. "To have a free relationship with a man is still not very widely accepted in Greece yet," she began. "It's the parents, the relatives, the neighbors—you know, everyone who will say, 'You [had] an abortion, what else did you do? Do you have a disease as well? What kind of a person are you?' In Greece it's not acceptable for a woman to present herself and say, 'I had an abortion,' for [whatever] reasons. This is not acceptable. So we hide these things. And also, if in women's organizations they speak about abortion, they don't talk about themselves, they talk generally about abortion. Not their own experience." Abortion has become an ethical *issue*, then, in that it is often a woman's moral responsibility to *hide* the abortion, and thus to hide the evidence of her own or others' sexual impropriety— the character flaws that would lead to the problem of an inappropriate pregnancy—from others who might use that knowledge against her and her family.

Of sexual transgressions, Katherine said, "If you don't talk about it, it doesn't exist." Robinette Kennedy (1986) reports Cretan women speaking of hiding extramarital affairs from others in order to contain "the evil" of the discretion. So too with abortion. The silences surrounding abortion up-hold honor or repute because these depend less on what one actually does, and more on what others believe about what one does. Although abortion throughout early modern Europe was framed in terms of sexuality rather than against ideals of motherhood (McLaren 1984; Schneider and Schneider 1995), I argue that women's experience of this in Greece has been somewhat different than, say, in Catholic Ireland, where women may hide knowledge of their abortion "to protect themselves from the criticism of others" who condemn abortion as wrong in and of itself (Fletcher 1995). As one Cretan woman told Kennedy, "When I don't say anything to my husband, the evil stops right there. Nothing happens. But if I tell anyone about it, the bad thing goes on. My husband will kill the man [her lover]" (1986, 125). Silence here serves both as a coping mechanism, as Kennedy suggests, and a way to reinscribe the conditions of suspicion that often mark conjugal and other family relationships.

Pressed into ethical service of family and community, the means of abortion are justified by the ends of preventing inopportune pregnancy and hiding inappropriate sexual activity. Young women, speaking of their own generation, assured me that legality and abstract (e.g., Catholic) morality are not issues with which a woman concerns herself at that moment. As twenty-five-year-old Toula said: "If [a woman] had to do it, she would do it. That is, she wouldn't be at all influenced by what she believes with regard to religion, how she thinks about the life that she has, what compels her to do this thing. She thinks about it and she does it." If a woman finds herself with a problematic pregnancy, then her task—for which she is ethically and socially accountable—is to rid herself (and her family) of that problem. Phoebe concurred:

> The decision for a woman to have an abortion—I believe it's not easy, it's a difficult decision. Of course, when a woman decides to have an abortion, I believe that she has no other choice at that moment when she hasn't taken any other protection. At that moment, of course, I don't think that she is interested in whether it is legal or not. What interests her is, she sees the pregnancy as some problem, and she wants to cease having this problem. Therefore she decides to have an abortion. Naturally, she also thinks about what repercussions this can have in her life—that is, to her psychological and emotional condition, and even in her relationships.

Phoebe clearly regards the decision to terminate an inopportune pregnancy through abortion as a matter inextricably grounded in the specific, immediate circumstances of that woman's life. The apparent pragmatism underlying Athenian women's past and present explanations for why women have abortions is not self-seeking. I do not believe that American women, or any other women, seek abortions out of truly selfish motivations, but unlike in the United States, where society is explicitly built on an ideal of inalienable human rights and property in one's person (Glendon 1987; Ginsburg 1989; Petchesky 1995), in Athens it is only pronatal nationalists who cast women who have abortions as selfish creatures. Athenian women are able to draw on the available understanding that, as social beings, women are members of families and communities, in order to point to the coerciveness of social obligations and economic restraints that compel one to seek an abortion.

To a Western purview the kind of virtue ethics I have been describing—in which the moral actor is not expected to avoid all inappropriate behavior but must hide impropriety—may seem far removed from any kind of morality that might find a Christian basis. However, there is strong support for this system of ethics, based on social recognition rather than actual deed, in Orthodox theology. As previously noted, Athenians frequently distinguish Orthodoxy from Catholicism on this point. Sophia, age twenty-seven, told me:

> We don't have intense problems with the church as the Catholics do.
> Our church doesn't make such a fuss. People are active in it in some
> way, but it's only the quaint grandmothers who yell about it. The
> priests said something [against abortion], but no one listened to them.

And forty-seven-year-old Artemis said much the same thing: "The church says no, but the state says yes [to abortion]. People hear what they want to hear. When the pope in Rome said no, so what? Not to use the prophylactic? He's completely—what with AIDS now—he's completely foolish." Nevertheless, the Orthodox Church clearly opposes abortion on theological grounds, since every life is sacred and human life is said to begin at conception. For Orthodox Greeks, that is a given. Young Nia, who conjured up multiple situations in which a woman might reasonably have an abortion, still believes "abortion is a sin; it's the taking of a human life."

To understand how Orthodox Greeks reconcile a belief that abortion is a sin with pragmatic acceptance of its practice, it is useful to recall John Campbell's ethnographic distinction between "personal sin" and original sin (what he calls "ancestral sin"; 1964, 324).[28] Because abortion is frequently employed to cover over inappropriate sexual activity, and since sensuality is regarded as original sin, abortion has been evaluated as a consequence of original sin. Both types of sin, Campbell writes, "divide man from God but[,] while the individual is wholly responsible for personal sins, he feels little sense of guilt for the other kind of sin which he sees as a pre-existing condition of the world into which he was born" (324). If original sin places the moral burden of sensuality on women, it also lets them off the hook for this: responsibility for controlling sensuality, or correcting the repercussions of uncontrolled sexuality, "is not to be confused with individual guilt" (327).

The Orthodox Church recognizes that life presents many difficulties and constraints, and that sometimes it is possible to create a larger sin or wrongdoing in trying to avoid another. Theologically, this is presented in terms of *ikonomía*, a notion that allows the church to turn away from a smaller wrongdoing (sin) in the interests of facilitating a larger good; as one Byzantine scholar and Orthodox believer put this to me, "sometimes it's better to turn a blind eye than to stir up trouble." In *Byzantine Theology*, John Meyendorff explains that the theological use of the term *ikonomía* derives from its New Testament application by the Apostle Paul, for whom *ikonomía* referred to a "divine plan for the management of history and of the world" or the stewardship of God's "house" (1974, 88). *Ikonomía* is the task that God entrusted to humankind—to be "servants of Christ and stewards *[ikonomoi]* of the mysteries of God" (1 Cor. 4:1, quoted in Meyendorff 1974, 88). In contrast to Roman Catholic dispensation, with *ikonomía* what "is at stake is not only an exception to the law, but an obligation to decide individual issues in the general context of God's plan for the salvation of the world" (1974, 89).[29] Rather than allow "exceptions to the rule," as a theologian put this to me in an interview, *ikonomía* recognizes that rules are selectively applied in relative social contexts.[30]

The logic that *ikonomía* brings to the issue of abortion is that it is the divine duty of a woman to be a good mother; if she cannot, for reasons of economics or age or marital status, be a good mother to the child she would have from an unintended pregnancy, it is ethical not to have that child. This does not erase the fact that she is putting an end to a human life, but in the eyes of most believers it would be a greater sin to bring a child into a life of inadequacy or shame. Particularly religious women might undergo a ritual purification or seek a special blessing from a priest after having an abortion. But the abortion can itself be viewed as a penitential discipline for careless or inappropriate sexual activity, one that women have undergone on behalf of men.

While no woman who spoke to me explicitly raised the Orthodox notion of *ikonomía*, I believe it is helpful in understanding whence prevalent attitudes toward abortion come. In speaking of the sin of abortion Eva stressed that it is also

> a crime to birth a child and not to want it and to create problems for it, or to have it and give it up for adoption—or many of them leave it, you know, in the street, or even kill their children. Is this not a crime which happens later? It's relative. The best thing is for there not to be an abortion; but from the moment that there is a dilemma as to whether or not to keep the child, there is an uncertainty. I, at least, cannot say

whether it's good or bad. It's better for it not to happen. If it [the situation] arises, however, you think about it differently.

Consistent with an ethic of service, this practical relativism recognizes that living a full human life entails the fulfillment of certain social obligations. But if contemporary women frequently call on an ethic of service to reconcile abortion with motherhood, *teknopiía*, or the making of children, is today more frequently addressed through an alternative ethic of choice.

"THESE DAYS": AN ETHIC OF CHOICE

While Greek women entered the waged workforce in significant numbers during and after the war era, women's formal participation in the workforce seems actually to have declined between the 1961 and 1981 census years (whereas from 1951–1981 it grew by 165 percent; NSSG 1992),[31] under pressure of conservative values imposed during seven years of military rule (1967–1974). Reminiscent of the Metaxas regime, the colonels' junta, led by Georgios Papadopoulos, was impassioned in its self-proclaimed mission to defend the traditional values of "Helleno-Christian civilization," and it reigned successfully under the nationalistic slogan "Fatherland, Family, Religion." The historian William McNeill has argued, "Their ideal was to live in a world where all Greeks thought and felt alike, conforming to an orthodoxy that was national as well as religious" (1978, 121). A resurgence of religious, patriarchal family-oriented values took root among vast segments of the population.[32] After democracy was restored in 1974 following a student-led protest, women began returning to the labor market.[33] By 1981, women accounted for 31.9 percent of the national labor force, with 56 percent of all employed women living in urban areas (NSSG 1992). Amid continuing inflation, their workforce participation has since been on the rise.[34] One sociological study suggests, "While up to 1980 there was a compatibility between rapid development and the adoption of Western European models of consumption, the economic crisis has led Athenians to seek other strategies of survival and continuing consumption. These include the growth of the 'black' economy, double and triple employment. These strategies, together with continuing family solidarity, have allowed Athenians to avoid massive poverty and unemployment" (Agrafiotis et al. 1990a, 18).

When, in 1981, Greece became a full member of the European Economic Community (EEC), this marked a sea change in Greek social, economic, and foreign policy. EEC membership came as the legacy of diligent efforts by the fiscally and socially conservative New Democracy Party, but at a moment when state leadership was handed over to a populist socialist party, PASOK, which in 1983 liberalized Family Law and other social legislation (see appendix 2 for a summary of relevant legislative reforms). Throughout the 1980s, Westernizing trends driven by both the free market aspirations of the political right and the women's rights platform of the left consolidated a rhetoric of individualism that appealed to multiple constituencies. Because the conflicting political ideologies of the two major parties met in their vision of a modern, free-thinking, self-actualizing individual, the opposition leader of the New Democracy Party, Miltiades Evert, was able, during the 1994 prime ministerial elections, to trade on his party's long-standing commitment to securing Greece's position in the European Economic Community to appropriate the feminist commitment of the incumbent Socialist Party in an appeal to women voters. Evert published a two-page open letter to the women of Greece in the popular women's magazine *Yinéka* (Woman), which began, "I didn't come to speak to you man to woman. I came for us to speak as humans who care about and share in Life, the Earth, the same Beginnings, the *Patrídha*. We live in a new Era, where new conditions are having us give a new meaning and content to human values." The letter goes on to explain that "the supreme value of the political philosophy of New Democracy is the Person. Free, Knowledgeable, Thoughtful, Informed, Citizen. Our political thought and practice has as its main charge the respect of the personal individuality of the person and the freedom of his/her choice." (1994, 132). But if Athenians have widely adopted the modern view that a woman can and ought to choose her life path and have children when she wants, because she wants to, women relate their *own* life stories in terms of the material and cultural constraints they face in exercising this control.

Choice may be the operative idiom of contemporary urban life—and of women's gender proficiency—but Athenians are well aware that their choices are rarely free or automatically obtainable. Explicitly contrasting with the older, coexisting ethic in allowing women virtuous behavior guided by personal desires, the ethic of choice did not fully take hold until the 1980s. In the stories that follow, women call on both ethical frameworks to make sense of their obligations, responsibilities, and decisions having to do not only with *teknopiía* but also with demonstrating that they are both good women and good at being women.

Achieving Modern Motherhood: The Virtues of Conscious Planning

In contemporary urban Greece, sexual activity for women as well as men is conceptually separating from reproduction. At the same time, a woman's chaste reputation is no longer sufficient to establish her as a good woman. Lela, returning from the kitchen with a plate of bakery cookies to where we were sitting on her wide balcony, overlooking the street where her father had set off for a walk with his young grandsons (Lela's son and nephew) so that she could devote her attention to our interview, described what she sees as an ethical shift:

> I think that with the young people the question is, what do ethics mean, what is the problem of ethics? The situation has changed. It's over: this [old] ethic no longer exists. Now what is it? People are now occupied with having a good *éthos* in society, in their families, with their fellow human beings—as opposed to ethics in the past, which had to do only with sexuality and nothing else. Ethical positioning [for women] had only to do with protecting your virginity. This was what ethics was. In other words, if you were the worst person, this wasn't an issue of ethics. Immoral [*aníthikes*] women were those who had had a sexual relationship without being married, and this relationship ended before they got married. If they got married the issue was over; it wasn't a matter of ethics or morals then. You couldn't say that this was an unethical [*aníthikos*] person. That's what happened here.

Attention that once focused on women's sexuality in evaluating individual social worth is being retrained on maternal practice: "People are now occupied with having a good *éthos* . . . in their families" when, ideologically, the moral center of the Greek family revolves around the mother. To be good at being a woman, one should be recognized as being a good mother. In theory, this is nothing new. In practice, however, the terms of what it takes for a woman to be recognized as a good mother are changing as women's domestic responsibilities are compounded by extradomestic responsibilities. Lela, acknowledging that her fifteen-month-old son is being brought up largely by her own mother and father, who live downstairs in the same building, continued:

> I do not think that motherhood has changed from the past. Motherhood is as it always was. That is, the relationship between mother and child hasn't changed. What *has* changed is the position of the woman in society. She gives more things, but it's not the issue of motherhood. Motherhood stays the same, but the woman who works doesn't sit at home and raise the kid, as happened before.

That "the position of the woman in society" has changed in the wake of capitalist expansion and women's increased educational and occupational participation rewrites the social meaning and experience of motherhood—

even as women are adamant that motherhood itself is eternal (or at least resistant to change). Women are thus prompted to rethink their strategies regarding *teknopiía*.

Women's maternal obligations are complicated as children are coming to be regarded as consumer projects. As Galena, a woman in her sixties, put this to me:

> Before, the family had children to work with them, to help as hands. Now this has changed. The baby is a mouth to feed, a body to clothe. It is not [a matter of] hands. We change as a society, we are not as we were before. Greece now has the same problem as Europe, other developed countries.

Today a mother's success depends not merely on bringing forth children who will inherit the family's name and assets but also on raising *successful* children—children with advanced degrees, who speak two or three languages, perhaps study abroad, and can succeed in a competitive job market; children who look smart dressed in tailored European clothing, who drive a car, who live in a good neighborhood. Since at least the early 1980s, parents have felt pressure to provide the best for their children and to produce the best children. *Teknopiía* is itself coming to be viewed as a productive process among the middle classes.

The ability to provide children with optimal opportunities and material comfort requires in the first instance the assumption of a proper, or responsible, approach to birth control. Nadia, who has never married, said to me:

> I tell you, only the foolish ones are having children; the intelligent ones are holding off. Because proper persons know what a child demands. . . . Perhaps because the Greek has undergone indigence, before and after the war—and Greece was always a little underdeveloped—back then they had children. And those who have grown up now tell you, "I don't want my child to go through what I went through then, I'll have one and it will live well, not many and live in poverty." At least the young Greeks think this.[35]

Phoebe agreed with her age-mate Nadia that people have fewer children out of an appropriate sense of responsibility, which she qualified as maturity:

> In Greece we have a low birthrate. For what reason? I believe that it's because things are a little difficult from the economic side. A couple thinks about when they will have a child, and wants to offer their child a good, comfortable life, meaning to have the money to be able to afford the good schools, to see to the child's education. You see, they have

had this economic deprivation, they begin to think that we can have one child only—or no children, if we don't attain the economic ease to enable us to raise our child. This is, I think up to a point, an issue of maturity.

These women enunciate an emergent approach to *teknopiía;* in their talk of propriety and maturity, they invoke what I call the ethic of choice, in which motherhood is a goal to be achieved, ideally through rational planning. In what follows, I explore how women go about being what Nadia calls proper *(sostós)* and demonstrating what Phoebe means by maturity *(orimótita)* when it comes to *teknopiía* in Athens in the mid-1990s. The ethic of choice is very different from a regime in which God wills it. And the nature that women are called on to realize is quite different, too. No longer are women asked to realize a self-controlling nature aimed at conforming to external standards. The nature they must realize is being internalized, seen, for example, as inner desire that should be actualized through conscious planning. That this has unfolded alongside major political and economic changes is no coincidence.

Young middle-class Athenian women described how women of their mothers' and grandmothers' generations apparently accepted motherhood when they first became pregnant (granted, the majority were presumably virgins at betrothal, and so were unlikely to face illegitimate birth), and they explained that today things are both different and more difficult. Women who are at least potentially economically independent, who by law enter into the marriage contract as equal players with equal rights and responsibilities (see appendix 2), who have possibly experienced several intense but impermanent romantic relationships, look to marriage as more than an economic arrangement or means of perpetuating lineages. Many hope their spouses will be their friends as well as life partners. And they anticipate having children as the ultimate, but not exclusive, indication that they have become full-fledged adult women. Occasionally, they depict having children as mutually exclusive with certain career paths. Women such as Eva and Toula, twenty-five-year-old friends—who, with high school diplomas, relocated to Athens from a northern village to pursue urban lives and full-time employment—do not view motherhood as exclusively defining of a woman's social person or character. Rather, they talk about themselves in terms of the work they do,[36] and they explain that the prospect of pregnancy and having a child can be regarded as a potential inconvenience. A woman must carefully schedule having children.

Yet for these young women, *whether* they wanted to have children was not at issue. They questioned their priorities: *when* do I want to become a mother? The narratives of two women who talked with me about wanting to have children illustrate how divisive this question can be. Both have studied abroad, living away from families with whom they remain close. Neither was in a serious romantic relationship at the time of our interview, so neither had a specific partner in mind when thinking about making a family. Although both Fotini and Despina are pursuing professional degrees, this must be read in a context where people frequently earn Ph.D.s to advance business or other nonacademic professional careers. The terms of their discussions about scheduling families are not unlike those voiced by their age-mates, such as Eva and Toula, who entered the workforce after high school.

Fotini was twenty-four at the time of our meeting and had recently completed a master's degree in France. I scheduled our interview at her parents' house in Pangrati, where she was living. Fotini was late for our appointment, and in her absence I spoke with her parents. Her mother, Irini, told me warmly how much she admired those who, like myself, attend university. She herself never studied beyond high school, halting her education upon marrying and having children. Irini boasted that Fotini had been offered a three-year scholarship to continue toward a Ph.D., although she had refused it, saying, "I want to do a doctorate, but at the moment I am more interested in having a family. I will do a doctorate, but I will do it as a married woman." Irini's younger daughter, who had two years remaining before completing her bachelor's degree in physics, will not go on to graduate school right away, not even for her master's. According to Irini, "She says, 'I will get my [first] degree, have a family, and then I will continue.'"

The thermostat recorded a steamy 40°C (102°F) that July afternoon, and when Fotini returned home she joined us out on the open balcony. Without knowing what her mother and I had discussed, she volunteered, "Yes, I have thought about having a family, and now that I have finished my studies it is the next thing to do." In the meantime, she was waiting to be posted to a secondary school teaching position. "To have a family," she explained, "you must have a job from both sides [mother and father]. I am thinking of doing it in the next five years, but if something came up tomorrow, I might say no." Fotini and her sister both depict having a family as a more immediate priority than advanced degrees. Since the elder sister, Fotini, recognizes that a level of material stability is prerequisite to this goal, her first move, even before finding a partner, is to find a job.

Despina took an alternative path, more common among middle-class Athenians. At the time of our interview, she was a twenty-eight-year-old doctoral student at a British university, who was back in Athens for the summer.[37] She and I were at similar points in our lives. We met through a mutual friend and spoke freely (and privately) about the dilemmas facing women "like us" who "want it all"—professional career and family—ruefully recognizing that only for women is this seen as "wanting it all." For men, anticipating both career and family is perfectly normal. Despina confronted the question of priorities before deciding to leave Greece. When I initially asked whether she wanted to have children, she replied:

> I've decided that it's a crisis you go through, and then you recover.
> When I first went to Britain, I was twenty-four and it was a big crisis. I
> think it was because I was supposed to stay for a long time, and by the
> time I would have finished my Ph.D. I would be twenty-eight, thirty. If
> I were to go, it would be five years before I could start to think about
> having children: this was the crisis. Should I do that, or just stay here
> and have a family? But after the first year the crisis passed. Now I think
> that it would depend on many things. Yes, you know, theoretically, I
> would like to have children. But then again, theoretically, I would like
> to have *many* children, and I know that I never will, because it's a mat-
> ter of money and many other things. But no, it's not an idea that freaks
> me out anymore: I like children a lot, but it's the circumstances.

At Fotini's current age, Despina passed through a crisis fearing that to pursue an advanced degree abroad would threaten her chances for having a family (which, she clarified, means having children). Subsequently, Despina is trying not to look at her life as an either/or decision between a Ph.D. and career, on the one hand, and children, on the other. Her happiness, she assured me if not also herself, does not depend on children. Being intermittently sexually active (she had recently broken off a transnational relationship with an Athenian man), Despina practices fertility control (primarily using condoms) so as to avoid any "unpleasant surprises."

Simultaneously drawing on traditional valuations of motherhood and contemporary feminist critiques of a structural lack of recognition for women's domestic labor under capitalism, Despina and Fotini regard having children as an achievement analogous to having a career.[38] They differ, however, on the degree to which this is something they can or should make happen through active will. Fotini is setting out to have a family as her first priority—toward which end, it seems, falling in love is merely a means—while Despina is waiting to see what direction her life takes after completing her education. Each woman spoke of this question of priorities as one that was hers to decide on her own terms, while well aware that such choices will always be constrained by circumstance.

This notion of achieved motherhood suggests it is not sufficient simply to want to be a mother; then again, at their young ages these women do not need to demonstrate the desire. It is assumed. But although research supports the public opinion that the vast majority of Athenian women want to become mothers (Symeonidou 1990), it remains difficult to differentiate desire from obligation because social expectations are so strong. One woman, who after many years of frustrated attempts was able to have a child using in vitro fertilization, told me, "A married woman who has no child is a topic of conversation. What is significant is that it is not acceptable for a couple to decide not to have any children." I met only two women in Athens, either socially or through my research, who told me they made a conscious decision not to have children. Neither has ever married, both are professionals, and the younger of the two (Maro) is thirty-eight.

Litsa, the bank teller, said to me:

> I don't see anyone getting married and saying, "I don't want to have children." Now it's another matter as to whether they do it because they *feel* it, motherhood, or because they *must* do it for the world, for others *[ton kósmo]*. Very few women have I seen who wouldn't have children. Let's say two to three out of ninety women would say, "It doesn't matter to me," or "I don't want to." It's very small, this percentage. Other women get married when they are young, they live two to three years without a child, and they tell you it's because "I want to live"; and then you see them later and in fact they do have children. I find this perfectly correct.

Litsa's comment that some women might really feel the desire for motherhood inside them (ethic of choice), while others must do it for others (ethic of service), is telling. Either motivation seems socially acceptable; I find it interesting that *some* motivation should be produced. This arguably undermines the persistent cultural claims that maternal desire *is* assumed of women. Lela, who at age thirty (after having inoperable damage to her fallopian tubes diagnosed) had her child after using in vitro fertilization, demonstrated a motivation consistent with the ethic of choice:

> For what reason did I want a kid? One thing is sure, it's not just because everybody does it. It's simply a matter of *nature*—I can't tell you exactly why. Certainly not just because they had one across the street. I wanted something that was mine. It could also be because of this that I got into it [IVF] at this age; I didn't feel that I would be able to have a child much earlier. I wanted to finish with my job, do some other

things; and somewhere along the way I felt the need to have my own child. To do myself something the whole world does—to do it myself too.

Here the nature Lela calls forth is an internal desire that provides the basis of personal choice. It is a matter of character that emerges from deep within the core of her being; this suggests a modern understanding of self that contrasts with an Aristotelian understanding of character as the result of properly internalized social norms. Nevertheless, that Lela also describes her need to do something "the whole world does" belies the social roots of her "natural" desire.

It remains the case in Greece that marriage is prerequisite to achieved motherhood (for a contrasting Mediterranean example, see Kahn 2000 on urban Israel). Eleni told me that her youngest daughter, having lived with her boyfriend for four years, "decided to get married because they want to have a child." Nia, the twenty-year-old anthropology student, said, "It's a dialectical relationship, marriage and a child. Why should a woman get married if she does not want to have a child, when she can just live with the man she wants, or have a free relationship?" Three women I spoke with volunteered that they were pregnant at the time of their weddings, and a fourth told me she tried (unsuccessfully) for a year to become pregnant before she married at forty. Haris Symeonidou's study with the National Center for Social Research calculated that, of 875 women surveyed who had been married for ten or more years and who had at least one child, 22 percent had conceived their first child before marriage (1990, 156).[39] I heard of eager relatives and friends engaging in the pan-Mediterranean custom of sewing blue glass beads onto the wedding sheets to ward off the evil eye and make procreatively auspicious the marriage bed; sometimes a healthy baby boy is rolled over the sheets in a gesture designed to encourage the on-site conception of a like creature. The updated-for-today version in Athens has friends and relatives throw five thousand drachma notes (around twenty U.S. dollars) onto the bridal bed in anticipation of the expenses to be incurred having children.

Underlying the claim that one marries in order to have children is the assumption that one need not marry in order to have sex. Toula acknowledged that, while many women her age (twenty-five) and younger are having sexual relationships with men they do not necessarily intend to marry, there are still "many women who save it for the first day of marriage." But her friend Eva countered that, although she knew young women who have never "made love," it did not mean that they were purposely "saving it." "Okay, it's fine to save something and do it when you want to," she explained, "but to save it only for [the sake of] getting married—it's different to want it yourself." Speaking of her daughters from her perspective as a sixty-year-old feminist, Eleni drew a similar distinction:

> When my children were teenagers—about ten years ago—things were more restricted than they are now. These days the young people see the sexual life as "make love with anybody, any time, any place." Without wanting it. If they want it, it's okay. But if they don't want it, if they feel they have to prove their progressiveness, that they are free by making love—it's something like it was with smoking, wanting to show off we were grown-ups.

If youthful, unwed, uncommitted sexual relations are coerced through peer pressure, then this is no liberation at all. Eleni continued:

> I think women have to learn how to control their own life and their own wishes. I'm not sure whether *control* is the right word[40]—*na katefthínoun* [to direct, guide]. And this has to do with what is called sexual liberation, and with how women feel about the liberation. I don't think that it's all liberated. It is another kind of oppression too. In my youth it was forbidden to have a sexual life before marriage or outside of a marriage. Now it is a must: to have a sexual life before marriage and at a very early age. And I think if it's a must, it's not liberated. I think women must learn now how to choose when and with whom [they will have sex], and they have to choose when and where and how many children to have.

At the same time, Eleni conceded that the diminished social monitoring of young people's sexual activity that is a feature of the ethic of choice may well be a positive development: "I think society now is more calm, more neutral about young people's sexual lives. Not only in the big cities but even in the small towns. I hear fewer comments, less judgment [about sex]." Indeed, sexually explicit and exploitative images of women are plastered everywhere in urban Greece: on billboards, magazine covers, television game shows. Major Athenian newspapers printed nude photographs of the (then) prime minister's wife, Mimi Liani Papandreou; subsequently, she gave an interview for a semipornographic men's magazine (Bonio 1996). Sex has lost much of its shock value, much of its ethical weight. People are seeking moral outrage—and moral security—elsewhere.

When I was in Athens, the newspaper stories about women that provoked outrage and problematized women's virtue were stories of maternal, not sexual, offense. Headlines for some of these stories included: "Babies Killed and Sold in Parents' Desperation" (*Athens News*, 11 November 1993), "Shock as Newly Born Baby Found Dead at Abandoned Basement"

(*Athens News*, 2 April 1994, p. 2), "She Buried the Baby Alive" (*Ta Nea*, 2 April 1994), and "Abandoned Kid's Mother Jailed" (*Athens News*, 20 May 1995). The women depicted in these stories acted in desperation to erase the consequences of an unintended pregnancy that developed into an unacceptable birth. The stories themselves call on both the ethic of service and the ethic of choice, demonstrating the dilemmas Athenians face in searching for a personally, nationally, and globally proper basis for their moral evaluations. For example:

> A thirty-year-old woman who buried her newly born baby alive said she had been "blinded by the shame" for conceiving out of wedlock. . . . Sofia Karakatsiani, a shy farm woman from the northern Greek village of Prosotasani, said she had hoped to bury her "terrible secret" along with the infant baby she bore out of wedlock.
>
> Concealing her pregnancy from relatives and neighbors, Ms. Karakatsiani checked into a local health clinic on Tuesday where, unattended, she gave birth to a baby girl in the bathroom and left. Desperate, she wrapped the infant in plastic bags and buried it by the roadside about one kilometre from the clinic.
>
> Health workers noticed the blood-stained floor and followed the tracks, discovering the distraught young woman. They said Ms. Karakatsiani showed them where she had buried the baby, but it was already dead when found by health workers.
>
> The young woman was later taken to the Drama State hospital for treatment.[41]

This story, like most others, is underscored with pity. Women who today resort to infanticide (a word that never appears in any of the accounts), or who act to control reproduction postpartum, are depicted as ignorant, peasant, naive, and backward—but not selfish, not pernicious. This woman claims in her defense that she acted to avoid the shame of being an unmarried mother, and implicitly to save her child from the shame of bastardization. The public—who number among them many women who have had abortions for similar reasons—can understand and even empathize with this woman's plight, even if they cannot sympathize with her ultimate action. The ethic of service continues to carry moral weight.

In September 1993 a newborn baby, still bloody from the birth, was apparently left to die behind the public toilets of a Patras bus station. This one was discovered still breathing. According to the newspaper account:

> Her name is Stavroula, a name she was given because she was born on the day that the church celebrates the name day of the Holy Cross on 14 September. Stavroula weighs just 1800 grams and is not among the

newborns born bringing joy to their parents. Because Stavroula will
never know her family. And it is better that she will not know them. If
ever they were found, the public prosecutor would seize them. . . . The
state prosecutor is studying the circumstances of her abandonment and
chiefly is pursuing the mother who preferred to throw [her] in the
trash. For little Stavroula it will be better never to find her.[42]

In this story, focused on criminal prosecution, the woman who "preferred"
to throw her child in the trash is seen to relinquish all claims to being that
child's mother. Unlike in the first story, where the postpartum woman
(lechóna) leads officials to the child's body and suitably demonstrates her
contrition, in Stavroula's story no woman is present to offer explanations—
a necessary component of modern moral praxis—and thus to engage public
sympathy. In her absence, the motherless child is consoled that she will
never have to know the woman who would abandon her. And yet this
mother, while held primarily accountable, shares blame with the rest of her
family, who will also never know Stavroula. The man who impregnated
Stavroula's mother, like the man behind Sofia Karakatsiani's shame, is immaterial to the story, a mystery in which no one is particularly interested.

I read in these stories ambiguity and conflict: Is the unwed woman who
"throws away" a maternal relationship with her child to be quietly admired, pitied, or castigated? Is she a martyr to tradition, suffering from the
unreasonable demands of honor? Or is she a "maternal monster," a practi-
tioner of unnatural acts of selfish disregard for human life and for her capacity to create it (Tsing 1990)? The stories bear witness to the uncertainty
Athenians confront when morally evaluating women as mothers and as
women. A traditional reading might see abandoning a newborn as a necessary evil on the part of an unwed mother, but the act itself would be un-
mentionable. That such private tragedies are now reported as news delivers
a modern evaluation of a practice deemed backward, and furthermore
reflects a very modern preoccupation with maternal duty itself.

Symbolically, what motherhood contributes to women's gender identity
is being transformed. In the past, when a woman demonstrated proper
femininity through sexual modesty, motherhood was important for establishing adulthood; as Dina intimated, motherhood distinguished girls
(maidens) from adult women (mothers). "Today," as Eleni put this contrast, "because unmarried women now . . . work, they *have* something."
When a childless woman can be clearly recognized as an adult in her capacity to work in the market, motherhood completes her as a woman.
Motherhood in turn becomes increasingly important for establishing gender, for distinguishing (working) women from (working) men. As women's

and men's social roles converge, biologically grounded reproductive difference is increasingly highlighted. This can have practical consequences. Men may be even more reluctant to share the burden of childcare and housework precisely because this has been made central to maintaining an obvious gender difference. In this sense too, the establishment of modern women's gender proficiency may, paradoxically, depend more fundamentally than ever on achieving motherhood.

Market-Based Economy and the Renegotiation of Femininity and Family

As we have seen, in strategizing how to meet their goal of motherhood and to be completed as women, middle-class Athenians are primarily concerned with reconciling *teknopiía* and their educational and occupational plans (rather than, say, with finding the "right" man). Discussing how women's experiences of *teknopiía* have changed since the 1970s, Eva told me that "today a woman is focused on social ascent, on careers, and sometimes [pregnancy] stands not as an obstacle but outside her plans." Echoing Eleni, Lela said, "Your participation at work gives you another existence, or sense of being *[ontótita].*" She suggested that external work rejuvenates a mother mentally: "You can get more tired by the work of bringing up a child, keeping a house. I think [working outside the home] is much better than staying here and just raising a child." She also stated that, with waged work, a woman's sense of self and range of responsibilities prompts her to look differently at the making of children. Women's participation in the labor force generates infrastructural needs that are not being met by the state or private sector, reshuffling family dynamics in ways that create new tensions between husbands and wives, parents and adult children. As forty-year-old Angeliki put it, "Now we are in a transition stage, because all our relatives *[óli i dhikhí mas]* had another mentality. What we call a generation is very significant."

Family and household, where group and individual interests intersect, represent key sites at which people confront conflicting ideas about gender and virtue. Lela, like my friend Moira quoted in the previous chapter, views the confusion regarding gender roles in families today as moral confusion: where once domestic roles were made clear, now they are muddled and no one is sure how to act ethically, begging the Aristotelian question of moral *and* conventional behavior. Soula, a forty-year-old who has continued to work as an embassy clerk following the birth of her daughter last year, elaborated:

It's not the woman in the house and the man outside anymore. Everyone grows up together, and I believe that it's a more contemporary way
of life. We're somewhat following the way of life of America, and of
other countries. It's not as it was in the past, when we lived more
calmly, had more free time. In the past decade the way of life has completely changed. Even in my own family, a young family, I see that five
years ago we had time to go out every day and to relax. Now you can't
do this. It's the rhythm of life, it's so demanding that we don't have any
time. We have increased our demands: we want a car, we want for our
children not just school but the *frontistíria* [private after-school
classes], their English, the gymnastics. We have all our hours filled each
day with many things.

Feminist theorists have argued that the household performs a contradictory role in social reproduction under market capitalism (Mitchell 1971;
Rapp 1982; Delphy and Leonard 1992). It is responsible for preparing individuals to be sent out into the social world ready to succeed in the market,
but it can provide a physical site for this precisely because it is kept somewhat sequestered from the outside world. "Out there in society," as Athenians conceive it, people are pitted against each other in an agonistic economy where their loyalties are demanded by institutional forms of power;
confounded and wounded, they return to the household, which is run and
symbolized by women and envisioned as a haven of safety and nurture
(Campbell 1964; Friedl 1967; du Boulay 1986; Dimen 1986). This dialectical relationship is exploited (and, in some contexts, created) under industrial capitalist economies, which wedge deeper the division between public
(work) and private (leisure) domains.

With this structural change accompanied by women's increased participation in the public sphere comes a reorientation of parental responsibilities. Aliki Andoniou, a psychologist who at the time of our interview was
pregnant with her second child, stated that having children today in Athens

is clearly the affair of the couple. In the past, it was the affair of the
family and of society. That is, you had to have a child for the society,
you owed it to the society, and you had to prove your fertility. Of
course even today people have to [have kids] by any means, with different reproductive techniques, but it is much more an individual affair, an
affair of the couple, than before. Previously it was a social affair and the
affair of the grandparents and others.[43]

In a modern society, *teknopiía*, the making of children, is ideally relegated
to the nuclear family. Consequently, the right to have and raise children,

and the responsibility for them, is placed solely in the hands of heterosexual parents (legal questions of childcare responsibilities under late modernity revolve around who is awarded the right of "true" parenthood). While this principle finds fullest expression in Protestant-based free-market capitalist societies,[44] in which individuals are expected to pay the price for their behavior and live with its consequences (Kertzer 1993, 17), in Athens, some, like Soula, view the trend toward consolidating nuclear families as a characteristic trait of modernity that Greece is coming to share with the more fully developed world. The privatization of childbearing is double-edged: on the one hand, young people may feel freer to make their own decisions in planning their lives and how children might fit into them, but, on the other hand, they run the risk of finding themselves overburdened if they try (or are forced) to shoulder the modern responsibilities of *teknopiía* without the extensive help of relations.

Another psychologist I interviewed added to what Andoniou stated: "The big difference between Greece and the rest of Europe is that the Greeks still have the big extended family. When you talk about family pressures, it's not only the husband, it's the mothers—two mothers—the in-laws, the parents of the parents, sisters, brothers, cousins, whatever. They press all together." Eva, who had been living with her parents in a village near Volos and commuting by bus to her office job in a factory, was relieved to put some distance (six hours' worth) between herself and her family when she was offered a position with the same company in Athens. She lives alone in a modest one-bedroom Pangrati flat.

> But I go [home] very often. I'm not cut off. Every two days or so [we make] telephone calls. And all the family holidays, Christmas and Easter, I have to go and see them, and I go. Plus every—at least two to three times a month I go to Volos. I haven't cut off contact with the rest of them. We're thick, but it's not that they have [a] hold over me anymore, that to make a decision I must notify them.[45]

She complained that Greek parents—"not like it is elsewhere, [where] they leave them alone"—tend to hover over their kids "to see what they do and where they go, how they behave." My encounter with the Stavropoulos family helped me recognize common points of tension between familial support and interference.

I met Maro Stavropoulou on a chilly afternoon at her combined dentistry office and home at Plasteira Square in Pangrati. After we had chatted awhile over coffee and she had copied out potential contact names and numbers for me from her address book, Maro realized her next appointment was fast approaching. She seized on the idea of telephoning her sister, who was that day eating with their parents—I could talk with them instead. After a quick call, Maro announced they would expect me in about thirty minutes. Finishing my coffee, I thanked her and left. My next stop was hardly three blocks away.

I rang the doorbell of a somewhat rundown neoclassical house just off Varnava Square and heard a high pitched female voice shrill, "She's here!" Niki Stavropoulou, Maro's younger sister, opened the door and ushered me in through a bare hallway to a simple room furnished with four chairs surrounding a table on which the bread crumbs and retsina tumblers of the midday meal remained. A television in the corner was switched on to a Greek game show. I was invited to sit at the table while *Kíria* Maria, her hair held in tight curlers, finished clearing it. Niki went to fix the coffee. After asking me how I liked Greece, "Papa" went off for his siesta. Soon we three women were sitting at the table with our requisite coffee. Someone turned down the sound of the television, but the set remained on. Maria often turned her head to fix her eyes on the screen, but paid continual attention to the conversation, which Niki led, interjecting regular comments that her daughter always paused to hear.

Maro had described her multigenerational family to me as "a classic Greek family" (her mother called it a "proper" one). The children grew up in a village near Pyrgos, the natal village of both parents. "My father worked, the mother at home occupied with the kids, the grandmother and grandfather living with us; and my mother's sister was also staying with us until she got married," Maro had told me. Before retiring, Maro and Niki's father worked as a carpenter. When Niki explained that, while she and her two siblings finished primary school, "Mama worked at home," Maria replied matter-of-factly, "One worked, one worked. I sewed at home. But just for us. Not for retail." Niki reiterated, in a tone suggesting that she would be hard pressed to sew clothes if her life depended on it, "But she sewed our own clothes! She raised three children!" Niki reported that her brother, now in Crete, works as a foreman in public works, concluding, "Myself, I have just the diploma from *líkio* (high school). I've worked from time to time, but now I'm unemployed." Maria averted her gaze from the television to announce, "Now she's an insurance agent!" "Now I'm not very involved with insurance," Niki gently corrected. "I've sort of given up on it." Later in our conversation, aware of her protective stance regarding her youngest child, I turned to Maria and asked, "You're a mother. What does it mean to your life?" She answered, "I'm happy because I have three children. I'm fine." Niki smiled. "I'm touched! We're good children and we love her. Both Mama and Papa." "The love is mutual," Maria said.

The next week I returned to talk with Maro, alone. While emphasizing that she and her siblings "are very closely tied" to each other and to their parents, Maro described her family as caught in the grips of conflicting desires for togetherness and autonomy. When there are family issues to resolve—they were then deliberating over what to do with the family home in Pyrgos which had suffered earthquake damage—all three children, who are in telephone communication almost daily, "must come to a common understanding." Before opening her private practice in 1980, Maro attended a university in Athens, where she and her sister and brother shared an apartment. "We would go out, the three of us, as a group with our friends; we were continually together. We continue to love one another [*aghapiómaste*]." Some discord set in among the family, however, when Maro finished her degree and announced her intention to open an office in Athens rather than return to her parents' town as had been expected. Although Maro conceded it would have been easier for her there, where houses are more affordable and she had a large circle of acquaintants who could have constituted her initial clientele, she wanted to live in Athens and, by that point, to live by herself. She sought independence, relatively speaking.

Her parents' response was to move to Athens themselves, to within a five-minute walk of their older daughter, while keeping the family home in Pyrgos. It is not uncommon for parents to follow their adult children—at least one Athenian mother even followed her daughter to Chicago while she attended graduate school. By this time Maro was a practicing dentist, a self-sufficient adult. Her father seemed to view things differently. Maro had to put her foot down—it was either that or sneak around like an adolescent:

> My father is very overprotective. Let's say I would leave their house to come here and it was late, one o'clock in the morning. He would tell me, "As soon as you get there, call." And I would say, "Call? No way." Say I'm on my way home and I meet a friend on the corner, and on the corner there's a souvlaki place; and she says to me, "Come, let's drink a beer," and I say to her "Fine, let's sit and have a beer." Well, if I weren't to come here and immediately telephone, what would he do? Wouldn't he be alarmed? This is why I live alone. Okay, now that he has health problems, generally I'll tell him where I can be found. Once I went to Spain. I gave the phone number to my sister and told her how to notify me if something serious happened. But it would be good if the phone didn't ring, so I didn't give the number to my parents.

Now Maria and her husband spend only the winter months in Athens, during which Niki divides her time between her parents' home and the home she shares with her husband in Pireaus. Each generation is faced with negotiating between traditional and modern expectations and demands when it comes to family relations. Making and managing money is often at the center of these negotiations. With Greece's productive infrastructure lagging behind its consumption rate, even middle-class Athenians are able to accumulate what are perceived as the basics—an apartment, a limited wardrobe of decent clothes, a regular diet of meat—only with the aid of others, usually their parents or in-laws. A professional woman I know, in her late thirties and single, lives alone in a suburban flat in Halandri purchased for her by her father, a flat she could not have afforded on her salary alone. Modern ways of living depend on traditional support networks.

I spoke with three unmarried, well-educated women in their late twenties who are slowly climbing the urban socioeconomic ladder with the aid of parents who, all living in villages, are not especially well-off. These women, friends since university days, are presently a physician (Rena), a Ph.D. candidate in archaeology (Athena), and a record store clerk who also tutors English (Sophia). They are quite conscious that they and others of their generation are the products of Greece's turbulent political history and recent economic growth.

ATHENA: Look. We were brought up within a rhythm of social life where we learned about goods, products. We want such [material] comforts that our social infrastructure doesn't support. When our parents were growing up after the [German] occupation, they had no money, they had no food. They say they grew up on bread and olives.

SOPHIA: My mother got her own first pair of shoes at the age of twelve. Until then she had only a pair of shoes from her older sister, which she wore every Sunday at church. Imagine that we are the children of these people!

ATHENA: And we have twelve pairs of shoes.

SOPHIA: My mother used to put cardboard in her shoes when her soles were worn out, and now she has twenty pairs of shoes. Because they grew up in that way, they did not want their children to be deprived.[46]

ATHENA: We grew up in a period of economic growth [the 1970s to the 1980s]. We learned [what it was like] to have relatively nice houses, to have nice clothes, a car. Unfortunately, however, we reached a point where we got stuck. When the basic wage is around a hundred thousand [drachmes], and you want a home

in a nice area, the rent will be seventy thousand a month.[47]
This is normal; it's not some absurd amount. You think that
you can't live. It's very hard. And if you want everything, this
is what you do: the parents of a friend of mine used to eat
bread and cheese, while their kids ate regular food, so they
could gather the money to buy a flat.[48]

Athena's parents made sacrifices to help finance her advanced degree from
a British university. Sophia explained that her own parents felt badly because they could not offer her more economic support and had to abandon
her in Athens:

I live alone. My parents had to go back to the village in Crete. I pay
rent, and every month they try to send me what they can—and I see
every time I go down to Crete that they worry they can't give me forty
thousand [drachmes] a month. If there's a month when they can't send
me money, they waste ten thousand calling me on the phone to tell me
they're sorry.[49] If my family were in Athens, I wouldn't try to live on
my own.

Tensions arise when young people recognize the moral system in which
their parents operate—based in an era when status flowed from parents to
children by way of inherited character and property—but at the same time
plan for themselves a life they must personally author.

The younger generation is more independent than their elders sometimes realize, in part because young adults consciously keep knowledge of
independent initiatives from parents. Despina works a part-time job in the
British city where she attends graduate school to supplement her modest
scholarship, which her parents already supplement every few months. She
cannot divulge this to her parents: they would feel that she had to take a
job because they had failed to provide adequately for her. The middle-class
women in their twenties that I knew in Athens recognize and respect their
parents' need to *feel* they are providing adequately for their children, revealing a new generation-based rift between the appearance of prestige and
the reality of power (cf. Friedl 1967). They negotiate a measure of independence without hurting their parents' feelings, because they have not
rejected the values of family solidarity. The ethics of service and choice are
not mutually exclusive.

Thinking about how she wants to raise her own daughter, and mindful
of the lingering effects of how she herself was raised, Soula tried, as we
spoke, to sort out the conflicting pressures of what I have framed as com-

peting ethics, and which she views as a struggle particular to the Greek context. She sketched two common, conflicting parenting strategies:

I believe that the institution of the family in Greece is still strong, compared with other countries. There is still the meaning that this is my child and I have obligations. Of course in certain cases I think it gets overdone: the kids get married and the parents think they still have obligations—surely this doesn't happen abroad? But there is also the other extreme, that as soon as the kids turn eighteen or twenty that's it, finished, the parents have no more responsibility, nothing on their plate. There are the two sides: the parents who say, "We brought you into life and we are obliged to serve you all our lives," and the others who say, "We brought you up, now you have to take care of us."

Both sides can be viewed within the frame of an ethic of service; the difference lies in whether the obligation to serve rests primarily with the parents or with the children. In prewar agricultural settings, filial obligations predominated; the pressures of a market economy that placed new emphasis on education as a means of upward mobility shifted the burden of obligation onto parents to provide new opportunities for their children. Soula's critical voice invoked traditional notions of children's responsibility for themselves, while at the same time calling on a modern understanding that parents (primarily mothers) should be given room to devote themselves to projects and interests other than the success of their children. Soula felt the pull of an ethic of service but, like Maro, articulated its unrealistic expectations:

What I'm trying to say is that there's something that I like and something that I don't like in the Greek family. While it's very tight, in certain ways it pulls you apart a little: they want to be continuously together, but you can't. I believe that when children leave home and get married, that's it for their own family, finished. The relationships that should be maintained with the parents are [maintained]. The child will go and see them, they'll eat together, go out together, but each is in their own home. They each have to have their own life. I don't know whether you have seen that most Greek families are like this—they continue to live together in such a way that, even if they are in separate houses, there's the same effect.

Having met the Stavropoulos family, I had in fact seen this.

What Soula did not mention, but which other women emphasized, was that this negotiation of parental responsibilities primarily affects women, as mothers and grandmothers. Angeliki, a forty-year-old civil servant married to a dentist, talked with me about the gendered difference in parental roles—a topic foremost in her mind as she negotiated her relationships with her thirteen-month-old daughter, her husband, her job, and her mother-in-law (who is much "more tightly linked" to her husband than she herself is with her own mother). "These days," she said to me,

> the father wants to be involved, to play; often the child and the father are tighter [than the child with the mother]. He's the child's friend. The mother gradually begins to obtain another role, she's the mother—she does the [house]work, she cooks, she bathes it, she takes it to childhood events, to parties, she reads to it. The mother is very much like an obligation, and the father like a toy: this is the difference. The mother is the must: "Don't jump on the sofa!" The father is much more entertainment. There is a difference; mother is one thing and father is another.

Because motherhood continues to encompass care of the household as well as care of children, freeing fatherhood to be "much more entertainment," family conflict related to paid employment can fall out along gender as well as generational lines. When family members "press all together," according to the psychologist Vaso Skopeta, often they demand of a modern woman who works outside the home, "How can you abandon the child?" Skopeta impressed on me that even "university women, women with Ph.D.s, tell me, 'My poor little girl, what's she going to think of me that I'm always at work?' " Despite progressive, PASOK-initiated legislation such as Law No. 1414/84, which calls for nondiscrimination based on sex in all aspects of employment, the cultural supposition that women should devote themselves to protecting the household, and should take responsibility for children's upbringing, leads most people to regard female employment as an extension of domestic duties (Sutton 1986; Symeonidou 1990; Vaiou 1992; Chronaki 1992). As Symeonidou puts it, "The female spouse is the one who maximizes the use value of the family" (1990, 172). In her 1989 research among Athenian women, conducted under the auspices of a comparative European Union (EU) study of women and poverty, Vaso Skopeta told me she found that a woman's salary is often that portion of the domestic income earmarked for the children's private schools, the children's clothes, and the children's shoes. Female earning power, meanwhile, has never reached the level of male earnings.[50]

That Athenian women experience a double bind, bearing the brunt of domestic labor in addition to performing externally paid work, is hardly exceptional (Hewlett 1986; Hochschild 1989; Segura 1994; MacLeod 1996). But Athenian women, often presuming that women have it easier in more solidly modern societies (supposedly populated by more solidly modern men), speak about their double burden in an idiom articulated with what to them is a distinctively Greek tradition of patriarchal power. (In speaking of patriarchal tradition, these nonacademic women use Greek words that have become part of Anglophone academic feminist jargon. While the meanings of these words are similar in both contexts, such words, when spoken in Greece, are as descriptive as they are analytic.) Nadia, whom I met when she appeared at my doorstep peddling foreign-language tapes, told me:

> Today's women work. From the moment that the woman works, she also has her personal vigor [*névro*], she has her own ambitions, she has many problems; and of course this unwittingly creates a situation in the home. For example, she would want her husband to help [around the house]. The man, the Greek man, is phallocratic [*fallokrátis*]. This means to have been raised to a way of life in which work is made to be either men's or women's. Somehow these don't agree. This creates innumerable problems in a relationship. To put it simply, the woman today is not the woman of the past who stayed under [*kathótane ipó*] the man. What does *under* mean? It means without voicing her opinion, without voicing her problems, without a lot.

Maro, like Nadia a middle-aged, single, working woman, voiced a similar view:

> The mother, for me, plays the most significant role in the house. However, because society is androcentric [*androkratikí*], the world appears male and the father thinks he has the upper hand. For although, anymore, they both generally work—say, in the shop—and, among the majority, also both participate in the home, the woman is the one who has the responsibility for the house, the responsibility for the kid, and the father has only the responsibility of work. He participates less in the common responsibilities of the house because he's tired, because he's going to go see his friends, because he'll read his newspaper, because he'll sit around—this is the classic Greek family! It's generally thought that the role of the father is more important, while in essence it's the mother's.

Nadia and Maro describe a situation in which women are beginning to see the world and their place in that world differently from previous generations, and in which they are faced with the task of getting men to share and act on this vision. While certainly there are Athenian men who concede in principle that the old ways are unjust, in practice, as women told me, "it takes generations for a society" to "move ahead."

I frequently heard Athenian women refer to that stubborn patriarchy as *líghi anatolikí,* "a little Eastern," and to the men who clutch onto it as *lígho píso,* "a little backward." Men are said to be backward because they hold tighter to elements of tradition that run counter to modern liberated gender relations. In being labeled Eastern, these men are additionally denigrated as being "Turkish."[51] Georgia Afxendiou (1996) reports similarly that Salonikan women who work at managing market and domestic responsibilities consider themselves more Western and progressive (e.g., more rational) than men, who work to keep a clearer distinction between social domains and, by extension, between men and women. And yet it should also be noted that the rigid, gendered division of labor is complicated by the axis of sexuality. A Greek Australian woman I knew who had lived and worked in Athens since 1983 told me the following tale of a woman she knew, who was about her own age (late forties or early fifties). This woman was married to a man who would wash the dishes and hang out the clothes. The neighbor women would gossip—is this man "otherwise inclined"?—that is, my acquaintance clarified, homosexual. He must be, the neighbors concluded; that's why he's doing women's work—and in the open too! It did not matter that he was married. Owing to the marriage mandate, I heard of many women who found themselves married to men who never really followed through with conjugal relations beyond what was required to produce heirs; gay men largely lead double lives in Greece. In this case, the women's gossip became so intense that it convinced the wife that her husband actually was homosexual, on no evidence other than his domestic help. The couple divorced.

In expressing frustration at men's (and some women's) comfortable complicity with the injustices of traditional patterns, Maro and Nadia do not view phallocratism or androcentrism as tyrannical or threatening, but they shake their heads at men's naïveté regarding social power. Women, they state knowingly, are the true backbone of the family; and the family, as they are repeatedly reminded by priests and politicians, forms the core of Greek society and the Greek nation. Phallocratism and androcentrism are ironical devices that urban Greek women, often with smug humor, employ among themselves to deflate male *eghoismós*—the masculine principle of social excellence (Herzfeld 1985)—to simpleminded (perhaps hypocritical) egocentrism *(eghokendrismós).* In so doing, they establish a moral differentiation between men and women that celebrates women's progressiveness and indicates their belief that women do more than men—and make wiser, more informed choices—to propel Greece forward in the global arena and to foster Greece's maturity in the family of nations. Changes in gender proficiency are articulated in moral idioms.

When Nadia, Maro, and others disparaged men's phallocratism or *anatolitikótita* (being Eastern) in my presence, they also signaled our shared "gendered intimacy" as progressive women living in modern patriarchal societies. I improvise here on Michael Herzfeld's "cultural intimacy" (1997a), a notion that gets at the confluence of contradictory cultural self-stereotypes—that "insiders" will own up to a given trait among themselves in a gesture of "rueful self-awareness," but, when confronted by powerful outsiders, will vociferously deny all association with that same trait. In a country where culture has been officially expunged of trace remains of Ottoman presence, Greeks admit among themselves that some of their most beloved and intimate elements of daily practice—coffee prepared in a copper *bríki*, for instance—are shared with Turks or are even traceable to Turkish origins. In blaming men for Greece's relative cultural backwardness in comparison with their vision of the United States, then, these women play on a form of cultural intimacy that crosscuts gender.[52] The strategic use of dualistic cultural stereotypes—women are "really" in charge of a decidedly patriarchal society—helps people negotiate inevitable tensions and conflicts at the level of everyday life.

"The Baby Costs Too Much": Refiguring Reproductive Agency under an Ethic of Choice

One arena where urban women claim greater maturity and responsibility than men is the realm of fertility control. Since the 1950s, this has been clearest in women's recourse to abortion. Because abortion was introduced as part of an ethic of service, many women view it as self-compromising, rather than self-fulfilling. An ethic of choice demands other options, alternative ways of avoiding a necessary evil. The remainder of this chapter addresses emerging ideas about the making of children in a market economy; the following chapter takes up Athenians' engagement with specific means of family planning.

Overwhelmingly, Athenians believe that it is more difficult today to decide to have children. As Niki said:

> Now, especially in Athens, because the woman works [outside the home] she doesn't decide easily to raise a child, [even] one or two. She makes that decision less frequently. With the economic difficulties that there are today, the middle-class Greek, I believe, thinks much more about raising a child. If they don't have the economic capability, how will they manage it?

Niki's statement not only realizes politician Miltiades Evert's call for the "knowledgeable, thoughtful" person and operates more within an ethic of

choice than of service, it also signals the economic basis of women's reproductive decision making.

Lela told a similar tale, adding that financial insecurity strains both the
household budget and the marital relationship:

> From discussions with friends and people at work, [I understand] it is a
> very difficult decision to have a child now. One problem is the relation-
> ship. There's a terrible crisis in human relationships, marital relation-
> ships, but I believe that this will get better once we have solved the eco-
> nomic problem, which is fundamental. People aren't deciding to have a
> child. My sister just birthed, and the maternity hospital cost her five
> hundred thousand [drachmes]. It takes a long time for someone who's a
> worker to collect such a great amount of money. And then there are all
> the other expenses, for the family and for you yourself—if you smoke,
> if you want to go out occasionally. You can't refuse yourself these
> things, not to go out because it costs money. There are many expenses,
> and I believe that the low birthrate is something to think about. I have
> a *koumbáros* [wedding sponsor] who's a civil engineer—he works at
> DEH [the national electric company], and his wife is at the Bank of
> Crete.[53] Beyond the fact that they have some problems between
> them—which I believe would be fewer if they solved their economic
> troubles—anyway, they don't think they'll have another child. He tells
> me, "How would we manage? We would have to find another house;
> the one we have now is too small for a four-person family. We'd have
> more expenses, . . . spend more at the supermarket." A baby has incred-
> ible expenses.

Although the requisite doctors' fees compare favorably to those in the
United States, durable consumer goods are exorbitant.[54] Few discount
chain stores operate in Greece, where nearly everything—strollers, baby
clothes—is imported and sold at specialty shops with high overhead.

Since Greece was propelled into the European market economy, EEC
and EU money has funded several works projects that employ a large number of people—most notably, in Athens, the expansion of a metro system—
but injections of projects and money had not fully revitalized the Greek
economy by the middle 1990s. Cheap food imports, including Danish
"feta" cheese, flooded the country via the new Alpha-Beta supermarkets
and did little to stimulate the country's underdeveloped industrial sector.
The Maastricht Treaty, signed in February 1992 and stipulating that a European Union member country's public-sector debt must not exceed 60
percent of its gross national product (GNP), forced a palpable 12 percent
inflation rate to bring down Greece's debt, stuck at twice its GNP into the

1990s.[55] Athenians felt deeply the effects of an economic crisis exacerbated by EU directives that the country "catch up" with other member nations.

In every interview I conducted, people spoke of *teknopiía*, the making of children, primarily in terms of requisite economic resources. This is not surprising, since debate over what responsibilities best demonstrate a woman's maternal and gender proficiency reflects a shift in the moral understanding of good mothering and proper womanhood under intensifying capitalism. Education in Greece, as throughout southern and post-socialist eastern Europe (Collier 1997; Kligman 1998), is superseding accumulated inheritance and business connections as the prime cause of social ascent, the securer of high status occupations.[56] For this reason, Athenian parents routinely spend money to send their daughters and sons to *frontistíria* for private classes held after regular school hours.[57] So many students learn a second or third foreign language at *frontistíria* that, while education generates cultural capital, it also works to level differences in class disposition or group style (Katsillis and Rubinson 1990, 274; Stewart 1991, 125–28). Parents feel they must push their children through high school, since entrance into the ten fully subsidized state universities is based on competitive comprehensive examinations.[58] Many students pay to attend one of the numerous private colleges augmenting the state system. Still others choose to study in the United Kingdom, Germany, United States, or Canada; many never return to Greece.

While choice and personal achievement have become the operating designators of status, reputation is largely based on cultural capital, a person's style *[ífos]* as reflected in how one chooses to spend one's money (Stewart 1991; Faubion 1993). Litsa astutely applied this to mothering:

> It is very difficult to have a child—these days we are a consumer society. Earlier—I tell you [this] from my own life—when we went to school, we used to wear [uniform] pinafores; one would last the year with its tears mended and patched. But now, there is this consumerism. Tomorrow my child will see someone wearing such-and-such shoes, and he'll tell me, "Me too!" You'll tell me I should fix it so [that] my kid is not interested in name brands; you say I don't have to send him to extra classes to do a foreign language, rent if I don't own a house— life is very expensive and the costs are many to raise a child. In the past we grew up in another way. I was the last child of five; what my sister would wear one year I would take the next. It didn't matter to us; we weren't bombarded by television. Of course *we have done this to our lives*. They [marketers, media, etc.] put this idea into our heads, but *we* are the ones who go and implement it, we are the consumers. Tomor-

row at the supermarket, we see something new, we try it, we like it—
and there's the good discount, so—it's difficult. [Emphasis added]

What Maila Stivens writes of middle-class urban Malaysia speaks equally to
Athens: "To be a modern mother is to be an active consumer under great
pressure to acquire all the commodities necessary for the satisfactory performance of motherhood" (1998, 63). Galena Skiatha, president of the Union
of Greek Homemakers (Sýlloghos Ellinídhas Nikokíras) a group that lobbies
the state to pension homemakers for their domestic labor, told me that this
was a major change that had occurred since her "generation of the war":

> I say our season was very hard, but they do not see that now. Now it is
> another epoch, the epoch of consumerism [and] the television program.
> All that means you must have money—first of all is the money, and
> then comes the baby. So the baby costs too much.[59]

Parental obligations have always been about parents wanting to enable
their children to get ahead. But today, when one cannot talk about motherhood apart from the quality of a woman's mothering, Greek consumerist
self-fashioning redefines being a good mother as providing the best material goods for one's children, rather than, say, spending quality time with
them. When others recognize that a woman chooses to spend her hard-
earned money on her children—to keep them in the latest fashions, to provide them with extracurricular activities—this demonstrates her moral
worth as a mother.

Contemporary women's role as consumers is best viewed not as a new
phenomenon but as an extension of their long-standing activities as
household managers (*nikokíres;* Gefou-Madianou 1992, 110). When their
"relationship to the economic framework of both the family and the community" is defined by their role as *nikokíres,* then "being a nikokyra also
serves as the central focus for self perception and for women's own observations of their changing roles" (Salamone and Stanton 1986, 103). Similarly, the notion that parents should provide their children with the best is
not a modern import but represents, as Athena suggested to me, a translation of the dowry system, intensified by the memory of famine and material lack from the war era as well as by the capitalist proliferation of consumer choice. The dowry, after all, has long served as a social mechanism
not only for propelling daughters into economically and socially advantageous positions as wives but also for handing down capital from one generation to the next (e.g., Friedl 1962). Athena explained:

Because now a family that has one child wants to give it everything. Education, English, French; it goes to the gymnasium, takes piano lessons. They want their kids to have everything that they need for when they leave home. This doesn't happen abroad, but it happens here. The dowry still exists. The girl herself will demand this help from the house because she can't cope and because she has been brought up to be a consumer. This is not just with girls. The same goes for boys. While in the past, the woman had to have a certain amount of money, or a house, now this holds for both of them. For a family to start out, they have to have the means.

Because the contemporary "education dowry" can be bestowed years before marriage, it is related less to winning a worthy mate and more to establishing the child as a self-sufficient adult (who will seem attractive to other self-sufficient adults). For women, too, now, adulthood comes before marriage and parenting, not with it.

Some Athenians are questioning the benefits that this contemporary, equal-opportunity "dowry" supposedly affords women: equality in marriage and economic independence. Despite its patriarchal tenets, the old dowry system often provided women with a measure of security in the admittedly unequal marriage partnership. When a woman brought a house with her into a marriage, that house remained legally hers, and, in the past, women were known to show husbands the door for misbehavior. Today, when property is held equally between spouses, a wife loses exclusive rights to a dowry. And whereas in the past brothers were obligated to help provide their sisters' dowry to marry them off, before they themselves married,[60] this is no longer the case. Niki and Maro's mother, Maria, echoed Athena's observation, saying, "Now whether you have a boy or a girl, you will spoil the same years in order to school both of them, to provide for them everything." The financial burden shouldered by parents—or, as Haris Symeonidou (1990) found, by mothers—is increasing.

In order to be able to provide properly as mothers, wage-working Greek women pursue one of two strategies when they have a first child (Symeonidou 1990). Many, like Fotini's mother, Irini, leave the workforce after marriage or childbirth; for these women, waged work appears to be a functional precursor to motherhood (Vaiou 1992, 255). Alternatively, they return to work right away, finding caretakers for their infants. Beyond the state guarantee of six months' unpaid parental leave to supplement four months' paid leave for the birth itself, there is little informal job security for women in the public sector. There is no state provision and little social precedent, Symeonidou explained to me in an interview, for women to reenter the labor market after dropping out (see also Papadopoulos 1998). Aside from poorly paid piecemeal manufacturing jobs, part-time employment is virtually nonexistent (in 1995, 8.4 percent of Greek female employment was part-time, compared with a European Union average of 31.3 percent [Papadopoulos 1998]). Many mothers who ceased working indicated on Symeonidou's surveys that they would like to reenter the job market but were unable to do so. The labor activity rate of Greek married women between twenty-five and forty-nine years of age is the lowest in the EU, at 40 percent compared to the EU average of nearly 60 percent (Eurostat 1994, cited in Papadopoulos 1998, 55).

The lack of quality, affordable day care is a huge concern of parents and aspiring parents. Maro, who meets many mothers in the course of her dental practice, said, "There must be centers where a woman can leave her child without having to pay her entire salary. There are very few day care centers, nursery schools. The ones we have are nothing for the needs that exist." Private day care centers *(pedhikí stathmí)* in the middle 1990s charged as much as 600,000 drachmes (U.S.$2,575) a year per child, or 50,000 (U.S.$215) a month.[61] If a couple has two young children, the fee matches the average monthly salary of a secretary or clerk. To offer another comparative figure, my roommate and I rented a three-room Pangrati flat for 85,000 drachmes a month; occupying identical flats above and below us were two families of three (downstairs: mother, father, toddler; upstairs: mother, father, college-graduate working daughter). At Varnava Square a block and a half away, a bilingual (Greek-English) day care center charged 80,000 a month. A few state-run day care centers are in operation, but here it is not uncommon for a sole child-care worker in a cement-walled building to have as many as fifty small children in her charge. For many families, this is not an option. State centers take only children whose mothers are employed full-time (Vaiou 1992, 253), and only (some of) the expensive private centers will accept children under the age of two and a half. Litsa, the working mother of a seven-year-old, told me, "This is something very difficult—where to take your child. I had him at day care until he went to school. I paid such money! Now he goes to [public] school. But he gets out at 12:30, and someone has to stay with him until 3:00 when I come home. I have anxiety." In Athens, employment does not reduce women's desire to have children; reduced childbearing is more the result of an infrastructure that cannot accommodate the needs of mothers who work outside the home.

While middle-class urban Greeks are beginning to join other southern Europeans in employing African, Filipina, and Albanian immigrant women as domestic workers and nannies (Anderson 2000; Lazaridis 2000), most Athenian families continue to rely on the unpaid labor of family members. Of the thirty-eight women I formally interviewed about their family lives, four had children at that time too young to attend nursery school, and nine others had children at school at least part-time. All mothers worked full-time. Two of them, professionals, employed live-in Filipina nannies-house-keepers, while the others, like Soula, routinely left their children in the care of their parents during the day. This common arrangement suits people not only economically but also emotionally, because they prefer not to have *ksénes* (meaning both nonfamily and non-Greek persons) looking after their children. Kalliroe, who employs a Filipina woman to look after her four-year-old, assured me that this has not excluded her own parents from contributing to her daughter's upbringing:

> When I was pregnant with my daughter—this is very important—my husband and I lived by ourselves. We were living in [the] city center [near Pangrati, walking distance to her office], with the air pollution and everything. A month before I birthed, we moved to my parents' house in Penteli [a posh suburb, maybe an hour by car from the city center]. We were all living together—the *kopélla* [girl] too, the Filipina—it's a very big house. And so things were easier—I could get back to my work, take trips—because my mother took care of her when I traveled.

Even professional women rely in part on what I came to call the *yiayiá* institution—the informal social institution by which grandmothers *(yia-yiádhes)* are willing and available to help with the domestic economy of their children's families. We might view this as an urban adaptation (or inversion) of some former village patrilocal residence patterns, where daughters-in-law were called on to provide much of the domestic labor for the households of their mothers-in-law (see Friedl 1962). That older generations help their adult offspring by means of unpaid labor, in addition to the material support of a dowry or inheritance, reveals the increasing emphasis and value placed on the younger generations, itself characteristic of modern family organization geared toward the generation of productive children (Saporiti 1989). However, with women delaying childbirth into their thirties, the gap between generations is widening: even if grandparents are at home during the day, they may be quite elderly. Ariadne will not try again to have a second child, "because I am too tired, even though I might like to, inside me. My mother used to look after him when he was five months old, but now she has had a stroke." The *yiayiá* institution may well be a dying one in Greece's cities (Symeonidou 1990, 149).

Secure in her savings and pension, seventy-year-old Dina complained to me that young women today do not exert enough effort to attain both *teknopiía* and careers. When she was young, Dina attended school and earned her teacher's certification. At age twenty-four, during the civil war, she was posted to a town school not far from Athens, where she met her husband. With a smile, Dina told me how they met after he arrived as a new faculty member. I asked Dina whether she took a dowry with her into marriage. Her smile faded to disapproving frown. "No, of course I did not take a dowry, because I worked!" As is common for women today, her dowry, back then, had taken the form of education and employment. Because this came on the heels of a decade of war, shortages, and economic collapse, it is hardly surprising that Dina and her husband could not rely on their parents to establish their new household: "Everything that we ended up with, we worked for together." Not only did Dina and her husband earn enough to purchase property and build two summer houses, they had two children. Dina was thirty-three when her first child was born:

> We had no grandmother at home; my mother was dead, [her husband's mother] was too old. I managed both work and family by having outside help. Many times I waited for the helpers at the balcony, wondering if I would be at work on time. But one thing I can be proud of is that, during my thirty-five years at work, I was never late.

If, in the 1950s, she could raise two children while working full-time without the benefit of a live-in grandmother or dowry, Dina saw little excuse for women not to do the same today:

> And so now some of these young women don't have children; they say, "My figure!" Ach! And other alibis they give: "We work!" You find a way. At least I did. I worked for thirty-five years. It was hard, without a dowry; it put a lot of pressure on me. However, I brought forth the children.

It may be, as Dina implied, that some young people today expect parental handouts without shouldering their share of the responsibilities. But it is also the case that Dina may not fully appreciate what has changed culturally since her early adulthood. For many women, it is no longer enough that one has brought forth the children. Elaborating on why she will not try to have a second child, thirty-five-year-old Ariadne, who has been married for twelve years, noted, "It would be economically impossible for them to grow *as I would want.* [Even] if my mother were well [and could help with childcare], it would be difficult. The economic factor is serious; we both work" (emphasis added). So while Soula, in sympathy with Dina, who is twice her age, commented that "a middle-class family today can comfortably raise two children," the question hinges on how people define comfort in view of new familial and economic realities.

Economic insufficiency, the physical and emotional stress of contemporary life, and a deficiency of human character are all frequently cited as reasons why couples these days are having fewer children than in the past, indeed fewer children than they would *like* to have. Athenian women tend to discuss reproductive agency not in terms of individual, self-interested decision making but rather by stressing external parameters that seem beyond their immediate control. And they depict many of the constraints that impinge on personal desire, that thwart the realization of women's characterological nature, as symptomatic of Greek modernity.

I heard of couples who decided not to bring children into the overpopulated, polluted city of Athens, and who will not have kids unless they, like Kalliroe, can afford to move to the tree-lined streets of middle-class suburbs. Casual acquaintances described to me at length today's medical problem of low fertility, holding air pollution largely responsible for purportedly lower sperm counts. Nadia, who walks the city streets extensively in her job as door-to-door salesperson, believes people are especially vulnerable to the modern pollutants of television radiation and car exhaust because the "stress" *(ánchos)* of modern life is making people "soft." Critiquing modern technology and ways of life for damaging people's "natures," both characterological and physical, she sees Athenians being drained of virility and fertility, as well as *kéfi,* the high spirits that can be viewed as Greek-style joie de vivre:

> People aren't as tough as they were [when they ate] wild foods—and television has radiation, do you know?—which taints the potency of the person. The person has lost sex because of this culture: they don't have sex with the frequency they used to. Here you hear of couples who have sex every five days, every two months—haven't you heard this?

And the less frequently couples make love *(kánoun érota),* she noted, the fewer children they make *(kánoun pedhiá).* Friends Eva and Toula also joked (but at the same time meant seriously) that today, with people working two jobs and commuting and running about the city, they are simply too tired at the end of the day to make either love or babies: "These days, if you get back around ten or eleven o'clock at night, you can't make babies; you have to go to sleep!"

Today, when sex is condoned, if not expected, before marriage, some say they are not getting it as much as when it was illicit.[62] Even Greek politicians may be concerned that people are having sex too infrequently. I was told that a state-run television station, at least in rural areas where siesta hours are universally observed, broadcasts at midday foreign soft-pornography videos.[63] My acquaintance theorized this as an attempt on the part of the state to encourage an increase in the birthrate, the logic being that, at midday, people are not yet tired out, and if they are at home for a few hours with their spouse, why not try and "get them in the mood"? Given political concern over the falling fertility rate, the theory is plausible.

CHANGE AND CONTINUITY: CRITIQUING FATALISM AND CHOICE

The partial transition from an ethic of service aimed at directing women's control over their sexuality to an ethic of choice guiding women's maternal practices entails a refiguring of reproductive agency for women. But, as I have argued, this is a difference of kind, not degree. When women left it up to God to decide whether and when they brought forth children, they were not fatalistic regarding reproductive outcome. Similarly, women today are well aware that their choices regarding *teknopiía* and motherhood are not automatically obtainable. I was struck by how pragmatically these women seem to regard the limits of choice. I was impressed by the political-economic perspective they brought to bear on obstacles they faced, and a bit envious of how they seemed able to shrug off feelings of inadequacy for failing to meet their own and others' expectations.

Incessantly one hears in Greece the refrain "What can I do?" (*ti na káno*). Anthropologists have interpreted this as a move to avoid responsibility for any act whose outcome is attributed to the whims of *tíchi*, "chance" (see, for example, du Boulay 1974, 95). Greeks ascribe events to fate (*míra*) in order to carry on in a world not under their immediate control. They do not act because it is their fate to do so; rather, fate—which can in modern settings be shorthand for the emotional, moral, and material factors seen to impinge on people's (supposedly) otherwise rational action—allows them to cope with events that do not accord with their ideals.

Furthermore, appeals to fate permit people to manipulate circumstances behind the scrim of public scrutiny without upsetting the dominant ideological order. I heard Athenians utter the phrases "What can I do?" or "What can one do?" to accompany actions that seem not to meet social, often gendered, ideals, such as delaying marriage or neglecting to have children. When the economic crisis is the most common justification Athenians offer for the country's low birthrate, women and men who nevertheless manage to have children are able to spin for themselves tales of heroic achievement and self-sacrifice: mothers are exemplary women. Alternatively, people can use the economic crunch as an alibi for choosing not to have children: "What can I do?" At the same time, people who for physiological reasons cannot have children, as well as others who may not want any, can hide what might be viewed as a moral or character deficiency under the alibi of material scarcity. Women's agency in *teknopiía*, I have argued, is in many ways continuous from past to present. Traditional appeals to fate have never been fatalistic, and modern appeals to choice are modest. The intensifying Greek modernity is making explicit women's very real, if always socially constrained, reproductive agency.

As they discussed their perceptions of cultural change and continuity over the past decades, I consistently heard Athenian women invoke ethics—and play the ethic of service and the ethic of choice off one another—to cast themselves as virtuous subjects and to level social criticism. This rhetorical strategy may involve claiming a gendered nature that at first glance seems essentialized. Recall, for instance, Lela's claim that, whereas women's lives have clearly changed, "motherhood is as it always was." And Phoebe remarked, "I believe that all mothers are the same. Of course, in past eras there were mother-heroines who dedicated their life to their children; they did terrific things. [But] I believe that every mother is prepared to do everything for her child. This is within the nature of a woman."

The nature that motherhood most fully realizes is a moral relationship of service—"every mother is prepared to do everything for her child"—evincing a more characterological than strictly biological notion of nature. As illustrated in Orthodox iconography—the most common domestic icon is the Panayía Vrefokratoúsa, Mary holding the Christ child—there is no love, *aghápi*, stronger than that between a mother and child. Distinguishing between *érotas*, passionate but flighty love, and *aghápi*, a greater and enduring love, Niki explained that *aghápi* obtains "mostly with the mother and the child, who is a part of her self—the child is a part of her self, from her body. She had it nine months inside her; it's something different."

Aghápi is an ongoing, transformative relationship that connotes a Christian sense of selflessness, and that, in the words of Caroline Whitbeck (1990), designates a "non-oppositional" ontology in which the self is defined not against "the other" but in mutually enabling relations with it. In their depictions of pregnancy, many Athenian women describe the fetus as part of the woman's body: the same blood runs through both. While mothers say they feel the bond of maternal love initiated at the moment of quickening in the womb, they do not view the fetus as a separate being with whom they have a social, maternal relationship. What exists between a pregnant woman and her fetus is an *ontological* relationship, and this leads to a stronger social relationship after birth.

In Niki's view, a woman's body naturally lends itself to cradling an infant in her arms:

> She's built to create a child. Because of this, you will observe that most times the man holds the baby completely differently than the woman. The body of the woman is built such that she can hold a baby, while for the father it's difficult. Usually the man is afraid to hold the baby.

Recalling that Niki believes that motherhood "completes" a woman, it is tempting to conclude that, for her, mothering—that range of responsibilities entailed in the gestation, birth, and proper upbringing of a child—is essential to women, something that "is most irreducible, unchanging, and therefore constitutive" of being a woman (Fuss 1989, 2). That women are primarily responsible for young children is, to Niki, clearly self-evident. But as Herzfeld reminds us, "self-evidence is made, not given. It does not rest on the existence of 'self-evident truths,' but on the presentation of contingent circumstances as self-evident truths" (1997a, 153–54). Niki and Phoebe may be making a moral claim by drawing on the pervasive image of a woman holding a child exemplified by the Panayía Vrefokratoúsa. Herzfeld notes, "Skilled actors, female and male alike, can deform . . . self-evidence for their own purposes, whether they succeed in incrementally altering the larger structure of values or not" (1997a, 153). Rather than assume these women are falling back on traditional understandings of a world governed by divinely ordained nature, we must ask why and to what effect they call on essentializing rhetoric (Fuss 1989).

For the most part, Athenian women seem content to assume primary responsibility for children. In this they are recognizably powerful and can take credit for their children's development and success—and realize their feminine nature. In drawing on the moral tenets of the ethic of service, women can also negotiate the modern tensions they experience in making reproductive (and other) choices. Some women address the double bind presented by their family's need for both domestic and extradomestic labor by referring (or deferring) to women's natural capacity to nurture and train children, especially infants, and a natural incapacity of men to perform such tasks. Their invocation of a revered tradition of maternal service, even sacrifice, effectively naturalizes and thus normalizes social conflicts and contradictions that have accompanied women's widespread emergence in the workforce: "What can we do?"

Dina, who is somewhat impatient with younger women's complaints, announced, "In our day, it was the women who were more responsible than the men. The men would go off to work, and it was the women who were with the kids. When the child was ill, a man would never stay up all night. A woman, however, sat with the kids." Nia asked her, "Why is it that a woman is the one who sits?" "This is due to the mother instinct, God's gift to women," Dina replied, in what I view as a moral, strategically essentialized claim. "You believe this?" Nia, the anthropology student, pressed, almost incredulously. "I believe, I believe." Men, in contrast, are often said to be ignorant when it comes to children, particularly infants. An American friend of mine said of her young Greek husband, usually so progressive in his thinking, that he claimed total incompetence when it came to their newborn. "He was afraid to get involved," she told me. "Like, he really swore that the baby was going to go sliding out of his hands, and he was going to drop the baby in the bathtub or something, actually kill the baby!" If a man cannot hold a baby without getting worked into a panic, many women reckon it is best not to hand them one. (Men play quite well with children who are able to walk about on their own; one recent mother noted, "As long as it's a baby, they don't understand. I don't think that men get it early on, what it means to be a father. From a year on, they begin to understand that there exists a little human being and they have some responsibility to care for it, to watch over how it will grow up.")

Furthermore, if pregnancy is recognized as an ontological relationship, childbirth is the dramatic, painful moment that marks the beginning of the *social*, maternal relationship. Far from acquiescing to the pain of childbirth as God's Edenic punishment to women, Greek women frequently deploy the pain and blood of birth to justify the active role they will play in their children's lives. Women told me they want to feel the pain of birth. Two said they felt cheated by cesarean deliveries. Ariadne, who had her child after pursing IVF treatment, expressed a bodily desire to birth and mother:

> I wanted to grow a child inside my belly. I wanted my belly to swell up. I used to go and stand in front of the mirror and try to imagine how I

would look pregnant. I wanted to feel all the emotions of motherhood. I wanted to feel the child get bigger, kick. As I told you, I birthed naturally; it hurt—I wanted to feel the pain to get the pleasure out of it. Afterward, I wanted the baby to be placed on me so I could kiss it. I wanted to feel all this, from inside me, not out of egoism.

Mothers demand the respect and gratitude of their children by pointedly reminding them, "Look what I suffered for you! My child!" (see Dubisch 1995, 225–26). The widespread cultural currency of such ideas is suggested by a story I heard about a male doctor: Eva's older sister had recently birthed her first child, and according to Eva, the doctor refused to give her an epidural "because, he says, 'You won't understand, you won't have the impression you should when the child comes out; you will have one response when you are drugged, and you will have another response when you are natural and you hear the child coming out. This is very important. For the child and for yourself.' " The pain of childbirth symbolizes the energy drained from a woman's body to flow into her children's bodies, giving substance and strength (dhínami) to a future generation of Greeks.[64] By aligning the *material* sacrifices mothers make for their children as they grow with the *physical* pain of childbirth, women garner moral credit under an ethic of service for consumption patterns in a political economy of the maternal body that literally and figuratively feeds their offspring. A rather extreme example of this is reported in Herzfeld's *Portrait of a Greek Imagination*, in which the writer Andreas Nenedakis describes how his mother went to great sacrificial lengths to provide him with food parcels while he was a political prisoner (an accused Communist) during the war (1997b, 46). When he returned "from exile" he noticed that his mother's row of gold teeth was missing. "I ate her teeth," he realized with a start. "Can you understand the meaning of such a thing?" The meaning that I, like Whitbeck (1990), take from this is that this kind of relational ontology seen to obtain between mother and child confounds the individualizing logic of essentialism.

Women deploy the rhetoric of self-sacrifice so well that Dubisch identifies sacrifice or suffering as a defining feature of Greek motherhood (1995, 212–17). Characterizing suffering as an everyday practice through which actors both express social identity and connection and validate their performance of social roles (206–28), Dubisch further notes that suffering can be "a means by which women—and men—can demonstrate to and remind others of the difficulties inherent in the performance of their roles" (217).[65] When, as under an ethic of service, one's acts are motivated by external convention rather than inner imperative, everyone suffers thwarted yearnings, affections, and ambitions. Women's ritual laments and complaints, as public displays of suffering (Danforth 1982; Seremetakis 1991), can be seen as a safety valve for releasing frustrations and inner contradictions compounded by an ethic of service. But if women believe they do or should reap precious emotional reward as mothers, at what cost is it gained? The rhetorical deployment of self-sacrifice is one thing, actual self-denial another. Within the more recent framework of an ethic of choice, Athenian women increasingly articulate and defend the difference.

If maternal suffering has helped define Greek mothering, psychologists, sociologists, and lay critics alike complain that many women today are choosing to sacrifice too much. Mariella Doumanis (1983) argues that, when only wealthy women can provide "the best" for their children without working in the labor market, the insurgence of women in the paid workforce has been accompanied by a professionalization of motherhood among the upper classes, to which middle-class women struggle to aspire, spurred on by imported, air-brushed media images of American supermoms. Eleni Stamiris similarly observes that, far from essentializing women's double bind as being within their nature, "the 'good housekeeping' role of women has become a fetish especially among the middle classes, leading to obsessions with extreme household cleanliness and the overindulgence of children" (1986, 101). Women I interviewed summed up the expectation that "a good mother is a giving mother" as an aspect of Greek *noötropía*, an everyday word usually translated into English as "collective mentality" but which describes something more akin to Bourdieu's notion of "habitus" (1977), in that it refers to an imagined common consciousness with a traceable cultural history and that triggers certain embodied responses. For all their allusions to a Greek mentality, no one means to suggest by this that all Greeks think alike. References to an *ellenikí noötropía* are interesting because they refer us to normalizing cultural pressures of which Greeks are themselves aware and often critical (Afxendiou 1996; Herzfeld 1997a, 79). Greeks evoke *noötropía* in calling out the limitations of a cultural tradition to which they still adhere. It marks the perceived pivot point between past and present, continuity and change.

Aliki Andoniou is critical of the consumerist drive of today's middle-class mothers, calling what they have come to regard as a basic tenet of parenthood—that providing only the basics is insufficient—a "mistaken *noötropía*." Mothers, she in effect warns, are pushing the ethic of choice onto their children too early, thereby robbing them of their childhood:

> Yes, the *noötropía* is that, for a child to be satisfied, it must go to a private school and have a lot of clothes, a lot of toys, and so forth. They

don't understand that these aren't what satisfies a child. They have given very great significance to material goods, and because of this, people aren't having kids. The mistaken *noötropía* of the parents predominates: that for a child to be raised properly, it must wear Kickers shoes and have a lot of expensive toys, video games. This mentality is passed along.

To professionals and to women like Dina who combined work and mother-hood in the 1950s, today's "overachieving" mothers seem excessive, if not naively misguided. I heard middle-class Athenians voice similar criticism of mothers—and it is mothers who are judged, as well as given credit, for how their children are raised—who push their children too hard. Litsa ex-plained, recalling comments by others:

Because the previous generation were deprived, now we all look to turn our kids into stars. I believe this too is wrong, to tire out the children. Just across [the hall] from us, they have a boy and a girl. The fourteen-year-old boy has a tutor for every class [and] attends French lessons. The girl goes to Greek dance classes. They can't go run around in the garden. Sometimes people forget that a child is a child. I think that some form of exercise and a foreign language are necessary; then as time goes by, you see what your kid is good at. You should not try and make him a star from the age of six. He has plenty of time to study later.

These days a daughter, instead of helping with the housework and looking after a younger sibling, will be driven to ballet class or will return late from *frontistíria*. Her mother, meanwhile, spends her time in pursuits different from those of her own mother or grandmother. Rather than take a couple of hours preparing moussaka from scratch, a woman will more likely stop by the supermarket after work to pick up a frozen casserole or a packet of instant béchamel sauce mix.[66] Her "free" time will be spent helping her children with schoolwork and chauffeuring them to their various activities. The relational ontology of motherhood makes it difficult for women, as Vaso Skopeta, who teaches women's assertiveness training workshops, complained, to separate their own needs from those of their children's.

Reciprocal ties of support and interference hold as well among adult children and their parents. As traditional practices such as the dowry and mothering are being reset in new economic and cultural frames, in many families the burden of accumulated demands falls to those who remain at home: the grandparents. Maro saw this, too, as a problem:

Because the economic situation is difficult, kids have returned to the family. This is not to say that they all live together, but they have a child and leave it with their parents, then they take it home for the weekend. Both parents work. Their mothers are hanging over them, and for I don't know how many it's becoming the same family bond. That is, the [grand]mothers are mothering again for their daughters' children. That is how self-seeking the situation is becoming anymore. "Since Mother will cook anyway, it's better; we are spared from fatigue, hardship, and a few minutes." That's the *noötropía* [collective, embodied mentality]. [The grandmother] puts in two casseroles instead of putting in one casserole, and she's willing. It's a willful situation.

Maro is suspicious of young women's willingness to rely on their mothers' domestic labor, just as she is suspicious of the complicity of the older generation of women willing to mother again for the next generation. She laments an apparent loss of female autonomy and independence when women devote themselves to mothering twice around: "It's becoming the same family bond." Again, this is not a new cultural development. "The child of my child is two times my child," a saying goes; or, as Artemis said to me, "The grandmother is like twice mother." But this is one tradition Maro would like to see truly banished:

> I see that we are turning back with this. I believe that one takes a step forward as one arranges one's own life. You want to have a child, you assume the responsibilities of having a child; you work, you assume the responsibilities of working; you have a house and assume the responsibilities of this house. I consider it to be a step ahead for one to stand up in one's life like this—having maintained ties with siblings, with parents, with friends—but to clarify one's life, to have it in one's own hands. And I think that anymore there's beginning to be a step backward in this. Always with different excuses: work, the economy, AIDS, this and that. I don't know anymore what all excuses they find to return to the home and to stay there.

For Maro, the properly modern woman should direct her life without relying heavily on her family, and she should be personally accountable for her own actions. Maro, feeling she has achieved this in her own life, regards the "unwillingness" of younger women to take similar responsibility for their lives as compromising the feminist (my word, but I think Maro would approve) gains made courageously by women of her peer group.

In this chapter, I described shifts in how middle-class urban Greeks approach the idea and practice of *teknopiía*, the making of children, as an ethic of choice becomes newly available to women. In the next chapter, I look at how this ethic of choice is being enlisted in the promulgation of an even more individuated ethic, one advocated by Western-style family planning organizations, that encourages women's emotional and physical well-being. To do this, I focus on specific fertility control methods.

3   Rationalizing Sex

Family Planning and
an Ethic of Well-Being

Family planning is a need broached by family reality in our era, an
essential need and one, in reality, with no return. We cannot return
to an era when the coming of a child was little more than a
fortuitous affair. Today, if you like, the general economic and social
demands of raising a child—just as with the position of women and
the changes which have supported this position—in order to train it
properly so it has the necessary education . . . and everything else
that it needs—all this creates a need for family planning. And it is a
need we must face. And, contrary to what some here are trying to
present, this does not diminish the significance of the coming of a
child. Precisely this need to raise the consciousness of parental
choice . . . underlines so importantly the event of the birth of a
child in contemporary society. This need for family planning
traumatically emphasizes precisely how great is the responsibility
of today's parents to bring a child into the world.

> MARIA DAMANAKI, member of Parliament for the Greek Communist
> Party, speaking on the floor of Parliament in support of
> legalizing abortion, June 1986

Family planning, as an institution and philosophy, first came to Greece in
1976 by way of a private center established by a British-trained gynecologist and a group of concerned housewives. Family planning—here signifying the calculated use of contraceptives—is forwarded in Greece as an
emergent and liberating practice, a clear alternative to traditional strategies
for birth control reliant on restrictions governing sexual activity and
backed by abortion. Consistent with the ethic of choice, the first principle
of family planning considers it a human right that people be able to choose
the number of children they want and when they want them—without
women having to resort to abortion. Toward this end, family planners want
men, but especially women, to reconsider the ideal point at which human
will enters into reproductive processes and to assume a more proactive

sense of reproductive agency. If traditionally it has been more acceptable to limit reproduction through social measures that control the natural impulses of human sensuality, a more modern woman should control her natural capacity to conceive by doing something to her body (regulating ovulation through hormonal intake, or inserting devices into her uterus or vagina) that could (supposedly) allow for unlimited, uninhibited sexual activity. Greek family planners, then, purport to give women the knowledge and tools with which they can more rationally control their fertility in order to better realize both their desires regarding *teknopiía* and their nature as women.

Despite both private and (more recently) state-sponsored efforts at family planning education, research suggests that Greeks overall have not significantly changed their contraceptive practices over the past several decades (the exception being a rise in condom use as a prophylactic against HIV transmission). At the time of this writing, the most recent statistics (from 2000) on oral contraceptive use put the national average at 5 percent, still the lowest rate in the European Union, where over the past decade the average rate has remained at about 35 percent.[1] The Greek percentage is also striking in comparison with neighboring countries that have been heavily targeted by international family planning organizations (with the assumption, perhaps, that women in Europe have already modernized their fertility control measures). In Egypt, for example, 15 percent of all women of reproductive age use the pill (National Population Council Report, June 1990) and oral contraceptive users constitute 41 percent of all Egyptian women who use contraception (1988 Egypt Demographic Health Survey). But if awareness of modern methods in Greece has not translated into their widespread use, new knowledge *is* encouraging Athenians to reconsider how they talk about contraception and abortion and morally evaluate women on the basis of their fertility control practices.

I argue, counter to modernization theory, that if knowledge of medical fertility control technologies enables a modern shift in the ideal site of reproductive agency—from the social realm of sexual relations and the post hoc arena of abortion to the medicalized space of conception and contraception—this does not signal a gain in human agency or women's autonomy in reproductive matters. My interviews reveal that patriarchy has been a stronger check than lack of knowledge on Greek women's reproductive agency. Market capitalism, alongside the material and political effects of war and urbanization, have colluded in eroding a procreative mandate by which women's compliance with an ethic of service restricted appropriate sexual behavior to marital sex aimed at reproduction. As production was moved out of the household, in Greece as elsewhere, children have been transformed from "hands" useful in increasing the family's wealth to "mouths" needing to be fed (Shorter 1975; Katz 1990; Abelove 1992; Greenhalgh 1995). And as the leftist parliamentarian Maria Damanaki notes in this chapter's epigraph, if Athenians continue to perceive children as necessities rather than luxuries, parents today must work to achieve them within the parameters of a socially and economically constrained ethic of choice. Equally committed to the principle of choice, Greek family planning efforts have worked to replace the procreative mandate with a newly alternative sexual ethic—what I call an ethic of well-being—that is permissive of pleasure and focused on personal health. The virtues of preventative personal health are supposedly available to both women and men, that is, they are gender neutral.

This chapter treats family planning as an ideology, as an explicit set of assumptions and opinions that organize and disseminate knowledge in such a way as to bring local practices in line with broader social forces and political ideals (Williams 1977). In Greece, these political ideals turn on the "European" status of the nation. At various medical and family planning conferences I attended in Athens, I heard policy makers and physicians speak of family planning in terms that Fotini Tsalicoglou would dub an ideological "passport to modernity" (1995, 86).[2] Westward-looking medical professionals and volunteers who advocate family planning view the rational consciousness and responsibility it touts as a marker and manufacturer of European status. Left-leaning politicians and feminist activists present family planning as a tool with which women can gain Western-style sexual liberation and reproductive autonomy. The ethic of well-being, like the ethics of service and choice, is enlisted to pursue a variety of political and moral goals. What counts as well-being (and what is emphasized as being Western) also varies. While medical professionals concern themselves primarily with the bodily well-being of women, feminists call attention to women's emotional or psychological well-being and quality of life. Politicians, as I discuss in the following chapter, speak largely about repercussions for the well-being of the nation. Biomedical, feminist, and demographic claims on women's "well-being" help to contextualize the ethical narratives of individual women, voiced in the previous chapter, and further complicate their sense of reproductive agency. While all these groups advocate better availability and information about medical contraceptives, in speaking of family planning advocates I refer specifically to organized family planning outreach by physicians and volunteer counselors.

Detailing the history and educational strategy of private and state family planning initiatives in Greece, I show how family planning advocates have sought to impose the modern logic of rationality onto sex. Sex, taken to be normatively heterosexual, is figured as a social activity and as the natural means of procreation. In rationalizing sex, family planners aim both to make sense in modern terms of the still common, but what they see as backward, practice of repeat abortions and to forward a more rational and healthy alternative in the form of medicalized contraceptive use. Family planning advocates also fully biologize the nature women are expected to control to regulate births and to demonstrate their virtue as modern women. As a result, whereas Athenian women I interviewed chiefly described abortion as an unfortunate "solution" to inopportune pregnancy and as a "necessary evil" forced by patriarchal gender relations and economic pressure, family planners and health professionals hold a reified notion of culture accountable for women's resistance to medical contraceptives. At the same time, they argue that tradition harbors a latent cultural logic that might yet be harnessed to persuade women of the greater rationality of prophylactic practice.

Family planning advocacy repeats a belief common among urban Greek professionals, that if people give up so-called traditional mentalities (*noötropíes*) based on folk belief or religion for more modern mentalities guided by rational calculation, personal liberation and autonomy will follow (Doumanis 1983; Papagaroufali and Georges 1993). But modern people require a tradition through which to define themselves. Juxtaposing the "contraceptive resistance" theory of Greek social psychologists, physicians, and family planning professionals with middle-class women's assessments of fertility control practices reveals how family planners, caught in the tradition/modernity dualism, overestimate the difference that knowledge, consciousness, responsibility, and cost/benefit analysis—the tools of modern rationality—can make in determining people's engagement in sex and fertility control. Rationalizing sex compromises the success of family planning goals and unwittingly contributes to the burden of women's sexual and reproductive accountability.

After outlining and assessing the history, programmatic strategy, and conceptual framework of institutionalized family planning in Athens, I present my own analysis of Athenian fertility control practices and attitudes. The stories middle-class women told me about sexual relations and contraceptive practice reveal that their personal decisions, or preferences, do not reflect an either/or choice between tradition and modernity but aim rather at negotiating behaviors and attitudes characterized as either traditional or modern that are simultaneously expected of them by a modern society. They are rewriting the moral implications of sexual and reproductive practices in the process. As Niki said when reflecting on changing gender roles since she moved to Athens from a Peloponnesian village nearly two decades ago, "Of course it's changed a lot, because they're trying to change us. From the television and in the schools, they speak to us, all the politicians; they're trying to change us, to make us European because we are third world. So the foreigners say that we belong to the third world and must become Europeans." I end by considering how Athenian women must position and reposition their modernity not only as women but also as properly *Greek* women. Much of Greek modernity is embraced as progress by its participants one moment, but is distrusted the next as foreign condescension and imposition. Changing gender roles and sexual mores are no exception.

FAMILY PLANNING IN GREECE: PASSPORT TO MODERNITY

Use of Fertility Control Methods

When I asked a demographer at the National Center for Social Research to comment on the condition of institutionalized family planning in Greece, she immediately replied, "Family planning does not exist":

> There was an effort within the so-called health centers when the previous PASOK government was in power [during the 1980s]. But it didn't work. I don't know why. It didn't have the personnel. They are in hospitals, in big hospitals in Athens and the cities, and the people are not really aware of them. They use the old-fashioned methods, and that means withdrawal and condoms.

The earliest formal statistics on birth control date to 1966–1967, when the (now defunct) University of Athens Center of Demographic Research conducted a large-scale survey of 6,513 married women (age twenty to fifty) throughout Greece. Their study—which set out to examine women's use of abortion—generated the following figures in response to a question regarding "methods used . . . for family limitation" (Valaoras and Trichopoulos 1970, 289):

Withdrawal	49.2 percent
Condom	22.0 percent
Induced abortion	20.6 percent
Other [pill, IUD, etc.]	8.2 percent
Total users	89.5 percent

Two decades later, Haris Symeonidou, on behalf of the National Center for Social Research, conducted an extensive nationwide survey of women living with their husbands in their first marriage to examine social-economic factors affecting fertility and family size. She came up with strikingly similar conclusions: 1,499 of 1,881 women (age fifteen to forty-four) returning surveys reported having used some kind of contraceptive method "in order to avoid an unwanted pregnancy" (not being a method of contraception, abortion was addressed in a separate set of questions, with 629, or approximately one-third of the women, admitting to at least one abortion; 1990, 124–25):

Withdrawal	44.0 percent
Condom	36.0 percent
Rhythm method	9.3 percent
Modern [pill, IUD]	5.4 percent
Other methods	5.5 percent

In Athens and Thessaloniki, the rate of women using either the pill or IUD ran closer to 12 percent, especially among more educated women and particularly those who had lived abroad (Symeonidou 1994). According to physicians and demographers I interviewed, the rates hardly wavered over the next decade.

What initially interested me about these statistics is that 85 percent of the women Symeonidou surveyed nationwide considered themselves to be using *some* kind of contraceptive method, just as 90 percent of respondents to the previous survey admitted to a "method of family limitation" from a list that included abortion. Even when using so-called traditional methods (for Symeonidou, this includes withdrawal, rhythm method, and condoms), these women were consciously not leaving procreation wholly to chance or to God's will. Traditional Greek reproductive agency has never been fatalistic, as some anthropologists and Greek professionals have suggested. But as with the concept of choice surrounding *teknopiía* (the making of children), contraceptive choice is never free, never solely at the discretion of any individual.

Male condoms, labeled by doctors and demographers as traditional birth control, remain the most common means of contraception after withdrawal. Several middle-aged women I spoke with indicated that they and their boyfriends used condoms before marriage (forty-seven-year-old Artemis recalled, "*I* was never the one who bought them; it was always the boy"). After marriage or making a commitment, however, it was understood that a woman should "relieve her husband" of the obligation to procure and use condoms by "paying attention" to her fertile days. Long available at kiosks, condoms are now stocked on supermarket shelves. In 1998, a Greek brand of condoms at the Extra supermarket in my neighborhood sold in packages of ten for about U.S.$4. Manufactured condoms are imported from the United States, Japan, Germany, Taiwan, and Korea and packaged in Greece without being subject to government control.[3] Not surprisingly, their breakage rate is frighteningly high—a significant number of abortions follow use of defective condoms. Spermicide and even female condoms are openly displayed in middle-class neighborhood pharmacies. Many forms of barrier and medical contraceptives are available and affordable in Athens and throughout most of the country, but as a study by the Athens School of Public Health conducted in the late 1980s found, "there is a gap between what people know and what they personally do" (Agrafiotis et al. 1990a, 105).[4]

The pill was first distributed in Greece in 1963. Gynecologists, cautious about potential links to uterine cancer, passed on to their patients a wariness that approached mortal fear. Women who were willing to ingest hormones did so under the guise of "menstrual regulation"; before 1980, by law a physician could prescribe contraceptive pills only by claiming to treat a woman suffering from menstrual disorder. The hormone levels of such pills have drastically declined since the 1960s, but in public opinion the link with cancer has not been severed. Since 1980, pills have been available without prescription, although it remains illegal to advertise any contraceptive method other than condoms. In the middle 1990s, provided a woman knew what to ask for, she could attain low-dosage (including combination estrogen and progesterone) contraceptive pills over the counter for between U.S.$4.50 and $9.00 a cycle. A pharmacist on Nikis Street near the central square of Syntagma gladly explained to me that they offered several versions of the pill—the "classic" pill, a dose of hormones that a woman ingests every day—as well as tri-phasals, which include a week of placebos. That pharmacy kept all contraceptives, mostly pills and prophylactics, in small boxes discreetly behind the counter, making it impossible for a customer to browse the selection casually. When I asked whether many girls came in for information, the pharmacist replied no, hardly ever. "Girls don't care, they aren't concerned. There is no center for information or counseling here," she erroneously informed me (as the following section demonstrates), "so they have to pay 10,000 drachmes (U.S.$45) to visit a doctor to learn" what to ask for in a pharmacy.

I visited a gynecologist, a woman I had interviewed, at her private office adjacent to her apartment in the fashionable neighborhood of Kolonaki for my yearly pelvic exam and Pap test.[5] I also wanted to learn which pills might be available in Greece that would most closely approximate ones I had taken in the United States. The physician gave me a list of tri-phasals to take to a pharmacist and also wrote out for me a list of *six* blood tests she recommended before starting the pill. For this task she handed me the business card of a medical technologist (a highly specialized entrepreneurial sensibility in Greece extends to health care services). The blood tests would have cost me another U.S.$30 (the doctor's fees were $35, reduced on a sliding scale from her normal $45, with an additional $22 lab fee for the Pap test). I opted to pass on the blood tests and had no difficulty purchasing a tri-phasal in a Kolonaki pharmacy. I was not asked about blood tests, nor did anyone at any point ask me whether I smoked (in the United States, physicians warn that smoking increases one's risk for heart failure while taking the contraceptive pill). The entire process involving a physician, lab technician, and pharmacist could dissuade women from obtaining pills. Moreover, the names of hormones used in oral contraceptives are long and difficult to pronounce; brand names are scripted in a foreign alphabet.

Nearly every woman I asked about "means of preventing pregnancy" named the pill. They had read about it in a magazine, or had friends who had tried it; but only five out of thirty-eight had ever taken oral contraceptives. Their narratives seem fairly representative of pill use in urban Greece (see Georges 1996a). Athena, a twenty-eight-year-old graduate student, got them "from a friend." Kalliroe, a professional who had spent several years in Paris, said she and her husband used pills before they got married. Now, after the birth of her daughter, her cycle has become so exact that they successfully avoid conception by refraining from unprotected sex during her five monthly fertile days. A doctor prescribed oral contraceptives for Artemis, a forty-seven-year-old college graduate who taught private lessons in French and Greek, and who had used condoms before marriage. But this was to regulate her cycle in order to increase her future chances of conceiving; her problem was not contraception but conception and pregnancy (she has had four miscarriages and remains childless). "But many of my friends," she told me, "they use only pills [for contraception]; but the doctor must tell you which ones, and after some years you must stop, because of cancer, you know. We don't know yet [how great a cancer risk it is]." Chloe, age thirty-four, lived for several years in the United States, where she was on the pill for a year before quitting because, as she told me, "I wasn't comfortable with it." She and her husband "end up using condoms more than anything. I guess the pill is the more convenient one, but messing around with hormones is not something I was very comfortable with." Despina, the Ph.D. student at a British university, quit using contraceptive pills after a brief time because, although "the pill is supposed to be more reliable," the decision to take it "depends on the situation that you are in." Despina was in a transnational relationship, "was smoking a lot," and "didn't want to stuff myself with hormones" whose benefit she was not utilizing. "I mean, it is a *pill*. It's not a natural thing, it's artificial—so what's the point?" Despina returned to using condoms and, occasionally, withdrawal—"when you don't have a condom and it [sex] just happens."

Women who believe that ovulation and hence conception *can* be regulated through hormonal treatment may yet feel uncomfortable with the idea of it, or are willing to "mess with hormones" only for a limited time, or seem relieved to find an excuse to discontinue taking oral contraceptives. These women, operating within an ethic of choice, are juggling competing understandings of the nature available to human reproductive control: they are willing to try controlling the biological nature of their fertility (specifically, the hormonal suppression of ovulation) as advocated by biomedical professionals, but they seem more comfortable controlling the social nature of their sexuality by introducing condoms into their sexual practice or by relying on their partners to withdraw. Owing to the ethic of choice, they must confront competing notions of what the nature of their bodies is and how best to protect, regulate, and realize it.

Ethical consideration of the nature women are to control in order to regulate births further illuminates the ongoing unpopularity of the other medical contraceptives introduced in Greece, the IUD and diaphragm. The chemically saturated contraceptive sponge is virtually unavailable. "They don't know the diaphragm!" Symeonidou groaned at me in an interview, saying that "0.2% [use it]. They don't even know it." Owing to low sales, diaphragms were regularly imported to Greece only for a short time in the 1980s. One gynecologist I interviewed keeps a box of them in a closet of his examining room to have on hand for patients who have lived (elsewhere) in Europe and are already accustomed to them. Chloe is the one woman I met who had tried a diaphragm, while living in the States, and she hated it, "felt it constantly." A Family Planning Association board member suggested to me in an interview that diaphragm uptake in Greece is low because women are generally wary of any product that requires personal insertion into the vagina.[6]

Similarly, anthropologists Marlene Arnold (1985), Eugenia Georges (1996a), and Joanna Skilogianis (1997) describe an ethnomedical discourse for women in Crete, Rhodes, and Athens, respectively, that distinguishes between inside and outside the body. These anthropologists report women's descriptions of the IUD as a foreign body that threatens the integrity of their own bodies, even asserting that the device could "become one" with their bodies or get lost in them. In Rhodian women's accounts, Georges writes, "use of the idiom of 'naturalness' appeared to reflect women's expressed anxiety over the health consequences of introducing 'unnatural' foreign substances and objects such as the IUD and the pill into the body on a long-term basis" (1996a, 514). I heard similar depictions from Athenian women. Despina told me of "friends who have tried the spiral [IUD] and all these kinds of things, but I think having a procedure and putting things in yourself is a bit dodgy—I have one or two friends who got it but then took it out." In comparison, withdrawal is appreciated as a more natural method precisely because it entails the social control of sexual practice and, in terms of the ethnomedical model, because it happens *outside* a woman's body (Georges 1996a, 514). Georges links this discourse to a broader cultural distinction between inside and outside that is used to police the boundaries of concentric circles of social and ethnic relations, separating "our own" *(dhikhí mas)* from "the others" *(i álli, kséni)* (Dubisch 1993).

I want to extend this analysis by highlighting the ethical implications of a model of bodily integrity concerned with policing boundaries: Since the nature with which women are concerned is at once physical and social, the notion of well-being that Georges and others describe is consistent with what I call the ethic of service. By not allowing physicians to implant IUDs and fit diaphragms, women see themselves as safeguarding not only their "organism" but also, at a symbolic level, the integrity of their families. This particular notion of well-being contrasts quite dramatically with the biomedical ethic of well-being promulgated by family planners. Both uphold well-being as a virtue; but under each model, what constitutes well-being, and what poses a threat to well-being, differs significantly.

Introducing Family Planning in Greece

A quarter of a century ago, family planning education began to emerge in Greece as a means and measure of a grassroots modernity. Confronting low contraceptive uptake and high rates of abortion, in 1976 the British-trained gynecologist George Kakoyanis helped organize a group of concerned housewives and politicians to establish the private Family Planning

Association of Greece (FPAG, Etería Ikoyeniakoú Programmatismoú), believing that if women were better informed about modern means of contraception—particularly the pill and IUD—the nation's soaring abortion
rate would decline.[7] By the 1980s, as many as three hundred thousand
abortions were being performed (illegally) each year, at nearly three times
the live birth rate (Margaritidou and Mesteneos 1992, 25)—that is to say,
as many as one in eighteen Greek women had an abortion in any given
year (compared with an estimated one woman in thirty-six in the United
States in 1988).[8] In this context, the Family Planning Association of Greece
has acted primarily in an outreach capacity, working to educate women and
men about modern medical contraceptives, the need to prevent the spread
of sexually transmitted disease, and the damage that abortion can do to a
woman's reproductive organs.

I met George Kakoyanis, who was at that time again president of the Family Planning Association of Greece, at his private office a few blocks down
from the prestigious Mitera maternity hospital along the stretch of Vasilissis Sofias Avenue that boasts the offices of many of the city's finest physicians.[9] The door separating his warm, scholarly office and stark, metallic-cold
examining room stood open, the contrast making me glad I did not have to
pass through the connecting door. This setup is typical of private medical
offices in Athens; gynecologists estimate that 90 to 95 percent of all abortions take place in such spaces. When (after the fall of the junta) Kakoyanis
returned to Greece following his studies in Britain in 1975, he was struck by
the comparatively large number of abortions being performed here each
year. "Abortion was, and still is, the main method of birth control in Greece,"
he informed me, shaking his head with dismay. Meanwhile, a group of feminist activists in Athens had also taken notice of the finding by the University of Athens Center of Demographic Research that abortions outnumbered
live births among Greek women. One of the early housewives-cum-activists,
who when I met her was a grandmother in her sixties and treasurer of the
Family Planning Association, told me she became involved because she "felt
that the liberation of the woman begins at the moment when the woman has
the responsibility and the possibility to control the body." Through the combined efforts of gynecologists and feminist activists, the Family Planning Association was founded as a private organization in 1976, without any
significant resource base and with no governmental support. Eventually, a
Greek industrialist donated a million drachmes to pay for the premises, the
phone lines, and other items needed to get the organization off the ground.

The FPAG published the first material in Greek on family planning and
sexual education. Some six hundred to seven hundred volunteer members

nationwide participate primarily by giving community talks on contraception. Biennially, the FPAG sponsors a three-day symposium in Athens,
"Sexual Education and Health," attended by members of the public, the
press, and health care professionals. This regular event occasions the FPAG
to engage state representatives and educators in important dialogue regarding sexual and reproductive health care issues. The feminist consciousness-raising movement that swept the United States in the 1970s,
and reached Greece a decade later, promoted the principle that knowledge
can lead to increased autonomy.[10] Greek family planners share this principle. One of the largest feminist political organizations in Greece in the
1980s, the Union of Greek Women, maintained an affiliation with the
reigning socialist PASOK party under the leadership of Margaret Papandreou, the American wife of the then–prime minister. Family planning was
high on the agenda of the Union of Greek Women (Papandreou 1984), and
its membership overlapped with that of the FPAG (Stamiris 1986). In 1985
the association became an affiliate of the International Planned Parenthood
Federation (IPPF), from which it receives funding.

In the 1970s, most public or political awareness of family planning concerned industrialized nations' desires and strategies for suppressing population growth in the developing world; this seemed threatening to Greeks
aware of the comparative demographics of the Aegean.[11] For family planning to be granted state support, women's health concerns were made to
speak to the nationalist anxiety over a declining population growth rate.
The same University of Athens study that revealed the frequency of abortions causally linked this, and women's (supposed) secondary sterility, to
Greece's demographic weakening (cf. Valaoras and Trichopoulos 1970). In
1980, swayed by the argument that, since family planning operates rationally, it can be employed to rationalize—in this case by stimulating—the
national birthrate, parliamentarians legalized female methods of contraception (the pill and IUD) and legislated the establishment of family planning clinics in a select number of state hospitals (Law 1036/80). Not coin-
cidentally, this act of rational modernization occurred the year before
Greece became a full member of the European Economic Community. By
1990, thirty-eight state-sponsored clinics were in operation throughout
Greece (thirteen others had by then shut down), eight of these in the
Athens area (Margaritidou and Mesteneos 1992). The state-run centers
operate quite apart from the FPAG; however, because the number of
qualified personnel is limited, private and public initiatives and member-
ships overlap.[12] Advocates of family planning within and outside the government stress that contraception is "in every instance" preferable to abor-

tion, saving women the emotional stress, financial burden, and risk of sterility said to accompany abortions. It is good for women, it is good for the nation.

The offices of the FPAG are located in a dingy office building on Solonos Street, up a few blocks from the University of Athens toward suffocatingly busy Omonia Square. After riding in a dubious elevator to the fourth floor, visitors are immediately cheered by the sight of colorful brochures and pamphlets, free for the taking, which line the office's antechamber. These include FPAG publications addressing AIDS, contraception, infertility, and a history of the organization. I paid my first visit unannounced and was warmly welcomed by the full-time secretary, the only salaried FPAG employee. In an adjoining room, I found Evangelia, one of the more experienced volunteer counselors, leading an informational seminar to a coed group of about forty university students. These seminars, given at their office and in secondary schools, at meetings of women's groups, and in village community centers—accompanied by numerous publications—represent the bulk of the association's activities. While Evangelia's work with the FPAG is strictly volunteer, she is employed full-time by a state family planning center run out of the Maternity and Child Welfare Institution;[13] her activities with both organizations, such as visiting schools to promote contraception and reproductive health awareness, are nearly identical.

In this and other seminars, Evangelia goes through the various methods of contraception—"all of them," she assured me in a later interview. Standing in the back of the FPAG seminar room during that first visit, I was struck by her inclusion of such traditional methods as withdrawal and counting one's fertile days as valid methods of family planning, if not as reliably effective as "technical" methods. For Evangelia, the methods themselves are not essentially traditional or modern; she is willing to see older methods employed by college students with appropriately modern attitudes. After all, the condom is essential in protecting against sexually transmitted disease. Committed to the ethic of choice, she is adamant that the particular method a person uses be selected by that individual. Keenly aware of the negative images of the pill instilled in the 1960s, in her presentation to college students she worked to correct misguided fears by emphasizing that today's pill, with its lower doses of hormones given in three-week cycles (some progesterone-only), is quite different from the early pills, which contained high levels of estrogen and caused notable side effects. Yet by no means did Evangelia seem to favor the pill as the contraceptive of choice. I found consistently that neither physicians nor FPAG counselors tend to push the pill as is often done in the United States (particularly in college settings) and developing countries (by U.S.- and European-funded nongovernmental organizations), whether because they share a concern about harmful side effects, or because they are accustomed to stubborn opposition. Evangelia demonstrated how to insert and arrange a female prophylactic, introduced as "the only female contraceptive that protects against AIDS"; a British-manufactured female prophylactic had been recently introduced onto the Greek market. She did not speak of abortion. Although it remains illegal to advertise abortion services, information on abortion may be given in family planning centers such as this.

At the end of the seminar, Evangelia distributed an FPAG-published booklet titled *What Do You Know about Contraception?* (Ti kséris yia tin antisíllipsi?). The pamphlet expresses well the philosophy of the organization and its programmatic strategy for effecting change in people's attitudes toward and use of family planning methods. It begins:

> This booklet aims to give basic information about how the reproductive systems of men and women work, how conception happens, and the methods you can use to control your fertility. Thus, you will be able not only to prevent an abortion but also to plan your family responsibly and consciously, without stress and worry and without danger to the health of the mother and children.

A childlike drawing on the cover depicts a happy heterosexual couple holding hands, the man attentive to the woman, both gazing lovingly at one another. A baby sits adjacent to them as if still an idea, a twinkle in the parental eye. The booklet goes on to describe the male and female reproductive systems, providing women with the opportunity to check their own understandings of the rhythm method of contraception against scientific knowledge: when a woman's cycle is "normal," it is explained, ovulation happens twelve to sixteen days before the beginning of the next cycle; when the ovum is not fertilized, it is expressed with the period *(to periódho)* that follows.[14] This reproductive biology lesson reflects the FPAG's commitment, as a board member explained to me in an interview, to teach women, in particular, "how their bodies work, what they're doing to them—in a sense to feel in control."

Waiting for Evangelia to finish answering one-on-one student questions following her presentation, I flipped through the rest of the pamphlet, in which family planning is depicted as the planning of one's family, supporting a potentially if not explicitly pronatal nationalist ideology. It does not emphasize fertility limitation or regulation. The FPAG booklet quickly aligns family planning with the unquestioned desires and expectations of a Greek audience in such a way as to placate nationalist demo-graphic anxieties. Above a drawing of a young girl with bows in her hair, holding a baby in her arms, the caption asks rhetorically:

"Who doesn't love a baby?"

This taken-for-granted desire for children is situated within a contempo-rary consumerist understanding of what being a good parent involves.

Every parent wants the best for his or her children:

- comfortable house
- good nutrition
- proper education

The matter-of-fact tone of a scientifically backed narrative deftly trans-forms material desires into the "needs" of what is simultaneously estab-lished as a middle-class audience. It also cites a cultural understanding of motherhood that encompasses household management as well as childcare and nurturing. A middle-class Athenian woman reading this pamphlet might well be reassured to hear a voice of authority acknowledge that the question of having children is rarely an existential one, but instead depends on the external conditions of material means.

The FPAG advises:

Plan your family.
When you plan when you will have a child,
you create a happier family.

This introduces the crux of family planning ideology—if people, but espe-cially women, accept more direct agency and take willful, premeditated control over their own reproductive fates, this will result in more people being able to have more children, happily: "The size of the family doesn't have to be a matter of CHANCE, but a matter of the couple's choice." In con-trasting chance *(tíchi)*, illustrated by a pair of dice and a roulette wheel, with choice, the FPAG presents family planning methodology as a rational alternative to cultural acquiescence to fate *(míra)* or to a notion that in the past people had babies when God brought them. Family planning situates chance as a customary recourse resonant with du Boulay's ethnographic depiction of villagers who appeal to fate in order to "abdicate from respon-sibility for an act whose ultimate outcome they cannot even guess with any degree of conviction" (1974, 95–96). In contrast, family planning sup-ports an ethic of free, conscious, proactive choice for women:

Family planning will help you decide freely and responsibly how many children you want and when you want them. There may be many reasons that compel you to plan how many children you will have and how far apart to space them, e.g., health reasons, social, economic, returning to work.

. Toward this end, the Family Planning Association offers you the knowledge and the means that you need.

Returning implicitly to the demographic issue, the pamphlet next distinguishes the general principle of family planning from population suppression programs such as China's one-child-per-family policy. When the FPAG was first getting under way in the late 1970s, Kakoyanis explained, "there was a bad coincidence" that, at the same time, "they started to realize" that the nation's population growth rate was slackening. "Because Greece is in a very sensitive geographic position and has some differences with [our] neighbors [who] really reproduce themselves quite quickly . . . , there was the misconception that family planning opposed the demographic situation." The FPAG continuously works to break down the equation between family planning and population limitation:

Family planning is not identical to limiting births; it is interested in your having healthy and desired children. With its responsible and objective information on the issues of reproduction and on health matters that have direct relation to reproduction, it will help you create a healthy and stable family. Furthermore, the objective of family planning is:

- to help those who cannot have children
- to supply correct and responsible sexual education to youth
- to acquire basic knowledge to protect the fertility of men and women.

After introducing the idea of family planning, the booklet returns to biology and answers in scientific terms the question "How does a human life begin?"[15] The point is to explain that, "in order for someone to prevent pregnancy, one must block the spermatozoa from joining the ovum. There are several reliable, safe and simple ways to block this meeting." The biology lesson in human reproduction and subsequent discussion of "reliable, safe and simple" contraceptive methods redresses the "ignorance" many family planning advocates perceive among Greeks regarding reproductive biology and available contraceptives. One study of sexual behavior and AIDS awareness reported that 25.9 percent of Athenian men and women surveyed "thought that condoms could climb up into the womb or stomach (!) of women," and that 18.6 percent responded they were "not sure" if this could happen

(Agrafiotis et al. 1990a, 109). Attending an FPAG-sponsored, three-day public seminar in November 1994, "Sexual Education and Health," I heard one gynecologist refute what he deemed to be "common myths" surrounding the contraceptive pill in Greece: that its use leads to subfertility, that it provokes weight gain, that it is cancerous, and that it is more dangerous than pregnancy. "It is a misperception," he declared, "that the pill harms the health of a girl."[16] But when women do not know others who have been on the pill for any length of time and remained healthy and fertile, why should they not be wary? Why offer their own bodies as test cases?

Physicians who have not been well schooled themselves in modern fertility control methods (owing to state-controlled curricula) cannot be relied on to alleviate women's misgivings. A psychologist confided to me that a particular physician associated with a major Athenian maternity hospital, at least during the 1980s, promoted *only* the pill among his patients, offering no information about the diaphragm or IUD, because he had some financial arrangement with an overseas pharmaceutical supplier (contraceptive pills are not manufactured domestically). This female psychologist, who was at that time working as a volunteer counselor at a state hospital family planning center, came away from the experience with a cynical take on the Greek medical profession as a whole, and with a particularly damning view of women's health care, presided over by predominantly male physicians:

> People in Greece see the doctors as gods.[17] They know everything. And they [the doctors] know it. I think doctors in Greece have deep complexes. And especially gynecologists. They chose the specialty just to get money from abortions, and they—I think they hate women, finally. That's what I saw [at the family planning center]. They have this power, since they get out of the university and they put on that white robe; they have this snobbish expression. So they look at women like they despise them; they don't answer their questions. They don't accept questions—with very few exceptions. There are exceptions.

While generally trusting medical advice, many middle-class women consider medical practice, particularly gynecological practice, as yet another means of institutionalizing patriarchy.

In 1990, members of the FPAG conducted a study to assess the effectiveness of their state counterparts and found that hospital-based family planning clinics operate more as women's health clinics than as contraception education centers (Margaritidou and Mesteneos 1992). Questionnaires sent to employees at these clinics revealed that just 2 percent of women of reproductive age (age fifteen to forty-four) had used the services at one time or another, and that the vast majority of these women visited the state family planning clinics for counseling and routine gynecological services such as Pap tests and breast examinations.[18] The authors interpret this as part of a wider cultural tendency to approach medical services for curative and therapeutic benefits, with little regard for health promotion and disease prevention (Margaritidou and Mesteneos 1992, 31). Thus, the study concluded, the use of modern contraceptive methods remains relatively low in Greece *because they operate preventively.* Precisely because women view abortion as a post hoc therapeutic measure, they reason, it continues to be practiced widely. Women, the authors imply, retain an old-fashioned mentality regarding reproductive agency. *What Do You Know about Contraception?* conveys this same frustration, suggesting by its concluding tone that the FPAG assumes readers take abortion for granted, as a birth limitation strategy:

> It's not necessary to end up having an abortion. There are other ways to plan your family. Family Planning is not a secret!
> ASK US

A post hoc, behind the scenes form of reproductive agency is not acceptable under family planning ideology: women should be able to take overt action to regulate their fertility and prevent inopportune pregnancy. In an interview, an FPAG board member spoke to me of how difficult their sex education work is when "nobody wants to talk about it. Everybody just wants it to go on quietly, nobody wants to do anything. We say this isn't good enough. Women have the right to know." An FPAG press release from 1993 elaborates:

> The basic aim of family planning is to instill reproductive responsibility
> and consciousness, with the objective goal of creating stable and
> healthy families with happy parents and desired, strong, and happy
> children. This is attained through the responsible and objective inform-
> ing of individuals on the issue of reproduction as well as on the issue of
> health, which has a direct relationship to reproduction.

Family planners set for themselves the immediate tasks of ensuring that women and men know what to request in a pharmacy, and of familiarizing people with the language and ideas of family planning so they will take advantage of the options available to them.

Explaining Traditional Culture through Modern Rationality

Knowledge, presented not only as a tool but also as a symbol of the autonomy awaiting women once they gain a scientific understanding of their bodies' reproductive cycle, appears as a well-rehearsed theme in much of the FPAG literature. Additional titles include *Do You Know? It Could Happen to You . . . Abortion* and *AIDS: The Known "Unknown": Knowledge without Prejudices*. Beneath such appeals to the liberating effects of knowledge lies a committed belief in human rationality, such that even sex, often regarded by "moderns" as the most chthonic of human impulses, is drawn into a realm of logic and calculated action. Institutionalized family planning operates on the rationalist assumption that, not only *can* people gain control of their lives but, given certain knowledge, they *will* make certain decisions and act accordingly. Lovers will not have sex without using prophylactics.[19] Women will choose contraception over abortion because they accept its scientifically backed promises of relative safety. Thus, rational models purport not only to influence how people act but also to determine or predict it.

Optimism that such programs can prompt people willingly and willfully to change their fertility control practices arises from the belief that family planning does not merely proscribe behavior but also forwards a new way of thinking, or *noötropía* (embodied, collective mentality). At the fourth FPAG "Sexual Education and Health" seminar, in November 1994, the former FPAG president Afrodite Teperoglou spoke of "the necessity" for people to accept family planning as a "philosophy of life." Editorializing in a 1995 edition of the journal *Planned Parenthood in Europe*, the IPPF consultant Evert Ketting explains that the organization's "broader mission indicates that 'family planning' is not an isolated issue; it is a philosophy of life. It is based in the conviction that human beings will act responsibly if they possess the knowledge, skills and means to do so" (1). Family planning promotes, if not inculcates, a particular way one should see oneself as a subject in society. This subjectivity will employ rational calculation in maximizing personal interest and is purportedly available to women and men alike. Viewed from Ketting's IPPF perspective, this subjectivity transcends local cultural idiosyncrasies; it is a unifying philosophy of life politically charged with seeing personal freedom flourish in the face of patriarchal domesticity, nationalistic population agendas, and other tradition-based regimes of reproductive control. But from an anthropological perspective, this appears to be a naive proposal.[20]

The family planning strategy presupposes that, to be modern, a person must think her way out from under emotional baggage and away from cultural biases. In their printed literature (if not the more spontaneous presentations like Evangelia's reported above), the FPAG describes family planning as a positive alternative to more traditional limitations on sexual activity, such as abstinence necessitated by the rhythm method and male restraint involved in withdrawal, not to mention prescriptions for female premarital chastity. In their literature the FPAG does not advocate sexual activity that is not oriented toward reproduction, such as anal or oral sex, although these have been mentioned in reports of traditional sexual practice in Greece both as means to prevent pregnancy and as means to avoid an unmarried woman's loss of virginity (Agrafiotis et al. 1990a, 36; on rural Turkey, see Delaney 1991). As Greek family planners tend to see it, traditional methods reinforce prevailing patriarchal norms that posit men as the active participants in sexual relations, and women as the passive recipients (cf. du Boulay 1986, 150). Painting the past as a backward and undesirable social setting, especially for women, family planning advocates often exclude cultural tradition and belief from the processes of rational decision making, which, for them, offer women the opportunity to overcome the burden of patriarchal tradition, what I have analyzed through an ethic of service.

Assuming that all human action is guided by rational decision making, family planning rhetoric sets up a paradox. The use of modern, medical contraceptives must be upheld as *the* rational choice, counterposed with a traditional reliance on less effective male-controlled methods and, in Greece, on abortion. At the same time, family planners must explain apparently irresponsible or irrational behavior either by stating that it stems from ignorance ("they don't know any better") or by situating the act in such a way as to rationalize it ("it has made sense to them because . . . "). So while women who supposedly rely on abortion as a "method of birth control" are chastised for acting in ignorance of their bodies or with insufficient information about alternatives, the analysts' very assignation of abortion *as a method* of birth control implies rational justification on the part of women. When the practice of abortion is rationalized, social and medical scientists can portray women having abortions as using a traditional method in a modern way. They must still code the practice itself, abortion, as traditional—even though it has been used in significant numbers only since the 1950s—to be able to encourage women to abandon it in favor of medical contraceptives. Family planning advocates thus reinscribe pejorative labels associated with tradition even as they insist that all women act on the rational, if misguided, basis of perceived self-interest.

Seeking rational reasons for why women have come to accept and even expect abortion, Greek professionals have chalked it up to a cultural resistance to contraception, reiterating a move common among social theorists in the 1980s to seek evidence of human agency solely in acts of direct resistance (see Abu-Lughod 1990). Proponents of what I call the resistance theory, which was widely accepted by Greek psychologists and gynecologists (Naziri 1989, 1990, 1991; Agrafiotis et al. 1990a, 38; Tseperi and Mestheneos 1994), try to make sense of the reality that, as one psychologist I interviewed put it, even women who "have all the knowledge, the information" still "have abortions, many abortions, and women are *expected* to have them."

The resistance theory begins with the observation that Greek tradition grants women adult status on the basis of becoming mothers. Elaborating on this, clinical psychologist Despina Naziri (1991, 13) writes:

> [The] limited diffusion of modern contraception . . . by women must be interpreted as a sort of "resistance" dictated by unconscious motives. This resistance is related to the symbolic and real meaning of modern contraceptives and conflicts related to the traditional importance of the mother role and, hence, the constraints concerning the expression of female sexuality. The "unwanted" pregnancy reveals the profound, unconscious need of both men and women to prove their fertility upon which modern contraception could cast doubt, even if temporarily.

A social psychologist affiliated with Athens's Alexandra maternity hospital rephrased this same opinion, telling me in an interview that "a lot of research in Greece says that a woman is not legalized, quote-unquote, in her sex unless she becomes a mother. And this is very evident. Many women who have not become mothers feel rejected . . . by society." Because it is as mothers that Greek women have gained social recognition and status, proponents of this theory, conflating pregnancy and motherhood themselves, leap to the conclusion that pregnancies are rarely unwanted even if births are. Naziri suggests that many Greek women actually *prefer* abortion because, unlike contraceptives, abortion does not disrupt a seemingly natural and valued link between sexual intercourse and procreation (for a version of this argument by anthropologists, see Loizos and Papataxiarchis 1991a, 224). Pregnancy is said to manifest female fertility, which contraception obscures (see also Arnold 1985). The child psychologist Aliki Andoniou explained to me:

> I think that it is considered taboo to be able to enjoy repeated sexual relations—there is this subconscious idea that the erotic act [*i erotikí práksi*], unchecked, is something for which one does penance [*timoríte*]. They can't enjoy it. That is, the erotic act is still linked to childbirth, to having children. For very many people. The erotic act is not autonomous, and if you want, you have children.

Assuming so great a causal link between sexual intercourse and procreation that Greeks can hardly separate them conceptually, she suggests they portray birth control as another matter altogether, one that enters into the picture after the fact of conception (by way of abortion). In this way Naziri, Andoniou, and others—including some FPAG members, who first put me on to Naziri's research—suggest that women's willingness to engage in unprotected sex manifests their often subconscious desire to become mothers.

In viewing abortion as the outcome of a woman's capitulation to a pre-supposed desire for motherhood or to "experience . . . the power of the fe-male body to be fertile, full" (Pitch 1992, 35), these analysts measure abor-tion against a woman's capacity for motherhood, much as Andrea Dworkin (1983), Faye Ginsburg (1989), and Kristin Luker (1984) have described in the United States.[21] I argue that, in so doing, Naziri and others are making an analytical mistake, superimposing one "modernity" onto another. Per-haps these professionals are led to oversimplify what motherhood means to Greek women because they implicitly locate the object of their analysis within a traditional Greece from which they—Greek women themselves—are removed by virtue of their professional education at western European universities, experience living abroad, and elevated economic and social capital. This kind of distancing move is common among urban profession-als (Doumanis 1983; Papagaroufali and Georges 1993; Tsalicoglou 1995). In any event, the resistance theory misses the point that Greek women, in contrast with many contemporary Americans, tend to view abortion more directly in relation to *sexuality* than to motherhood. This does not merely follow from a traditional preoccupation with female chastity under an ethic of service but relates as well to an understanding that motherhood must be demonstrated by the proper care of a child (Doumanis 1983; Georges 1996a). Pregnancy is one thing, motherhood another.

Motherhood in Greece is seen as a set of social relationships. Only after the umbilical cord is severed does the child become its own living creature, and only *baptism* "makes" social personhood. Chloe, who was preparing to baptize her eight-month-old son, described what would happen: "They lift him and set him in a basin of water—it's to do away with any evil that there is. And they are given their names. That's when they are official. Be-fore he is baptized he has no name; [on] the papers for the state [e.g., the birth certificate], they write *aváftistos*, unbaptized, in place of the name." Charles Stewart observes, "Baptism is the portal through which humanity is entered. At this rite the child is forcibly separated from the realm of the demonic by means of a series of exorcisms that expel any malevolent spir-its lingering in or around its person" (1991, 55). Neither maidens nor mothers, gestating Greek women have experienced pregnancy as a liminal time of suspended identity after which childbirth arrives as a relief, even as a source of freedom. This, too, stands in contrast to the way childbirth is commonly met in the United States, where women spend their pregnancies "expecting" birth and, in the company of onlookers, view it as the culmination of the lengthy process of gestation.[22] The modern Greek *noötropía* is sustained through a combination of religious belief, regional customs, and medical confirmation.[23] Health warnings on cigarette packages and bottles of alcohol do not explicitly address pregnant women (in comparison, see Oaks 2001).

What is more, even if we acknowledge that fertility can be called on to link heterosexual relations to gender proficiency, this holds at least as much for men as it does for women. Eleni recalled to me that when, in the 1970s, her women's groups would go out into the villages to talk with women about contraception, they frequently encountered women who were afraid to use the pill, but for reasons other than ethnomedical concern for bodily integrity: they feared their husbands would discover it. Men did not want women to use contraception, Eleni explained, because they thought that, if their wives had many children, this would magnify their manhood.[24] A conflation of *male* sexuality and fertility is common enough to be played up in advertising a home pregnancy test: a full-page advertisement for a brand of pregnancy indicator, featuring a black-and-white image of a ruggedly handsome, shirtless man with a washboard stomach, appeared in a 1993 issue of *Yinéka*, a popular women's magazine. The caption reads, "Appearance isn't enough," suggesting that despite this man's exceptionally virile appearance, he may not be potently fertile—so buy a pregnancy test kit to find out.

Reinforcing the argument that, if female fertility requires proving, this is because male fertility (conflated with virility) is assumed, a diasporic Greek friend of mine in her early thirties told me the following story dating back a few years, to when she was making plans to live in Athens with her Greek fiancé. My friend was anxious about telling him she had had an abortion when she was nineteen, back in the United States. Although she had long been reconciled to it, her mother had hammered it into her never to tell anyone, especially not the Greek relatives. Finally, carefully, she told him—and was amazed at his response: "You had one abortion? So what? My sister has had four. And now at least you know you can conceive." This story reminds us that the issue of fertility is not reducible to a conceptual equating of motherhood and womanhood, but that having children is fundamental to *marriage*. Furthermore, what my friend's fiancé neglected to realize, and what proponents of the resistance theory also overlook, is that my friend's previous history of conceiving with a former boyfriend was no biological guarantee that she would be able to do so with her husband; as it turned out, they endured years of strain and multiple infertility treatments before she was able to conceive and birth a daughter. Here too, my friend's husband failed to recognize precisely what physicians and family planning advocates emphasize: abortion may do just the opposite of proving a woman's future fertility—it may damage it.

I read the widespread resistance theory—that some women resist contraception because they are culturally driven to test out their fertility by "letting themselves" get pregnant without intending to have a child—as an attempt to rationalize a seemingly irrational practice, namely abortion. In this regard, the Greek resistance theory resonates with Kristin Luker's 1970s study of contraceptive risk-taking among American women. In this work, Luker argues that risk-taking behavior, despite potential outcomes (in this case, including abortion, disease, and inopportune childbirth), is the product "of a 'rational' decision-making chain produced by a person who is acting in what he or she perceives to be his or her best interests, although often in the presence of faulty data" (1975, 138). Women who proceed with risky sexual behavior, who do not take the pill or insist their partner use a condom, according to Luker, do so only if they view contraception as relatively costly and pregnancy as potentially beneficial. It is easy to see how psychologists and family planners employ these terms to rationalize Greek reliance on abortion. The relative *costs* of modern contraceptive use for Greek women would include physiological harm to their organisms; the embarrassment of asking a doctor or pharmacist for the means; the challenge to dominant gender, sex, and power relations by which men play the active role in initiating sexual relations while moral women either resist their advances or submit to them (according to the sacrament of marriage); and the stigmatization of being considered "easy" if they carry condoms (Iordanidou 1992) or take the pill when unmarried. The relative *benefits* of even temporary pregnancy are said to include signifying womanhood, proving one's fertility to a prospective husband, and providing impetus to get married sooner rather than later. Naziri, Luker, and family planners who apply a cost/benefit analysis in understanding women's engagement in unprotected sex are well intentioned in that they are trying to prove the rational will, and hence fundamental intelligence, of women who might otherwise be criticized for their ignorance. Family planners do not want to question women's rational capacity—after all, they need women to be rational actors if they are going to act appropriately (i.e., prophylactically) on the basis of the new knowledge that family planning provides. What family planners question are the *premises* with which women are working in making rational decisions.

Much of the FPAG's literature is therefore directed toward changing and, for some, modernizing the premises women accept when thinking about sex, pregnancy, and having children. First, telling women they should be able to choose motherhood when they want it, family planning rhetoric calls on the ethic of choice to insist that motherhood is not the defining feature of womanhood but is something upon which (modern) women decide. This was precisely what middle-class women, fully sharing in this modern attitude, expressed when talking with me about motherhood: it was something to be planned around, saved for, even scheduled into one's life. Second, in such pamphlets as *Do You Know? It Could Happen to You . . . Abortion,* the FPAG warns of abortion's associated dangers and actively challenges the popular belief that abortions in Greece today are safe, and even, as Eleni claimed, "the safest in the world." Evangelia explained in an interview, "Today we try to enlighten people to see that the [physiological] effects of whatever contraceptive method she uses will be fewer than [the effects] of having an abortion." Physicians and FPAG members I spoke with in 1993 and 1994 supported the importation of mifepristone (RU 486) as a nonintrusive alternative to induce the abortion of an early-term pregnancy; not until 1999 was the drug approved for marketing in Greece. Finally, the FPAG encourages women (and couples) to regard sex as something recreational, pleasurable in and of itself.[25] They want to dissociate sex from procreation so that contraception will not create the cultural dissonance they fear. But it is one thing to rationalize abortion post hoc and quite another to present medical forms of contraception as *the* choice any rational woman would make.

In order to forward medical contraception as the rational choice they assume it to be, family planners must portray the experience of sexual relations as an event subject to rational deliberation within both traditional and modern framings. Distinguishing between the two, family planners describe a move from a subconscious to a conscious application of rationality. In this way, they cast both practices, and the women who follow them, as rational while still retaining a distinction between traditional and modern mentalities, or modes of rational application. Here their reliance on strict cost/benefit economic models undermines their own best intentions. Even if analysts root a driving desire for motherhood in specific cultural pressures facing women, they relegate culture to a realm separate from rational decision making procedure when they dismiss this desire as something traditional that women can overcome through proper education. As a result, as Anthony

Carter writes in his critique of Kristin Luker's early work, "agency collapses under the demands of abstract rationality and is reduced to a mechanical implementation of cultural prescriptions that ill-accords with observed outcomes" (1995, 82). This critique can be extended to the Greek case.

In suggesting that a young woman's first abortion is often the result of a "trial pregnancy," Naziri ignores the historical fact that Greek women began to "discover" abortion later in life, after having four or five children. At that point, not only was their fertility fully validated, but they also were demonstrating their ongoing gender proficiency by being good mothers. How can her theory account for women's agency in such circumstances? I need only think of my friend Katherine's abortion narratives (whereas she decided her first "had to be done," her second was coerced by her husband and female in-laws) to be dissuaded by Naziri's argument to explain the phenomenon of repeat abortions: that once a woman has undergone the experience of abortion, it becomes "psychologically easier" for her to have another and then another. Not one woman I interviewed ever mentioned anything about a woman wanting to prove her fertility through abortion. And yet this remains a popular explanation among Greek professionals. A study of Athenian adolescents' awareness of HIV transmission, extending the fertility theory to men, claims:

> The "unwanted" pregnancy which usually ends in abortion is used as evidence by both men and women of their continuing fertility, and modern contraception would create doubts about this. Thus one can understand that Greek women use modern contraceptive methods usually only after the completion of a pregnancy. Repeated abortion can be seen as the expression of different ideological and psychological conflicts affecting her sexual life which relate to the constitutions of female identity. (Agrafiotis et al. 1990b, 38)

This leads, the study concludes, to women's reliance on abortion "as a method of birth control."

FPAG president George Kakoyanis, dismissing my suggestion that the Orthodox Church might impede family planning goals, offered an interesting variation on the cultural resistance theme:

> The problem is more cultural. I think it's more the people's ideas. Because the church is not so strong a tradition as the Catholics. The Orthodox Church is more flexible.[26] Abortion is traditional birth control. I would say that Greek people are more conservative in these kinds of things, despite easily adopting new ideas; in *this* aspect I think they are more traditional. Despite all this education, they are still resistive to the pill.

I asked whether they resisted because they disliked the idea of taking chemicals.

> Yes, they don't like to take chemicals—but they are *resisting;* this is very cultural. They don't like to interfere with the spontaneity of inter-course, or with—I think it's . . . the attitudes of people. Because every-body knows that contraceptives exist, especially young people. And the stranger thing is that the doctors . . . you're trained, as a doctor they know about contraception—but they don't push it. It is, I think, a deeply rooted attitude.

Kakoyanis astutely recognizes that physicians live within the same cul-tural system as their patients and can be disposed against contraceptives for reasons similar to anyone else's. Yet he, too, relegates culture to tradi-tion, setting this apart from rational thought as something that can impede proper decision making and action. From the position of family planning advocacy—his position—the comment is discouraging: the element of Greek society considered most conservative is neither the church nor the government—institutions that could be lobbied—but people themselves. Kakoyanis sees Greek cultural tradition as static and sustained in the *noötropía,* or habitus, of the populace, more resistant to change than any policy-making institutions.

In formulating a modern mentality deemed requisite to contraceptive uptake, these family planners underestimate the impact of things cultural on what they regard as rational action. When this happens, human agency becomes a matter of degree: how much or how little does an individual think her way out of cultural assumptions that neither accord with sci-entific knowledge nor maximize her own interests? Women who remain mired in tradition are implicitly portrayed as lacking both consciousness and conscientiousness, possibly incapable of feeling guilt, as suggested by the title of one of Despina Naziri's (1991) publications, "The Triviality of Abortion in Greece."[27] This kind of judgment is borrowed from Enlighten-ment ethical theory, which "regards rationality both as a natural property belonging to all normal human adults and as the only reliable guide to dis-tinguishing right from wrong action. Viewing emotions as contaminants of pure reason, it defines moral rationality in terms of individuals' abilities to consider dispassionately the interests of all those affected in any situa-tion" (Jaggar 2000, 356). I suggest therefore that it is not merely the prem-ises but also the model of rational action itself that may be unhelpful in understanding sexual behavior and fertility control practices, in Greece as elsewhere.

IN THE FUTURE? AN ETHIC OF WELL-BEING

Family planning advocates tend to see their program as introducing morality to issues of abortion and reproductive control in Greece.[28] But contrary to Naziri, who writes that "abortion is not a moral issue in Greece" (1991, 13), I view virtue and morality as absolutely central to the related concerns of sex, fertility control, and abortion. Because I believe that morality has *always* been central to Greek women's abortion practice, I view institutionalized family planning as an attempt to promulgate a *new* morality, a sexual ethic for women alternative to that organized by the virtue of service to others. According to this ethic, sexual practice is to be regulated so as to minimize personal bodily harm, as opposed to a traditional or cultural concern with minimizing social outcry. What I call the ethic of well-being is exemplified in the "Mother to Mother" column of the May 1993 issue of *Yinéka* (Woman) magazine. Here, Anthi Doxiadi-Trip observes that "the problem with prophylactics is not that no one has told [adolescents] about them, or that they've never heard of them. The problem is that, because they do not have the proper 'psychological training,' it goes in one ear and out the other" (321). She advocates training that will encourage preventative practices early in life: if kids grow up using sunblock to prevent skin cancer, and brushing their teeth to prevent tooth decay, she reasons, they will be more inclined in later years to use condoms to prevent inopportune pregnancy and sexually transmitted disease. The author champions a distinctively Western type of modern agency consistent with biomedical preventative care, "to give them the sense, the pragmatics [to realize] that many of the things that seem to happen to them are in their hands to make happen, not let happen[,] to them" (321). Through this kind of formulation, family planning advocates enlist the ethic of choice in a particular kind of reproductive agency, one that has as its moral object personal health and well-being.

Since the ability to exercise self-control has long been integral to the moral development of gendered subjectivities in Greece, particularly with regard to sexual (if not necessarily contraceptive) behavior (e.g., avoiding being in the wrong place at the wrong time), the ethic of well-being cannot be seen to offer individuals an emergent sense of reproductive control. The terms of a family planning-sponsored sexual and reproductive ethic are new, however, in several regards. The first concerns understandings of reproductive (and nonreproductive) agency. Several women I interviewed pointed out that human will is accountable only for part of the process of procreation and *teknopiía*. Not every sexual activity leads to intercourse, not every act of intercourse leads to conception, and not every conception leads to the birth of a baby. Spaces of uncertainty are given over to fate, chance, nature, the will of God, practical magic, or more recently, science (Stewart 1991). Nadia instructed me about natural uncertainties which, in her view, do not square well with medical science:

> There are women who can conceive only two to three times in all their life, and not because of abortion. It's clearly this fertility of theirs, you understand. Now some scientists admit it and some don't admit it. Whatever the scientific research says, I believe that the woman does not conceive every month during her dangerous days. I know this both from personal experience and from friends, that when you make love one day it doesn't [necessarily] mean you conceive a child. When conceptions are dangerous [i.e., during the fertile days of the menstrual cycle], it happens more easily; this has happened, and it has also happened that you can't conceive a child. I had a friend who birthed a child—she wasn't able to conceive a child for a long time, and she [conceived] the child during her period. Yes, it's true. And her three children were all like this.

I agree with Nadia that the scientific and rational basis of modern family planning strives for an unrealistic degree of knowledge about and control over procreative processes and that this puts undue pressure on women.

A second distinguishing feature of this ethic of well-being concerns how it imagines the ethical subject. Under traditional moral codes of sexual relations aimed at upholding God's will and group solidarity, the repercussions of premarital or adulterous sexual activity have had to do primarily with what others would say about the transgression. The new ethic personalizes the arbiter of moral behavior more deeply than would an ethic of choice, for each person is held morally responsible for her or his own actions in terms of possible health consequences affecting oneself and others, such as infection from disease or sterility from abortion. It is not merely moral codes that are changing, then: the bodily ethic of health requires too a change in "the way in which the individual establishes his [sic] relation to the rule and recognizes himself [sic] as obliged to put it into practice" (Foucault 1990b, 27). The new ethic does more than ask people to act to prevent inopportune pregnancy and the transmission of disease, rather than rely on post hoc solutions (i.e., abortion) to such problems: it demands that individuals take full responsibility for controlling a deeply biologized sense of their own nature. This notion of reproductive agency conflicts with the ethic of service as underwritten by an ethnomedical sense of well-being based on a fundamental inside/outside distinction. The ethnomedical model by which Georges and others have understood Greek women's reluctance to use the IUD asks women to direct their efforts at regulating external social relations. The biomedical ethic of well-being internalizes that effort, requiring women to regard their own bodies' regulated maintenance as a moral good in itself.

But, of course, bodies are not isolated entities (Scheper-Hughes and Lock 1991). As Doxiadi-Trip notes in her magazine column, "The difficulty is the meaning of prevention, the meaning of 'I have control over things that concern me,' [and] the meaning of communication, of discussion as a form of intimacy" (1993, 320). To help facilitate a shift in people's understandings of control, especially in regard to fertility control issues, family planning pamphlets and newspaper articles quoted in this chapter frequently replace the Greek word *érotas* with the English word *sex*. While socializing with Athenian teenagers as an American exchange student in 1988, anthropologist Joanna Skilogianis never heard the word *sex*. "Back then," she told me, "people 'made love' " *(kánane érota)*. An Athenian friend recalled to me, "My grandmother wouldn't talk about 'The Act'— that's what she would call it, *I Práksi* with a capital *I* and a capital *P*." But today, public use of the foreign word *sex* (the word is strewn throughout magazines and newspapers, heard on television, voiced by doctors) expands the allowable parameters of acceptable and valid sexual practice beyond vaginal intercourse.

Being Western, the word *sex* simultaneously connotes pleasure and rationality. Use of the foreign word likely contributes to these practitioners' own rationalizations of sex. But sex on the model of Western modernity, as Carole Vance (1984) has noted, is, if pleasurable, simultaneously dangerous. The FPAG literature can be quite explicit about the medical dangers of sex acts. One leaflet cautions readers to remember that "oral sex *[to stomatikó sex]* is very dangerous during menstruation or if the active partner has a cut in his mouth, swollen gums, ulcers, bleeding wounds, etc." In saying that any sexual contact is potentially risky, the literature acknowledges that any sexual practice, regardless of procreative potential, is indeed sex. Under an ethic of well-being, any sexual contact counts as sex. This is a necessary move in the Greek family planning program to disentangle sex from pregnancy and reproduction. The foreign word *sex* (transliterated into Greek) signals the advent of nontraditional sexual practice: primarily guilt-free sex outside marriage without intent to marry, but including anything that is not monogamous marital sex, men having sex with female prostitutes, or incest—all of which might be considered more traditional.[29] The ethic of well-being tells people they can have sex, any kind of sex, as much sex as they want—*and* do good—so long as the sex is "safe." Meanwhile making love can remain linked to procreation.

HIV, AIDS, Gender, and the Ethic of Well-Being

Not surprisingly, the AIDS pandemic has been called on in applying the ethic of well-being to sex. Informational literature by the FPAG and the Ministry of Health and Welfare Center for the Control of Infectious Disease (KEEL) on how to prevent the transmission of HIV rarely refers to *káni érota* (making love). Rather, it is *seksoualikí epafí,* sexual contact, that transmits disease as well as causes inopportune pregnancy. The AIDS awareness campaign provides a window onto how family planning and its attendant ethic of well-being must reconcile the promises and perils of being modern. In Greece, people's fear of AIDS has been focused on the virus itself, which has not been appended to any particular social group; it looms out there in "today's world." The first cases of AIDS in Greece were reported in 1983.[30] According to popular opinion, AIDS appeared in Greece via tourist "carriers." AIDS, always otherized (like *sex*) through its English acronym, is depicted as a symptom of modern times and not as, say, a disease put on the earth to punish individuals for engaging in certain practices. It was striking to me how infrequently AIDS was mentioned in conjunction with homosexuality or gay men; more often, Greeks connect it to intravenous drug use, another modern import.[31] Given the collective memory of a centuries-long struggle against occupation and foreign rule, this view is in keeping not only with Greece's historically rooted sense of victimization or what Nikiforos Diamandouros (1993) has called Greece's "underdog imagination" with respect to the West (Diamandouros 1993) but also with a local understanding that homosexuality reflects a weakness of will or peccadillo of preference. It does not concretize an essential sexual identity. Homosexuality, like overenthusiastic heterosexuality, is a natural (if morally questionable) phenomenon that can be blamed on the human condition of original sin. In contrast, HIV is seen to come from outside Greece. When HIV is not ghettoized among a sexual minority, the health message is that *anyone* can contract the virus: "All sexual acts are dangerous without prophylactics"; "Any kind of sexual activity without proper use of a prophylactic is very dangerous"; "AIDS attacks anyone regardless of sexual orientation."[32] The standard *noötropía* seems not to be "It could never happen to *my* child (or to me)," but rather, "Oh my God, it's going to happen to my child (if not to me)!" Only 50 percent of Athenian secondary school students (age twelve to eighteen) surveyed as part of a comparative study of attitudes toward AIDS sponsored by the World Health

Organization "agreed" they were "not the type of person who would get AIDS" (Agrafiotis et al. 1990b, 10).

Playing to this collective fear, the AIDS-information campaign presents its message as the light at the end of the tunnel, as a glimmer of hope in a fallen world. Family planning fights modernity with modernity by retooling and reapplying (for instance, within marital relations) that ancient technology, the prophylactic:

> The surest method of PROTECTION is to INSISTENTLY DEMAND that your sexual partner wear a PROPHYLACTIC.
> Don't make love in any way with a man who refuses to wear one.
> Your own life, and your partner's, comes first.[33]

Using the vocabulary of safe sex, the planning rhetoric forwards good health as a matter of moral responsibility. Unlike the ethic of service, the ethic of well-being also promises gender-neutrality.

Consider the following advertisement for condoms, which appeared in the 11 July 1993 issue of *Epsilon,* the magazine insert of the Sunday newspaper *Eleftherotipía.* This ad, pitched toward heterosexual adults, calls forth the autonomous moral agent that family planners hope to encourage:

> HEALTH AND FAMILY PLANNING IS YOUR OWN CHOICE
>
> For each man, for each woman, the partner and the character of every relationship is a personal choice. *It is your choice, health and family planning.*
>
> Respect your choices and protect as well as you can yourself, your partner, your relationship. Protect yourself from unpleasant surprises, and enjoy life and erotic love *[érota].*
>
> DUO condoms have been designed to respect the desires, needs, and mutual pleasure that is possible in a couple's life.
>
> Manufactured from natural latex material and covered with a special coating that assists, they are electronically examined one by one for absolute *certainty* and *safety.* You, the man, but also you, the woman, ask for the name DUO at SUPERMARKETS and kiosks. It isn't necessary to be bold. What is necessary is for the modern person who respects himself and his partner to act responsibly.
>
> DUO? Certainly![34] Make the correct choice and ask for the name of the authoritative contraceptive protection, DUO.

Men and woman alike are told they can enjoy life and erotic love without "unpleasant surprises" so long as they demonstrate respect for themselves and their loved ones and make the correct choice to use prophylactics. When such behavior is said to demonstrate the responsibility of "the modern person," the ethic of choice is harnessed to an ethic of individuated care. The ethic of well-being follows Western models of modernity in that it asks people to realize morally appropriate behavior by enacting responsible decisions that are explicitly self-interested, rather than by finding self-interest through service to others.

Personalizing responsibility in sexual relations itself represents a break with tradition. As Lela explains in the previous chapter, in the past courtship was carefully chaperoned by a girl's parents, brothers, and other kin protective of her maidenhood (du Boulay 1974; Hirschon 1978). Women's sexual responsibility a generation or two ago—protecting their honor by safeguarding virginity prior to marriage or engagement, and getting pregnant soon after—is today recollected not as the sole responsibility of a woman's choice but as the result of people collectively following imposed convention (the mandate of female chastity is surely recalled as being more strict than it ever was in reality [Herzfeld 1983, 1997b, 160]). While Athenian women are not troubled by the notion of controlling fertility per se (the notion of restricting births is far from new, after all), they do see the locus of control shifted from parents and other relatives to couples. When reproductive agency is to be directed *through* the act of (rationalized) sex, this directly involves only those having sexual relations. The very name of Greece's most popular condom reveals and reinscribes this move: *duo* means "two."

What is omitted from the DUO condom advertisement, and what many family planners neglect to examine critically, is that this burden of personalized contraceptive responsibility is gendered feminine (Luker 1975). Promotional campaigns for condoms frequently act on traditional stereotypes of gender and sexuality and pitch their message toward women and not men. The August 1992 issue of *Diva*, a glossy fashion magazine targeting middle-class young adult women, was prominently displayed at kiosks covered in plastic encasing a silver-wrapped condom. I once bought an slim-fitting skirt of Greek manufacture from a Monastiraki shop that had affixed to it a paper packet labeled "AIDS" and containing a male condom. While it is unequivocally good that condoms are becoming commonplace, a feminist gynecologist I interviewed, Eftyhia Leontidou, complained that condoms had never been advertised extensively when their primary purpose was to prevent pregnancy:

> You see how unfair it is. How many years have we tried as women to make men use the condom? The woman would try to make him use it,

but the partner would not accept, because he didn't like it, et cetera. But now, with the AIDS problem, it's really advertised everywhere. This was never done for pregnancy. Not to save the women's life [by reducing the need for abortions], but it's only to save the man's life. It's terrible. I find it, you know, outrageous, actually.[35]

Just as Greeks have traditionally viewed limiting family size as a woman's maternal duty, current condom advertising and family planning advocacy makes it a modern woman's duty to protect the heterosexual family from disease. But if women are persuaded to buy male condoms, it is left to them to convince their male partners to wear them. When condoms are marketed to both men and women, whether in the DUO advertisement or in government-sponsored informational AIDS leaflets—such as one featuring a heterosexual couple frolicking on a beach—this feminizes a traditionally male contraceptive.

Committed to the liberating promises of women's rational contraceptive practice under an ethic of well-being, Greek family planners adhere to a "medical sexual ideology" that underestimates "the issue of power in gender relations" (Van Eeuwijk and Mlangwa 1997, 38–40). A brief story illustrates: A gynecologist at the FPAG public seminar "Sexual Education and Health" voiced his frustration that while women "refused" to take the pill because of the cancer scare, they did not stop smoking.[36] If women are willing to take a certain health risk for the pleasure of smoking, he reasoned, they should not fuss over an unverified health risk associated with oral contraceptives but, indeed, should weigh the costs and benefits of smoking versus the pill and quit smoking to minimize the risks of pill consumption.[37] Blinded by the gender-neutrality of rational models, this physician cannot see that weighing the costs and benefits of smoking and of taking the pill are *not* culturally equivalent practices in Greece. Because contraception takes place in the context of heterosexual relations, its practice is never exclusively "male" or "female." At the same time, responsibility in sexual relations entails more than working to avoid inopportune pregnancy and the spread of disease. Sexual relations are profoundly shaped by cultural pressures and, in Greece, men's and women's sexual responsibilities include upholding asymmetrical gender relations intimately bound up in the meanings and practices of sex and love. The individualized ethic of well-being will remain unrealizable when it comes to sex—in Greece as elsewhere—so long as heterosexual relations continue to be informed by patriarchal gender inequality.

What Women Say: Reconsidering
Abortion under an Ethic of Well-Being

"The last few years now," Maro said to me, "since AIDS appeared and they began the campaign about AIDS, the prophylactic has begun to enter into people's lives." Vaso Margaritidou of the FPAG agreed in an interview for a leading daily newspaper, *Ta Nea*, that "fear of the disease has led many to understand the need for prophylactics" (19 April 1995). Consensus among the family planning community holds that the number of abortions has been falling since around 1992 as a welcome by-product of the increased use of condoms to prevent HIV infection.[38] An earlier *Ta Nea* article reports, "The male prophylactic is almost the only method of contraception that young men know[,] and the majority of them use it—not for contraception but for their own protection from the diseases that are transmitted by the sex act" *(me ti seksoualikí práksi).*[39] While, as Eftyhia Leontidou stated, this does not represent the significant improvement in women's control of reproductive issues that family planners anticipated, Athenian women are rephrasing their moral evaluations of abortion and women's reproductive agency in light of what medical experts declare.

Several women mentioned to me having seen American-style television talk shows featuring health professionals discussing the medical dangers of abortion. Doctors in Greece are highly respected; their word is rarely questioned (Arnold 1985; Lefkarites 1992; Tsalicoglou 1995). Nadia, who had seen such programs, volunteered that, while repeat abortions could lead to female infertility, she believed new techniques were making them safer:

> Does abortion clearly damage the organism? I believe this is not a matter of opinion, because it's a medical issue. Of course the doctors say that some methods [are better]; for example, not to scrape a piece of the uterus [in English, "dilation and curettage"] but to use suction, like with a cupping-glass [vacuum aspiration]. Now, how successful is it? I believe that after some two or three abortions you always do harm to the organism for the next time you want to keep a child. I have heard of cases where [women] have had around two abortions, with the result that they can't have a child.

Other women spoke from direct experience. Litsa, who at age thirty conceived her child using IVF, confided to me that she was unable to conceive naturally after having an abortion in her youth.

Now that the medical dangers of abortion are known and contraceptive methods are widely available, a fully responsible attitude toward regulating fertility ideally entails planning ahead, taking preventative measures, and safeguarding one's health. Whether or not they feel able to exercise this kind of agency, the women I met often set these as expectations for themselves. By adopting new moral evaluations, women are enacting an ethic of well-being, although not in a way that results in the liberation envisioned by family planners. Having for generations turned to abortion as a lesser-evil solution to the problem of inopportune pregnancy, Athenian women increasingly see abortion as fraught with considerations for their own health. Chloe, a thirty-four-year-old graphics designer, observed, "When I was growing up, nobody ever said that you can damage your own reproductive system, which is maybe something that might make you think a little more. It wasn't really—I never remember it being drilled into our heads. That's probably why [women use abortion so frequently]."[40] A university-educated, upper-middle-class woman who has lived in the United States, Chloe believes that Greek women of her mother's generation approached abortion as a method of birth control or means of family limitation because they did not know it could lead to infertility. If they did know, her rational logic implies, they would have sought alternatives.

Twenty-year-old Nia also called on the ethic of well-being in tentatively supporting the resistance theory, which states that some women actually *prefer* abortion as a birth control method:

> From what I've heard from friends of mine, many women get pregnant and prefer to have an abortion—married women—[rather] than use a contraceptive method. Indeed, I've heard of women who have had an abortion, married with older children already—they feel ashamed that, having a child of twenty, they go and get pregnant again. And they and their husbands know only this, no other way [to limit births]. It is for them the solution, a method of contraception [sic]. They consider the problems they might face. They have had children, it can't harm their system.

Like Chloe, Nia makes a secondhand evaluation of past practices in light of present scientific knowledge. Nia believes women who might regard abortion as a deliberate method of birth control must be *older;* they must have the children they want. She rationalizes their "ignorance," even suggesting that abortion may not be a bad option for them since, at their age, and because they are already mothers, it cannot harm them. "Younger women," however, "avoid it [abortion] because they think that it might cause them problems, and they might not be able to have children later on." Realizing that the ethic she might apply to her own generation is not fairly applicable to older women, she excuses herself from judging them. "Since women are today more informed; they believe it is better to be preventative, and so they consider abortion as a last resort. If you can't do anything else, and a child comes to you suddenly and at an [advanced] age when you can't have a baby, I think you resort to an abortion."

Chloe and Nia are clearly conversant with the argument that "a great number of sterilities among women are the result of previous abortion."[41] At the FPAG's fourth public "Sexual Education and Health" seminar, a physician described "abortion in our country" as a "catastrophe of life and women's health." The organization's 1983 publication titled "Conclusions of the Seminar on Women and Family Planning" warns:

> Abortion is a violent dilation of the cervix and scraping of the fetus out from the uterine cavity by mechanical means. It is not a natural medical practice, but a violent intervention that terminates the natural protection for the preservation and development of pregnancy, causing complications leading to devastating consequences for the woman's mental and physical health.[42]

Fear tactics such as this harshly worded statement are common in biomedical sexual education efforts not only in Greece but in other countries as well (Rivkin-Fish 1999).

An ethical understanding of abortion based on protecting one's physical well-being, including future fertility, poses moral challenges to a now customary understanding of abortion as a necessary evil articulated with an ethic of service. These challenges may well compromise women's reproductive agency. While Athenians are talking more openly about abortion and sex today than in the past, people wanting to espouse modern views may be quicker to label abortion a shameful resort—perhaps particularly when talking with a young American.[43] Today the shame of abortion can emerge from a woman's supposed ignorance of contraception. Or, a woman who has an abortion may be viewed as being too backward in her perception of sex to be capable of taking preventative measures and, thus, likely to damage her body unwittingly and threaten her future fertility. Properly modern women should know better than to view abortion as a method of birth control or to find themselves in the passive position of having to resort to it.

Unfortunately for women, judgment can be levied against them today according to both modern and traditional criteria. This kind of ethical indeterminacy is played out in assessments of women's virtue as self-controlling. Midwives at a state-operated Athenian family planning clinic (with a more solidly working-class patient population than is represented in this study) were heard remarking of a woman seeking yet another in a long series of abortions, "What's her problem? Can't they control themselves?" (Skilogianis 1997). These midwives, certainly schooled in the latest contraceptive techniques, arguably castigated this woman not for her failure to use an effective means of contraceptive protection but for having too much sex with her husband. As Marina Iossifides writes of a southern Epirus village, "Couples who have sex without intending to marry are considered to be 'like animals,' unable to judge or control their passions" (1991, 138), calling to mind Ernestine Friedl's observation in a Viotian village that "parents who have more children than they can adequately feed and care for are accused of behaving like animals; they are said to have neither brains nor self-control" (1962, 50–51). The exercise of self-control over natural impulses such as sexual desire is what helps differentiate humans from animals; sexual self-control characterizes a *kalós ánthropos*, a "good person," who properly realizes his or her human nature in both an Aristotelian and an Orthodox sense. More resistant to change than penal codes and other institutional parameters, as Kakoyanis noted, this *noötropía* (embodied, collective mentality) continues to inform the moral assumptions of policy makers, physicians, family planning workers, mothers-in-law, and prospective lovers.

The moral questions deliberated are significant—and the moral doubt understandable—because, while matters of sexual propriety are decided on the basis of a woman's established character, meaning that a woman must pay continual attention to her public appearance and others' opinions, procreative matters entail discreet actions that occur in specific contexts. In these cases a woman's good repute may not be sufficient to excuse a momentary lapse or "mistake." Middle-class Athenians voice the ethical *ideals* of Western attitudes toward reproduction, but remain uncertain as to which actual *practices* count as appropriately modern in the urban Greek context.

Repeatedly, I heard Athenians consider ethical issues of reproduction by assessing the maturity of the populace: were Greeks or was Greek society mature enough to meet the challenges of the modern world? Maro, the thirty-eight-year-old dentist, positioned sex education within the broader context of health education and, echoing Kakoyanis's frustrations, castigated the same adherence to tradition:

> Here there is no education of bodily health in the schools. Health education generally doesn't exist. . . . And I think that a society which isn't advanced enough thinks that these things are easily solved if you leave them to their fate—"I'm not concerned." Is it possible that children do not know how to use contraception? Isn't that somewhat serious? This is unacceptable for a contemporary society.

Voicing a somewhat contrary perspective, Phoebe rehearsed a cogent summary of the modern mentality that family planners both respond to and encourage, but on closer examination she is more lenient than they in her evaluation. Explicating her perspective on Greece's declining birthrate, she said:

> This is, I think up to a point, an issue of maturity. You see in other countries where there's some lack of maturity that children are continually born who, in the end, they don't know what to do with them— how to raise them, how to feed them. And the state tries to dissuade the people from having children. That is, [the state tells them] either to take some prevention or even to have an abortion, which *we* consider anymore something terrible—to go and have an abortion in our era. In Greece it [the low birthrate] means exactly the opposite. And I believe that Greeks are very mature on this issue.

Phoebe asserts that to have an abortion is something "we consider anymore" to be "terrible," a traumatic last resort—not because it is morally ambiguous, as she made clear elsewhere in our discussion, but because "it was very dangerous, it can have the repercussion of a woman not being able to have kids, not to get pregnant." Today, she told me, evincing a modern mentality that would make family planning advocates proud, "the doctors, gynecologists, sociologists, continuously try—on television, in books they've written—to inform women about abortion and to show them that there are other, better ways of protection." But at the same time, Phoebe is also suggesting that Greeks have only the number of children for which they can properly provide, and that they do this by employing some self-imposed birth control strategy (yes, including abortion). The state has not imposed measures to suppress fertility; quite "the opposite." And *this* Phoebe sees as being "very mature." Family planners would not necessarily agree, because they do not view every birth control method as equal.

For Phoebe, as for most women I spoke with, any method of birth control is ultimately justifiable if a woman uses it in good faith, in service of both her family and herself (to the extent that they might separate these sets of interests). Moral character still creates morally appropriate behavior: as discussed previously, if a woman demonstrates that she is or wishes to be a good mother, the act of abortion or contraception is deemed morally sound. According to family planning ideology, in contrast, character is immaterial to the act. Abortion is damaging to a woman's body: it is avoidable and hence morally unsound, and therefore a woman who has an abortion lacks forethought and moral judgment. The fundamental clash between imported Western family planning programs and the traditional Greek *noötropía,* which family planners see themselves as being up against, results from the way ethical subjects and reproductive agency are imagined.

The Gender of the Choice

While the modernity that Greek family planning efforts strive to realize does not give women reproductive agency, I have shown that it does move the ideal site of control from the social realm of orchestrating sexual relations and the post hoc arena of abortion, to the individuated, medicalized space of conception and contraception. As medical professionals work to redefine procreation as a physical rather than metaphysical event, they encourage a shift in the nature to be controlled: from the impulse to engage in sexual activity to the physiological processes governing conception and gestation. If women can be held responsible for "controlling" not only sexuality but now also procreation, these each carry a different moral valence. The implications for conceptualizing gender, and responsibility, are significant.

Greek femininity and masculinity have been differentiated in part by the appearance of male sexual dominance (Friedl 1967). Because male sexuality is seen as naturally potent and omnivorous, manliness is questioned, in Greek slang, by the derogatory word for "passive homosexual" *(poústis),* one who puts himself in an "open" feminine sexual position with respect to another man. Women have been trained to expect and resist men's advances unless it is socially appropriate for relations to occur (an ever broadening, but contested, category), in which case they are to be seen to "submit" to male desire (Hirschon 1978; du Boulay 1974, 1986; Cowan 1990) while, often, hoping that men will cooperate in preventing inopportune pregnancy by "pulling out." Although young women today are allowed greater social and sexual mobility than before, and despite family planning efforts to validate a wide range of sexual practices, gender inequality continues to underwrite popular understandings of sex-*érotas.* Vaginal intercourse, according to forty-two-year-old Koralia, tends to define heterosexual relations.[44] While "97 percent of people have oral sex," she asserted in probable hyperbole, "it's not the only sex, you see. I don't think people feel it is completed if it doesn't have vaginal intercourse and if it doesn't have orgasm. Especially on the male side. On the female side," Koralia laughed wryly, "it's different." In contrast to the association between virility and manliness, hetero sex can be complete without female orgasm, and without compromising women's femininity.

Perhaps the greatest challenge to the gender-neutral family planning strategy is one that advocates seem hardly to notice: a woman who assumes control over sexual relations must, in patriarchal settings such as Greece, still guard against disempowering or emasculating men in their relations.[45] Family planning advocacy tends to forget that the choice to use modern contraception is deeply gendered. It is understandable that family planners view the exercise of female control as an absolute good. Following the "our bodies, our selves" line made popular in 1970s American feminism—motivated by the Lockean supposition that people hold property in their bodies—family planners want to enfranchise women in the arena of contraceptive control, since women risk more than men in sexual relations. But when sexual practices that would challenge male authority are viewed from an implicitly male perspective, the problems this can create for women are obscured. It is *not* an easy matter of rational choice to ignore or defy dominant gender ideology. Greek gender stereotypes, for instance, contrast men's "intelligence" *(eksipnádha)* and women's "cunning" *(poniriá)*. Whereas male intelligence is conversant with modern scripts of premeditated action, women's cunning is far more consistent with post hoc, behind the scenes maneuvering (such as abortion). For a woman *to prepare* for nonprocreative sex by inserting a diaphragm or by ingesting a daily pill—or even by insisting that her partner use a condom—is to act with more foresight than cunning, or in other words, rather like a man. This has been the case, too, in Britain and the United States; Linda Gordon has suggested, "It is easier and more 'normal' for men to be lustful and assertive, for women merely to surrender, to be carried away by a greater force" (1979, 126).[46] We cannot simply think our way out of culture or ideology. Critically, even painfully, aware of the gender of the choice, twenty-eight-year-old Athena, the only woman I interviewed who was at the time taking the pill, shook her head and said, "Greek women . . . believe that contraception is the man's problem."

My punning here on Marilyn Strathern's *The Gender of the Gift* is of course intentional. In this monumental book, Strathern challenges the human universality of a notion of gender, of "dichotomous natural difference biologically conceived," and warns of the analytical pitfalls of cross-cultural comparison (1988, 40). Here, I have tried to do with family planning's embedded assumptions about choice what Strathern does in critiquing the gender neutrality of anthropological theories of gift exchange in Melanesian societies. She writes, "To ask about the gender of the gift . . . is to ask about the situation of gift exchange in relation to the form that domination takes in these societies. It is also to ask about the 'gender' of analytical concepts, the worlds that particular assumptions sustain" (1988, xii). The premeditated decision to use medical contraceptives not only means something different for women and men, but it also is differently enlisted in what it takes to be good at being a woman or man (gender proficiency)—and in what it means to be a good woman or man (demon-strated virtue).

Consider the example of the DUO condom ad. Viewed more as prophy-lactic against disease than against pregnancy, condoms have long been as-sociated with casual affairs and prostitutes. For a woman to try and intro-duce condoms into marital relations can therefore be seen as shedding doubt on her own or her spouse's sexual fidelity.[47] Again, this is not to say that traditional birth control methods, practiced according to the preroga-tive of men, have negated women's sexual and reproductive agency. Katherine, who lived out her twenties in Athens in the 1960s, assured me that "it was never a problem" to convince her husband that "today it's safe or today isn't safe." Male withdrawal *can* work rather successfully in con-cert with the "female" rhythm method of pregnancy prevention. And yet the terms of this cooperation are not equal. Indeed, when women, espe-cially older women, impressed on me that communication *(epikinonía)* and sympathetic understanding *(katanóisi)* are the key components of a suc-cessful marriage, I wondered how frequently their minds jumped to birth control issues. As Katherine noted, "I was *expected* to be the responsible one—you know, to make the decision, to say today it's safe or today isn't safe." She began to mimic herself in a singsong voice, "Yes, you can, dear! No, I don't think it would be appropriate, dear! Fine, my precious!" And of course Katherine was the one who had to face an abortion when she "goofed" on her days or her cycle shifted. If men retain the upper hand in *contraception*, Greek women, since they are accountable for bringing chil-dren into a family—and only so many children as can be properly raised—have often taken *birth control* into their own hands, correcting for "sur-prises" through medical abortion, performed efficiently and quietly.

As a means of family limitation, abortion has enabled women to better care for the children they already had. It has also provided women with a means of coping with a careless or uncaring husband, with a too-forceful lover, with an incestuous male relation. Indeed, abortion often belies an at-tempt to cover over the evidence of inappropriate sexual relations (includ-ing extramarital affairs, incest, and as Nia implied, sex between spouses after "a certain age") or, today, "irresponsible" (nonprophylactic) relations. For this reason, women who have abortions have been able to call on the ethic of service in casting themselves as good women, often as good moth-ers (Georges 1996a; on the United States, see Petchesky 1990; on Italy, Pitch 1992). Very often women have abortions, I was told, when men do not shoulder their responsibility in sexual relations to avoid conception. Eleni, an active feminist now in her sixties, stated clearly that abortion

practice in the Peloponnesian village where she was raised and married related largely to a lack of male responsibility in sex:

> I know a woman who had forty-one [abortions] and five children. I
> know that particular woman feels horrible about it because she felt sex
> as a rape, not at all as sex—because her husband would get drunk, come
> home, make love to her, and the next month she would have an abor-
> tion. I know some women who never had an abortion because their
> man was very careful about, uh, keeping so the abortion wasn't needed.

The husband of the woman who had forty-one abortions clearly conceived
of marriage within an ethic of service for women. Indeed, at that time there
were legal grounds for regarding marriage as a property agreement
whereby a husband owned access to his wife's body for the purpose of sat-
ing his sexual desire and for producing heirs. By necessity *she* limited the
number of heirs through abortion. This kind of reality led the gynecologist
Eftyhia Leontidou to pronounce abortion—and patriarchal complicity with
it through the institutions of family, church, and medicine—as "part of the
violence against women" in society.

Abortion, incorporated into an ethic of service for women and revamped
by an ethic of choice, can symbolize women's patriarchal obligation and dependency *or* represent a woman's free exercise of personal choice. I was
struck by how many middle-class Athenian women of various ages emphasized the former over the latter. Maro, after commenting on how "almost
all" her friends have had at least one abortion (one has had five), told me, "I
think it stays deep in their hearts, it bothers them, you understand? Because
most of them do it at a young age. It's not that at any moment you'll do it
consciously, it's because they got pregnant and had to—either because they
weren't working, [or because] there was no opportunity to get married by
the time they would have the child, or because they were very young." Her
sister Niki, in a separate interview, told me of "one friend who was already
married and wasn't able to keep any more; she had two children and couldn't
have any others. And because there wasn't this understanding between the
couple, and she got pregnant, of necessity she went and had an abortion."
"Why?" her mother asked; "didn't they use condoms?" "At that point they
had started having children," Niki replied. Here again, condoms are described as antithetical to a committed relationship consummated through
parenthood. "Now he's gotten over it," Niki said in an attempt to placate her
mother. "Her husband became aware; he understood that anymore it's a
matter of health, for the woman, after so many abortions." Maria muttered

under her breath and looked unhappy. In being ever-gendered, choice in using fertility control is ever-constrained.

Significantly, a few women stressed that patriarchy's historical relationship to heterosexuality, and thus to abortion, has never been subsumed by the institution of marriage. Discussing reasons why a woman, or even a young girl, may be compelled to have an abortion, Artemis, a forty-seven-year-old schoolteacher, told me, "And you know, many times—I don't know if you found this in your research—many times the father was the father of the girl."[48] "Incest?" I asked, seeking clarification.

> Yes. Usually in the villages, because they have often the one room, everybody was, you know, [sleeping] in a row. Maybe the father was drunk when he comes back from the *kafenío*, or in the house they have wine. And many times, I think more than we know—because after that they couldn't speak of it, because no one would marry this woman if they knew. So many times, you know, it was done. The mother knew, I think, but she never said anything. And for the girl it was more difficult. It was not only in the villages, but it was more easily done there. In the villages it was easier for the father to go to his daughter. Because of the way of life, the way of the family, the space. . . . The girls went with their sheep, goats; they went out, somebody found them, nobody to hear you. I think—no I'm *sure*, well, I'm not sure about *how* big it was, but it was a phenomenon.

A study by the Children's Health Institute of 743 schoolchildren and university students in 1994 suggested that 1 out of 6 Greek girls, and 1 out of 16 boys, has been sexually abused by older male relatives or friends (see also Blum and Blum 1965, 49).[49]

The tendency for families to close ranks around members to serve the collective interest causes a protective silence to blanket the occurrence of incest. Artemis, born and raised in Pangrati, may have drawn on an urban/rural version of the modern/traditional divide to speak more easily about the unspeakable. Katherine, symbolically distanced by being raised in Canada by Greek parents, spoke to me more explicitly in a voice that became increasingly hard, bitter:

> If you don't talk about it, it doesn't exist. It doesn't happen. I feel very strongly about this. Because my father was—I have a family history. Of, ah, of rape. You see. And nobody would believe it of anybody in my family. My father was a real bastard. And he was a nice Greek man. A pillar of the community and all that shit. In my case, I was very small and frightened into submission and into keeping quiet.

"Did you ever talk to your mother about it?" I asked.

> My mother? [She laughs without humor.] You've got to be kidding. My
> mother? No. No. Mothers don't know these things—they don't want to
> know. Mothers don't want to know, because whether they do or not
> [they can't do anything about it], especially if they are dependent on
> the husband, on the father.

Of course, as Artemis intimated, when mothers have been forced by their
daughter's pregnancy to "know," they have colluded in the crime by helping the girl procure an abortion.

Having returned to Athens after raising her children in Canada, Katherine is determined to have her childhood story heard, to bring this hidden
crime out into the public sphere.[50] She has told female Greek relatives
about her experience, often finding that her confidence inspires others:

> I've talked to people. It's quite interesting, the response. A relative said
> to me, "I'll tell you something I've never told anybody before . . ." And
> then I'd hear a story, interspersed with whispered comments—"Don't
> tell anybody, I'm only telling *you*." Why didn't she say anything about
> it? Well, I mean, I understand, I just wonder. And then somebody else:
> "Well, you know what happened to *me* when I was six years old. There
> was an uncle." It's only when you open up that they'll talk about it.

Since for these men, the point of incest is to manifest physically the symbolics of patriarchal power and, perhaps, to achieve sexual satiation (in such
cases sex has nothing to do with inheritance ensured through women's
conjugal fidelity), abortion has always been permitted by both church and
state when pregnancy results from an incestuous encounter. In threatening
the proper flow of consanguineous blood by which kinship is constituted
(du Boulay 1984), incest (the Greek word is *emomiksía*, blood mixing) has
been viewed as a crime against the family and lineage, not against the child
raped. Acting within the ethic of service once again, women have papered
over this crime with abortion. In Greece, as throughout modern European
American settings, incest poses more of a social problem than extrafamilial
rape because, as David Schneider (1976) suggests, incest is analogous to
treason in that it threatens the family as a transcendental moral object necessary to the related ideologies of patriarchy and nationalism.[51] In that
case, as Katherine implied, with incest it is "the secret-tellers who are the
traitors" (Burton 1997). Susan McKinnon has argued that "the role of the
father in paternal incest is 'normalized' to the extent that paternal authority and [male] sexual agency and female nurturance and sexual acquiescence are, themselves, considered to be 'natural' and, therefore, normative"

(1995, 36). In Greece, this patriarchal logic is compounded by a tendency (perhaps particularly among inhabitants of Crete) to label violent acts of a general nature (e.g., blood feuds and sheep raiding) not as violence but as an expression of *eghoismós,* or masculine virtuosity (Astrinaki 1994; Herzfeld 1985). When male behavior in incest or marital rape is seen to represent an exaggeration of the norm (whereas mother-son incest, an inversion of the norm, is pathologized), marital rape and incest become structurally incorporated into the architecture of the patriarchal family. Abortion, built into the same patriarchal system, hides (or denies, or both) and thus protects incest and domestic sexual abuse. For women and children, the strategies of silence surrounding abortion are not merely a matter of honor or virtue; as Katherine emphasized when she read an early draft of this argument, to keep quiet is frequently a matter of safety.

Such cases demonstrate a contrast between the appearance of male authority and the reality that women act from behind the scenes (here by covering over men's compromising behavior) to safeguard the family's moral well-being (Friedl 1967; Dubisch 1986), reflecting and buttressing the traditional Greek ethical system that appears to privilege outer act over inner state. We see evidence too that, when ethical evaluation is focused on appearance, space is opened up behind the protective facade of the family and household, which allows morally ambiguous behavior to go unchecked. It is not the case that Greeks would view hidden behavior as exempt from moral evaluation; rather, morally questionable behavior that is not discovered is allowed to continue. Abortion allows sexual immoderation to continue.

Because abortion happens after the fact of sex—and because, in Greece, it has been fully medicalized—it can be viewed separately from sexual practice, if not always separately from the complexity of a heterosexual relationship. This permits a woman to assert control after a couple leaves the bedroom; a woman can hide her intervention from the man if necessary. Abortion mitigates but does not challenge the power dynamic of heterosexual relations. Modern medical contraception such as the pill or IUD does not provide women with the same escape clause as abortion; since it is forwarded as an exclusively female method of contraception, it *does* challenge both male dominance in sexual relations and the wider social inequalities this helps engender. Significantly, the pill is often referred to in Greek as contraception *(antisíllipsi)*—traditional methods employed by women that predate the language of family planning are implicitly *not* contraception but are described instead as being careful or paying attention. In this patriarchal context, where the virtue of service still has purchase on women's propriety, the only truly feminine forms of birth control entail the management of sexual appetites—what in modern terms would be called emotion—either by dissuading a male partner from trying anything ("it's a bad time, dear"), or by managing the consequences of succumbing to sexual appetites by being prepared to have an abortion or birth a child she may or may not be able to raise properly.

Love, Sex, and Reassessing Risk

Women's lives are easier when men behave, I was told repeatedly. In this light, I wish to reconsider the ethics of women's choice to take risks by having unprotected sex (see Paxson 2002 for an extended analysis). Family planning has clearly couched the notion of sexual risk in terms of risk-management and avoidance aimed at maintaining emotional and physical well-being by avoiding inopportune birth and sexually transmitted disease. Taking into account the gendered aspect of heterosexual relations in urban Greece sheds light on why Despina, fully within the biomedical ethic of well-being, cited her smoking as a factor in deciding to stop taking the pill, rather than the other way around. From this perspective a new meaning of risk comes into focus, one not well captured by the English word connoting "the possibility of suffering harm or loss" and implying willful accountability: "To incur the risk of," as defined by the *American Heritage Dictionary*. In contrast, Greeks talk about "being in danger of" something *(kindhinévo)* or "playing" the odds *(pézo)*—risk implies leaving matters to chance, abdicating responsibility rather than incurring the responsibility of miscalculation. As depicted above in the FPAG pamphlet *What Do You Know about Contraception?*, chance is more akin to fate than to calculation or choice. Alexandra Bakalaki (1993) observes that an "element of risk" afforded by having sex without using technical contraception is often said in Greece to heighten sexual desire. Koralia—an educated professional who knows her contraceptive options, has never married, and has chosen not to have children—confided to me that "the idea of reproducing has always come up in my sex life. I have to admit that the idea that [conception] might happen is a very exciting fantasy I have used." Risk, she implies, can be sexy. Risk suddenly appears to be something a woman in certain circumstances might not wish to manage or avoid.

The risk Koralia finds sexy is her own. As an unmarried woman, she would have to confront the decision of how to proceed with an inopportune pregnancy by deciding between abortion or motherhood (formal adoption is uncommon in Greece and is virtually never presented as an option to pregnant women). What Koralia finds sexy is giving herself up to risk, very much as one relinquishes the self in modern romantic love—a submission that Greek women are trained to effect more consistently, more completely, than are men. The fear of pregnancy can of course also detract from women's sexual pleasure (Georges 1996a, 514). Because modern heterosexual relations have been defined by male orgasm and initiative, relegating women's pregnancy risk to the category of side effect, heterosexuality has been concomitantly organized around a preconception of female vulnerability (Cowan 1990, 76). Implicitly, when modern women "give themselves" to men in *érotas*, in passionate sexual relations, they challenge men to do what is right—and perhaps gain clarity regarding the state of their relationship. Is this a man who can be trusted, relied on?

If a "not nice" man causes his wife to have repeat abortions, the wife of a "good" man, as we have heard, will never have to undergo one. Withdrawal and condoms, the most accepted forms of contraception in Greece, may be additionally valued by women precisely because they are male methods. Despina, who prefers condoms over pills, implied she does so because she *wants* men to take responsibility for contraception. Drawing on her cigarette, she told me she did not like the new female condom being marketed in Athens, "because I think it's too much. I mean, you know, women have to take the pill, women have to do everything—now we have to do the condom as well? I hate this idea, I would never try it, just for this reason." In performing withdrawal and by using condoms, men can be seen to take responsibility for the sexual encounter so that women are able to "submit" to emotion (and, indeed, to men) without having to worry about "unpleasant consequences." Despite not advancing the cause of feminism, succumbing or surrendering to men, at least within relatively stable relationships, may offer women strategy and agency. Women may be testing out their *men* as much as their fertility in risking pregnancy. Agency does not always come in the form of overt, unilateral control or, for that matter, resistance (Scott 1987; Abu-Lughod 1990; McNay 2000). The expression of male love *(aghápi)* is for many self-proclaimed modern women more meaningful an aspect of heterosexual relations *(érotas)* than is the possibility of pregnancy or any symbolic connection with procreation. As Phoebe explained:

> *Érotas*, with the meaning of sex, or passion which you feel for an individual, is something that is passing. *Aghápi* is something that stays forever. That is, I believe, as you set out in your relationship with an individual, you start out first with *érota*, this attraction between two persons; and then either it will fade, it will never become anything else, or it will be followed by *aghápi*; and this lasts, certainly, for all the years of your life.

Eva concurred, noting that "after *érota* comes *aghápi*. When I'm *ero-tevméni* (in *érotas*) I have a passion for this man. I like him, I want him; then after awhile, I believe that the passion and my *érotas* will continue to exist, but *aghápi* will prevail." The relationship between sex and risk may indeed be fundamental to notions of *érotas*, a form of love distinguished from *aghápi* by virtue of its physicality, unreliability, and fleetingness.

In rationalizing sex, then, family planners neglect to consider that many (certainly not all) heterosexual encounters are experienced in the context of gendered ideals surrounding passion and love where women's risk can either test men or express trust in them. Some women may view leaving it up to men to perform withdrawal or to supply a condom as an opportunity to discern whether this is merely *érotas* or has become something else, something more sustaining, something that contemporary women are demanding more vocally than in previous generations. It is clear that women and men regard sexual love, *érotas*, as coming from the heart, or from the gut, but certainly not from the mind. Thus the family planning ideal—that women are supposed to choose medical contraception over abortion—constitutes a problem at the contestable level of ideology: namely, that modern people tend to see sex as something that *defies* rationality. After all, rational calculation follows its antecedents in Cartesian epistemology as it "regards all sense experience as illusory" (Bordo 1986, 452; Jaggar 1989). Implicitly, in the view of modern subjects, sex is rational only well before or well after the fact. Women can make the most careful plans—keep condoms in purses and bedside tables—they can come up with a creative array of explanations and alibis in hindsight. But, as Despina noted above, sometimes "it [sex] just happens." Nadia, who shares Koralia's age and never-married status, but not her education or economic status, explained in all earnestness that the actual experience of sex is something "crazy," something that happens outside the realm of abstract rationality. Regardless of one's best intentions in the light of day, Nadia told me, how one behaves "in the heat of the moment" is another matter entirely.

Risky, crazy—these are by no means the irrational rantings of misguided peasants. These narratives reflect ways in which middle-aged, heterosexually experienced urbanites come to terms with innumerable, always contingent, personal encounters. Rather than voicing a supposedly traditional view of sex bound up in procreative possibility, Koralia and Nadia voice the very modern conceptual opposition between reason and emotion, in which reason is associated with rational, market-oriented, cost-benefit analyses, while emotion is associated with the home, women, and noncontingent love *(aghápi)*. As good women, Koralia and Nadia are obligated to appeal to emotion in their justificatory narratives and to succumb to male initiative in the heat of the moment of heterosexual contact. And, as Verena Hillmann and Therese Vögeli Sörensen similarly note about modern Swiss women's ambivalent approaches to motherhood, "A rationally justified decision is demanded, although many factors for women cannot be determined rationally" (1997, 180). Precisely because modern rationality is defined apart from emotion, morality, and tradition, when the most modern of subjects either resist or fail the particular demands of rational calculation (here owing in part to hegemonic gender directives concerning heterosexual relations), they are able to call on emotion and morality in their defense. Louisa Schein writes, "People not only position themselves vis-à-vis modernity through multifarious practices but also struggle to *reposition* themselves, sometimes through deploying the very codes of the modern that have framed them as its others" (1999, 363–64). Thus, the narratives women tell to others (and probably themselves) "outside" the moment to explain what is increasingly viewed as laxness in prophylactic practice draw on the distinction between rational calculation and emotional impulse that the very idea of rationality depends on. "Sex is crazy," Nadia said to me, "and within this madness you can think of nothing. . . . At that moment you can't think to [use a condom], and in the sight of the person you're going with . . . you don't know how you will act at that moment." *Ti na kánis?* What can you do? The view that sex is exempt from the demands of rationality lets women off the hook for "failing" to meet family planning directives.

Every family planner's nightmare? Perhaps. But I argue that family planning rhetoric has helped fuel the sexual paradox as professionals continue to rationalize sex, insisting that while sex *is pleasurable* (and dangerous) it is *not crazy*. Despite family planning rhetoric imploring women to approach sex rationally, with emotional detachment, Greek women have been—and often continue to be—the guardians of a double standard. While the gendered ethics of appropriate behavior dictate that women demonstrate greater sexual control because they are morally weaker (in theory) and hence in greater need of physical restraint, in demonstrating such restraint they actually prove themselves morally stronger (in practice) than men, who "can't help themselves" in any event. This paradox has worked out well for men, as women are left to shoulder (behind the scenes) the burden of reproductive accountability. Far from disrupting this paradox, family planning rhetoric has unintentionally tended to reinforce women's accountability, demonstrating that "ideologies of modernization, so often thought to challenge traditional gender roles and relations and, in particular, to benefit women, have just as often reinforced the 'traditional' sexual division of labor" (Cowan 1990, 49; see also Stamiris 1986; Sutton 1986; Collier 1997). Fully aware of modern contraceptives, women I talked with voiced skepticism about family planning's efficacy by calling on aspects of their experience that have been categorically excluded from the terms of rationality. In so doing, they rightly point out the limitations of rationality as a guide to or predictor of sexual practice. While people's increasing awareness of their bodies may prompt them to reconsider actions they may not have thought about previously, self-knowledge is a misguided *symbol* of change. When people who are genuinely concerned about reproductive freedoms reify self-knowledge as a symbol of choice, not only do they overlook the material and symbolic factors that impinge on people's choices (Rothman 1984, 26; Haraway 1997, 196–97), but they also miss one of the most significant changes when it does occur: the reworking of people's moral positioning (see also Rapp 1999).

If rationality has a place in academic analyses of sexual activity and fertility control, it is because self-styled modern people discuss such issues in rational terms. This must be established ethnographically, not assumed universally. And when those of us who are modern subjects ourselves suspend deep-seated belief in rationality as the fundamental guide to human action, we can move beyond the moralistic judgment entailed in rationalizing women's use of abortion as preferential. We can better comprehend, too, the ways women and men continually negotiate emotional, moral, and social concerns in the course of their sexual and reproductive lives.

SAVE (SAFE) SEX: THE SEXUAL POLITICS OF NATIONAL IDENTITY

Institutionalized family planning operates within an international context of relative, often competing modernities. The wider political culture of a nation-state such as Greece, where gender and sexuality provide a framework for debate over national identity (Dubisch 1993, 281), further contributes to Athenians' reception of Western family planning. How does a new, self-oriented sexual responsibility for women articulate with what it means to be a properly Greek woman? And what does this entail for potential relationships with properly Greek men?

Gendered power dynamics of heterosexual relations are frequently reinforced through dominant notions of citizenship (e.g., Prokhovnik 1998). Greek national character has leaned on a sexual double-standard: where the state and its institutions are charged with defending the honor and boundaries of the nation, the state represents and is represented by men (political leaders, soldiers, husbands), while the nation is metonymic of the nation's supposedly vulnerable, symbolically "open" women (Hirschon 1978; Parliament of Greece 1993). When nationalism relies on patriarchal family metaphor, only women can ensure the reproduction of a pure, legitimate nation (Delaney 1995; Kanaaneh 1997; Paxson 1997). Greek politicians and the Greek press exhorted this patriarchal figuring of the nation-state at the end of the century as the country's declining population growth rate (blamed widely on repeat abortion and shrinking family size) was declared a problem of "national integrity" (Halkias 1998). What is more, gender stereotypes consistent with women's behind-the-scenes responsibility for birth control and men's overt sexual initiative, as Herzfeld points out, provide "an apt analogy to the Greeks' view of their general cultural and political subordination to 'Europe' *(Evropi)*" (1986, 222). While Greece struggles to conform to a more efficient and fiscally dominant Europe, Greeks also cling proudly to an antiestablishment sense of spirit *(pnévma)* not unlike feminine wile *(poniriá)* and decidedly Greek (Herzfeld 1986, 1992, 1997a). Dominant images of women's subjugation to men are reflected in orientalist self-stereotypes that recognize Greece's cultural and economic subjugation to Europe: proper women are to proper men as Greece is (improperly) to the West. Thus the Westernizing influences of family planning rhetoric—particularly in pushing for sexual equality modeled on a masculine standard—induce moral conflict for women and men, questioning not only people's gender proficiency but also their Greekness. In this context are formed distinctive responses to broader modernizing trends, including family planning's "philosophy of life."

As in the DUO condom newspaper advertisement, women and men are coached to believe that they will best be able to act appropriately—that is, prophylactically—in the heat of the moment if they adopt a modern mentality regarding sex. We have seen that traditional sex—making love—is defined by a concern for reproductive potential that also considers it taboo to talk about sex as a nonreproductive act in which sex can be enjoyable in and of itself. Schooled in biomedical models, Greek professionals call on the notion of traditional sex to explain people's reluctance to talk about contraception with their children or partners or doctors, or to consider mandating sex education in schools. Younger, "liberated" people, the "sexual revolution" generation, have rebelled at least in practice from restrictive sexual codes and adopted a more contemporary outlook on sex which, in keeping with Western media images and following the example of summer tourists, considers it fun, "crazy," a sign of liberated youthfulness, and above all, pleasurable. Finally, there is a more sanitized, medicalized family planning version, which decouples sex from reproduction in order to encourage contraceptive practice. All three takes on sex come together in an article, "Save Safe Sex," featured in the August 1995 issue of the racy men's magazine *Flash:*

> We would never tell you (like your mother) to find a good girl so you can have a family and put your mind at ease(?). We tell you, "Great, go out and screw this summer," because winter is miserable, because all the country's babes are now unwinding and you can't miss the party! (Koukiou 1995, 72)

Young people are being told: sex is not shameful, so don't be ashamed to carry a condom. Sex in this view—safe sex—can be enjoyable, but still it is not something to be engaged in freely, with abandon. As this article's title reveals, sex for pleasure will not be much fun if it leads to disease or inopportune pregnancy. Family planning rhetoric is thus similar to old-fashioned tradition in placing restrictive codes on sexual behavior and warning that irresponsible sex acts will result in personal tragedy. (The article also suggests that sex is less fun now that it is no longer illicit.)

Semantically, if *kánoun érota* (making love) refers to an almost quaint ideal of traditional relations between romantic or conjugal partners, then *seksoualikí epafí* (sexual contact) is a tarnished, contemporary form of the old ideal. But again, there is redemption after the fall: *seksoualikí epafí* has been brought out of the silenced realm of the family and into the public domain of scientific medicine. The cure for the ills of modern sex lies with the ancient prophylactic. There can still be joy in sex, in *érotas,* but only if one takes the necessary precautions: sex is *not* crazy. The responsible sex advocated by family planning organizations thus is presented as both new and liberating in that it allows room for the kinds of sex-for-pleasure supposedly valued by modern individuals. Indeed, the modern subject promoted by family planning rhetoric not only acts responsibly by consciously exercising calculated reason but also finds *pleasure* in behaving as a responsible adult.

Sexual pleasure is thus figured as a matter of mental attitude toward not the beloved but the body. The narcissism of this subject is made explicit in Doxiadi-Trip's magazine column: "The meaning of love" *[érota]* must include a "profound respect for the body—our own and others" (1993, 321). As an FPAG pamphlet expresses it: "AIDS is combated if each one *individually* takes measures! Looking out for myself means looking out for the one I love!"[52] Under the ethic of well-being, a properly moral attitude toward sex approaches it rationally, each instance of sex being morally equivalent to any other. Divorced from reproduction, safe sex is morally divorced too from the specificity of particular relationships. Family planning advocacy tries to accommodate a sense that love *(aghápi)* often motivates sexual behavior without confronting the paradox that "looking out for the one I love" turns out to mean "looking out for *myself.*" The family planning philosophy of life thus depends on a new object of sex—personal health and well-being—that is encouraged by a new object of erotic love: one's self. Passionate love, being swept away by pure emotion and physical urge, is immaterial to the pleasure of rationalized sex.

What? Take passionate love out of the *ideal* picture of sexual relations? Recall what Phoebe and Eva explained above: according to the Greek *noötropía* (collective mentality), sexual passion *(érotas)* is defined as a matter of physical attraction and recognized as a natural impulse, but it is frequently *valued* (perhaps especially by women) because it may become a path to *aghápi,* the enduring love of the heart exemplified by maternal love. Physical attraction and sexual relations come before, and potentially lead to, love, a point that Athenians explained to me as a contrast to the more puritanical American or British way of doing things. Family planning and safe sex rhetoric, cast in this foreign mold, asks Greeks to bring *aghápi* to their *érotas,* so to speak. It is not surprising to find a backlash, a proliferation of romantic visions. In Greece, this backlash is unleashed in the context of a cultural imperialism where the safe sex campaign is viewed as a threat to sanitize a wild, unruly—even Eastern—sexuality that many Greeks claim as a traditional aspect of national character. *Flash* magazine's "Save Safe Sex" article appealed to

> the person who wants to live and not to survive. Who isn't closed up in his room, traumatized by hysteria, paroxysms and forbiddings, who has no taste for either "abstinence and temperance" or self-service. Greek folk wisdom said it years ago: "Masturbation *[malakía]* is fine, but with sex you know the world." *Save sex!* And do it *safe!* (Koukiou 1995, 72, emphasis designates English, in the Roman alphabet, in original)

At the same time that Athenians signal their identity as modern individuals by using emotion as an excuse for not acting rationally, they can claim this "irrational" behavior as distinctively and importantly Greek. The *Flash* magazine article portrays Greeks as customarily incurable romantics and insatiable lovers. But as the tourist T-shirts remind us, this idealized tradition has revolved around gender asymmetry in sexual relations: "Greek men are the world's greatest lovers."

In the early 1990s, the virile component of a Greek national character may have been most potently portrayed by the country's late septuagenarian prime minister, whom the male-stream press could not help but admire for his bold move to court and marry a "tall—taller than 80% of the men in [his] PASOK party—blonde and sexy" woman, a contemporary of his children (Bonio 1996). Far from being raked over the coals of media morality for leaving his (American) wife of several decades, the mother of his children, for a younger (Greek) woman and Olympic flight attendant at that, Andreas Papandreou was credited with rekindling the national flame of *érotas* "in the years of a spiritually crippled Greece." An article in another men's magazine waxes poetic in stating:

> Oh men of Athens, anatomists of History. Come let us avenge the prime-ministerial member for the adolescent pursuits of dawning *érota*. . . . It's true. Andreas Papandreou, this fearsome generator of *aghápi* and myths, did it for you. He, whilst having a rendezvous with death, collided with *érota*. He dressed his feathers and set off on a solo journey, an odyssey to the depths of the soul. . . . *Érotas* swept like a conflagration over the hypocritical "don't" and "must" of constipated neohellenic society. He came like a spring rain to sweep away the dust of aged ideas. (Bonio 1996, 59)

Papandreou's much-publicized exploits were seen to breathe new life into the "Greek spirit," which had been flattened, presumably, by institutionalizing forces whose parameters for sanctioned behavior today include safe sex mandates. (He was reelected following the biggest financial scandal in recent Greek political history.) If Papandreou could let loose and find happiness at his age and in his position, hope was not lost for the Greek masculine-national ideal, according to which Greeks are mortal (male) adventurers in a land of female sirens. This article belies a mixed view of the West: in a magazine modeled after Western prototypes lurks implied "condescension toward the effeteness of the West" (Herzfeld 1986, 222). Just as women's supposed sexual weakness (their need for control) ultimately reveals their strength (their exercise of control), Greek (male) lack of sexual control ultimately testifies to the nation's virility. This contradiction (or better, inequality) is not particular to Greece but appears in the nationalist rhetoric of many modern nation-states. David Horn, for example, writes of early-twentieth-century Italian fascism that "the virility of the social body, like that of the individual male, was seen to depend crucially on women" (1994, 65). Rational safe sex mandates threaten symbolically to stanch the sexualized flow of Greek spirit through which the nation's perpetuity is guaranteed.

What is perhaps most striking about this sexual idealism in the Greek case is that it revolves around *men's* romantic, emotional inclinations. A decade or two ago, men's magazines were more apt to celebrate the "calculated, unemotional skillfulness" that a certain subculture of men (*kamákia*—literally, harpooners) applied to "the hunt" of foreign women for recreational sex (Zinovieff 1991). When the promise of sex (along with sea, sand, and sun) is seen to draw tourists to Greece from wealthy nations (Zinovieff 1991), the irresistible, charming, and sexually prolific Greek (male) carries national value as a marketable commodity. The practice and social status of *kamákia* has declined since fear of HIV-infection has induced more men to use condoms in casual sex, or abstain from its practice, or settle down with nice girls. In the wake of rational safe sex campaigns, and inspired by Andreas Papandreou's amorous adventures, in the early 1990s the Greek media added a romantic, marital "happily every after" (itself a televised Western vision) to the lure of Greek male heterosexuality. The virile and fertile Greek lover is, after all, not only a marketable tourist commodity but a national resource as a sexual service worker in the production of new Greeks—if, that is, he stays home and marries the Greek girl. While the stereotype of virile masculinity may help ease government anxiety over a declining birthrate, Greek men (including politicians) can still hold Greek women accountable for this decline.

What all this means for (heterosexual) Greek women is that now more than ever they feel pressure to be alluring to men, make themselves sexually available to men, and flatter men's sexual egos by letting men sweep them off their feet. Greek men in Athens and tourist areas around the country complained to me repeatedly that local women were not nearly so exciting or accommodating as foreign women (see also Zinovieff 1991). The highly visible marketing to urban women of new image-enhancing commodities such as nonfat yogurt and aerobics classes compounds the dilemma of feminine gender proficiency. In the early 1990s, when she was in her late thirties, my friend Moira divorced a television producer to live with her many cats and teach in a private school. Discussing her marriage over dinner one night, Moira advised me, "A woman must be interested in what the man is interested in." As soon as Moira began expressing interest in her own projects and goals, rather than devoting her time to cheering on her husband's career as she had been, the marriage fell apart. How are women to reconcile pressure to play the supporting conjugal role with articles and advertisements exhorting them to take control of their sexual and reproductive lives? Debate ensues: how are modern Greeks supposed to talk about sex and go about romantic relations?

This play of mixed messages draws national concern amid anxiety over the population size. While Greeks are berated for having far fewer children (producing a far smaller army) than Turks do, Greek politicians praise their constituency for being modern enough to validate Greece's membership in the European Union, the privilege of which Greece officially finds Turkey undeserving. But at the same time, Greeks frequently view proudly their sexual proclivities as being more Eastern or Mediterranean (mesoghiakés), more in line with the Turks, who are similarly "hot blooded" and "passionate" as opposed to, say, the "cold" Brits, who, in being stereotyped as overly rational and unemotional, are depicted as emasculated, effete. Gendered, sexualized imagery figures widely in national stereotyping since "like gender—nationality is a relational term whose identity derives from its inherence in a system of differences. In the same way that 'man' and 'woman' define themselves reciprocally (though never symmetrically), national identity is determined not on the basis of its own intrinsic properties but as a function of what it (presumably) is not" (Parker et. al 1992, 5). Nationalism colludes with patriarchy in demanding that family planning, responsibly employed by modern citizens, rationalize not only sex and families but also population growth.

Athenians' commentary on having sex, making children, and practicing fertility control echoes what David Sutton has written regarding residents of the Greek island Kalymnos, that they are attempting "to navigate the Scylla and Charybdis of either a loss of identity that they fear modernity brings, or of veering too close to 'tradition' and being 'left behind' " (1994, 240). This illuminates the Athenian query: Are Greeks or is Greek society mature enough to flourish in the contemporary modern world? In pushing a rational, calculating, and Western model of proper sexuality, family planning programs have alienated many Athenians, men and women alike, who have responded by reclaiming a virile masculinity (defined against a submissive yet controlled femininity) immortalized in Greek national character. The model citizen may be portrayed as a (male) soldier of love who knowingly returns to a waiting wife willing to succumb to his needs and manage any "surprises" thereby created. When gender remains crucial to the construction of the Greek nation-state and is symbolically enacted by male-dominant heterosexual relations, it becomes easier to understand why Greek women can eagerly consume a biomedical model of pregnancy (Georges 1996b; Mitchell and Georges 1997) and birth (Arnold 1985;

Lefkarites 1992) while remaining wary of medicalized, female contraceptive practices. In this view, we can also see how those among the Greek medical establishment who advocate family planning construct their own orientalizing stereotypes of Greek women to explain an irrational "preference" for abortion. Herzfeld elucidates this Greek dilemma: "As self-styled Westerners discursively seek to distance themselves from the 'atavistic' Balkan and Muslim worlds, usually by decrying a supposed lack of rationality in those populations, they find themselves imitating precisely the same paradoxical strategy of simultaneously exoticizing their own past and pointing to it as the source of their national character" (1997a, 110). In rationalizing sex, family planning advocacy threatens the natural flow of that masculine sexual energy (responsibly channeled by women's post hoc birth control) that helps distinguish and reproduce Greeks as a unique and special people.

I argue in this chapter that Athenians approach fertility control in the context of a cultural modernity where the categories "traditional" and "modern" are fluid, shifting, and mutually dependent. In vainly attempting to get women to choose modern, Western contraceptive attitudes over traditional ones, family planners exacerbate what Sutton identifies as "the most significant moral issue" facing Greeks today—the question of where people stand on the shifting terrain of "East" and "West," "Greek" and "European" (1994, 240). Far from ensuring modern women's liberation, family planning rhetoric, in overstating the power afforded by scientific knowledge of procreative processes, has furthered women's lived contradictions as Greek women. In the following chapter, I consider how particular rationalizations of sex, and the reproductive statistics generated by social scientists, have been called on to foment nationalist sentiment and to hold women responsible for the well-being of the nation-state.

4 Maternal Citizens

*Demographics, Pronatalism,
and Population Policy*

The family, being the cornerstone of the preservation and the
advancement of the Nation, as well as marriage, motherhood and
childhood, shall be under the protection of the State.

> Article 21, Constitution of the Republic of Greece, "In the name of the
> Holy and Consubstantial and Indivisible Trinity"

During my time in Athens, I heard all sorts of people exclaim over the immediate certainty that "Greece is getting smaller." An elderly lady once
lectured me sternly about "people these days not having children anymore" as she clutched my arm for support while darting through stalled
traffic on Vasilissis Sofias Avenue. A surprising number of Athenians can
quote the country's fertility index: 1.4 children per woman of reproductive
age while I was in Greece (dropping to 1.28 by 1999; see Council of Europe
2001). Everyone has a theory. As noted earlier, popular explanation pins
blame on the pollution-filled haze that hangs over the nation's capital,
which, as a kind of symbol of the toxic side of modernity, is held responsible for declining sperm counts. In a radio commercial broadcast during
record-breaking heat in the summer of 1999, one that played to the common perception that people are having sex less frequently these days, an
air-conditioner manufacturer promoted its product as a solution to the
country's "problem of underfertility" (Athanasiou 1999). What is more,
nearly everyone I spoke with about it described *ipoyenitikótita* (underfertility) as a threat to the nation or to the Greek "race." Nadia said to me
darkly, "There will not be a next generation. . . . And history will end."
Soula commented, "A people will disappear if this rate continues." Although many laugh self-consciously even as they deliver the party line,
Greece's demographic weakness, abbreviated simply as *to dhimoghrafikó*
(the demographic), is a popular topic of conversation and concern.

Capturing Greeks' historical perception of themselves as political under-dogs (Diamandouros 1993), the demographic problem has become a politi-cal hot potato tossed between the major parties, metonymic of nationalist concerns. Greece's birthrate, measured as the ratio of live births per deaths in a given year, has fallen since World War II, from 12.5 (in 1954) down to .87 (in 1990), well below replacement level. In 1998, deaths for the first time outnumbered births in Greece, producing a birthrate of −.2 (see appendix 3). Declining birthrates have combined with consistent Greek emigration throughout the last century to produce one of the weakest population growth rates in Europe. In the early 1990s, demographers predicted a total population decline by the year 2015 (Parliament of Greece 1993, 11; Emke-Poulopoulou 1994). These statistics are not only consistent with the repro-ductive narratives of Athenian women but also may seem unsurprising from the perspective of demographic transition theory, according to which low fertility has helped establish modern economies, signal national wealth, and demonstrate civic maturity. Demographic transition theory, however, obscures variation in how symbolic and practical consequences of fertility decline might be read across European, let alone other, contexts. While Greece's fertility decline might be viewed positively as final evidence of its modernization or true "Europeanization," within Greece it is widely de-picted as a terrible problem, a threat to the nation (Emke-Poulopoulou 1994; Paxson 1997; Halkias 1998). Because Greeks most frequently measure their demographic situation against that of "Eastern" (and ambiguously modern) Turkey, rather than definitively modern "Western" European countries, Greece's demographic transition to plummeting birthrates signals a rever-sal of the proliferative traditional patriarchal imperatives of Hellenism that have been essential to maintaining Greece's break with its Eastern past.

My purpose is not to argue whether the demographic situation actually constitutes a problem for Greece. Nor is it to calculate the average number of children that women birth and determine why, which is primarily what most published studies attempt (e.g., Symeonidou 1990; Parliament of Greece 1993; Emke-Poulopoulou 1994). Following Foucault, I am most in-terested in learning how the demographic problem is talked about, who does the speaking, what audiences are reached, and what understandings are pro-duced (see Foucault 1990a, 11–12; see also Halkias 1998; Athanasiou 1999). In 1991, the PASOK government convened a special nonpartisan parlia-mentary commission to study the country's demographic situation and to recommend relevant policy measures. Issued in 1993, the commission's re-port *(Praktiká Voulís)* explicitly compares Greece's depressed population growth rates with the flourishing ones of Albania and Turkey (it reports that Albanian women have twice as many children on average as Greek women; Turkish women three times) and proclaims, "In our country, in which today the fertility rate is among the lowest in Europe, the demographic problem reaches terrific national proportions that can threaten our national independence and territorial integrity" (Parliament of Greece 1993, 1). My fieldwork coincided with the issuing of this report, and I heard demographers, family planners, physicians, and feminist activists explicitly respond to it at medical conferences, a symposium sponsored by the Family Planning Association of Greece (FPAG) to address the demographic issue, and meetings of the Greek chapter of the European Forum of Left Feminists. Only at gatherings of the latter, throughout the winter of 1994, did I hear direct refutation of the claim that *to dhimoghrafikó* constituted a problem. As forum members made clear, culturally and historically specific notions of nationalism, ethnicity, gender, and sexuality come together in the creation of Greece's demographic problem.

I examine the discourses that have surrounded the demographic problem over the past couple of decades—including debates over legal abortion, family planning, and sex education—for what they reveal about relationships seen to obtain in Athens between the nation, the state, and its citizens, as well as ideas about gender, family, and sex. Significantly, the "demographic problem" and the "problem of abortion" are frequently mentioned in the same lecture or the same publication. "Modern states and their citizens alike claim rights to the regulation of diverse reproductive concerns such as contraception, abortion, and adoption," writes Gail Kligman; "hence, reproduction serves as an ideal locus through which to illuminate the complexity of formal and informal relations between states and their citizens" (1998, 3; see also Gal and Kligman 2000). Attending to such relationships in Greece illuminates the following paradox: despite the vehemence of nationalist pronatalist rhetoric, which I trace to the late 1960s, the government, as previously noted, decided in 1980 to establish family planning clinics in state hospitals, and in 1986, it legalized abortion on demand.

I make sense of the apparent contradiction between a pronatalist government agenda and liberal reproductive rights legislation by arguing that the Greek government has forwarded liberal family planning legislation as pronatal population policy. Here Greek policy is in keeping with what Jacques Donzelot (1979) has argued of the historical position of families within modern industrial states: the government expresses an interest in domestic and family life first through institutional measures and then by inculcating in people a sense of responsibility for bringing about the state's ends. Swayed by the rationalizing promise of family planning ideology, policy makers have assumed that good Greek citizens can and should exercise rational choice in such a way as to reproduce Greece as a distinct cultural and political entity by choosing to have larger families. In so doing, Greek politicians displace demographic responsibility not only onto individuals, but onto individual *women*. The parliamentary commission report, observing that at least half of all pregnancies in Greece end in abortion, goes on to attribute 40 percent of the nation's declining population growth rate to women having repeat abortions (Parliament of Greece 1993, 19; see also Comninos 1988, 211). By first giving women the right to free and safe abortions, and then by singling out abortion as the nation's number one demographic foe, the government's reproductive policies and rhetoric reflect a confluence of national interests and paternity rights that essentially frames the condition of the nation's population as the nation's "woman problem." The Greek chapter of the European Forum of Left Feminists succinctly titled their critique of the parliamentary report appearing in a leading Athenian newspaper: "Demographics: Women Are Again to Blame" (Evropaïkó Forum 1993, 44).

In what follows, I unpack the symbolic logic underlying the parliamentary commission report by situating it in the political history of the modern Greek nation-state, providing context for why the declining birthrate is regarded as such a serious problem. I explore a strategic shift in Greek nationalist projects, from territorial expansion to biological reproduction; drawing on ethnographic materials providing local critiques, I examine the gendered and racialized imaginaries animating these strategies. I next recount the history of the legalization of abortion in Greece, from grassroots protests to the corridors of Parliament (punctuated by a brief account of the pro-life movement in Greece).[1] This sets the stage for understanding *how* family planning legislation can be configured as pronatal policy. Finally, I consider why the state, despite its vehement rhetoric, has failed to implement a family policy that successfully stimulates the fertility rate.

DEMOGRAPHIC HISTORIES AND THE WELL-BEING OF THE NATION-STATE

When the Hellenic Republic was founded in 1830, fewer than one-third of Greeks in the Ottoman Empire were living within the territory originally allotted to the new nation-state (Pollis 1992). To solidify a unifying Greek national culture following emancipation from four hundred years of Ottoman rule, early state leaders "looked to the past as a model for creating their self-image" (Augustinos 1977, 3). Athens, a dusty village at the time of independence, was selected in 1834 to be the capital of the fledgling nation-state because it boasted the stately Acropolis (Clogg 1992). Evincing Greece's glorious and democratic past, the Acropolis has provided a solid cornerstone for nation-building ever since. According to Hellenism, Greece's nationalist historical narrative, a continuous line can be drawn between ancient Hellenic traditions and contemporary national identity: modern Greeks are said to be the rightful heirs of classical Greek civilization (Herzfeld 1987).[2] What is interesting—and crucial for understanding contemporary Greek politics—is that the ideology of Hellenism was essentially imported from Europe. A Greek-speaking intelligentsia learned the ideals of Hellenism in eighteenth- and early-nineteenth-century German and British universities, and took them to the Aegean, where they instigated the Greek War of Independence from Ottoman rule (St. Clair 1972; Clogg 1992). Europe first claimed spiritual and intellectual ancestry in classical Greece, famously perpetuated by the eighteenth-century phil-hellenes (hellenophiles) who traveled about the Greek countryside composing odes to Grecian urns and the piles of marble rubble they found amid cultivated olive groves (St. Clair 1972). In transforming rubble into historic relics demanding respect, the philhellenes reinstated classical monuments and, some would argue, "saved" that past and the legacy of classical Greek civilization (see Herzfeld 1982, 1987, esp. 20–21). The West's image of contemporary Greeks continues to be filtered through the rose-colored glasses of cultural nostalgia. A feature article in a 1993 issue of *The Economist* announces: "Their Parthenon-building ancestors began that culture, and their Byzantine ancestors kept it alive when the rest of Europe had fallen into the dark ages. If the West eventually gave the world Enlightenment, it was Greeks who had provided much of the light" (22 May, p. 3).

Imported along with Hellenism to forge a Greek nation-state was, of course, the very idea of a nation-state, that modern construct based on the Rousseauian notion that a "nation" of people suitable for legislation as a state is one "which is already united by some bond of interest, origin, or convention" (Rousseau [1762] 1967, 53).[3] When the very existence of the modern Greek nation-state has been justified at home and throughout the West, then as now, as a natural extension of an age-old Hellenic tradition (Herzfeld 1982, 1991; Jusdanis 1991; Clogg 1992, 1996), the defining features of Greekness are presumed to be passed down from each successive generation to the next in a legacy of custom, language, and—reflecting the enfranchisement of Byzantium within this Hellenic tradition—Orthodox Christianity. Modern Greek nationalism is heralded as a cultural and historical renaissance, even as a sacred rebirth. Jill Dubisch notes that 25 March is celebrated "as a day of double import, for it is both Greek Independence Day and the day of the angel Gabriel's announcement to Mary that she would bear the son of God. In other words, two rebirths—of humankind and of the Greeks—are combined" (1995, 164). National and ethnic identity have become conflated in the ideology of Hellenism, a phenomenon facilitated by the fact that, in Greek, both meanings are contained in a single word: the adjective *ethnikós* refers to both "national" (citizenship) and "ethnic" (language, custom, religion) criteria.

The apparent homogeneity (from the Greek *omoyénia*, "same birth or descent") of cultural, linguistic, and religious markers of ethnic Greekness is by no means a natural phenomenon, let alone an ancient one. Early Greek nation-builders entered into the collective "forgetting" and reinvention of tradition that brokered the emergence of modern nation-states throughout Europe (Renan [1882] 1990, 11). Historically, many of modern Greece's most important cultural figures—important both in codifying a national character at home and in exporting positive images of Hellenism elsewhere—have been *omoyenís* (of the same origin or birth), persons who identify as Greek—who are Greek—but who live outside the borders of the state as citizens or residents of other states. The historian Gerasimos Augustinos writes, if "Hellenism for the Greeks has been the imperative to maintain their country's territorial integrity and cultural uniqueness . . . that uniqueness in cultural matters, paradoxically, has been best served by remaining open to varied influences from abroad" (1995, 204). This is paradoxical because the rules of modern nation-statehood dictate that members of a nation ideally should live within that nation's state's territorial borders. Indeed, the purpose of the modern state and its institutions "is to guarantee the survival of [a] people as a unique entity" (Augustinos 1995, 170)—that is, to protect a nation. Considerable demographic movement throughout Greece's modern history has meant that national and ethnic criteria have never overlapped as cleanly and continuously as ideology would suggest. The modern assumption that a nation should map onto the boundaries of a state—be coterminous with its citizenry—is rarely realized (Anthias and Yuval-Davis 1992, 21). What is interesting in the Greek case is how national ideology has tried to erase diasporic loss, even as it perpetuates a vision of national strength that depends on what is simultaneously erased (Greece's poet laureate George Serefis spent most of his life in London; two of Greece's four gold medal winners in the 1996 centennial modern Olympic Games in Atlanta were born outside state territory).

In an effort to obtain a better fit between the nation, that constellation of cultural characteristics, and the citizenry circumscribed by the state, early domestic policy of the modern state worked to diminish reliance on outside examples of Greek character by exercising what amounted to a cultural purge within the country of many elements having origins external to the Hellenic ideal (i.e., were reminiscent of Ottoman occupation). A concentrated, centralized effort to expunge at least the written language of borrowed Turkish words hampered the country's educational system for generations, until the 1970s, when the spoken demotic Greek was instated as the official language (Herzfeld 1987). Being Greek has meant embracing those elements that highlight cultural uniqueness: speaking the Greek language and adhering to the Greek Orthodox faith. And when being Greek has meant doing as a Greek, great emphasis is placed on cultural training. According to the Constitution of 1952, education should propel the "development of the national consciousness of the youth on the basis of the ideological directions of Hellenochristian civilization" (quoted in Augustinos 1995, 190). Toward this end, the nation's school system is overseen by the Ministry of Education *and* Religion. People who are not Orthodox Christians are forbidden to teach in primary and secondary schools for fear that "she or he would subvert Orthodox spiritual values," which have been consistent with Greek nationalism (Pollis 1992, 182). Until 1983, children could enter the public school system only if their parents produced for them a certificate of baptism (registering their legal names).

Citizenship laws provide a further example of the link between Greek culture and *éthnos;* persons who wish join the Greek state by law as opposed to birth must undergo a process of being "written as a citizen" *(politoghráfisi)*—not, as in the United States or United Kingdom, a process of "naturalization." Of course, in a sense citizenship or national belonging is still naturalized, made to seem inherent and eternal (Yanagisako and Delaney 1995). In the Greek case, however, it is not so much one's physical birth that is simulated and appropriated by state institutions but one's moral and cultural training. The "transubstantiation of . . . heredity into heritage," Herzfeld writes, is conveyed through popular reference to early intellectual leaders of Greek independence (whose American counterparts are remembered as "forefathers") as " 'Teachers of the *Genos*'—the mind directing the blood" (1992, 42).

Blood metaphors of Greek kinship and national identity can be traced to the word *yénos,* which originally referred to agnatic groups, usually of the aristocracy, from which contemporary Greek notions of "stock," "race," and "a national people" have developed (Herzfeld 1992, 41–42; 1997a, 40–41).

Anthropologists have pointed out that, within monotheistic traditions, membership in a kindred, race, and nation is in each instance secured by metaphors of "sharing" blood seen to trace common descent (Schneider 1969; Just 1989; Anthias and Yuval-Davis 1992; Yanagisako and Delaney 1995; Herzfeld 1992, 1997, 41; Kanaaneh 1997; Linke 1999). Because kinship bonds, bonds of blood, are seen to be natural, biologically given, they appear unbreakable, permanent, even sacred. Under the legal ideology of Greek family law, "kinship by blood" *(syngénia eks ématos)*, unlike "kinship by affinity" *(syngénia eks aghistías)*, "can never cease to exist" (Koumantou 1985). In 1882, Ernest Renan noted that the common interests of civil society are insufficient to make a nation: "Nationality has a sentimental side to it; it is both soul and body at once" ([1882] 1990, 18). "Blood" provides the biological counterpart to the transcendent, never-ending and morally charged Greek "spirit" that "civilizes" its citizens as Greek (Just 1989; Herzfeld 1992, 22–32). But more, this blood of national cohesiveness, the blood of the *patrídha*, is agnatic blood; continuity in Greek national culture is reckoned through the male line. We can see traces of patriline in the very word *dhiasporá*, meaning "the scattering of seed"; the diaspora extends the masculine, culturally enlightened "spirit" of the *éthnos* through the scattered "seed" *(sporá*, whence "sperm") of its "sons."

Beyond referring us to a kinship system traced through men, the word *diaspora* "suggests the questions of *legitimacy* in paternity that patriarchy generates" (Helmreich 1992, 245, emphasis added). While the symbolic meaning of blood makes a romanticized petition to some natural and precious bond, blood is at the same time precarious. It is "easily spilled, subject to drying up, too readily mixed" (Foucault 1990a, 147). Author Irini Dorkofiki bemoans the territorial "areas which hemorrhaged from the blood-letting of the population" as more and more families abandoned village homesteads for life in the big cities (1985, 134–35). Similarly in 2000, an Athenian newspaper editorial warned, "The most crucial aspect of the country's demographic problem is the fact that the population bleeding is more intense in Thrace, the northern Aegean and Epirus—the regions, in other words, that comprise the nation's frontier and suffer the greatest impact of the upheaval in the Balkan peninsula."[4] Under an early modern politics of sanguinity, as Foucault describes it, the blood that stands for the life force of a nation requires careful definition and protection by state institutions (1990a, 147–50).

If early Greek domestic policy worked to produce and protect the nation's cultural uniqueness, the foreign policy of the fledgling state was driven by the Meghàli Idhéa (Great Idea), a plan to take back from Ottoman Turks the city of Constantinople (Istanbul) and coastal territory in

Asia Minor stretching to Smyrna (present-day Izmir). In a sense, the Great Idea was to resurrect the Byzantine empire in the form of an independent Greek state (Augustinos 1977). The Meghàli Idhéa flickered out on the shores of Asia Minor when the 1919–1922 Greek-Turkey War, remembered by Greeks as the Asia Minor Catastrophe, ended as Mustafa Kemal (later Ataturk) sacked the predominantly Greek city of Smyrna. If historically the ancient Greek diaspora represented territorial expansion and cultural dispersion, for much of the twentieth century the wider-flung diaspora has represented the residue of demographic change, military failure, and economic weakness.

Indeed, according to Augustinos, "The most significant factor affecting Greek nationalism in the twentieth century has been the demographic transformations and attendant social changes that the country has experienced" (1995, 171). Large-scale urbanization, emigration, and foreign immigration throughout the past century challenge the rural foundation of traits such as language, patriarchal custom, and Orthodox cosmology that come together in a "national character" to name ideal inhabitants of the nation-state. The redrawing of national boundaries following the 1912–1913 Balkans War marked the beginning of this century's demographic upheaval, as Greece gained land equal to 70 percent of the state territory held to that point, and the state's population nearly doubled, from 2.8 to 4.8 million (Clogg 1992, 83). These new citizens constituted a mixed population of Greek, Bulgarian, Serbian, Albanian, Turk, and Vlach peoples. Soon, however, an "exchange of populations" mandated by the Allied Powers in the wake of the Greek-Turkey War (1921–1922) saw 1.25 million Greek Orthodox people from Asia Minor migrate to Greece, and nearly as many Muslim Turkish speakers uprooted from Greece and relocated in Asia Minor (Hirschon 1989; Clogg 1992). After Nazi Germans invaded in 1941, one hundred thousand Greeks (7 percent of the 1940 population) perished of starvation alone. In 1943, Thessaloniki's prosperous Sephardic Jewish community—some fifty thousand persons constituting one-fifth of that city's population—was deported to Auschwitz (Clogg 1992). The famine, warfare, emigration, and urban migration that began during Axis occupation carried over into the consequent civil war (1946–1949). Shortly thereafter, the junta period (1967–1974) brought a second wave of out-migration; from 1951 to 1970, at least 25 percent of the national workforce emigrated (McNeill 1978, 117). The 1970s saw the subsequent return of many Greeks who brought with them continental and North American sensibilities.

Demographic calculations are purported to be about power in numbers (Hacking 1982), enumerations of citizens representing bodies paradigmatically generated through women's birthing them and men's conquering them. The parliamentary commission report declares that "the people [*o laós]* is the most valuable asset of the state, propelling production, economic and social progress, and guaranteeing its existence and security" (Parliament of Greece 1993, 30). Persons, as members of a populace, become politically significant in that they constitute the labor force, elect politicians, reproduce new citizens, and embody national character. Because the Greek army is composed of men fulfilling their mandatory two years' military service, the size of the Greek army directly depends on the number of young male Greek citizens in residence. Diasporic Greeks are viewed under the demographic gaze as errant children, perhaps lost sons, of the *patrídha.* Demographic change challenges not only a country's purported demographic strength (size of army, labor force, etc.) but also the supposed cultural homogeneity of the nation, which the state must try to protect. Greekness is not confined by state boundaries, and thus it has the potential to pull attention and loyalty away from the nation-state, which is fixed by borders that are apparently still under negotiation (Cyprus) and that remain vulnerable to foreign interests (Greek Macedonia and some eastern Aegean islands). Concentrated attention on Greek emigration and declining fertility actually obscures the most significant site of demographic movement during the last decade of the twentieth century: the immigration of hundreds of thousands of political and economic refugees, Greek and non-Greek peoples, women as well as men, from Albania, regions of the former Yugoslavia and the Soviet Republic, East Africa, and the Philippines, many of them seeking eventual relocation to Canada or the United States (Vidali 1999).

In a rather successful effort to deflect attention from all this demographic movement happening on the ground, nationalist rhetoric—fueling such state mechanisms as education and the Greek Orthodox Church—appealed to the transcendent nature of a Greek spirit, to an *éthnos* seen as a set of cultural ideals believed to inhere in the person of a Greek. In a 1966 tract, Andreas Papandreou proclaimed, "There exists something called a Greek character and Greek ideals and which expresses our common origin in the Greek earth. Also, there exists a way of being and thinking which is clearly Greek."[5] When Greeks feel themselves under attack by Muslim enemies or European benefactors, Alexander the Great's triumphs can be dusted off and paraded as evidence that Greeks are to be taken seriously; out, too, come reminders that Greeks were the inventors of democracy. *The Economist* observes, "When Greece can present itself as a lonely outpost of western ideas, defying the barbarians; then the West rallies round" (22 May 1993, p. 3). But because these moments have been few and far between (witness the extended and yet unresolved struggle for Cypriot union), Greece's ambiguous global positioning and relative cultural and geographic isolation breed external indifference and internal insecurity—a situation ripe for defensive hypernationalism. This has been most clearly expressed in recent years through rhetorical claims to "Macedonia" as both name and historical legacy. Such claims resounded throughout Greece at the end of the twentieth century, following international recognition of the independent Balkan state, which Greeks persist in calling FYROM, the Former Yugoslavian Republic of Macedonia. Tourism posters, government postage stamps, the cover of the Athenian yellow pages, envelopes for my electric bill, even bags of state-manufactured cement proclaimed in the 1990s that "Makedonia is Greek" or "Makedonia has been Hellenic for 3,000 years." When Greek politicians talk about Greece (Hellas) as a transcendent ideal, they avoid having to address the ambivalently welcomed "return" of Pontic Greeks from the Black Sea region or the grudging reception of Sudanese and Filipina domestic workers—not to mention the frequent hostility vented at Albanian refugees (Seremetakis 1996). The *éthnos* viewed as an everlasting spirit *(pnévma)* transcends the particular messiness of history (and of the gendered foundations to which national identity is secured). Guided by an ageless national ideology, Greece's telescopic view of history has proven convenient for generations of policy makers.

Consequently, when Greeks today (and not only politicians) talk about populations and nation-states, their temporal horizons are great indeed. It is written in the 1993 parliamentary commission report on the demographic situation, "The demographic aging of classical Greece and of Byzantium, according to reputable witnesses, drove Hellenism into subjugation for centuries and virtually to complete extermination" (Parliament of Greece 1993, 30). In this dramatic statement rings a warning to contemporary Greeks that they are responsible to and for the distant past as well as the future.

The contemporary demographic problem is so pervasively framed as a threat to a millennia-old Greek nation that it surfaced in a medical lecture on contraceptive technology given as part of the panel discussion "Women and AIDS," presented at an Athens conference I attended on AIDS and sexually transmitted diseases.[6] At this meeting of doctors, medical researchers, and health care workers, a leading physician and researcher in adolescent gynecology prefaced his presentation on recent advances in contraceptive technology by comparing the population size of Greece as it has progressed throughout the twentieth century to the "Greek" population under Alexander the Great (who arguably may have thought of himself as Macedonian). He projected a slide comparing population figures for the modern state relative to what "the Greek population" was at the time of Alexander:

POPULATION OF GREECE SHOWN AS A PERCENTAGE OF THE GREEK
POPULATION DURING THE EPOCH OF ALEXANDER THE GREAT

1928	3 percent
1971	2 percent
2000	1.2 percent

I offer this rather striking choice of analogy, in which a modern state is juxtaposed with an ancient empire—begging questions about who gets counted in demographic calculations—to illustrate how the time frame within which contemporary Greek national and demographic interests are discussed is the monumental time of millennia. When this happens, the actual twentieth-century events that can help explain the current demographic situation get drowned out by rhetorical appeals to an age-old nation. This rhetorical move further exemplifies how the Greek nation constitutes a paradox in that it refers both to a diasporic set of persons sharing a common language and cultural heritage and to a modern state delineated by national borders whose supposedly homogeneous population is in reality not so homogeneous as official ideology would have it.

But why did this essentialist form of nationalist rhetoric show up at a prestigious medical conference? The physician's intention was to acknowledge the validity of the demographic problem and to reassure patriots that promoting condom use and other contraceptive practices will not further imperil the demographic situation by suppressing the birthrate. In fact, doctors at this conference argued that family planning programs can actually help the demographic situation by enabling couples to have the children they want.

Nation-Building: From Territorial Expansion to Biological Reproduction

What has happened in the last century is that the state, its dreams of territorial expansion put to rest, shifted strategies for securing national continuation. Greek irredentism (previously articulated as the Meghâli Idhéa and written into the Greek constitution by the name of Hellenism) is not much spoken of these days, with a stalemate as usual in Cyprus, the potential threat of a unified "Macedonia" looming throughout the 1990s, and near-battle with Turkey over a few rocky islands populated by goats at the end of the century. Following the 1920s, the field of Hellenism has moved away from the sphere of empire to the bedroom and maternity ward. During this time, too, in proper modern fashion, the government has organized and provisioned demographic, medical, and sexological institutions designed to study and rationalize the population (Donzelot 1979). Under what Foucault (1990a) has called a modern regime of "bio-power," where individuals are linked to the population through the nexus of reproductive sex, the enduring spirit of the nation, understood as hereditary substance and symbolized by blood, becomes an entity that can be monitored, quantified, and managed. In this policy shift, Greece has joined other European countries in recognizing that "the basis of a state's wealth and power" lies "not so much in the extent of its territory, but in the size and productivity of its population" (Gal and Kligman 2000, 18–19).

Greece's first census, really an enumeration, was taken by hand in 1828 as Greece was on its way to establishing sovereignty.[7] In 1860, it was constitutionally stipulated that a census be taken every ten years. Because the census is de facto—that is, it counts the people who are present on a given day—and because state aid is made locally available on the basis of population density, civic-minded citizens may scramble "home" to be counted in their natal villages. But while the census calculates the de facto population, Greek elections operate on a de jure basis, depending on where people "belong" irrespective of whether they are present during a census. Greek citizens are required (until they reach seventy years of age) to return to their place of birth, the locale where their mothers' birthed them and where they are registered with the state, to vote in national elections. Athens itself falls eerily still on election days. The de jure population is thus formed by a conflation of national territory and women's bodies, such that elections in effect reenact and reconfirm the moment of citizens' political births.

As Foucault has argued, in the biopolitical harnessing of populations by nation-states we witness the premodern "symbolics of blood" overlaid (i.e., not fully replaced) with a modern "analytics of sexuality" (1990a, 148, emphasis omitted): "At the juncture of the 'body' and the 'population,' sex became a crucial target of a power organized around the management of life rather than the menace of death" (147). Historically, at the heart of population studies, lies sex: the necessity for states to analyze fertility rates, legitimate and illegitimate births, ways of making people sterile, and the impact of contraceptive practices. Biopolitics is about directing rationalized sex and reproduction at rationalized populations. It is no coincidence that the demographic problem was first identified as such following the publication of a study of women's birth control practices, conducted in 1966 and 1967 by the (now defunct) University of Athens Center of Demographic Research (cf. Valaoras and Trichopoulos 1970). It is this survey, which found that the abortion rate had overtaken the live birthrate in urban areas, that the parliamentary commission report cites in attributing the low birthrate to women having abortions (see also Comninos 1988; Naziri 1991; Emke-Poulopoulou 1994). Recently, a professor at the University of California, Los Angeles, Michalis Giokas, himself part of the Greek diaspora, predicted disastrous social and national consequences from the falling national birthrate (which, typically, he compared to Turkey's) at the Third Scientific Congress of Greek Medical Students.[8] His policy recommendation was "that a demographic institute be established to monitor research and family planning programmes" (*Athens News*, 9 April 1997).

Citing statistics on the increasing numbers of Greek women who have "only one child," the parliamentary commission report declares, "In order to put a stop to the reduction of births and to ensure the rejuvenation of the population and the survival of Hellenism, achieving the goal of the third child must be given great importance" (Parliament of Greece 1993, 11). In the distant past, in the time, say, of Alexander, Hellenism was born or carried by the diaspora, marked as male; but contemporary Hellenism is primarily birthed by women back home.[9] In 1986, at the height of the debate over the legalization of abortion, Irini Dorkofiki published her polemical treatise, *Abortion: The Annihilation of the Race*, in which she presents abortion as an enemy of the Greek people, a mechanism of race "suicide." "Demographics are the most underhanded enemy of our race [*filí*] and the first national order, the Meghàli Idhéa of today," she writes (1985, 130). Today's Meghàli Idhéa counts on the creation of larger families. As a demographer at the National Center for Social Research said to me in an interview, "Usually when you speak demographically [in this country], you speak about demographic policy having to do with family allowances, and with the care of children and mothers, with housing for families, with incomes and taxation, all to improve and attenuate the situation of the family with many children." By reducing the demographic field at home to matters of biological reproduction and cultural regeneration, this again skirts issues of migration and movement. For Hellenism, what this means is that, by inciting general awareness of Greece's declining population growth rate—juxtaposed with the cultural stereotype that Muslim Turks "reproduce like rabbits"—politicians can rally the patriotic support of the public. In this way demographics quantify what nationalism qualifies.

Nationalism, Racism, Sexism: A Local Critique
of the Demographic Problem

In early 1994, the Greek chapter of the European Forum of Left Feminists met regularly at the home of a feminist publisher, Eleni (introduced in chapter 2), to plan a public meeting titled "Nationalism, Racism, and Gender." Their project was undertaken in response to the 1993 parliamentary commission report on the "demographic problem" (I acquired my photocopy of the report from one of the members). One January afternoon I visited Eleni for an interview, and she told me about the forum and their concerns about the tensions, violence, and suspicions that had escalated in recent years between Greeks and Balkan refugees. Forum members were critical of a Greek nationalism based on racial and cultural purity. When I expressed interest in the forum's activities, Eleni remarked casually, "They're coming over tonight. Would you like to stay?" So I drank some more coffee, ate some more of Eleni's delicious semolina halvahs, and positioned myself by the open window to watch this eclectic, nonacademic, well-read group of Athenian feminists assemble under a burgeoning cloud of cigarette smoke. To these critics, the "demographic problem" constitutes a problem *not* because women are having fewer children and young adults are continually emigrating, but rather because the nation-state is conceived through latent racism and sexism.

These women are committed to refuting the common claim that "there is no racism in Greece," a statement that depends on an erasure not only of increasingly visible instances of racism but also the very presence of ethnic and cultural diversity within Greece (Karakasidou 1997). As a reader of a draft of this book pointed out, denials of racism and intolerance of immigrants might be analogous to incest denial—both incest and immigration of non-Greeks threaten the construct of natural family solidarity to which both the ideologies of nationalism and patriarchy appeal for moral validation. Furthermore, while the rhetoric of exclusion most frequently articulates a cultural racism, the fact that nations have been figured as families, and demographic concerns have been framed through biopolitics, has permitted government officials frequently to recast the issue in terms that collapse into biological racism. When ideals of modern nation-statehood demand that Greeks—defined by a cultural tradition seen to inhere in people as if it were some national birthright—live in Greece, politicians are less interested in sheer demographic numbers than in generating the right sort of numbers. Indeed, the population of Greece increased by over

537,000 persons between 1983 and 1993 (Council of Europe 2001), and the 2001 census revealed that the national population increased by 6.6 percent since 1991—owing to net migration (NSSG 2002). An Athenian newspaper article published in 2000, warning that the "demographic time bomb is ticking while governments are fiddling," qualified a recent leveling off of the dropping birthrates as the result of "births to foreign women who came to Greece during the great influx of migrants in the 1990s. Between 1976 and 1999," the article emphasized, "the number of births [among primarily Greek women, that is] fell by 30.9 percent" (Drettakis 2000).

Meanwhile, the parliamentary commission report on the demographic problem acknowledged that the successful repatriation of "political refugees" and the mass arrival of Greeks leaving homelands in the Pontus region of the Black Sea and northern Epirus (southern Albania) could have a "positive effect" on the Greek demographic situation: "The common cultural roots and Orthodox Christianity help greatly in their adaptation to and assimilation into Greek society" (Parliament of Greece 1993, 15). In contrast, "other" immigrants, "chiefly Muslims from Afro-Asiatic countries," are said to "create serious socioeconomic problems," since "they cannot adapt to Greek society because of the completely different culture of Islam, which is not only a religion but a way of life" (15)[10]—a claim that forgets the significance of the Ottoman Empire's millet system, whereby people of many faiths were ruled through the authority of local religious leaders. Greek national culture, working to conform to the Western mold of the nation-state, continues to depend on generating differentiation from Eastern forms: "Muslims have other models, other ideas, and inculcate other, different societies of eastern populations" (32). By focusing on the reproductive aspects of demographics and national expansion, the Greek state obfuscates the xenophobia and racism that underlie migration issues.[11]

At this and other meetings of the European Forum of Left Feminists I attended, members discussed how contemporary Europe, not only Greece, echoes with new discourses on national belonging that collapse it into racial or ethnic identity (Anthias and Yuval-Davis 1992; Anthias and Lazaridis 2000). They acknowledged that racisms are plural and specific to national and social contexts, arguing that education and economic class divisions exacerbate racism against even Greek immigrants ("there is even racism against the Pontics, who are Greek!"). Pontic Greeks are poorer, from rural backgrounds, and they joined the working-class immigrant ghettos established following the "exchange of populations" in the 1920s (Hirschon 1989). Greeks who descended from merchant families in Cairo or Constantinople, on the other hand, tend to be wealthier and better educated than the average indigenous Greek and are able to fully participate in Greek society, even as they may be looked on by locals with jealous mistrust. "We have a Greek diaspora," Eleni explained to me. "That is [one reason] why we say that we don't have a demographic problem—because we have so many Greeks who come back. They are a very strong race and they give; they are very good workers and it's good for the Greek economy. If we [Greeks] say we have a demographic problem, then we are racists."

Other (non-Greek) immigrants fill an equally important role in the economy, taking up the lowest paying jobs, which Greeks disdain. Greeks favor Filipinas as domestics and nannies; as Catholic Christians, they are seen as being "less other" than Islamic Africans or Albanians (Lazaridis 2000). Several generations ago, things were different, forum members collectively recalled. Families migrated from Albania and other Slavic areas to settle in Greek villages (Seremetakis 1991; Panourgia 1995). They "became like natives" and were accepted. Not so today. Since the 1980s, most Balkan migrants, men outnumbering women, have come to Greece hoping to move on to the United States; they are not so interested in settling and sending out roots.[12] Today, people seem "more conscious" of "difference," these women observed. When I was in Athens, Greeks routinely witnessed on television thousands of Albanians—illegal, destitute immigrants—corralled in shipyard warehouses outside Athens to await being packed into military buses, driven north, and dumped off at the border. Albanians have become the unfortunate scapegoats for the ills of modern society, blamed repeatedly for crime, harassment, and the drop in wealthy tourists (Panourgia 1995; Vidali 1999). Someone at a forum meeting mentioned that these days Greeks commonly identify people as Albanian by how dirty and ill-clothed they appear to be; Seremetakis has noted that "Albanian" is often taken to be a generic label for immigrants (1996, 489). The parliamentary report baldly states, "The demographic aging of the population leads to social downgrading with the slackening and degeneration of many institutions (family-child-motherhood), and with the appearance of the socially weak there is an elevation of criminality, narcotics, and acts of arbitrary violence in general" (Parliament of Greece 1993, 32). Here, figured as "socially weak"—that is, improperly civilized as Greek—foreigners are blamed for a rise in crime, drug abuse, and violence that alternatively could have been viewed as endemic to urbanization and a weak economy.

When being Greek means doing as a Greek, the report ultimately implies, politics of inclusion and exclusion are based on cultural racism that is best avoided by reproducing one's own kind (see Stolcke 1993). In a 1993 newspaper article, the Greek chapter of the European Forum of Left Feminists directly challenged the Parliament on this point, charging that "the report's direct incitement is racist [*ratsistikí*], that we birth children in order to replace the economic migrants with a pure national labor force, when a migration policy that would include the equal recognition of foreign migrants in Greek society with the same rights and obligations would be able—according to the logic of the authors of the report—to invigorate our country demographically" (Evropaïkó Forum 1993, 44). That is to say, if immigrants were accommodated and welcomed, rather than excluded and mistrusted, they could solve many facets of Greece's "demographic problem" having to do with labor and national defense. Reluctance to accommodate them suggests that political concern is not about sheer numbers of population but about the future of "Greekness" itself.

Members of the forum base their critique on an analysis of how gender becomes a technique of racism and nationalism. Women, they noted at their meetings, are primarily figured as symbols of the nation, while men are its representatives and agents [*forís*]. This leaves women at the borders to serve as the guardians of the nation. When the category of race marks a nation's or a people's "own" women from "others," Eleni noted, racism is often used to exploit women sexually. The group discussed the systematic rape of Bosnian Muslim women by Serbian soldiers as a weapon of ethnic cleansing in the early 1990s, a clear act of defiling not only these individual women but also the nation for which they stand—and of cuckolding their symbolic husbands, Bosnian soldiers (see Allen 1996; Gal and Kligman 2000). In Greece, I learned, the word for prostitutes, *pórnes*, is often synonymous with *Póntes*, or women from the Pontus region. Someone mentioned that women from Smyrna (forced to migrate from the coast of Asia Minor in 1924) are also stereotyped as prostitutes, as illustrated in Kostas Mourselas's popular novel (serialized on television while I was in Athens) *Red Dyed Hair*. The label *Smirniári*, or "woman from Smyrna," is another slang expression for whore.

The use of a female figure to symbolize, rather than represent, nation-states has been widely noted (Anthias and Yuval-Davis 1992; Delaney 1995; Kanaaneh 1997; Nelson 1999). This is a fertile female, a mother: the French revolution's *la patrie* figured a woman giving birth to the nation. Such symbolism reinforced and helped reproduce a strictly gendered model of state citizenship, elaborated from the so-called natural rights of man based on such political philosophies as Rousseau's social contract among free and rational men. Women, legally and politically dependent on men and therefore not free to enter into the social contract on their own account, have been accorded a maternal citizenship that has come at the price of full inclusion in the so-called public sphere, or political citizenship (Rich 1986; Pateman 1988; De Grazia 1993; Kligman 1998). In Greece, where an ethic of service to the patriarchal family has been extended to service the paternalistic state, a woman's sexual and political identities have been construed as coterminous. A Greek newspaper article from 1928 identified menstruation as evidence of women's essential reproductive role that simultaneously disqualified them from direct political participation:

> Some Greek women ask for the woman's right to vote. About this issue
> a very famous scientist had discussed in Parliament the scientific fact
> accepted globally, that every female succumbs to an unbalanced and
> frantic condition some days of every month. Since these days of the
> month are not the same for all females, it is impossible to find a day of
> mental balance and psychological calmness that all females could share,
> so on that happy day to run the elections. Therefore, a woman's vote is
> a dangerous thing and as a result repulsive. (*New Day,* 3 March)

Women in Greece did not win the vote until 1952, only after demonstrating a masculine-style citizenship by fighting alongside men in resistance against the Italians, then the Germans, and then (depending on whose side they were on) the Communists or the Greek national army (Fourtouni 1986; Hart 1996). Women have won enfranchisement throughout the world, but nowhere has this supplanted expectations about maternal citizenship.

Women continue to be called on by states to serve in two senses as the symbolic "bearers" of nations (Anthias and Yuval-Davis 1989). *Qualitatively,* women's traditional service in raising children within patriarchal families has been harnessed to national interests. Women's natural capacities for mothering are expanded to encompass a "natural" capacity for reproducing the cultural traditions and values that bind together a nation and preserve a people's uniqueness. Women do this by civilizing nationally or ethnically identified children and by setting the patriotic example. *Quantitatively,* women have been responsible, and frequently commended, for birthing new citizens and workers (Kanaaneh 1997; Kligman 1998; Krengel and Greifeld 2000, 205). Pregnant women have been depicted as carrying the perpetuity of the nation in their wombs. It is through such practices as census taking that women are held responsible for demographics: national identity is born of women. What I mean is not simply that women are seen to make babies, but that the science of demographics, the tool of the state in defining its population, examines the reproductive productivity of *women,* not men. In census-taking demographics, there are two measures of natural population growth: the rate of population increase occurring through births, and that occurring through immigration or territorial expansion. While the birthrate measures the percentage by which live births exceed deaths in a given year, the fertility rate is a raw measure of the number of children *per woman* of reproductive age (fifteen to forty-nine) within the population. A quick glance at the research supported by and published out of such institutions as the University of Athens Center of Demographic Research reveals that the vast majority of state-sponsored studies of sexual behavior and reproductive outcome take as their subjects women and adolescent girls. When one looks at demographic statistics, one is looking at women: Do women practice contraception? Do women have abortions? How many children on average do women produce?[13] (The exception has been studies that focus on AIDS awareness and HIV risk.) If the nation-state as *patrídha* represents the land of the "fathers," in proper patriarchal style the *patrídha* is founded on control of the "mothers" (Pateman 1988).

When the strength of the nation-state can be measured in terms of fecundity, as it is when demographics are effectively reduced to the fertility rate, a fertile Hellas can be represented by—as it depends on—the fertile *ellinídha*, or Greek woman. In this way demographic policy can be framed as a women's issue. When women are made responsible for reproductive practices, often they are held accountable for all accidents, errors, and failures to meet rational ideals (Tsing 1990); thus the demographic condition of a nation-state can be viewed as the country's woman problem. As Daphne put this:

> For me the solution is better conditions for the women and for the people generally. There isn't the kind of problem that they show us, the government and the state and the ministries. Okay, there is a problem, Greece is a country that has more old people than young, but it's not only about women and families, whether they have children or not. It's economic, but it's also a lot of other factors, like children's death—it has nothing to do with women."

"Do women get blamed for it?" I asked provocatively. "Yes!" she nodded. "It is put on women."

The maternal symbols of nationalism have helped shape the formation of Greek population policy, revealing *how* responsibility for demographic strength has been placed on women.

Legalizing Abortion

Fewer than thirty years after Greek women's enfranchisement, Andreas Papandreou's socialist-populist PASOK party was elected in 1980 on a platform espousing the consolidation of national interests and the social equality of the sexes. In the first two of PASOK's eight years in power during that decade, Parliament overhauled the family law (see appendix 2) and added a special governmental office, the General Secretariat for Equality, to the Ministry to the Presidency to oversee institutional and occupational equity for women and men. It took a grassroots women's movement, however, to spur the government to bring before Parliament the promised legislation to legalize abortion. Public and parliamentary debates from this time reveal contests over what constitutes appropriate ethical terms in which to judge (or forgive) women who have abortions (and the doctors who perform them) in a newly modern society that had just joined the European Economic Community. On the Parliament floor, much of this debate centered on the potential consequences of legal abortion, and implicitly women's responsibility, for the demographic situation. To examine parliamentarians' arguments is to witness the reinstatement of an ethic of national service for women in a way that seeks not to undermine the politically expedient ethic of women's choice.

The motion to legalize abortion in Greece was never driven by a need for safe and readily available abortions. As Daphne said to me, "Of course you might have to pay a lot of money, but it was safe. You could have as many abortions as you like." Even when illegal, a safe abortion performed by a competently trained gynecologist was far more accessible throughout much of Greece than it is in the United States today when legal. Instead, activists were driven to define abortion as a normative medical procedure. Legalization would introduce abortion into the national health care system, thereby making it available to even the poorest and most rural women. Daphne, active in student feminist groups in the 1980s, and the feminist gynecologist Eftyhia Leontidou each narrated to me the story of how the grassroots campaign to legalize abortion coalesced as various feminist groups rallied behind the initiative of the Autonomous Women's Movement (Aftónomi Kínisi Yinekón), one of the few feminist groups not aligned with a political party. This campaign was always pitched alongside a call for public informing on contraceptive methods and their use. "The real problem for us was contraception, not abortion," Daphne told me. Abortion's illegality, these feminists rightly pointed out, never deterred physicians from offering the service but in fact flung wide open the door for doctors' profiteering. Eftyhia, a founding member of the Autonomous Women's Movement, said to me, "We thought it was a feminist issue and it was very important to raise because," for reasons previously discussed, "abortion is part of the violence exercised against women."

Feminists hoped that, beyond economic considerations, legalization would mitigate the stigma that abortion could impress on a woman's psyche and character. If abortion were sanctioned as a standard medical procedure, they reasoned, perhaps women would feel more able to talk about their experience, helping to dispel any lingering sense of shame. In effect, the feminist movement wanted what the FPAG did: to extract abortion from an ethic of service, where it often compromised not only women's integrity but also their bodily health, and reinstate it within an ethic of choice. Under either ethical model, they declared, women who resort to abortion are certainly not criminals.

Beginning in 1983, the Autonomous Women's Movement, a group with a nucleus of about ten women, which swelled in those years to around thirty, plastered the capital city and suburbs with posters designed to bring abortion out from its hidden place in the domestic sphere into the public eye. One afternoon Eftyhia pulled poster after poster from storage in her apartment, spreading them out carefully as she talked me through the three-year campaign. The first poster went up on 8 March 1983, International Women's Day, and it created "really a shock." People in Athens discussed its dramatic query for months:

Woman
How much do you pay for an abortion?

"We thought weeks and weeks before coming up with this slogan," Eftyhia told me. "How much? How much is an abortion? Woman! How much do you pay? Meaning not just the money, but how much do we pay in dignity, in your body, things like that."

Soon followed a poster asking questions aimed to hit at the heart of family planning issues—questions about the flow of information and knowledge:

Woman
Were you ever informed by:

- your home
- your school
- your church
- your political party
- your job
- the I.K.A. [National Health Insurance Institution]
- the hospitals

- the maternity clinics
- by the abortionists

that there is such a thing as contraception?
autonomous women's movement

"We really got them all," Eftyhia commented happily. A striking poster proclaiming "Get the laws out of our body" (see figure 1) draws on liberal discourse familiar to U.S. abortion politics. The following year, again to mark International Women's Day, the movement brought out a two-part poster series beginning with the announcement

> Today, 8 March
> International Day of the Woman
> we do not celebrate
> nor do we receive social calls

The accompanying poster explained why:

> And abortions are still illegal
> Contraception nonexistent
> Rape in marriage legal
> Abuse of women every day

Remarking on the accompanying drawing of a woman's head and upper torso wrapped tightly in a strip of cloth from the nose down, Eftyhia quipped, "Shut up and open your thighs, you know?" By 1984, the campaign of the Autonomous Women's Movement had been joined by the women's groups of various political parties and by autonomous women's organizations, such as the local Women's Group of Ambelokipi (an Athens district that includes a concentration of hospitals).

On 18 January 1985, several women were detained in Athens for police interrogation, charged with having had abortions. Postponed again and again, the case never went to trial. Eftyhia's group protested outside the building where the women were being held. Television crews arrived. The women were never officially exonerated; charges were simply dropped. But one week after the arrests, on 29 January, five to six hundred women marched through the streets of central Athens behind a banner emblazoned: "State, Doctors, and Church—Complicity and Hypocrisy." Women carried plastic lilies, a symbol of the Panayía (All Holy Mary, Mother of God), as if to say to all women, Eftyhia explained, "Here, see, it can happen to you too." She and her peers circulated among the crowd listening to women boldly claiming an ethic of choice yet apparently feeling account-

Figure 1. The 1985 campaign poster of the Autonomous Women's Movement for the legalization of abortion. It reads: "Get the laws out of our body. To abolish the law that criminalizes abortion / free abortion on demand / promulgation of contraception / women's health centers." Photo by Heather Paxson, courtesy of Eftyhia Leontidou. Reproduced with permission.

able to an ethic of service as they whispered to one another: "Well, abortion—yes, I have had one. But are we supposed to *talk* about it?" Men whose manliness seemed safely sequestered from the issue heckled from the sidewalks. Women proceeded through what was then the red-light district on Athinas Street, intent on provoking public reflection. Politicians, actresses, singers, and physicians among them dared the Ministry of Justice as they passed by Omonia Square: "I have had an abortion! Arrest me too!" No further arrests were made.

The January 1985 march drew gratifying front-page newspaper coverage. Magazines devoted articles to it. Debates unfolded in the letters sections of newspapers, some complaining about medical profiteering; others, drawing on opposing rhetoric borrowed from the United States, said of women who had had abortions: "They killed their children." In a separate interview, Eftyhia, a practicing gynecologist, told me of witnessing women break down in tears after or before an abortion, an emotional response she views as having to do with their fear of the medical procedure and the anesthesia. They worry, "Will I be all right?" not "I'm killing my baby!" she said. " 'The baby' is not a baby for anyone but the journalists" (see also Halkias 1998). Public debate continued for over a year, until, in 1986, Parliament finally took up the matter and proposed legislation. "It was only since then that *abortion* became a political word, and was not just the sin to forget about," Eftyhia said to me. "This was the difference I think we made."

From the altars of many Orthodox churches at this time could be heard appeals invoking the sanctity of human life and maintaining that it begins at conception. But in Parliament, some of the most impassioned arguments heard against legalizing abortion aimed outside a woman's body, beyond the family-planning ideal of focusing on her physical and mental well-being, and focused instead on the well-being of Greek society and nation as a whole. I read the parliamentary debate and its public aftermath (see Halkias 1998 for a corroborating analysis of letters published in Athenian newspapers) as being not only about policy measures designed to confront the nation's demographic crisis but also about the relationship between the government and its citizens—particularly female citizens—in an age of ambivalent modernity. The government had already been compelled to address family planning under the watchful eye of the European Economic Community (Emke-Poulopoulou 1994, 66). Ever since the demographic problem captured national attention, politicians have had to question the potential role of the national health care system in safeguarding the health of the national population. As Donald Light (1994) notes, state health care systems reflect not only a society's values concerning quality of life but also government goals and issues of legitimacy. In legalizing abortion, Greece could be seen to comply with European Union directives and encourage political liberalism while acknowledging the reality that abortion had become a primary means of birth limitation.

Parliamentary debate, extending over five days between 26 June and 5 July 1986 and 171 pages of photocopied transcript, broke down along partisan lines. Conservatives (members of the New Democracy Party) espoused Greek tradition by appealing to Christian morality and a fundamental connection mediated by Orthodoxy between the Greek family and nation. Members of the left (belonging to the incumbent PASOK party as well as the Greek Communist Party) drew on Western rhetoric to emphasize the state's political commitment to women citizens and "democratic policy." What comes through in the rhetoric is an overlap of moral political visions, an overlap that allowed legislation to pass without forcing either side to concede total defeat, and, for that matter, without allowing either side to claim total victory. Legal abortion in Greece is indicative of, and helps constitute, a hybrid modernity in which elements of Western rational will and Eastern collectivity unite in the name of a "Hellas" that can strategically gesture in either direction.

Citing the study conducted by the Center of Demographic Research in the late 1960s, the opposition New Democracy Party, which customarily aligns itself internationally with the West and particularly the European Economic Community, argued against legalizing abortion by foregrounding the female sterility that results from repeat abortions. This was deplored not only on behalf of the woman who took her fertility for granted before "ruining" herself but also, in its multiplication and elaboration, in consideration of the resultant sterility of the nation. They argued that abortion accounted for 50 percent of female sterility (male infertility is not mentioned) and thus 40 percent of the country's *ipoyenitikótita* (underfertility). Nikolaos Anastasopoulos, a gynecologist who addressed the Parliament, declared, "The demographic problem of Greece, my dear colleagues, which has a direct relationship with abortions, is very severe" (Parliament of Greece 1986, 7017). A member of the New Democracy Party, Vasileios Sotiropoulos, elaborated:

> I do not want to mention the demographic problem, because they may judge us to be polemical and that we always have war on our minds, while today everything is being done for disarmament and peace. And we accept all this about disarmament and peace, but a little realism is needed. In the year 2000, Greece will be 11 million and Turkey 90 million inhabitants. From then on, no one can shirk its implications. I wish that it amounts to nothing and that we exchange olive branches. I hope with all my soul. I believe, however, that this will not necessarily come to pass when the rate of increase in the Greek population in the last 5 years has fallen to .6%. Let us not forget that many states do a great deal in this area to increase this rate. (Parliament of Greece 1986, 7015)

Members of the New Democracy Party argued against abortion by proclaiming that "human life" is an absolute good that "begins at conception." The moral claim that fetuses have the right to life, or to personhood, is fundamental to the nationalistic appeal (see Haraway 1997). For abortion to impact upon demographics in a significant way, fetuses must be regarded as viable, human beings, often as "children" (merely "unborn") that can thereby be accorded rights or national identity as citizens (see also Halkias 1998). Certainly this is the assumption of Irini Dorkofiki who, opting for the high end of abortion estimates, laments in her book that, in any given year, "in Greece 400,000 little Greeks weren't born" and that between 1951 and 1971 "1,000,000 Greeks, that is to say, 10% [of the population], *were not born* because of abortion, and another 10%, 1,000,000, migrated" (1985, 139; emphasis in the original). If polemical in her rhetoric, Dorkofiki's words demonstrate that aborted fetuses and émigré citizens are accorded equal status under the demographic gaze.

The idea that Greekness begins at conception, however, clearly contrasts with the notion that Greekness must be learned, an idea consistent with a sense that human nature is actively realized through proper self-regulation and social interaction. Indeed, several conservatives qualified their argumentation in keeping with this local conceptualization of personhood. Valuing the cultural event of childbirth for ushering infants into the natural world of humans, they acknowledged a qualitative distinction between fetus and baby. The New Democracy member of Parliament Vasileios Sotiropoulos clarified the distinction: "Birth is a fact of life. Here, clearly, the embryo is really appointed personhood, legally whole, but the embryo is human life from the beginning, from its conception" (Parliament of Greece 1986, 7013). In other words, even if the fetus cannot claim rights on the basis of civic personhood, we should honor the sanctity of this life for its *potential* to gain human personhood. Sotiropoulos stated further, "Okay, if we accept that yes, the act [of abortion] is punishable, but for different social or medical reasons this punishable act is elected, then we are being very frank. But to try and say that the fetus is not life until the 12th week, and consequently this act isn't punishable and every woman can, with simple consent, by her will and hers alone, without discussing it with her spouse or with the supposed father, do this operation, then many problems are created" (7013–14). The consequences of abortion are too great and too weighty, he implied, for a woman to responsibly undertake on her own the decision to have an abortion. Recalling precisely the move in 1951 to criminalize abortion in the first place, the threat posed by abortion is revealed to be a transgression of male rights in paternity, as well as (paternal) state interests in increasing the fertility rate (see Heng and Devan 1992).

The incumbent PASOK party, which proposed legislation to legalize abortion, and which is historically wary of American and western European influence, began its case by arguing moral philosophy to uphold a liberal, progressive view of gender equity with a distinctly Greek, as opposed to American, flavor. The PASOK member Athanasios Filoppoulos stated, "Prevailing within our understanding of moral standards, within a new social problematic, within an ethical problematic," is the notion that the "life" of a fetus is *not* an "absolute good" but is of "relative value" (Parliament of Greece 1986, 7011). PASOK reasoned that the life of a mother in every instance outweighs that of "her" fetus. In his opening remarks, Filoppoulos stated that the *emvrío* (embryo or fetus: these are not linguistically demarcated in Greek) is an inseparable, dependent part of a woman's uterus that obtains true human existence from its separation from her body at birth. A fetus may embody human life or a human soul, but not human personhood. It is not a citizen. Again, this reasoning accords with a notion of realized nature; the "ethical problematic" to which he refers is compatible with a feminine ethic of service in valuing human life on the basis of lived social relations. It is further consistent with a customary understanding that social personhood, registered with a name, is accorded upon a child's baptism, not its birth (Blum and Blum 1970; Georges 1996a). It is this same reasoning to which Sotiropoulos appealed in his clarification above. Yet his socialist opponent, rather than appeal to cultural tradition, sought authority in modern science: "The suitable answer, according to science, is that throughout the duration of pregnancy the *emvrío* is not biologically autonomous, it depends on the organism of the mother and obtains human existence upon biological separation from the mother; from then it lives as its own organism and from then is entitled to rights" (7012). Intimating that his party's secular view is more progressive than the opposition's, the PASOK parliamentarian couched a culturally Greek view of fetal life—one his New Democracy colleagues could recognize as inflected with the religious tradition they wish to uphold—in the Western terms of individual rights and personal freedom:

> As ideas unfold about the freedom of an individual's self-determination, freedom that is directly interrelated with pregnancy, at least during the first stages, and with motherhood as an expression of a woman's personal freedom to become a mother whenever she can and whenever she wants—such perception is extended to all social levels, that the freedom of a woman's self-determination within a fixed time and space, during the first trimester, is a good greater than the life of the *emvrío*, in every case. (Parliament of Greece 1986, 7011)

Liberal and conservative, modern and traditional, arguments blurred, building a bridge between party positions across which the legislation could pass. Conservatives invoked the tradition of the Greek family and lauded the social and political value of women's mothering while espousing a very modern claim to the sanctity of fetal personhood (McLaren 1984). Liberals voiced a traditional distinction between fetal life and fetal personhood, while calling for the modernization of women's civic participation as workers and as mothers.

For both parties, however, legal abortion constituted a political issue of national importance because, one way or another, they saw it as contributing to the demographic strength of the nation. Proposing that abortion be institutionalized and regulated through state family planning clinics, socialist members of Parliament such as Ioannis Zigdis claimed that, with legal abortions performed in appropriate circumstances, there would be fewer resulting sterilities, fewer deaths of women of reproductive age, "far fewer women who are high-strung," and ultimately more babies born into happy families—in short, just what the country needed (Parliament of Greece 1986, 7150). To be sure, everyone anguished rhetorically over the mental and physical health of women who undergo abortions. But significantly, as Maria Damanaki, then of the Greek Communist Party, pointed out, it was not until abortion was linked to demographics that anyone seemed to notice or care that upward of three hundred thousand women each year were undergoing this potentially traumatic operation. Irini Lambraki, a member of PASOK, noted similarly, "It is certain that, if the life or social regard of men were in danger, this issue would have been resolved hundreds of years ago" (7153).

Legal abortion seems, in the end, to be aimed at defending the social body, reflecting what David Horn, writing of mid-twentieth-century Italy, describes as a "new kind of social contract," neither strictly liberal nor totalitarian, founded on reciprocal duties: "Society was engaged to preserve the life of its members, while the members were obligated to contribute to the well-being of the social organism" (1994, 39). In this modern system, "medical and economic assistance were, in theory if not in practice, provided to individuals not because of moral obligation, as under liberal regimes, or because individuals were considered to have a right to live free of disease or economic hardship. Instead, they were provided because it was perceived to be in the best interests of a nation that a statistically significant number of individuals be healthy, productive, and fertile" (44). The ethic of well-being becomes a matter of civic responsibility and national concern.

According to their own explanation, parliamentarians finally agreed to decriminalize abortion in order to acknowledge "a reality." The gynecologist Nikolaos Anastasopoulos laid neutral groundwork for this compromise when he accepted, speaking before Parliament, that "biologically . . . life begins at conception and the *emvrío* is neither of the woman nor of the man. The fetus is of the fetus. It is a separate organism that is maintained within the uterine cavity" (Parliament of Greece 1986, 7018). "And it is of two," interrupted a member of the New Democracy Party. "And it is of two constituents," Anastasopoulos conceded:

> It is an abridgement of two generative cells, but as an organism it is its own organism, and no one has the right to kill this organism, neither the woman, nor the man. . . . Our own constitutionalists say this. . . .
>
> The Church of Greece—both the Orthodox and the Catholic—bear witness that it is homicide. Other organizations say that it is homicide. I accept that it is homicide. It is. But what is happening?
>
> In Greece, there are 300,000, 200,000 or 100,000 [abortions per year], that's what the different people who take statistics say. Do you accept it, sir colleagues, that there are 300,000 Greek women who must be considered criminals, and 1,000 or 1,500 gynecologists who are to be characterized as callous criminals?
>
> I don't accept it. (7018)

Neither did parliamentarians. The government owned that it could not have three hundred thousand criminals running about, perhaps especially since many of these "criminals" were married to (or were themselves) parliamentarians. As Eugenia Georges writes, "That Greece's high abortion rate was common knowledge, discussed openly in the mass media, signified to many a breakdown in the moral authority and political legitimacy of the state" (1996a, 511). Abortion is now available on demand to women sixteen years of age and older through the twelfth week of pregnancy, giving Greece one of the most liberal abortion laws in Europe (Kaplan 1992).

The Pro-life Presence

Although I argue that women have widely incorporated abortion into an ethic of service aimed at enhancing the quality of mothering as well as protecting family repute, a relatively small pro-life presence in Athens calls for women to reverse their moral stance toward abortion, in the pronatal service of the nation. Although Greek pro-life activism waned following the unsuccessful bid to block abortion's legalization, it showed signs of revival during the late 1990s amid increasing public concern over the *ipoyenitikótita*.

Organizationally, the Panhellenic Association for the Protection of the Unborn Child exists alongside a private welfare-type organization that weds nationalist and religious discourse, the Panhellenic Union of Friends of the Polytéknon (mothers of many children). Their Athens offices are housed at the same address. While my letters to them went unanswered when I lived in Athens, in 2001 the Union of Friends of the Polytéknon not only responded favorably to my request, posted from New York City, to reproduce here one of their posters (see figure 2), but they also sent me a huge mailer filled with additional copies of this poster and several issues of their newsletter. It seems their budget has grown since the middle 1990s. Previously, at least some of their funding, and much of their rhetoric, came from American pro-life groups. Eftyhia showed me from her activist archive a copy of the American antiabortion video classic *The Silent Scream*, which the Panhellenic Association for the Protection of the Unborn Child dubbed in Greek in the 1980s (for an analysis of the video in the context of the United States, see Petchesky 1987). By the end of the 1990s, the association had gained the support of the Greek national telecommunications company (OTE), which sponsored the association's website (Athanasiou 1999).

"OTE Phone Cards Carry Pro-life Ads, Say Feminists," ran a headline in the 17 February 2000 issue of the *Athens News*. Four feminist groups, including the Greek chapter of the European Forum of Left Feminists, accused the telecommunications company of illegally permitting the Association for the Protection of the Unborn Child to "promote its views": the messages "What price an abortion? A human life!" and "Thousands of people are sentenced to death before they are born!" had recently appeared on government-issued telecards. In a letter released to the press and addressed to the telephone company's management demanding the telecards' withdrawal, the feminist coalition noted that this kind of rhetoric represents a Greek version of "movements that in other countries [read: especially the United States] culminated in a climate that led to violent—and often homicidal—attacks against women and doctors."

While the telecard slogans reflect pro-life views based on an assumption of fetal personhood (Petchesky 1987; Ginsburg 1989; Morgan and Michaels 1999), the imagery used in the poster put out by the Union of Friends of the Polytéknon fuses Western and Orthodox Christian images to create a countercultural, yet recognizably Greek, depiction of abortion as antimaternal. I first saw this poster in the spring of 1995, when I took a job lecturing to touring Americans about Greek village life through the Elderhostel program. On one tour, we visited an Orthodox cathedral on the island of Evia, near the coast of Attica, where Athens is located. The poster was prominently displayed, encased in glass, beside the cathedral's en-

Figure 2. Poster condemning abortion outside an Orthodox cathedral on Evia. Printed in Athens by the Panhellenic Association for the Protection of the Unborn Child and by the Panhellenic Union of Friends of the Polytéknon. Seated on the throne is the "New Herod—Abortion." Reproduced with permission of the Panhellenic Union of Friends of the Polytéknon.

trance facing a large public square. Explaining that I was an American student studying abortion in Greece, I made polite inquiries of the priest, who happily pulled me away from the rest of the group and into his office, where he presented me with a copy of the poster.

Borrowing religious figures (Christ, the Panayía, an angel) and using iconographic costuming and scripting for other characters, the modern-day political poster, jointly produced by the two Greek pro-life organizations, is rendered as an Orthodox icon. Its two halves depict Good and Evil. On Christ's side (as is spelled out in the lengthy caption at the bottom) reside His Church and all who rightly dwell there: the "chosen" and many-children family, the Unwed Mother who has assumed the responsibility of motherhood and "carries her cross," as well as "she who succumbed to abortion and is a 'Repentant' Mother." On the side of Evil presides "The

New Herod, Abortion," personified by an enthroned woman with snakes for hair crowned by a circlet of skulls. The caption reads in part:

> For a scepter she holds the scythe of Blood-red Death. She welcomes the Woman-Personifications of Coldheartedness, Fickleness, Indifference, and Voluptuousness [the latter is the prostitute figure dressed in fishnet stockings], and they offer her their flesh-and-blood fetuses, which she aborts . . . and tramples on! To the right, a doctor-butcher, with a pocketful of banknotes, who murders a fetus as it is being gobbled up by the Dragon of Hades! Above, an Angel of the Lord cries and averts His face.

The poster constitutes a fascinating, if horrifying, hybrid of gender ideologies and ethical systems. The pro-life message itself is largely borrowed from American or Roman Catholic traditions; to name a woman who repents an abortion a "Repentant Mother" is inconsistent with a cultural understanding that women must demonstrate continuing service to children to establish themselves as mothers. The iconographic mode of representation, on the other hand, is clearly Greek, as is the choice to focus on the character flaws of women who abort, rather than on the sanctity or purported individualism and rights of the fetus. Women who have abortions (and do not repent) are depicted as coldhearted, antimaternal; they fail to realize fully their natural feminine capacity to nurture and care for others. (In Greece, no one, not even among these pro-life activists, expects a woman, having experienced nine months of pregnancy followed by the emotional and physical trauma of childbirth, to give up her child for adoption.) They are fickle, shallow, frivolous, flighty (all these meanings are denoted by *epipoléotis*). They are indifferent. They are voluptuous. In this poster, the woman who aborts is Eve: she fails to overcome her base sensuality and to realize her salvation in motherhood (du Boulay 1974, 1986). Her coconspirator, the mercenary physician, is blamed alongside the weak-willed woman, equally doomed to Hades.

FAMILY PLANNING AS DEMOGRAPHIC AND DEMOCRATIC POLICY

In the midst of political scandal and intensifying nationalist fervor, the New Democracy Party superseded PASOK at the end of the 1980s. Prime Minister Konstandinos Mitsotakis, a member of the New Democracy Party, placed ultraconservatives in positions such as the Secretariat for Equality, this office going to a woman whom one person I interviewed described as "one of these 'fatherland, religion, family' people." She apparently "sat on" the state family planning programs by restricting their funding. Centers closed. And the fertility rate continued to fall. After regaining political power, in 1991 the PASOK government convened the nonpartisan parliamentary commission to "study the country's demographic problem and formulate recommendations for its effective confrontation" (Parliamentary of Greece 1993, title page).

In its report, the politically motivated commission called primarily for retooling state family planning clinics so that the meaning of family planning would not be "identified with contraception, abortion, and sterility," but would aim to "protect the family" and embrace the "support of motherhood, which must be forwarded as a supreme social value" (Parliament of Greece 1993, 19). The report concludes, "With the correct information about the harmful consequences of abortion to the health of women and their families, it is possible that 40% of women *will decide* not to resort to abortion" (1993, 19; emphasis added). In failing to recognize that women use the state clinics primarily for routine gynecological services, not contraception or abortion (Margaritidou and Mesteneos 1992), and in overestimating the power of women's "choice," the commission fell back on the same kinds of gendered assumptions about the responsibilities of citizenship that led, unwittingly, to pronatalist arguments supporting legal (and thus at least nominally state-regulated) abortion. Pronatal Greek demographic policy once again tried to adapt family planning to its purposes, to extend the ethic of well-being to encompass the well-being of the nation, and once again to reintroduce an ethic of service to women's reproductive practices.

In this, Greek population policy followed one of the many alternative models to demographic transition proposed since the 1970s to explain cross-cultural fertility decline, namely, a "cultural or diffusion" model. Contrary to demographic transition theory, as Susan Greenhalgh explains, culturalist interpretations begin from the premise that "changes in the economics of childrearing, and thus parental demand for children, do not explain when and why fertility falls. Rather it is ideational change—more specifically, change in ideas about the acceptability of birth control—that explains when fertility falls" (1995, 7). Nationalist Greek politicians complain that contemporary women "are refusing" to have children. If the problem is one of attitude, they reason (sharing many of the assumptions of the resistance theory of low contraceptive uptake discussed in the preceding chapter), so too is the solution. In short, the Greek government extends an ideational or cultural theory of fertility decline in forwarding family planning as an education-based population policy aimed at enabling women to plan rationally and space—not limit—births.

In 1977 the state first offered maternity leaves for women employed in the public sector. In 1983, as required for membership in the European Economic Community, the PASOK government ratified International Convention 103, which includes the "protection of motherhood" and makes provisions for three months of paid maternity leave, job protection for pregnant women, and other such benefits for women, regardless of age, race, religion, or marital status (see Law 1302/83 in appendix 2). Law 1539/85 increased maternity leave in the private sector from twelve to fourteen weeks, while in the public sector the leave became sixteen weeks. However, Greece has paid the lowest maternity benefits in the EU (Eurostat 1993, cited in Papadopoulos 1998). In 1984, additional parental leave was introduced, amounting to three months for each parent to devote to "the upbringing of a child"; an unwed mother is allotted the full six months. Since this applies only to those employed by companies with more than fifty employees, it excludes the majority of the labor force, which is employed in small enterprises (Papadopoulos 1998). A host of subtle and not-so-subtle pronatalist incentives are offered to young Greek couples. The government, for instance, is willing to exempt a father of two or more children from the mandatory term of military service and reduce the requirement for fathers of a single child. (I did hear of an Athenian couple who decided to have a second child, or at least to have it earlier than they might have liked, for this reason.) In 1993 the PASOK government extended the tax incentives for families.[14] The prohibition on advertising contraceptives in the media, with the exception of condoms advertised for their capacity to prevent disease transmission, may also be read in a pronatal light. However, implemented measures intended to protect the family are concentrated in provisions for the *polýtekni mitéra*, the mother of three or more children, offering most women too little too late.

Granted, the report advocates a comprehensive family policy that would encompass a range of measures: state health insurance coverage for couples "facing serious problems of sterility" to pursue "contemporary fertility methods" (primarily IVF); a housing policy that would provide free housing for larger families of the lower socioeconomic strata; the establishment of additional child care centers with expanded hours to accommodate working mothers; tax breaks for each child; and simplification of the current law governing adoption (Parliament of Greece 1993, 38–41). All measures focus on enabling couples to have more children than the current average. The idea is that Greek women should birth more babies. The report refers to this as family planning. Nevertheless, the comprehensive suggestions of the nonpartisan report have never been fully implemented as successive governments continue to make do with minimal measures.[15]

Greek family policy is limited in its goal of increasing family size by its own notion of family. Chapter 8 of the parliamentary commission's report on the demographic problem, "Aims of the Greek Demographic Policy," begins by distilling demographics to matters of reproduction. Reproduction is firmly situated in the family, where it is reduced to the maternal roles of women:

> There are . . . measures that can influence the size and structure of the population, such as social policy programs for the protection of the mother and child, for the confrontation of family burdens, for the encouragement of education, for the position of woman in society, for the regulation of the number and spacing of children within the family, etc.
>
> Although these programs are situated more in family planning and less in population policy, this is not to be underestimated because of the positive effect that it has.
>
> The problems of population *pass from the family* and bring about social consequences that, for our country especially, have a direct relationship to our territorial integrity and national independence. (Parliament of Greece 1993, 33, emphasis added)

Here politicians reason that, if the "problems of population" begin in the family, they must be solved *by* the family. Noting that, "compared to other European and Western countries[,] Greece ranks very low in terms of childcare provision (especially for children up to the age of 3), parental leave arrangements, levels of maternity benefits and welfare support for families with children," Theodoros Papadopoulos concludes that "the Greek family policy, through its inaction, implicitly nurtures and reproduces the ideological assumption that the family is the main provider of welfare in society" (1998, 54). What Papadopoulos refers to as a process of "Greek familism" not only holds families responsible for population issues but also singles out women's maternal responsibility.

In the parliamentary report, demographic policy takes the form of family planning appropriated to do educational work designed to promote the well-being of the nation:

> Today the meaning of family planning in Greece is identified with contraception, abortion and sterility. This conception is misdirected and needs to be reconsidered. Appropriate infrastructure with specialized personnel is called for that will correctly inform the large rural population on the issues of sterility and fertility as well as on policy measures

that support motherhood, which must be forwarded as the highest social value. (Parliament of Greece 1993, 19)

As with the legalization of abortion through the state insurance system,
the Greek government continues to offer population policy that aims to increase fertility by changing people's ideas about birth control. This
ideational strategy reflects a recent trend in international population discourse, solidified at the September 1994 International Conference on Population and Development held in Cairo, to abandon setting numerical population targets in favor of stressing better education as the key to both
women's emancipation and rationalized fertility regimes. As to how the
state can "correctly inform the large rural population," mentioned in the
parliamentary report, the report emphasizes the need for the state education system to "stress at every appropriate moment the Greek tradition [of
the family] and religious sentiment," so that women will indeed choose
motherhood and couples will choose to have more than the (then) average
of 1.4 children (Parliament of Greece 1993, 36). Feminist critics have recognized here a not-so-subtle return to promoting the "Fatherland, Family,
Religion" triumvirate that flourished in recent years under the colonels'
junta.

Members of the European Forum of Left Feminists and others are concerned with what they perceive to be a thinly veiled threat to legal abortion
in the demographic report. Indeed, it is written in the report that

> Law 1609 of 1986 "regarding the technical interruption of gestation
> and protection of the health of the woman," which decriminalized abor-
> tion through the third month following a certain procedure, today is
> not being implemented in practice, and all roads lead more easily than
> in the past to the operating table. Reexamination of the direction in
> which family planning is being implemented is deemed worthwhile for
> serious national, religious and demographic reasons. (Parliament of
> Greece 1993, 20)

In a 1993 newspaper article, forum members charge that the views of
politicians behind the report attempt to lay blame

> on women and youth for the tensions being raised between their eman-
> cipation and autonomy and their social worth. In propaganda opposing
> abortion, religion is called upon, as it is even proposed that women be
> informed that with their personal choice they cause the violent death of
> hundreds of thousands of lives. This propaganda refers, then, to willful
> abortion = murder, and this view, if not abolishes, at least constrains the

right to an abortion, such an important conquest of the women's movement. (Evropaïkó Fórum 1993, 44)

What the feminists view as propaganda, politicians deem "appropriate" information:

> Among the large agrarian social strata, abortion is considered even today as a method of birth control and as an innocent act. This notion must be overcome with the appropriate enlightenment of women and of couples generally, because of the serious psychic and somatic consequences that are brought about by these interventions, but more important, because of the violent death of hundreds of thousands of human lives. (Parliament of Greece 1993, 19)

That Greek politicians feel family values should be reinforced, if not taught in the public schools, harnesses the proper cultural training of young Greeks to an ethic of service in which nation and family are coextensive. Such training is viewed as particularly necessary in today's society, where outside influences, imported through foreign immigration, tourism, and television, threaten to corrupt Greek tradition. Elsewhere in the report it is written, "The elimination of traditional Greek paragons of life and social decay by undermining the values of marriage, family and childbirth have important effects on demographics" (Parliament of Greece 1993, 24). What is more, the report implies that women today can no longer be trusted to fulfill their qualitative service to the nation by properly socializing patriotic children. The modern woman who "severely" limits the size of her family is almost by definition, inescapably, *a traitor* to national tradition (Kanaaneh 2000). She is therefore blamed, as the European Forum of Left Feminists points out, for tensions created between modern expectations of autonomy (ethic of choice) and traditional expectations of social and national worth (ethic of service).

Responses and Critiques: "Women Are Again to Blame"

In response to the 1993 parliamentary report, the Family Planning Association of Greece organized a public symposium titled "Contemporary Demographic Trends and Family Planning in Greece." Held on a rainy January evening in 1994, the symposium aimed first to refute the parliamentary commission's stubborn reiteration that abortion, and hence women and physicians, are chiefly responsible for demographic weakening. A second goal was to clarify the activities of the FPAG and to demonstrate that their work does not undermine state demographic concerns—an understandable objective considering that restrictions on their activities had been imposed when the state first became interested in family planning in 1981. About 125 persons attended, gray-haired men in suits and middle-aged women, the latter muttering a running commentary on the evening's presentations. These presentations, along with audience questions, represented another confluence of traditional and modern ethical framings of the ways family, gender, reproduction, and nation-state intersect.

The speakers, who numbered among them demographers, gynecologists, economists, and family planning educators, agreed that the demographic problem is more complex a matter than just the birthrate, and that it depended as well on the death rate, the age spread of the population, migration, and the population distribution between rural and urban areas. But consensus could not be reached as to why abortions continued to outnumber births in Greece. A state representative from the Finance Ministry's Department of Population and Occupation stated confidently, "As research tells us, young couples and women *are refusing* to have children or are refusing to have the third child, which is exactly the goal of demographic policy" (emphasis added). This sentiment was shared by Irini Dorkofiki, never one to mince words, who laments in her book that today "they speak about the child and not about children [owing to] the famous 'emancipation' of women" (1985, 133). Member of Parliament Maria Damanaki refuted this charge during Parliament's debate over legalizing abortion, informing her colleagues that "someone here gave me the impression, mostly from the side of New Democracy, that he regards abortion as the caprice of today's women—indeed, this was based on a characterization of progressive women—as a whim that they indulge with the ease that they would in doing something else around the house or in their work or I don't know where else" (Parliament of Greece 1986, 7019).

The ethical tensions surrounding the very definition of progressive women are palpable. During the 1986 parliamentary debates over legalizing abortion, Ioannis Zigdis identified the issue ultimately at stake as gender parity: "Today the emancipation of women is a fact, we all accept it. No one doubts the equal rights of a woman to a man. Therefore, as she bears the burden [*város*, also meaning responsibility] of the *emvrío*, she will decide" (Parliament of Greece 1986, 7151). Thus in the debate, when members of Parliament interrogated Greek women's attitudes toward having children and found a general absence of liberal guilt for aborting, they reevaluated abortion—a practice rooted in an ethical understanding of women's service—through an ethic of choice. It is the same kind of ethical tension seen when women who seek abortions for reasons motivated by ethical service to family are castigated for damaging their fertility, that is, according to an ethic of well-being. Damanaki expresses frustration that modern women are today caught in an "impossible ethics" in which virtue is virtually unrealizable (Visakowitz 2001).

Significantly, Rena Lampsa, the former General Secretary for Equality under PASOK, who at the time represented Greece on the Council of Europe, countered government claims at the FPAG symposium, arguing that the real issue was not a problem of sheer numbers, nor was it women's supposed attitude toward motherhood. Crucially distinguishing the means *(ta mésa)* from the causes *(ta étia)* of birth control or family limitation, Lampsa and others underscored the very real economic and infrastructural constraints that influence couples' decisions regarding family planning (see also Emke-Poulopoulou 1994). Abortion has been the *means* by which women have met those economic, psychological, and social constraints; it has not been the *reason* why women are having fewer children—and thus abortion cannot be blamed for a declining fertility rate. Lampsa, calling implicitly on the ethic of service, pointed out that women, far from refusing motherhood, find themselves economically and socially unable to have the number of children they would like.

Thinking of friends who hoped to start families, and taking the critical and interested viewpoint of feminism, Daphne echoed Lampsa, stating that, because people are more interested in offering their children higher education and other opportunities for a better life, parents raise fewer children. Daphne added, "It's not only a matter of the family and how it works; it's also the everyday problems in this specific country. This is my opinion: that a lot of women want to have more children, but they can't for many reasons." Speaking with dozens of middle-class Athenian women who wanted to have more children than they had or expected to have, I saw no appreciable evidence of the motherhood backlash intimated by the parliamentary report. Women told me:

> I would like to have another child, yes. I would like at least one more. It's difficult because I'm working, and because now we want to have everything for our children. You don't decide easily to have more children, because you want to provide them everything.
>
>> —Anna, a thirty-one-year-old secretary, with one child, age eight months

> And I'd like to have more too! I would like many children. It's a matter of organization, because I am away many hours, and so is my husband. If we can be sure that there will be someone at home, at least two peo-

ple, then we will have four kids. We simply can't raise them by ourselves.

—Aliki Andoniou, a thirty-four-year-old professional,
four months pregnant with her second child

I would like to have kids . . . if I had the means to raise them. I don't
know how things will be when I have my own house, but I would have
no problem having even four children—only whether I would have the
capability.

—Nia, twenty-year-old unmarried student

These women are well aware of Greece's *ipoyenitikótita* (underfertility);
they shake their heads and remark that they live in a "country of aged people." Nia said to me, "We should all have children, but—" and then she
launched into a litany of economic and social reasons why this is was an
idealistic, impractical pronouncement. In a similar conversation, another
friend simply shrugged her shoulders, tossed back her head, and said, in effect, "Sure, Turkey is so big and we are so small, and we ought really to get
our population up; but then, nobody can have more than one kid, two at
most." A great rift opens between ideal and practice, a rift that never seems
to bother anyone. The ideal—that people should have bigger families—
"stays in the air," this friend told me. It is as if what journalists delight in
decrying as governmental *efthinofóvia* (literally, "responsibility phobia";
Herzfeld 1992; Faubion 1993) gives license to people's everyday avoidance
of responsibility.

For instead of investing significant funds in providing adequate subsidized child care, or overhauling the civil service to offer part-time job options, or revamping the split-schedule public school system, the state's
major family policy—*and* its major demographic policy—is to offer
women monthly allowances, price reductions on automobiles, and meat
and fruit during winter months, after the birth of a *third* child. Ignoring
the concerns of their constituency, as well as the best advice of their own
demographers (cf. Symeonidou 1990), the government persists in focusing
its pronatal moneys on an effort to reach the "goal of the third child," leaving the majority of people to fend for themselves with children numbers
one and two.

Athenian women I knew laughed at the *polýteknes* allowances, calling
the monthly U.S.$150 and free lamb at Easter to support three or more
children a "joke." The fact that private child care for one child costs more
than the rent on a three-room apartment in a neighborhood near downtown Athens illuminates their point. Of course, the state's aid may seem
more significant to women in rural areas, at whom such provisions ar-

guably are aimed. To put it bluntly, as did one person who reviewed a draft of this book, urban politicians may see the rural population as an emergency supply of "cannon fodder." The "give birth for Greece" (Halkias 1998) rhetoric is, indeed, strongest in the northern regions of Florina and Thrace; in Thrace the nationalist slogan is "Give birth and don't sell your land" to the Muslims (Anastasia Karakasidou, personal communication). Nevertheless, a former director of the National Statistics Association of Greece conceded to me in 1994 that "inflation has played its role in these allowances, and it seems that that measure has not played any important role in affecting the families that have more children."

Dina, the seventy-year-old retired schoolteacher, told me she believed the state should motivate women to stay home and have more kids, but that politicians have yet to find the best way to do this. "My sister," she explained, "takes thirty-five thousand [drachmes a month] because she has four children. But one [child] is a lawyer, the other a forestry commissioner, the third a translator for the European Union, the fourth is married. And now my sister gets a pension that she doesn't even need. She's got a kid who's a lawyer!" Dina is not alone in this complaint. The undersecretary of health for the socialist PASOK Party, which succeeded New Democracy in the fall of 1993, the next year voiced public disapproval of the "unjust" structure of the national insurance system that doles out benefits regardless of need, calling for reform of the pensions for the *polýteknes* mothers (Daoudaki 1994, 15).[16] The nonpartisan parliamentary report, for its part, simply advocates an increase in the size and duration of these monthly allowances and supports the full pensioning of *polýteknes* mothers.

If, as Athenian women repeatedly told me, "the state does nothing" when it comes to actual policy, many politicians—who are also citizens in their own right—seem to share many of their fellow Athenians' complaints, at least according to these politicians' writings. Even the parliamentary report recognizes that "the child is not only a matter of the parents but also of legislation and other social agents" (Parliament of Greece 1993, 24). Such things as "the new notion of the family and society that urbanization occasions (a notion that the countryside is also adopting), housing problems, the cost of education, the lack of appropriate child care centers, etc., [all] lead to smaller families and the postponement of marriage" (15). Family planners at the 1994 FPAG symposium worked to situate changing social norms in the kind of historical context presented in this book. They argued that what Greeks consider an appropriate family size has diminished with the transition from a localized, subsistence based economy to the national market economy. Women's participation in the labor force, as well as factors attendant upon urbanization, are forcing people to renegotiate how they reconcile work and family life. Several speakers intimated that Greece is at a cultural crossroads, and that "the Greek family" is undergoing some sort of transition.[17] Out came accusations of *efthinofóvia:* speakers charged parliamentarians with resisting changes already unfolding. Here again, politicians, said to prefer to decry some loss of traditional values and not to compromise on their expectations for families, were criticized for being too conservative. Certainly this rhetorical strategy is easier, and cheaper, than establishing proper day care centers. But as Rena Lampsa said that night, the question people should be asking is: What can the state do to ensure that people are able to have the kids they desire? The FPAG's strategy at the conference, then, was to take on the demographic situation, recognize it as a problem, and forward a specific kind of family planning policy that could serve as a tool in realizing state demographic goals. Greece's private Family Planning Association has learned, after having to fight legislative limitations on its services, that it is expedient to speak the language of demography.

Although the government and the FPAG may differ as to what kinds of family policy to forward, they share certain assumptions in identifying family planning as a form of population policy: namely, the related ideologies of rational action and an ethic of choice that supposedly extends to women as well as men. Politicians and family planners alike persist in the belief that, with the proper education, women will make proper decisions regarding fertility control. Nikolas Loizos of the Department of Population and Occupation stated at the FPAG symposium that central among the nation's demographic objectives is the "rational analysis of the Greek population." He also reiterated the parliamentary report's idealistic claim that, with "correct" information on the harmful risks of abortion "to the health of women and their families," and with proper teaching of the national and religious tradition that greatly values having children, "it is possible that 40% of women will decide not to resort to abortion." This thinking ignores the kinds of life situations and practical constraints that the FPAG is trying to get policy makers to address.

At the surface, members of the FPAG recognize the fallacy in regarding reproductive practices as the outcome of personal choices made rationally according to available information (for a similar argument by a state demographer, see Symeonidou 1990). Family planners try to shift the burden of responsibility from women and doctors back onto the state, charging it with the task of providing sufficient economic and infrastructural support for individuals to create families. As Lampsa told me in a later interview, "The demographic problem is a matter of free choice, first of all. And then, at the national level, the obligation of the state, of the government, is to provide the infrastructure needed for people who wish to have children."

As we have seen, the mission statement of the FPAG posits reproductive choice as a basic human right. Although a petition for individual human rights has wide political appeal these days, and although it resonates particularly well with women struggling to throw off the domesticating yoke of the patriarchal family, those who promote it play right into the hands of conservative demographers. In the first instance, to regard reproductive practice as an inalienable right, at least when hedged by pronatalist apologies, naturalizes women's *desire* to have children, even many children. Furthermore, the family as a social institution is brought into the realm of human rights to be ensured by the state; here government officials can legitimately record and regulate its development. In this way family policy in Greece is forwarded as demographic policy. Policy makers look on the family, as Donzelot (1979) argues of modern states, more as a "mechanism" than an "institution" of state interests. Moreover, Evyenios Koumantakis, a professor of obstetrics and gynecology, was able to proclaim at the FPAG symposium, "Family planning is demographic policy and democratic policy."

Law 1892/90 (Article 63), established in the early 1990s by the New Democracy government, provides for the *polýtekni* mother who has obtained her third child a monthly allowance equivalent to one and a half times the daily wage of an unskilled worker, multiplied by the number of her unwed children under the age of twenty-five. The allowance is paid so long as she has qualifying children. Furthermore, it is paid to the mother independently of any other allowance, salary, pension, or compensation (General Secretariat for Equality 1993, 18–19). The government also established old-age pensions for *polýteknes* mothers—a kind of retirement pension for "professional" mothers in gratitude for their service as employees of the state. The government expressed its appreciation in a press release sent out by Undersecretary Fanni Palli-Petralia of the Ministry of Health and Welfare on 8 May 1993, Mother's Day:

> On the occasion of the Mother's Day holiday, as propitious for family policy as for the mothers of many children, I send to all Greek women warm greetings.
>
> The government, honoring the mother, valuing the difficulties that she faces and wishing to ease what is becoming very heavy and institutionally imposed work [will offer]:

- monthly allowance of 34.000 drx. for the third child
  [U.S.$150]
- lifelong pension to women with four or more children

And all this is because we believe that the mother is the foundation of
the Nation. Without her, there would be neither manna nor future, nor
Greece.

In punning, intentionally or not, on *mána* (mother), the bureaucrat writing the press release reveals that women are held responsible *as mothers*
for the production of national identity by reproducing citizens.

A further danger in figuring reproduction as a right, especially in the
midst of pronatalist sentiments, is that the right to reproduce is made
equivalent to the right to produce, or to work. Women's maternal citizenship is thereby reinscribed. At the FPAG symposium, the Department of
Population and Occupation's Nikolas Loizos proposed that a woman receive 5 million drachmes (nearly U.S.$22,000) a year for her third child.
This is not a laughable sum. Although his generous offer met with a rous-
ing response from the crowd, one woman rose from the audience in indig-
nation. This was Eleni, the formidable feminist and mother of three, whom
I met that night for the first time. She challenged the state employee in her
booming voice: "I heard with astonishment that the state is ready to buy
the womb at 5 million! Who will speak to the ambitions of the child, what
my child can expect in life so that I can get 5 million! We [women] are
being confronted by the state as little machines!" Eleni took umbrage with
this contemporary, state-endorsed valuing of reproduction as the production of children, which deflects attention from, and hence undermines, the
subjectivity and agency of women who mother. The struggle, she rightly
points out, comes down to how women are perceived. To pay a woman
$22,000 a year to birth a third child is to give her a salary for producing her
quota of citizens. Even as the law stands, with benefits for the *polýteknes*
mothers—the $150 monthly allowances and nominal pensions—offered
regardless of family income or economic need, they are best regarded as an
amount paid for services rendered, rather than as a form of economic assistance to those who need it. And this is precisely how the pronatalists
speak of it. For example, in an article published in the March 1991 issue of
Gonís (Parents) magazine, the president of the Athens Union of Mothers
of Many Children, Vasilios Theotokatos, declared:

> It's known that our country is in danger of becoming a country of aged
> people, since the low fertility rate has today reached a very dangerous
> point and the demographic problem of our fatherland has been classi-

fied [as] the number one national concern. For this reason . . . a minimum allowance must be given to the mother of many children for her
offering—that is, a national offering—to solve our demographic problem. (Delidhaki 1991, 21)

In this way, fertility is rationalized as a form of productivity and women
are celebrated as professional mothers, monetarily rewarded for their ethical service and ultimate, maternal offering to the nation.

The Question of Sex Education

Given the political emphasis on education as the key to instilling national
values, and the demographic policy aiming to root in female citizens a
sense of autonomy and responsibility that will drive rational decisions not
to abort, one might expect the government to promote sex education
classes in the state school system. As it turns out, sex education *(seksoualikí aghoghí)*—that is, material covering conception, contraception, sexually transmitted diseases, and safe sex practices—has been absent from the
curriculum. Because this seems so at odds with recent legislation and a
general eagerness to consume and defer to modern reproductive knowledges (on ultrasound, see Georges 1996b), I routinely asked Athenians
what they thought about the lack of sex education in the schools. Athena
and Sophia agreed that its absence in both schools and homes accounted for
the population's low contraceptive uptake:

> It's a problem of information. It's the parents' fault. The generation
> that was born or raised during the [Nazi] occupation does not talk
> about it, and if you don't have someone to tell you what to do, you
> don't do anything. Our parents waited for us to learn these things on
> our own. So I don't blame the young people for making mistakes some-
> times, as they had no advice.

The question of *why* sex education is not included in the school curriculum
provides a topic through which Athenians comment on the ethical responsibilities incumbent upon the Greek family, the maturity of Greeks with
respect to Westerners, and the failings of state bureaucrats in their duty as
political representatives.

In addressing the absence of sex education classes, educators and parents
alike point their finger first at the many infrastructural problems plaguing
the school system, which suffers from a severe lack of funding. So many
"more basic" things require immediate attention—dilapidated classrooms;
the lack of maps, science equipment, and other fundamental materials—
that sex education is not a priority. Moreover, sex education would require

significant funds, I was told, because it should not simply be added to the regular biology lessons but must be taught by scientists specially trained in this field. Having been medicalized, sex requires a trained specialist to teach it. That is, middle-class Athenians have come to identify medical or scientific training as sex education. An anthropological perspective might identify exhortations to girls and adolescent women not to walk alone along public roads as a form of sex education, one that follows a social, as opposed to a medical, sexual ideology. That Athenians view issues of sexual training in *ethical* terms reveals an important local distinction: in matters of sexuality, schools are responsible for conveying an ethic of well-being. Without the training to do so, it is best for teachers to say nothing. Lessons about sexuality conveyed through an ethic of service should remain the responsibility of family members and are not included in the formalized meaning of sex education.

Keeping in mind the frequently voiced complaints regarding the conservatism of the Greek mentality, the question becomes: To what extent are parents and politicians ready to support a sexual ethic of well-being that has the potential to overshadow an ethic of service? School administrators and teachers who might otherwise advocate sex education are often wary of offending parents, who are said to consider sex shameful or embarrassing to discuss. One middle-aged schoolteacher attributed such ideas to virtually everyone involved (except implicitly herself): "Oh, I think they're a little puritanical. I think so. Not only the state, I mean the minister [of education and religion]—no, I mean also the parents. I think many parents will say no [to sex education], more than we think. Why? Because they have inside them this taboo. They don't talk about these things." But if some parents and teachers attribute the lack of sex education to a sexually modest *noötropía* (collective, embodied mentality) and school officials' unwillingness to upset the church by crossing the institution of the family, a professor of theology at the University of Athens emphasized to me the potential political (and demographic) repercussions associated with sex education.

While I had expected to learn from Dr. Sotiris Angelopoulos about theology and religiosity and morality, he repeatedly turned our conversation to politics and economics and nationalism, impressing on me that one cannot talk about the cultural effect of religion in Greece without addressing secular politics. This is certainly the case with public schooling. When I asked Angelopoulos what factors he thought accounted for the lack of sex education, he replied:

I think it's purely political. First, the fear that we are a small country, and there are people who fear that the application of a liberal program—oh, it would be detrimental, if you take into consideration what would be the advantage to some of our neighbors with this kind of thing. This [resistance to sex education in schools] is absolutely baffling. It's not the church, no. The church influences the attitude of the people very generally, but to tell you to do this or do that—no, we are not used to taking commands from the church. We have reverence for the church, just like the ancient Greeks. It's like a public service; it gives some kind of security, okay, but this is very general. More responsible for guiding the people is the government. But I tell you, this being a very small country among other small countries, and not being in good relations with everybody—as is natural, most of the time—*this* is prohibiting the introduction of modern programs of education, more awakening programs for the people. They [the politicians] are afraid of the results. Which [party] is going to try this? And then comes the political cost and the other factors that [lead to the conclusion] "Let the other [party] do this."[18]

To illustrate his point that political agendas are at stake, Angelopoulos told me of his involvement in the middle 1970s in drafting a policy recommendation within the Ministry of Education and Religion to teach Darwinian evolution alongside biblical creationism (which was already being taught) in public schools. The committee came to a unified decision to support the teaching of evolution, much to Angelopoulos's astonishment ("with theologians, we do not agree among ourselves"); however, the policy recommendation was struck down at the word of the minister of the New Democracy Party, whose attention was fixed on upcoming elections. In retrospect, after the minister won reelection by a very slim margin, Angelopoulos recognized the political necessity of the minister's refusal to introduce this educational reform: "I give you this as an example to tell you what factors are influencing the Greek society. . . . There are politicians and lay people who understand very clearly all about matters like this, but it is not easy to introduce [progressive policy]. It is not the reaction of the church—No! The people are conservative, and you will lose their votes. These things are more important to the government than what the archbishop would say about such things."[19]

Just how conservative are the people? When I raised the question of sex education with Daphne, who teaches secondary school, she wanted to affirm that Athenian children were prepared to take classes on sexuality and reproduction, but then hesitated. The children are still "close to the family," she explained, and are therefore not altogether open to such topics. A moment later she reconsidered, saying that children *must* be ready for this instruction, since they are already exposed to it by television, by their friends, by magazines. Whether or not kids are culturally or emotionally ready, information is available in the modern world, Daphne reckons, and thus schools should take an active interest in ensuring that at least some of the information they receive is scientifically correct and practically helpful. An ethic of choice requires a new kind of training: the training to assess competing information and make responsible decisions.

In her indecision, I see Daphne struggling to come to terms with the politicized tensions between the so-called traditional and modern expectations that are ubiquitous in Athenian life. Soula invoked these same tensions in explaining that, while she supported the introduction of sex education in schools, many other parents are not ready in comparison with the Western world: "In 1981 they ended school uniforms, and that was met with a lot of disapproval. We are a bit backward [*píso*] in these things. A little Eastern [*anatolítes*]. But fine! I'd never want to be anything else but Greek." Acknowledging that many traditional views and customs are to her admittedly "backward" or Eastern (i.e., Turkish), she engages in what Herzfeld (1997a) names "cultural intimacy" by associating such nonmodern traits as a prohibition on the open discussion of sexual matters with something distinctively Greek and therefore worth preserving. As we saw with the backlash against the sanitizing threat of safe sex, the "self-stereotypes that insiders express ostensibly at their own collective expense" play an active role in Greek cultural engagement by helping to solidify national character (3). Understanding this process is crucial to comprehending why family planning advocates have been more successful in changing the legal infrastructure than people's *noötropía* (collective mentality) and everyday practices.

I talked with three trained professionals who have lectured to school children about sex and contraception. Evangelia, the full-time family planning counselor who splits her time between the FPAG and one of the state social insurance organizations, visits schools after consulting both teachers and parents' groups. She reports that kids ask a lot of questions and are eager to learn. A professor of midwifery, Ourania Katsigianni, who trains graduate students to give guest lectures on sex education in high schools, shared this view as well as that of the church's limited influence. In a 1993 study of Athenian schoolteachers, her research group learned that about half were open to the idea of introducing sex education to their students. While some teachers try to do the lessons after giving themselves a crash course, others ask midwives, family planning volunteers such as Evangelia, or doctors to visit their classes. "The people's" resistance to sex education seemed to me not so strong as Athenians commonly make it out to be. But when I asked Katsigianni what she thought blocked its institutionalization, her response was strikingly similar to Angelopoulos's:

> I don't think it is the church, no. . . . Perhaps the church might have some opposition to certain things, but for sex education as a whole they are very supportive. I think it's—in the Ministry of Education they told us that they don't take the responsibility because some parents don't like it. In the schools they told us that the Ministry of Education doesn't like it and they don't have their acceptance. I think it's, you know, teachers, parents, minister of education—all of them have the responsibility, but they don't want to *take* the responsibility; they drop it.

Here again, the story told is a tale classic to modern Greece, a tale "of *efthino-fovia* ('fear of responsibility'), the stereotypical unwillingness to take any initiative in even the most marginally anomalous situations" (Herzfeld 1992, 143).

Athenians I interviewed agreed that talk of sexual matters should ideally stay in the home, but since most parents do not discuss such issues with their children, the schools should take up sex education: let the teachers do it. Many teachers, for their part, feel they lack the proper training, and besides, some parents might object. For politicians who are in charge of setting the curriculum, adherence to cultural tradition—something no proper Greek should claim he or she wants to eradicate—provides a convenient alibi for avoiding the issue altogether. Maintenance of Greece's cultural uniqueness (which *efthinofóvia* often facilitates) has led many Greeks and non-Greeks alike to look on the nation as European but non-Western (i.e., premodern).[20] When the vast majority of political officials and parliamentarians are men, this reinforces a *gendered* aspect to the cultural politics of maturity.[21] The debate over who should do what regarding sex education is part of the same wider discussion as debates over reproductive responsibility and family planning: the Western mentality is regarded not only as more forward-thinking but also as Greece's future, in contrast to the mentality—as Nadia and Maro said of men's phallocratism—deemed Eastern, backward, and of the past. The question becomes: Who will assume the role and responsibility of moving Greece forward? Family planners and politicians alike tend to look to *women* to fulfill their moral duty in "bearing" the nation forward in this new millennium by socializing children to act according to the rational demands of the contemporary capitalist era.

IDEOLOGICAL INVERSIONS

Recognizing that politicians look to rationalized reproduction as a means of modernity points us toward an understanding of why the government has failed to implement a comprehensive family policy, despite the national import read into the birthrate. Because demographics have been reduced to reproduction, and reproduction is seen as the domain of women, it is not surprising that family policy reflects ideologies of motherhood and ethical expectations for feminine gender proficiency. Official forms of power must negotiate social developments and adapt to shifts in cultural ideology.

These days, as I have argued, motherhood is supposed to be a matter of women's free choice, as opposed to her obedient service. This poses no fundamental challenge to state interests. It means that the government can simply direct its policy efforts at encouraging women to make the choice that will further state interests. This is precisely the aim of current Greek family policy, which works toward the goal of producing the third child by rewarding women for choosing motherhood *over* any other sort of employment or livelihood. Meanwhile, many women are asking alternatively for infrastructural measures that would allow them more easily to choose motherhood *and* a career or full-time occupation.

Athenian women want to be mothers. But when the government targets measures for the protection of motherhood in order to support large families, it misses the idea that what is socially and culturally important about *teknopiía* (the making of children) for women is completely filling the family form and gaining social recognition as mothers, *not* amassing multiple children. If motherhood is seen to constitute a choice, policy makers regard this as an either/or choice: so long as a woman is going to be a mother, according to this logic, she may as well produce many babies. The patriarchal state, then, falls back on traditional gender and kinship constructions that assume women either are mothers or they are not—but this is a rhetorical mask that obscures the cultural work being done by government policy. At the same time that women are hailed by the state as mothers, classified as baby producers (Althusser 1971; Herzfeld 1997a, 29), the ideology of choice puts the burden of responsibility on individual women.

As Verena Stolcke argues, this ideological sleight of hand reflects a more general shift throughout modern, capitalist Europe in the conceptualization of women:

> In an increasingly competitive society, fragmented by the social division of labour into a milliard of hierarchically ordered functions, indi-

vidual achievement and function are thought to determine a person's social position almost to the exclusion of such other criteria as family origin. A person's place within the social division of labour, however, in contradiction with the value attached to individual achievement, is also attributed to natural ability. (1993, 35–36)

A shift from traditional to modern subjectivities does not write nature out of the equation. What it does do is hold individuals personally, individually responsible for *realizing* their natures. As motherhood is recast as a goal toward which proper women must strive, the government sees women consuming family planning methods in order to maximize their natural desires for sex and children. But at this point, says Stolcke, mothers become an exception: not only are they held responsible for realizing their own natures *as women,* but also, *as mothers,* they are held responsible for realizing those of their children:

> Whenever social condition is attributed to natural deficiencies, women move onto centre stage as mothers, be it as bearers and reproducers for a class or for a "nation." If class or nation are conceptualized in essential terms, women's procreative capacity needs controlling to perpetuate class and national-cum-racial privileges. And control implies domination by men. (37)

When gender is a matter of personal responsibility, when mothering "completes" a woman's nature, and when actions are governed by choice rather than fate or convention, women have a moral obligation to aspire to motherhood. In this way, women are shown to be good at being women, and good Greek *citizens.* In this way, too, we can make sense of the apparent contradiction between a pronatalist government agenda and legislation that legalizes abortion and makes available modern family planning methods. Liberal family policy measures are implemented with the aim of enabling women to fully achieve their "biological mission" as women and to reproduce for the nation. The ideology of free choice that prompts legislators to provide economic encouragement for women to realize their supposedly natural desires to mother large numbers of children at the same time justifies the state's easy reliance on a combination of nationalist and superficially progressive rhetoric, without legislating significant, expensive institutional measures such as childcare provisions.

5 Technologies of Greek Motherhood

> For women, the experience of motherhood passes through their
> bodies, whatever they do with motherhood. I mean, deciding
> against motherhood is just as hard as deciding for motherhood.
> But it's a decision you have to make. You cannot pass through your
> life and forget about it. . . . Motherhood you have to consider, in a
> positive or negative way.
>
> KORALIA, forty-two-year-old professional

In *After Nature* (1992a), Marilyn Strathern contends that over the past
few decades "the English" have been pressed into reconsidering their previously taken-for-granted views on how nature and culture relate to one
another. Until recently, she argues, the English, and Euro-Americans more
generally, have regarded the domain of Nature as a resource for the production of Culture and as a constraining model for human endeavor.[1] In regarding their cultural projects as both built on and imitating nature, modern Euro-Americans have taken "after nature." Today, however, when
consumers gladly part with extra money to acquire specially grown organic produce, when researchers look to genetic therapy for cures for diseases, and when biodiversity must be politically claimed and secured by national and international agencies, nature no longer sits so obviously apart
from cultural intervention: "Nature as a ground for the meaning of cultural practices can no longer be taken for granted if Nature itself is regarded as having to be protected and promoted" (Strathern 1992a, 177).
What was once held implicit—that nature grounds culture—is being made
explicit, with the result that people are widely coming to see nature as culturally constructed. Thus, not only are Euro-Americans "after" nature in
acting with Nature in mind, they are today also postnature. Strathern does
not find this surprising. This process of literalization, as she calls it, is fully
in keeping with the Enlightenment proposition "that one should aim for a
state of permanent revelation, to demystify and make things more and
more apparent in consciously conveying it to others" (Strathern 1992a,

132). Today Euro-Americans have become more or less comfortable with "enabling" nature to be "itself." For them, being "after nature" at the end of the twentieth century means seeing oneself as living in an era when nature is no longer sustainable without technological intervention and legal protection, while harboring nostalgia for some sense of "real," untouched nature with which one can feel affinity.

In this book, I argue that the nature Athenians call on to legitimate their actions and choices is not quite the fixed, grounding nature whose logical demise Strathern diagnoses. For many Greeks, nature is not the simultaneous opposite and source of culture. Rather, I describe for Greek sociality—and gender construction—an understanding of nature that is more metaphysical, active, and unpredictable than the Enlightenment version. Even "proper" sexuality, the normative heterosexuality men and women are supposed to exhibit, is ideologically more a matter of learned, controlled behavior than raw essence. We have seen that women have been expected to realize their sexual natures as conspicuously self-controlling, particularly under an ethic of service. For men, in contrast, sexual urges are naturally more indiscriminate, meaning that it can be a point of honor for men to approach *ksénes* (foreign women with no protective family around), but it is equally expected that they will back off if this interest is not immediately reciprocated. Greeks further call on the indiscriminateness and strength of men's sexual impulse to explain incest and male homosexuality: homophobia among men turns precisely on the phobia that, "if you try it, you might like it," and thus one will find oneself negotiating a double life of married respectability and hidden sexual affairs with other men.[2] In this regard, gay men's engagement in compulsory marriage and fatherhood can be seen as ethically analogous to some women's recourse to abortion: it appropriately hides weakness of will or sexual indiscretion. As demonstrated by these examples, Culture and Nature have not been ideologically sequestered as separate, mimetic domains in Greece. Realizing one's nature through social practice does not require nature to be prior to, as grounds for, that practice.

Rather than "after nature," then, modern Greeks depict cultural activity as being *with* nature. I use the preposition *with* to signify that the characterological and physiological nature of *ánthropi* must be socially realized. It is notable that the Greek words for "in practice" and "in reality" are one and the same: *stin pragmatikótita*. What is "real" about human nature for Greeks is not its a priori fixity or inevitability or grounding capacity, but rather its realization through collective recognition of moral character established through behavior. In this sense the phrase "technologies of motherhood," in the title of this chapter, takes on an illuminating set of meanings stemming from the root of the Greek word *technologhía*. *Téchni* primarily signifies art, mastery or artistry, and craft; it indicates something made or in the making. This book discusses the *téchni* of urban Greek motherhood. Although calling to mind Anglophone conceptions of culture, such aspects of *téchni* are not presumed to be opposite of *físi* (nature). Indeed, I argue that Athenian women today approach motherhood as something to be worked at, achieved, and continuously demonstrated. Subsequently, this contributes to their gender proficiency, illustrating that they are good at being women. Gender, too, is *technologhikó*, as de Lauretis (1987) has argued following Foucault (borrowing from ancient Greek philosophy).

Gender inequality and sexual power are still legitimated by reference to nature, that is, they are "naturalized" in Greece. Witness the expectation that men will lust after women of all ages, family members, boys—whoever is at hand and socially and symbolically subordinate. Men's sexual power does not follow naturally from their greater size or musculature or genetic predisposition; indeed, physical power is largely stigmatized. Rather, it is social and symbolic power—the sexual threat they pose to subordinates—that is naturalized, as is women's and youths' vulnerability. Women's recognized source of power—they are cunning, wily, able to manipulate circumstances to their (and their family's) advantage—is naturalized as the definitively womanly character trait of *poniriá* (cunning). Nevertheless, using Strathern's work as a basis for comparison, I hope further to demonstrate that naturalization in Greece does something other than suggest fixity, inevitability, or a sense that there is nothing humans can do about the matter (Yanagisako and Delaney 1995). When customary behavior is naturalized in Greece, there is always room for strategic maneuvering or *crafting* so long as this action can be morally justified; customary behavior and ethical behavior, after all, are fundamentally intertwined.

Strathern takes English kinship as her paradigmatic example of a literalizing shift in Euro-American perspectives on nature because kinship has been regarded by modern anthropologists and others as a system for the social organization and, now, construction of "natural facts." As Lévi-Strauss ([1949] 1969) posits, kinship, produced by and after human reproduction—the "facts of life"—is where the domain of Culture follows Nature but also gains autonomy from it. Recognizing the ethnocentric specificity of this claim (MacCormack 1980; Goodale 1980; Strathern 1980), and building on critical commentaries of this pervasive formulation among Euro-Americans (Schneider 1968; Rubin 1975; Yanagisako and Collier 1987), Strathern argues that the implicit fact of kinship's social construction (as something that follows nature) is being made explicit (and not only to contemporary anthropologists), in large part owing to the recent media visibility of such reproductive technologies as in vitro fertilization (IVF), fetal ultrasound, and surrogacy. When reproductive technologies doubly assist the natural and social axes of kinship through medical technological and legal means, "there is little now to be taken for granted" (Strathern 1992b, 20).

In this final chapter, I take up the challenge of exploring what, if anything, is happening to the Greek notion of realized nature when these same technologies are imported and made (more or less) openly available on the consumer market. I suggest that in Greece IVF does not so much make explicit the social construction of nature as it is accommodated by a prior, conscious understanding of nature as socially realized. The ethical questions raised by IVF in Greece are, therefore, not entirely the same as in the United States and Britain. Strathern writes of the latter, "What is in crisis here is the symbolic order, the conceptualization of the relationship between nature and culture such that one can talk about the one through the other" (1992a, 177). Gender, by dominant Anglophone definition a cultural construct that is seen to influence embodied experience—and for women particularly, the experience of reproductive events—has centrally figured in this "crisis." Feminists, journalists, religious leaders, bioethicists, and medical scientists have, over the past couple of decades, debated in the English-language media whether IVF and other reproductive technologies enhance women's reproductive choice or primarily oppress women by serving as medical tools for rationalizing female reproductivity in contexts of gender, class, and racial inequality (Arditti, Klein, and Minden 1984; Corea 1985; Rothman 1989; Spallone 1989; Treichler 1990; Pfeffer 1993; Raymond 1993). Others worry that reproductive technologies will irrevocably rend the normative fabric of the nuclear family (Alpern 1992) (while still others celebrate this possibility) or, alternatively, may reinforce traditional patriarchal patterns and meanings (Corea 1985; Tabet 1987; Stolcke 1988). Although about a dozen IVF clinics, public and private, operated in Athens in the middle 1990s, these kinds of questions were hardly ever debated in the Greek newspapers, on television talk shows, or among acquaintances. In Greece, the central ethical questions turn on whether using IVF counts as proper parenting and demonstrates appropriate gender proficiency.

Consistent with a notion of achieved motherhood, one of the most controversial issues regarding IVF in Athens concerns the *quality* of mothering that a woman will be able to offer her child. Artemis, who remains childless after suffering four miscarriages, and for whom, as she put it, IVF "came too late" to Greece, explained:

I think after forty it's not an age to raise children. You do not have so
much—okay, you have some, but not so much to give, is my opinion. I
think when parents are younger they have more courage and fortitude;
when you're older, after work you come home and you are all exhausted. And it's not only that the body is more tired when you're
older, it's the mind too. And the soul. So you must think. And I think it
must be forbidden after a certain age to permit people to be parents in
any way, not only with IVF—with adoption, for example. I don't think
they should say, "I will take a child to have when I am old." It's one
way to think, but I think it's very wrong. You don't take the child for
you: you must for him, for the child.

In the newspapers, too, the only ethical aspect of IVF debated while I lived
in Athens concerned maternal age and ability: Was the fifty-eight-year-old
postmenopausal Athenian housewife who gave birth to a child conceived in
vitro from her husband's sperm and the ovum of a "close friend" too old to
become a proper mother? (cf. Neta and Sterghiou 1995). Many felt it was
not responsible of her to have a child she will be too old to play with, one
whom she will likely orphan before it reaches adulthood. Showing twenty-
five-year-old Eva a newspaper clipping, I asked for her opinion on this case
(*Athens News,* 18 Tuesday July 1995). She wanted first to get straight the
participants in the IVF, whose sperm and egg were involved. She stalled for
a few minutes, glancing through the article, before declaring, "Probably I
would say yes, why not?—with IVF. Probably if it was from sex I would
say no," she added, scrunching up her face in disgust at the thought of a
fifty-eight-year-old woman having sex. "To think of my mother [having
sex]? No." That the IVF took sex out of the reproductive equation helped
make the thought of late motherhood palatable for this young woman.
Eva's comments reminded me that marital sex between persons "after a
certain age" has constituted one of the sexual improprieties that women
have covered over by having abortions.

Frequently, too, Athenians pose this ethical question of IVF: Does it operate "with nature" or "against nature"? In other words—and not surprisingly—the ethical and social questions surrounding procreative technologies are similar to those surrounding contraceptive technologies: Is this a
proper way of realizing nature? Alternatively, is the "nature" realized
through assisted conception—including kin relations, gendered selves, and
a new child—going to be "proper," "normal"? I argue below that IVF is
adopted and institutionalized in Greece—far more readily than the IUD or
oral contraceptives—not only because it is consistent with a pronatal political sentiment but also because, imported as an "enabling technology," IVF

can be viewed as being consistent with a local understanding of realized nature. But as soon as IVF is normalized as being consistent with nature, this sets up the question of whether and when it might also be seen to go against nature. This query—with or against nature—retraces major points of cultural tension and lines of constructed difference explored throughout this book that concern both gender difference and a distinction between so-called modern and traditional mentalities.

In keeping with a Strathernian project, I am not out to argue whether fertility technologies are good or bad in any absolute sense, but instead find it interesting and instructive to explore "how we should think them and how they will think us" (1992b, 33). I address this question comparatively, juxtaposing as I go the Athenian case study with the literature on reproductive technologies, gender, and kinship in the United States and Britain. How people "think" and approach reproductive technologies is contingent on local metaphysics of procreation, meanings of maternity and paternity—and how these may or may not translate into mothering and fathering, economic and infrastructural constraints, and the political-economic currents through which this increasingly global practice is made known locally. To understand what people do with IVF in Greece, we must consider not only their understandings of nature itself but also ideas about the gendered realization of human potentialities.

As I reread *After Nature* in Greece, I thought about how the new ideal of achieved motherhood not only is underwritten by techniques of biomedicine but also is facilitated more pervasively by the ideological power of consumer choice—howsoever constrained this is in practice—to realize people's naturalized desires. How does consumerism, which after all figures so prominently in Athenian women's discussions of achieved motherhood and the making of children, match up with notions of realized nature? I began to look more carefully at commoditized maternal images in popular women's magazines; a survey of what I found regarding this kind of technology of motherhood trails my discussion of IVF. Consideration of assisted conception will lead us back finally, full-circle, to the question introduced at the beginning of this book: how and why do childless women like Phoebe and Niki claim that motherhood completes a woman?

ATHENIANS' USES OF IVF

Although IVF was not part of my original research proposal, I found myself fortuitously introduced to an established, private suburban IVF clinic not far from Pangrati. When the topic of infertility treatments came up during an interview with a social psychologist, my interlocutor, growing excited by our discussion, picked up the telephone to call an obstetrician friend of hers, Michalis Stamatis, who runs an IVF clinic, and scheduled an appointment for us for the next day.[3] I had written several papers in graduate school about contract pregnancy and IVF and was thrilled to interview members of the clinic staff, attend informational seminars given to prospective couples, and tour the laboratory. At a party thrown to celebrate the birth of five hundred babies conceived through the clinic, I distributed written questionnaires (which the head of the clinic's laboratory, Zoë, helped me edit) to fifty mothers and fathers who number among the clinic's success stories. Nine questionnaires were returned to me. Eventually, I visited and interviewed seven mothers and one father of children conceived as a result of doing IVF at the clinic. Some of these women have already made appearances in this book. I call the clinic the Ekso clinic after the Greek term for IVF: *eksosomatikí gonimopíisi,* literally, "out of body fertilization."[4] In everyday Greek, IVF is referred to simply as *eksosomatikí.* While I did hear people speak of the process as "artificial fertilization" *(techniti gonimopíisi),* I never heard a Greek translation of the phrase *assisted conception,* which has come to be the preferred term among Anglophone scholars and reproductive rights activists (cf. Franklin 1997; Kahn 2000) so as to avoid drawing an explicit contrast between the "artificiality" of IVF and an implicitly "natural" heterosexual method. In my discussion of IVF in Athens, therefore, I use the phrase *external fertilization,* which better captures the Greek phrasing and meaning.

Given the external and internalized pressures on Greek couples to "complete" a marriage by "making children" *(kánoun pedhiá),* it is not surprising that couples who encounter physiological difficulty in so doing seek a medical solution. IVF may be a technological import to Greece, but today Greek women are accustomed to medicalized birth (Arnold 1985; Lefkarites 1992) and prenatal care (Georges 1996b), and they realize that Greek physicians have been at the forefront of gynecological research (a statue of Dr. George Papanikolau, who introduced the Pap test, stands in the public square of his natal village; his likeness graces the new ten thousand drachma note). Women who pursue IVF cite the same reasons for wanting a child as do others: responses to my questionnaire included such ideological citations as "It's not a marriage without children" and "Basically our life was asking for it—and my completion as a woman—I wanted to become a MOTHER. To feel the creation inside me." In other words, Athenian women on a "quest for conception" seem more to focus on fulfilling their marriages and transforming themselves into mothers than on antici-pating the presence of a child (see also Inhorn 1994).

With Nature: The Technological Making of Mothers and Children

The women I met who had successfully used IVF to become mothers de-scribed more than their desire to mother as being "natural"; they also de-scribed the actual procedures of IVF, the process of external fertilization, as "a natural, normal way of reproduction," and a "proper" one at that. As the biologist Zoë put it to prospective and first-time patients in one of her in-formational seminars, "There's nothing strange [*parákseno*] about it." Most emphatically, the naturalness of IVF in Athens is not merely an ex-tension of the naturalness of a woman's desire to mother and a man's de-sire to father (although this is part of the picture). IVF is regarded as natu-ral and normal because it is viewed through the ethic of well-being and seen as consistent with both an ethic of choice and an ethic of service. Women can and do depict themselves as morally responsible for maintain-ing or treating their bodies in ways that facilitate *teknopiía*, overcome their childlessness, and complete the family form and their own womanly na-ture. These women's use of IVF demonstrates how technology and culture do not stand apart from nature. By choosing to pursue IVF, a medical cor-rective, women may (if successful) fulfill their expected role as mothers and, at the same time, service their husband's paternity and their family's expectations for another generation. In this way IVF works *with*, not after, a socially realized nature.

My observations at Ekso clinic indicate that staff present the concept of IVF to childless Athenian couples in much the same manner as successful parents talk about the procedure: it is a means to an end. One of Dr. Michalis Stamatis's patients informed me that, during a network television appearance, the doctor insisted "that every woman wants a child, and so everything else is secondary." As is often the case with abortion, Athenians depict IVF as an unfortunate necessity that some women encounter in their morally appropriate efforts to create a proper family (one female re-spondent to my questionnaire called *eksosomatikí éna anangéo kakó*, a "necessary evil"). Angeliki told me that when she tells people about IVF,

> I explain to them that it's a procedure, that the woman does some
> preparation of the organism so that she has many ova, that the spouse
> gives the sperm, fertilization happens in a tube [*sic*], and then, after cell
> division happens, they give you the implantation. What they put in
> you is an embryo. This is what I tell them. And then you wait and see

what happens—which ones will grab on [to the uterine lining] and which will leave. They say "Bravo."

Thirty-five-year-old Ariadne asserted similarly that she and her husband "accepted it very easily, as all the doors had closed. We had to do something to have a child." Soula, a thirty-nine-year-old bank clerk who birthed her child the year before I met her, said this about doing IVF: "From the moment a couple is faced with such a problem, they try to find a solution to their problem. Isn't that how it is? I believe this is a very good solution, very efficient." After she and her husband had spent several years trying to conceive, and after they had seen innumerable doctors who could find nothing "wrong" with either of them, a laparoscopy finally revealed endometriosis. Soon after, Soula had her fallopian tubes tied. Stamatis was the physician who performed the laparoscopy, and he suggested IVF to Soula and her husband as a treatment option. "I said this thing must be done," Soula told me. "I decided it, and I had no problems with it." Using rhetoric that sounds remarkably similar to many abortion narratives, Soula, Ariadne, and Angeliki all sought a medical cure for their social problem.

Childlessness, let us be clear, is a social condition (Inhorn 1996; Becker 2000), one that can become a social problem when notions of gender proficiency and kin relationships are linked through family-laden religious imagery, kin-based means of transmitting wealth and conferring social status, and project-oriented desires to produce quality children. Infertility—which also gains meaning in relation to ideologies of gender, kinship, and procreation—is, however, frequently represented as a medical problem. When infertility is pathologized, couples are able to seek (with no guarantee of success) a medical cure for their social problem of childlessness. This was evidenced in Athens when I asked about health insurance; even people who had no immediate experience with infertility told me "of course" IVF should be covered because, as one woman who had been through it said, "one turns to IVF because one has a *páthisi*," an illness. The government agrees. One of the state's pronatal measures is to offer partial health insurance coverage for "the expenses of contemporary fertility methods to couples who face serious problems of sterility" (Parliament of Greece 1993, 38).[5]

At first glance, the pathologization of infertility—viewing it not only as a medical condition but as a medical illness—reveals that the social problem of childlessness is folded into nature. This kind of naturalization of a social problem—turning childlessness into a medical condition—is what Sarah Franklin (1997) and others argue has occurred with IVF practice in Britain and the United States. But more is going on in the Athenian case.

In a context where having children realizes people's nature as men and women, seeking a cure for the apparent cause of childlessness—namely, infertility—can be incorporated into the natural order of things. I asked women who had nothing to do personally with IVF to comment on it. Most agreed with Maro, who said, "In the advancement of science, *eksosomatikí* is a positive step for women." Her sister, Niki, who spoke as a married and unhappily childless woman (not owing to fertility problems but because she and her husband cannot afford to raise a child in the manner they deem appropriate), said, "I don't think that any ethical issue enters into [IVF], because the Greek society loves the child. It wants there to be a child in the family." One woman who had successfully used IVF responded to my survey query "For what reasons did you want to have a child?" by asking back, "Who doesn't want a child?" Because this desire is not only taken for granted but also is viewed as *moral*, any recourse to science or technology in the aid of fulfilling that desire is not merely justified, it is deemed natural. In the Greek case, the naturalization called on to explain IVF does not signal inevitability, but allows for (limited) human intervention in nature if morally justifiable. To rephrase this in terms of an earlier argument, when Greeks invoke nature—be it organismic, characterological, or divine—they are not engaging in the fatalism of which early Anglo-American ethnographers accused them. Accusations of fatalism entail the ethnographers' imposition of their own version of fixed nature.

Athenians are in the first instance able to incorporate external fertilization into an understanding of "natural" and "proper" motherhood because, as I have discussed, it is gestation and birth, rather than conception, that is both definitive and emblematic of true motherhood. As Phoebe said to me:

> I believe that there's no problem created with *eksosomatikí* because it's clearly a technical matter. That is, from the moment that a life is started up, you feel it in your body; and you have this life inside your belly for nine months and you have the child—there is no ethical problem, or any other problem. It's simply a technical matter that helps two people to feel this joy of life. To have a child.

Owing to the significance of birth for creating mothers, Greek kinship ideology suggests that a child who enters a family via external fertilization does so more naturally than, say, a child adopted into one. For women, childbirth is both what demonstrates IVF's validity in making them real and proper mothers and what is problematically displaced by adoption. Most of the couples I met through the Ekso clinic had considered adoption, and a few had initiated the bureaucratic process before turning to IVF, but

IVF is not so much an alternative to adoption as an alternative to remaining childless in Greece. This is true in part because so few Greek women give infants up for adoption,[6] but also because the "blood" that establishes maternity is conferred through gestation and shed painfully through childbirth. Lela, who had clearly thought carefully about the possibility of adopting, said to me:

> At work they all knew that I got pregnant by this method—which is a method that helps people who have such a problem. If it did not exist, then I would have been in an unpleasant situation—not to have [a child] at all, or to go and adopt, which I can't accept. Not that I would not love the other [adopted] child—in the name of God, from the moment that you raise it, it's more what you have done [than where it came from]—but I just could not accept it. If you are older and have no more margin of time, then maybe you can accept an adoption.

In this regard, it is significant that gestational surrogacy has been practiced in Greece only a handful of times and, at the time of my research, within extant families; that is, a mother might gestate and birth on behalf of her daughter, in a sense literalizing the Greek saying that "the grandmother is twice a mother."[7] When women's recourse to external fertilization is accepted as a form of working "with nature," women are seen to be properly making themselves into mothers.

With *eksosomatikí*, Greek women depict themselves as taking charge of a natural process. Procreation results, when it does, from the bodily regimen that a woman elects to undergo—the series of injections to hyperstimulate ovulation and produce multiple ova, the taking of her temperature, and minor surgical procedures. Women told me that one of the features they liked best about IVF, as now practiced in Athens, was that it is a women-centered event. At the clinic, nearly everyone I encountered was a woman: the smiling receptionist, the lab technicians, two out of three biologists, and the clients (only occasionally accompanied by husbands) attending informational seminars and awaiting their turn in the operating room. It is common in the British and American literature on reproductive technologies to read that IVF is something to which women "submit" (Pfeffer 1993; Arditti, Klein, and Minden 1984; Spallone 1989; but see Becker 2000). In Athens people talk about it as something women "do"—and to which husbands agree.

These women successfully incorporate IVF into an ethic of maternal sacrifice and see it as an opportunity to experience even more fully—and get even more credit for—procreation and birth. Angeliki, who works for the electricity board, was thirty-five when she birthed her daughter, now four and a half. "When I chat with women," she told me, "and tell them I had Ioanna with *eksosomatikí* and now I'm trying to have a second child, again with *eksosomatikí*, they think I'm a heroine. Why? Because there's some procedure. They tell me, 'Hail to your courage.' 'Bravo that you've decided it.'" In other words, precisely because Angeliki went to such lengths become a mother, onlookers are impressed by the tenacity of her maternal desire (see also Franklin 1997). "It's one thing to make love and get pregnant," she explained, "and another thing to want to have a child, to enter into a procedure and have a baby like that. You have to want it a lot." According to some women I met, their commitment to having a child using IVF makes them "better" mothers, especially when others around them seem to have children merely because it is expected of them. Not only has their maternal desire been proven beyond a shadow of a doubt, the efforts they make to reach the goal of motherhood are incorporated into the long-standing ideology of maternal suffering. The pain of repeated injections and the ordeal of going under general anesthesia for ova retrieval augment the desired pain of childbirth.

One thirty-five-year-old woman wrote on the questionnaire she returned to me, "For me, I just wanted to become a Mother, to birth, *to be pained,* and to bring into the world a living creature who will fill our home with joy, happiness, love" (emphasis added). For Litsa, a bank teller married to a plumber, the most difficult pill to swallow in her years of battling the infertility caused (she believes) by an early abortion came after having finally become pregnant with IVF: she was told she had to have a cesarean section. She resents being denied the crucial experience of childbirth, and fears it will have repercussions on her mothering:

> It means something to me that I couldn't learn how I'd control myself
> the hour that the child comes out, not for the pain—what feeling could
> I have, what repercussions—can there be no repercussion for the child?
> I thought of it [childbirth by cesarean section] like an operation after all
> that I had done. I went in and okay, I came out with a child—not that
> the child wasn't my own—but I wanted to feel that specific [she mumbles something inaudible]. It didn't happen. It doesn't matter.

In keeping with a notion of achieved motherhood, every mother I met who did IVF intended to tell her children an IVF origin story. Angeliki showed me an archive she kept for her son for when he was older, containing a video tape recording of an interview Dr. Stamatis gave on television, various examination results, and fetal sonograms.

I also wish to contrast this sense of "taking charge of nature" with a depiction common in the United States and Britain that the naturalness of IVF comes from "just helping nature to do what it would have done anyway" (Franklin 1997, 103). Most Athenian women I spoke with who had done IVF described it as an intervention to correct damage that had been done to them *by* nature. By "nature" they referred to injury of their internal organism, as with Soula's ectopic pregnancies, or perhaps to metaphysical forces that denied them easy conception. Nature could wrong a woman regardless of whether infertility problems were diagnosed in her or her husband—either way a woman suffers, pointing to an indeterminacy between infertility and childlessness. Litsa's heartbreaking maternal success story indicates that even human error can count as "natural damage" that one can, following an ethic of well-being, appropriately try to repair. Unable to become pregnant after having had an abortion in her youth ("before we knew better"), Litsa suffered in her childless marriage. Following years of being told there was nothing to be done for her infertility, an Italian doctor gave her hope that she might be able to conceive if she agreed to surgery on her fallopian tubes. Within six months of that, she had an ectopic pregnancy, and her one functioning fallopian tube was removed. A couple more years passed before she met Stamatis, who had just established his IVF clinic. In 1987, she became the first woman at Ekso to become a mother. "I haven't hidden from anyone that the child is with *eksosomatikí*," she told me. "I didn't consider it—and I don't consider it—shameful what I did. I consider it my honor. I did something on my own that nature denied me—back when I had the abortion, by my own error or by the doctor's, I don't know what. I tried to redress something that I know nature damaged. I don't feel badly about this."

When a Greek woman cannot "do" conception inside her body and takes it into her own hands, so to speak, she tries to do it *outside* her body, with *eksosomatikí*. It always startled me when I telephoned the Ekso clinic and the receptionist would inevitably answer in a pleasant voice, "*Eksosomatikí?*" (literally, "Out of body?"). Significantly, this word designates the procedure as happening outside a woman's body, rather than stressing its "technological dimension," which Franklin suggests is the case with the acronym IVF (1997, 105). Extending Marlene Arnold's and Eugenia Georges's analyses of the "inside/outside distinction" that Greeks apply to health maintenance (1985 and 1996a, respectively), I suggest that performing fertilization outside the body, in a petri dish, importantly contributes to the "naturalness" of the procedure. "For both the social and the physical body," writes Georges (513), "the 'foreign,' with its disruptive potential, is usually suspect, potentially polluting and injurious to well-being. Maintaining health, then, involves upholding the integrity of bodily boundaries, with the orifices representing sites of special vulnerability." She quotes one woman explaining that to use an IUD would be "doing something not entirely natural. I've introduced something inside me. I do damage to nature, to my organism" (513). Just as withdrawal is seen as a more natural contraceptive than the IUD or pills because it operates outside a woman's body, IVF poses no threat to the integrity of a woman's inside—specifically to her womb, which is crucial for the validating process of gestation to occur. The phrase *eksosomatikí gonimopíisi* similarly makes explicit the fact that what happens outside (with assistance) is fertilization; pregnancy is the same as always. In establishing maternity, after all, fertilization is not at issue in Greece. Gestation and birth are the natural components of maternity. The movement of a "natural process" (fertilization) to the outside of a woman's body supports my contention that nature is naturally and appropriately realized through human action.

How, specifically, Athenians approach the procedures of IVF further contributes to their sense that IVF is a natural thing that helps women realize their gendered natures. Zoë described Greek patients as being "completely different" from clients she has worked with in the United States and England, arguing that indeed Greeks who pursue IVF act more like patients than clients.[8] "Greeks," she explained, never "ask things like, 'Tell me the percentage of my chances for getting an ectopic out of so many tries,'" as they do in the United States.[9] Greeks want to be told what to do and when, but "some people don't want to know any details; they'll just worry the more they know." Several women I met downplayed the strenuousness of the procedures. Angeliki, who when I met her was in the midst of superovulating for her first attempt at a second pregnancy, described to me the exhaustion and depression of seeking fertility treatment from gynecologists before learning about IVF—"after going through those four years, *eksosomatikí* was a game. I had a better experience with the *eksosomatikí*, the injections, than waiting to go to the doctor for him to see you, come again in two days to see the sperm, to think about this or that." Rather than process the technical details and weigh their statistical odds, Zoë continued, "in Greece patients want to be fathered or mothered a lot . . . , they want to call you all the time. If they could call you at home, they would for things like, 'Oh my God I coughed today; is this bad for the IVF?'" Zoë and the other biologists frequently found themselves performing ad hoc marriage counseling. For a time, a psychologist friend of theirs (conducting doctoral research on the psychological effects of IVF on mother-infant bonding) informally counseled patients at the clinic. In a later interview, I asked this psychologist what the women most wanted to talk with her about. "First of all they cried," she told me. "I mean, we had to spend about half an hour for them to cry, before they talked, which means that the tension had piled up that much."

In the informational seminars she gives to interested women and couples, Zoë does not warn that the hormonal treatment may manifest emotional effects, an omission first brought to my attention by a Greek-American friend who had been through two unsuccessful IVF cycles at Ekso clinic. (Comparing the emotional effects that many women in the United States feel with the pill, which suppresses ovulation, she speculated that many women undergoing IVF must be emotionally affected by these hormones, which promote superovulation—"It's like getting your period tenfold!") In response to my query about this after sitting in on one of her informational seminars, Zoë replied, "Usually they just complain about bloating, headaches, weight gain; not any emotional effect." The emotional aspect of pursuing IVF, which in the United States or Britain is often pathologized as a hormonally induced emotional side effect, is here normalized, even naturalized, in quite a different way—as a social performance regarded as a reasonable response to stress. Alternatively, it is seen as an aspect of cultural tradition, according to which social relations are frequently organized as kinds of kin relations (in this case, the medical setting offers paternalistic as well as scientific support). What medical science in Euro-American settings sidelines as psychological side effects (Cussins 1998, 67) centrally figure in Athenian women's success stories. Everyone I interviewed who had been through the clinic praised Zoë and the other staff for their warmth and emotional support. "Above and beyond their science, they are very positive as people to help you overcome your problem," one of them commented. When Ariadne first met Stamatis, "He looked me in the eyes and said, 'You are going to have a child.' And so I did. For me the human [element] plays a role—that they remember you by your first name, the fact that they will call and ask how you're doing. This is why I think they are so successful, because they are humans."

Zoë and Dr. Stamatis have accepted the honor and obligation of godparenting many of the children born to their patients. In this way, the medical technology of IVF is incorporated into the natural and ethical process of reproduction through the framework of spiritual kinship *(koumbariá)*. Traditionally, the godparents of a couple's firstborn child should be already in a *koumbáros* relationship with that couple as their wedding sponsors. When Zoë and Stamatis godparent their patients' children, they not only become lifelong participants in the coming-into-being (procreatively and, later, socially) of these children but also contribute to the valid constitution of couples' marriages by helping them complete the family form. *Koumbariá* is a spiritual kinship constituted in Schneiderian terms (1968) through substance (the oil with which the infant is anointed in baptism) and code of conduct (sponsorship of both the parents' marriage and the upbringing of the child). The relationships obtaining between *koumbariá* in these cases is perhaps especially intense because Zoë and Stamatis also "sponsor" the shared substance of "blood" that connects the generations.

The currency of spiritual kinship in this instance alerts us that the nature into which IVF is incorporated in Greece encompasses not only biology but also the supernatural forces of the divine. Again, IVF here is not so much about reproducing and reemphasizing biological parenthood per se (Becker 2000) but more about transforming women and men into parents. Athenians further invest *eksosomatikí* with naturalness by crediting God with their reproductive success. In response to my query asking, "Do you think you will try for an additional child?," a thirty-eight-year-old physiotherapist wrote on her questionnaire, "I don't think anything. I believe that a lot of things are a matter of chance, and I thank God for the child that he gave me." Another questionnaire, returned by a woman who tried for a year to get pregnant before she married (at age forty) and for four months after marriage before turning to IVF, wrote, "For me, motherhood is a gift of God."

The Orthodox Church has not come out with any official pronouncement against IVF; this can be read in a couple of ways. First, the church celebrates motherhood more than conception—Mary is far more frequently hailed as the Bearer of Christ (Theotokos) than as the Virgin—and this, as I have discussed, represents an important point of theological and cultural difference from Catholicism.[10] In our interview, Ariadne, who owned that she "was never very religious" before trying to become pregnant, narrated to me the following account:

> One day we happened to be on the island of Chios, and we visited a monastery where you can see the only icon of the Panayía not holding Christ in her arms. This icon carries many offerings for children. When I went to venerate this icon, it touched me very strongly. This was the only time that I kneeled and prayed with passion and said that, if I had a child and it were a boy, I would name it Panayiotis—after the Panayía—or Nicholas, after my father, who is a saint in his own way, and if it were a girl, Maria. I came back to Athens, did an IVF, and got pregnant. The day that the test came back positive was the name day of Aghios Nectarios, so I decided to have the child baptized in the church

of Aghios Nectarios. I birthed; then, when the day of the christening came and I went to church, I saw the font between two icons, those of the Panayía and of Aghios Nicholas—what a coincidence, as I was naming him Panayiotis Nicholas. The baptism took place, and then one day I was talking to a friend of mine who follows the church very closely, and she told me that the child was given to me by Aghios Nectarios. She said that he became a monk at Chios, and that that icon of the Panayía was his most beloved, and he had written many letters and Aghios Nicholas was his favorite saint, for whom he built a church in Alexandria. She told me that when I prayed in church he heard me. So I believe that it really did help me. I was helped by my faith. To some people, it might seem strange, they might laugh at me—but it never existed for me before either.

Such narratives evoke an understanding of procreative agency consistent with an ethic of service, which sees humans as undertaking some kind of social activity (be it heterosexual relations or IVF), after which, recalling Nadia's phrasing, "if God wants, He gives you a child."

Theological distinction between Orthodoxy and Catholicism on the matter of IVF also returns us the theological doctrine of *ikonomía*, which can be applied to IVF as it is to abortion: since "God wants there to be a child in the family," the end—completing a marriage—can be seen as justifying the (nonstandard) means of reaching that end.[11] That IVF and abortion can be brought together in a coherent narrative of contingent maternal responsibility emerged in my conversation with Varvara, a forty-year-old mother living in an affluent suburb. When I asked whether she would like to have another child, she replied in terms that were quite familiar: "I would like to, but practically, for us it's not easy. It is very difficult, and not just the economics." But she went on to tell the following story. Shortly after the birth of her daughter, Pani (conceived via IVF), she missed her period. At first she assumed this was due to the hormone treatment she had had, but indeed she was pregnant. The pregnancy ended in miscarriage, but a few years later she found herself again pregnant, without doing IVF. "Unbelievable," I commented. "Unbelievable," Varvara nodded. "But the more unbelievable thing is that I had an interruption [abortion]." She had stopped working when Pani was born (previously she had held two part-time jobs, as a bank clerk and doctor's office receptionist), and her husband's shop was doing poorly. Beyond their financial troubles she had some health problems (which she chose not to detail, although she assured me she was now "fine"): how could they have had another child? "And as [her husband] says—and he's right—at forty-one it's a different age to have a child." She was thirty-six when she had Pani. Her voice sounded matter-of-fact, but sad. If she were to become pregnant again, she would not have the "interruption." She repeated this at least twice.

By interweaving the moral virtues available to them—service, suffering, behind-the-scenes agency, personal choice, and caring for one's physical well-being—women in Greece have made IVF a natural means of reproduction. Although many of the women who birthed with the aid of IVF thanked God for the "gift" of a child, they formulated the prayers which God had answered in terms of the ethic of choice as well as that of service. Litsa described her recourse to IVF as a conscious rejection of the "motherhood as destiny" model:

> I felt a very great void without the child; I couldn't get over it. I couldn't accept my "fate," as they said, and say, "That's it. Finished" *[telíose]*. Psychologically I was in very bad shape. How to explain this? I had this need. Other people said to me, "It doesn't matter," "What's wrong?" [and] "Lots of couples don't have any kids." I wasn't able to process that this could happen to me. God, power, science—I don't know to what [to direct] my spite. I'll throw up my hands [and give up] only when they tell me—not one doctor, I don't know how many I'll endure, as many as I can to pay for [having had an abortion] again, inside me. I had the problem; I wouldn't say, "It doesn't matter."

Similarly, Ariadne emphasized that "we wanted the child; it wasn't luck. Patience and persistence bring results." An ethic of service provides direction for pursuing the end of motherhood by any means necessary; an ethic of choice gives women a vocabulary to articulate the strength of their desires for maternal experiences; an ethic of well-being offers women a chance to "correct," by bypassing, damage that "nature" has done to them—to their bodies, their sense of self, their social lives. Even when employing the most modern of technologies that promise women increased control over their ability to make babies, and even under the most justifiable of moral conditions, Athenian women often express a limited, even humble sense of reproductive agency whose most positive aspects are not without ambivalence. If nature both causes and permits women to pursue external fertilization, nature can yet be blamed if the IVF fails to lead women to the desired and virtuous goal of motherhood.

Gay Becker says about middle-class America that "reproductive technologies reinforce the cultural ideology of biological parenthood, diverting people from their primary goal to become parents" (2000, 64). In Athens, what is currently reinforced by IVF is the social and cultural significance of motherhood, as well as the increasing importance of demonstrating control over one's biological fertility (rather than sexuality) for feminine gender proficiency. This is not to say that ideologies of motherhood and maternity are immune to change. It could be that Greek women may, in the future, be able to choose to make paternity extraneous to their plans to mother. As Litsa argued,

> When someone wants something desperately, they will find a way of achieving it. Every woman should be allowed to have a child. Let's say a woman is divorced, works, and does not want to remarry at the age of forty, but she wants to fulfill her life's ambition, every woman's life ambition. Such a law should be passed to allow this. There are today many mothers who bring up their children alone. Now, I'm not saying they have no problems, but nothing so serious that it can't be over-come. Let's say that I have a child with IVF and then I divorce—is my doctor responsible? Of course not. I never had to sign anything that said I will never divorce.

At present, and this is significant, fertility technologies are available in Greece to a socially limited extent. The particular clinic I visited is not alone in accepting as patients only heterosexual and, with few exceptions, married couples. Same-sex partners have not organized to seek parenting rights in Greece. In addition, contract surrogacy, where a childless couple pays a woman to gestate and birth a child on their behalf using either al-ternative insemination or IVF techniques (see Ragoné 1994, 2000) has only begun to be practiced, covertly, in parts of Greece.[12] At the time of this writing, no legislation had been passed to govern the commoditized use of reproductive technologies.

It will be interesting to see whether Greeks will follow the example of Britons and Americans in parceling out component parts of procreation into marketable skills and contractual labor relations. Consistent with the low overall percentage of single-parent families during the 1990s (just 5 percent nationwide, including children raised by widows), independent sperm banks in Athens during the time of my research barred single women from purchasing donor sperm for home use via turkey baster. But as Litsa's words attest, and as presented throughout this book, IVF in Greece is adopted into a sex, gender, and kinship system that treats procre-ation and child raising as events that are more centrally feminine than masculine. Considering the extent to which women aspire to become mothers, and given increasing divorce rates and postponement of marriage, I would not be surprised to see single women (regardless of sexual preference) seek single-parenting through assisted conception in Athens, as is becoming relatively common, for instance, in Israel (see Kahn 2000).

Against Nature? Confronting Technological Anxiety

Even when Athenians frame their own use of external fertilization as a natural way of reproducing and becoming parents, they are well aware that others may see things differently. Ariadne, who learned about IVF with her husband only while researching infertility treatments, mentioned during our interview that a morning television program (airing after an earlier Ekso party celebrating the birth of two hundred babies) had interviewed women on the streets of Athens, asking whether they would do IVF. Seemingly contradicting the above discussion, "most said, 'No, because I can't go against nature' *[dhen boró na páo enántia stin físi]*. They were young, inexperienced," Ariadne explained. Her husband, Yiannis, who participated in this interview, elaborated: "When you don't have a problem, things look rosy. When you develop the problem, from then on it's on your mind and you think about it. And you say, 'I accept it,' one way or another." Angeliki made a similar argument, explaining that when a friend of hers "told me 'I would never do [IVF] myself,' I said to her, 'You have two kids and you don't need to do it.' When you don't have any [infertility] problem you don't know whether you would do it." Nevertheless, I was told that "misunderstandings" about what external fertilization actually entails are legion among people who do not themselves face the problem of infertility, and that in negotiating these misunderstandings, women and men who pursue IVF confront head-on the overlapping mentalities and ethics that texture Greek modernity. Specifically, IVF brings into focus the conflicts women face when an ethic of service (directed at obscuring morally ambiguous acts from public scrutiny and maintaining social cohesion) and an ethic of choice (encouraging individuals to pursue their inner desires and personal goals) suggest divergent paths for being virtuous and gender proficient.

The literature on reproductive technologies is full of cautionary tales about choice. Scholars and activists warn that the choice to pursue a child via IVF may become for childless (and married) women a mandate, and that soon the choice will be *not* to pursue every technological possibility regardless of financial or emotional cost (Rothman 1984; Strathern 1992b; Raymond 1993; Franklin 1997; Becker 2000). The motherhood mandate is a valid concern in the Greek context, too. Varvara told me that, before she had a child (via IVF), she felt both "different" and left out by "the others"—specifically women with children—who were, she owned, her "number one problem": "I wanted to have a baby, of course, but I also felt alone." Dina, who knew about IVF from television, commented with only mild interest, "*Eksosomatikí* shows the need that women have to make children." At the risk of repeating myself, the term *choice* can be a misnomer when applied to the decision of women and men to pursue infertility treatment as a means of establishing "normal" adult identities and family relationships (Becker 2000; Inhorn 2000). Perhaps the most significant choice Athenian couples confront comes after having decided on the IVF route: will they be open with family and friends about this, or will they keep it hidden?

Most people I spoke to were open with others about doing IVF, and, as we have seen, they have been congratulated for their courage and strength of commitment. Of course, this is a self-selected group who chose to be interviewed about it. A significant number of Athenians who turn to IVF, I was told by both Zoë and the psychologist who works with IVF-mothers, opt not to tell a soul, or they tell only a very small number of close friends. Varvara confided to me that her greatest fear about the entire procedure was that her mother would find out. A friend of a friend who had done IVF told her mother, who "couldn't accept it. She is afraid, perhaps, how the baby will be." Soula, who invited me into her home to speak with her about IVF, warned me the moment I settled in my chair that only the staff at the clinic, her husband, and now I knew about this. She explained her silence as an outcome in part of simply being too exhausted to take on the burden of having to explain the technicalities to skeptical ears: "I did not want any negative influence from outside. My husband and I didn't have any problems with it, but I don't think the Greek society is mature enough for some things, and they don't understand."

As they do when evaluating attitudes toward *teknopiía* (the making or having of children) more generally, urban Greeks frequently deploy the question of maturity to distinguish and evaluate urban and rural, younger and older people's understanding of external fertilization. One thing "they" often "fail" to understand, according to those who pursue IVF, is a scientific explanation of procreation. Athenians told me of parents and older relatives who live in villages: they do not know the word *ovum* and thus cannot be expected to comprehend the process of externally fertilizing one in a petri dish, after which point the embryo can be returned to a woman's uterus for "normal" gestation. As Varvara suggested, such persons may assume that "an *eksosomatikí* child" will be somehow different. It must be acknowledged that disability is stigmatized severely in Greece. The residents of Greek orphanages sadly attest to the fact that, here, unwanted babies are primarily physically and mentally abnormal babies.

Even Eva, before weighing in on what she thought of the fifty-eight-year-old woman who birthed a child after using IVF, first asked me whether the baby was healthy, signaling some kind of anxiety about biology (perhaps in reference again to an inside/outside model of bodily health, but this time from the subject-position of the infant, rather than the mother). Thus, "real" motherhood is predicated on producing a "normal" child—an important topic that Gail Landsman (2000) has discussed in the context of the United States.

Lacking an understanding of female gametes, traditional Greek procreation theories trace bilateral inheritance through the shared substance of "blood" *(syngénia eksématos)* (du Boulay 1984; Koumantou 1985; Iossifides 1991). But if blood, a biologizable idiom of relatedness (Schneider 1968), normatively constitutes Greek kinship and is the first component of establishing a child's normalcy,[13] the social practice of parenting fundamentally contributes to the development of a child's identity, the shaping of his or her individual nature. As previously noted of nationalist rhetoric, the blood of kinship is often said to contain the "Greek spirit" evocative of ancient cultural and philosophical achievements. Dina, speaking as a grandmother and former schoolteacher, expressed this to me: "A child's character is created by the way you bring it up, but also by what comes from inside from its parents. If it comes from alcoholic parents, say, this creates problems for the child. It will not just depend on the way that you bring it up." Wariness of institutionalized adoption is augmented by a belief, which Dina intimated existed, that when blood bonds are questionable you do not know what you are getting.

While descent is traced bilaterally, two sorts of "blood" commingle in the developing fetus. In addition to the lineal descent of hereditary genetic-like substance transmitted through paternal and maternal blood, blood also flows laterally through the umbilical cord from gestating mother to fetus ("the same blood flows through both" mother and fetus). This gestational, rather than generative, blood contributes to the uniqueness, and special strength, of maternal relationships. Both forms of blood are significant in that they entail *social* repercussions.

External fertilization is most dramatically misunderstood, then, as external *gestation*. Does blood still flow between a woman and the *emvrío?* This is the most threatening fear of unnaturalness that Varvara and Soula worried others might have about IVF. Ariadne's husband, Yiannis, owned, "I was a little guarded myself. Not that I was ashamed to say it, but because someone else might not know what IVF meant—because the term 'test-tube baby' [*to pedhí tou solína;* literally, baby of the tube] is widespread."

"They hear 'test-tube baby,' " Ariadne interjected, "and believe that the child grew inside a tube. That is, we're talking about primitive *[pro-tóghona]* things." A baby that "grew inside a tube" clearly would not benefit from the maternal blood of gestation—and the mother would not benefit from the bond this creates with her child.

And yet, Ariadne takes a strategy opposite of Soula's, telling everyone that she used IVF, but emphasizing, "I don't let them misunderstand me":

> I haven't hidden it from anyone. I have even told Yiannis's parents, and they live in the countryside. They are elderly, educated, but completely different. I have explained everything to them. We can't expect an eighty- to eighty-five-year-old woman in the countryside to know these things. She has lived all her life in the fields, she has had six children— and I told her. She told me not to tell anyone that I did it with *eksoso-matikí*. But I told her that it makes me even prouder than otherwise because I struggled to do it; and I feel prouder because I managed to have a child despite all these problems. I tell her she should not be ashamed that her grandchild is by *eksosomatikí*. It is a bit difficult for her to understand, but I believe she has. I haven't given anyone the room to miscomprehend it. Everywhere I pose it as a natural thing, as it is.

Ariadne's husband added:

> She tells everyone that this child is by *eksosomatikí*. They say, "Bravo." They all give their best wishes. The fundamental thing is to not be ashamed of what you have done. My wife never had this problem. She would go to try on a maternity dress and would say, "I'm pregnant by *eksosomatikí!*"

Greek women such as Ariadne who go public with IVF frequently figure themselves as missionaries of modern science and set out to inform and help others who suffer childlessness. Many happily donate ova (most donor ova used at this clinic are the unneeded ova of others doing IVF). With Ariadne's consent, doctors have given her telephone number to many women seeking infertility treatment. "I have sent complete strangers to Stamatis," she boasted.

Ariadne seems to view IVF similarly to how it is presented and accepted in the United States and Britain: as a medical means to bypass or surmount fertility problems in order to "cure" childlessness. It does not "fix" abnormal sperm or "mend" damaged fallopian tubes and thus does not cure infertility (Strathern 1992b, 37). Taking into account the multiple ethical systems at play in urban Greece, however, complicates this seemingly straightforward analysis. Couples such as Soula and her husband who choose to hide IVF may—provided they meet with success—for all intents and purposes "cure" their infertility as well as their childlessness. So far as "the others" were concerned, their prayers were answered and Soula birthed the child everyone awaited. If appearances suggest that pregnancy occurred on its own—that is, without technical assistance—infertility has been obscured rather than bypassed. Infertility no longer exists, in the sense of having social relevance. Because in Greece fertility is by nature socially realized, arguably Soula used IVF to expand her biological fertility, rather than surmount her biological infertility. In contrast to the Euro-American cases documented by Sarah Franklin and others—in which assisted conception, when favored, is seen as "giving nature a helping hand" (assuming an a priori nature that knows what it wants) or as a typical and natural use of technology by culture-bearing humans—in Greece, as I have argued, it is natural to help direct nature: external fertilization is not the same as assisted conception. Women view IVF as a technology of motherhood whether they approach it as a means to obscure or erase or to bypass infertility, but in either case it contributes in distinct ways to gender proficiency. The difference comes down, in part, to how Athenians deploy ethical models of tradition and modernity.

When Athenians, like Ariadne, share proudly with others the technical procedures they have followed to achieve parenthood, they are applying a modern technology taking what they view as a contemporary ethical stance (consistent with both the ethic of choice and the ethic of well-being), one that evaluates a particular action in the particular context of individual interest and intent. Here, women use IVF as a technology of motherhood in the sense that it opens up a new means of mastering their fertility and crafting themselves as mothers. When people like Soula use a modern technology but hide it from others, they are applying it within an avowedly (in their evaluation) more traditional ethic of service rooted in proximate village life, holding that it is morally appropriate to keep hidden an act (such as abortion or IVF) that might call public attention to such family matters as sexual activity (or lack of it). The ethical impulse to hide a potentially controversial means to an unquestionably appropriate end keeps the act (means) itself from being subject to moral evaluation: If you do not talk about it, it did not happen. When women use IVF as a technology of motherhood in this way, they implicitly draw on a final set of meanings contained in the word *téchni:* artifice, ruse, subterfuge, wile. The behind-the-scenes use of IVF consistent with an ethic of service is also consistent with the stereotypical understanding that women are by nature cunning. Athenian women use IVF, therefore, in ways that *both* challenge and reinforce dominant ideologies of kinship and gender.

If Athenian couples can choose either option—can openly assume an ethic of choice and share with others their strategy of external fertilization, or can negotiate this with an ethic of service in allowing others to assume that infertility was never a problem—then these entail different kinds of moral ambiguity and experiences. Couples such as Ariadne and Yiannis who use IVF within a modern ethic—in the open where they can receive extra praise and emotional support—seem more satisfied and settled with the experience. In this vein, Lela commented that I was likely not to have difficulty finding women willing to talk with me about IVF, because

> by talking you solve a lot of your problems. By telling you and a couple of others, to get it out from inside me, it's a great help. I saw this in my own situation, although I wasn't hiding it from anyone. I had a problem, I searched for what to do, I found it, and I talked about it—because that's how I got over it. Otherwise . . . , if I had shut myself up in the house and said, "What happened to me?" and didn't talk about it, I wouldn't have gotten over it at all. I was helped a lot, and I realized that other people had the same problem. I work at the electricity board, and I saw that, by talking about what I was going through, others who had been hiding this same problem went to seek help.

Those like Soula, on the other hand, who hide their IVF practice from fear that they will confuse and antagonize relatives and friends (usually those who are older and who have less formal education), experience more evident frustration living in an ambiguously modern society. By *ambiguous* I am not suggesting Athenian society is not quite fully modern, but instead that modernity, as noted earlier, never exists without the tradition by which it is defined.

Fully contradicting what she had said to me at the outset of our interview about Greek society not being mature, Soula later said equally adamantly:

> I believe that our society today is mature enough to accept IVF. Maybe ten, twenty years ago, I don't know how they would have seen it then. I don't think they would have accepted it. But today, because there is this problem and it seems quite a widespread one, I think it is natural *[fisiologhikó]* that they should accept it. It's a natural way of reproduction. Proper *[sostí]*.

Soula is not only claiming that external fertilization works "with" nature but also arguing "it is natural" too that urban Greeks "should accept it" by adopting a more modern *noötropía* (embodied, collective mentality). And yet by hiding her IVF, Soula painfully demonstrates how fraught and tenuous her position is. IVF pushes prospective parents to take seriously and reconcile what they view as old-fashioned ideas about procreation and family in making claims to be modern, at the same time that other traditionally held notions, such as the virtue of maternal sacrifice, help facilitate wider acceptance of IVF.

That IVF forces people to shoulder the paradox of modernity's reliance on tradition in a most personal, intimate, and gendered way emerged too in Litsa's recounting of her IVF experience. Usually, Litsa told me, she is a person who wants "the doctor to be my friend and not just a doctor—not because I pay him to be concerned with me, to give me explanations, but because I want to know what is happening to me. With the dentist, I hold the mirror and see what he is doing to me." In contrast, when she pursed IVF,

> it was the only time that I wasn't interested in anything. It was the only time that I didn't want to know anything, only the result that I got every midday from Zoë—and I knew that when the cells go up it's good, when they don't go up it's not so good. This is all I knew. I didn't want to be inside this. I wanted to think that it was happening to someone else, not to me. I was afraid of the result. The feelings were very strange.

I read the "strange" feelings Litsa felt, and her aversion to learning about the procedure for the sake of knowledge, as testimony to feelings of ambiguity about pursuing such a resiliently rational method in the attempt to realize the most virtuous aspect of female nature recognized by Greek society. What IVF makes explicit in Athens is the contradictory nature of modern Greek femininity.

Virility, Fertility, and Masculine Gender Proficiency

Fears that others will view their child as "not normal" constitutes just one reason couples opt not to make known their recourse to IVF; frequently, this is aimed at protecting the social potency of the father's paternity. IVF is more readily incorporated into Greek notions of realized feminine nature than realized masculine nature. When fertilization occurs outside rather than inside a woman's body, definitively maternal processes are not impacted: women who become pregnant with IVF still get morning sickness, still dread cesarean sections or elect for epidurals, still get their forty days off work *san lechónes*, as newly delivered mothers. As one woman put it, "After birthing a child that you have had in your belly for nine months, I don't think it makes any difference whose sperm or ovum it was." Zoë, my biologist friend at the clinic, assured me that 80 percent of the women who have been through the clinic were indifferent to the possibility of donor ova or donor sperm: "A lot of women say, 'If my husband's sperm is no good, just use any other sperm. I don't care.' Of course," she added, "we don't use it without the husband's permission."

Maternity is legally defined in Greece by childbirth: "The biological process of childbirth manifests, still, the *syngénia* [kinship] relation of the offspring with its mother (maternity/motherhood). For this reason the law accepts that only with birth is *syngénia* of the offspring founded with its mother and her *syngenís* [kindred]" (Dheligianni and Kousoula 1984, 3). Paternity, however, is theoretically about fertilization, the contribution of "seed" *(sporá)*, and the recognition of that contribution; legally, this has been secured through the institution of marriage (Dheligianni and Kousoula 1984; Koumantou 1985, 1988). Reproductive technologies with the potential of using donor sperm complicate matters. Litsa told me that, when they learn about the IVF, people sometimes ask about her child,

> "Is it your own?" But they mean is it your husband's especially, because you're fine. They don't know what the ovum is, they see your belly inflated: "She birthed, it's hers." For the woman, since it came out of her belly it was her own. They take issue that it isn't the spouse's.

When maternity is defined by childbirth, hiding infertility through concealing external fertilization is often directed at protecting paternity and male ego. Women's choice to hide their IVF is thus incorporated into an ethic of service where what they service is paternity, or more precisely, a conceptual link between sexual virility and manliness rendered through fertility and proven by recognized paternity. Men often "confuse virility with potency" in the United States (Becker 2000, 46) and elsewhere. In Athens, as in urban Egypt (Inhorn 2000) and Israel (Kahn 2000), male-factor infertility is increasingly treated with a variation on IVF called intracytoplasmic sperm injection, where a single sperm is injected into the cytoplasm of an oocyte. This procedure facilitates couples' biogenetic reproduction, eliminating the need for donor sperm. Intracytoplasmic sperm injection has been used in Athens since 1993, although it does not address some of the most significant Greek concerns about paternity.[14] In the first instance, moral concerns are not always directed at what *actually* happens (that a husband's sperm is used in IVF) so much as what others might *believe* happens. Second, Greeks, like the Israeli Jews of whom Susan Kahn (2000) writes, are not so concerned with biogenetic connection in and of itself. What is primarily at stake for Greek men, by way of biological paternity, is their gender proficiency.

When knowledge that a man's wife has pursued external fertilization may throw into question whether the sperm used was his, what is thrown into doubt is not so much his genetic connection to the child but rather his virile capability to inseminate his wife through sexual intercourse. Maro cited the ideology of masculine sexual "capability" as a reason why infertility problems are immediately assumed to lie within a woman's organism (see also Inhorn 1994, 2000):

> There is the following phenomenon in Greece when a couple tries to have a child and, for whatever reasons, a child doesn't come: usually the weight falls on the woman. The responsibility is the woman's, not the man's—when of course it may well be the man's [physiological problem]. Why does this happen? Because men are capable *[ikaní]*; the women have the problems in Greece. That's what they [men] think, that's what they are taught—that it's not possible that they are unable to have a child. It's the male egoism that all this social conditioning has cultivated in them. Men are phallocentric *[falokendrikí]*; very few are not.

And as a woman who turned to IVF after having "problems with my fallopian tubes," explained to me:

> Greek society is male-dominated *[androkratoúmeni]*. The man might have the [fertility] problem, but it would never come out that he had the problem. It would come out that the woman had the problem. And now, the man still has a hard time going to get checked out, even though I believe the percentage is even, of men and women who have the problem. It is very difficult for Greek society, which is patriarchal, to admit that the man might have the problem.

The *kalá 'ndras,* meaning a "well man" or one who is "good at being" a man, as Herzfeld (1985) has discussed, is one who asserts a sense of self-regard *(eghoismós)* through agonistic or competitive display. To demonstrate masculine gender proficiency, men continue to enlist women's help (whether by request or demand) in hiding a weakness, perhaps especially one associated with sexuality, be it lack of restraint, lack of virility, or infertility. The resulting double standard, these women recognize, compromises *feminine* gender proficiency.

MARKETING MODERN MOTHERHOOD

When evaluating contraception, abortion, and other fertility control methods, including IVF, the women, family planning advocates, physicians, politicians, and mass media discussed in this book refer increasingly to a "women's nature" that is "made" through appropriate maternal, rather than sexual, behavior. The introduction of IVF helps constitute a parallel shift in how women's proper relationship to *teknopiía* is assessed: the having of children is no longer a taken-for-granted aspect of marriage that "just happens," but has become an achievement based on techniques of motherhood that are both newly proliferating and increasingly scrutinized. A notion of achieved motherhood is further constituted by a capitalist market economy (of which medical technology is part) and the increasingly diversified participation of women in this economy as workers and consumers. Jill Dubisch asks:

> With increasing affluence, does Greek women's maintenance of family reputation now rest more on their role as consumers, demonstrating a family's material status in both urban and village settings, and less on the control of sexuality and the maintenance of the integrity of the "inside"? (1993, 282)

As I have detailed, the substance of the nature that women must control to demonstrate gender proficiency is also transforming: women's need to control their sexuality is giving way to a need to control, even rationalize, a biological capacity to bring forth babies. Choice is the prevailing modern virtue governing *how* one should control one's nature and, thus, have the sex one wants and make the babies one wants. Athenians consume contraceptives and abortion to work with and regulate natural sexual desire; they turn to IVF and other medical technologies to work with and enable natural fertility and parenting desire. Family planning, as private and governmental initiatives present it, is meant to enhance both; as such, it is forwarded as a means of modernizing or Westernizing the Greek *noötropía*.

Institutionalized family planning in Greece also begs the question of *whose* choice, ultimately, is to be realized by such practices. While the ideology of family planning brings together individual rights discourse and enabled desire, thereby upholding the right of couples to build a life that revolves around a "desired, happy family," all too often this vision is blind to the patriarchal gender dimensions of supposedly shared choice that still persist in modern societies. The choices enabled by the tools of family planning do not always prove liberating for women. Contraception may facilitate coerced sex (as American and British feminists argued generations ago), and IVF may exacerbate the pressure on women to pursue emotionally and physically demanding procedures that they may feel compelled to hide, thereby denying themselves the support of even their closest friends and family. In addition, family planning potentially undermines women's traditional ability to use fate or God's will as a cover for unconventional desires not to have children.

While I was interviewing women who had successfully used IVF, and, on occasion, while I enjoyed a leisurely dinner with Zoë and mutual friends, I grew aware of a proliferation in Athens of public images of pregnancy. I thought not only about how childless women might respond to such images but also about how they affect each woman who, as Koralia noted in the epigraph to this chapter, must come to some kind of understanding of how she relates to the idea, if not the reality, of motherhood.

Because Greek media often adopt Western formats, their representations offer an incisive view of the ambivalence that characterizes an urban Greek gaze—and indeed, cultural movement—toward the West, often epitomized in Greece by the United States. Public representations found in commercial advertising and political activism are always produced and consumed by people in specific contexts where dominant meanings can be resisted and negotiated as well as reinforced. Looking through women's magazines, I found that marketing firms operating in Greece have been quick to respond to, or even anticipate, the changing assumptions, desires, and insecurities of their target audience. They work particularly hard to reassure women, as Dubisch suggests, that they can demonstrate their moral worth through appropriate consumerism (1993, 282). The advertisements I collected from Greek magazines during my fieldwork reflect a vision of women working to achieve motherhood—as well as a sense of ambivalence about what this means for viewing oneself as a woman. Such ads constitute part of the modern ethical elicitation and performance of gender in contemporary urban Greece.

Consider this ad, from the April 1994 issue of *Yinéka* (Woman), for a fancy Italian stroller named Marianna, presumably after the Virgin Mary (see figure 3). Giving the stroller a personal name suggests iconicity for the imaginary child that the device is built to contain. Material goods do not come cheaply on the import-heavy Greek market (an American friend of mine married to an Athenian complained that she paid U.S.$300 in 1994 for a relatively cheap stroller); having the will and purchasing power to obtain this stroller can be viewed as analogous to saving and planning for that child. Peering into the carriage named Marianna, the woman in the advertisement, fashionably dressed as a professional, supposedly sees the object of her longing: her own child. A baby container, the carriage is marketed as a fetish object; a female viewer is invited to see her own fantasized child in Marianna.

The caption for the advertisement suggests a second identification with the stroller, superimposed on the first, visual identification: "The Marianna

ΤΟ MARIANNA EINAI
ΟΠΩΣ Η ΜΗΤΕΡΑ:
ΩΡΑΙΟ ΑΠ'ΕΞΩ
ΩΡΑΙΟ ΑΠΟ ΜΕΣΑ.

Το παιδί σου το επιθύμησες, το περίμε-
νες, το χάιδεψες και γι' αυτό διαλέγεις
πάντοτε το καλύτερο. Όπως το Marianna:
συγκεντρώνει όλα όσα ψάχνει κανείς σε
ένα καροτσάκι και κάτι περισσότερο.

Την κομψότητα.
Το Marianna είναι ωραίο εξωτερικά: Ξε-
χωρίζει για την κομψότητα των φινιρί-
σματων και την ιδιαίτερη επιλογή των
υφασμάτων, την αρμονία των σχημάτων
και για την κλασική βάση του με τα ακτινω-
τούς τροχούς.

Την άνεση.
Το Marianna είναι ωραίο εσωτερικά: το
πόρτ-μπεμπέ είναι πολύ ευρύχωρο και
άνετο. Στο εσωτερικό είναι εφοδιασμένο
με μιά άνετη και ρυθμιζόμενη πλάτη. Η
ειδική ανάρτηση με σούστες παρέχει μία
μεγαλύτερη άνεση στους περιπάτους
του παιδιού σας.

Την ασφάλεια.
Το Marianna έχει αξονικό φρένο για ένα
ασφαλές σταμάτημα, το σύστημα Secur-
block, για να τοποθετησετε στη βάση με
διπλή ασφάλεια, το πόρτ-μπεμπέ ή το
καθισματάκι. Και όλα αυτά συνδυάζονται
με το περιορισμένο βάρος μιάς κα-
ταπληκτικής και ανθεκτικής βάσης από
αλουμίνιο.

Την εύκολη χρήση.
Το Marianna μετατρέπεται σε ένα άνετο
καροτσάκι περιπάτου, αντικαθιστώντας
απλώς το πόρτ-μπεμπέ με το καθισματάκι. Επιπλέον είναι εφοδιασμένο με ένα
πρακτικό και μεγάλο καλάθι για τα διά-
φορα αντικείμενα.

Δυνατότητα επιλογής.
Το Marianna διατίθεται σε μία μεγάλη
σειρά υφασμάτων και σχεδίων μεταξύ
των οποίων μπορείτε να διαλέξετε το
καροτσάκι "σας". Οι εσωτερικές επενδύ-
σεις, οι οποίες αφαιρούνται και πλένο-
νται, έχουν επεξεργασθεί με την ειδική
μέθοδο Sanitized για μία μεγαλύτερη
υγιεινή.

Marianna.
Μία βάση
για απλό καροτσάκι
και καροτσάκι
περιπάτου.

Marianna

Peg PEREGO
Ασφάλεια σε τέσσερις τροχούς.

Αποκλειστικός Αντιπρόσωπος ΠΕΡΑΜΑΞ Α.Ε. Λ. Αλεξάνδρας 7 - 114 73 ΑΘΗΝΑ - Τηλ. 6437607

Figure 3. Advertisement for the Marianna stroller, by Peg
Pérego. *Yinéka* magazine, April 1994, p. 207. Reproduced with
permission of Peg Pérego.

is as the mother: beautiful on the outside, beautiful on the inside." The flat-
tery of this slogan operates at two levels. First, it implores the woman
voyeur to appraise herself positively as her baby's original "carrier," during gestation, in the same way she—discerning, savvy, responsible consumer—would appraise this product, another baby carrier. The text states:
"You desired your child, you awaited it, you caressed it, and for this reason
you always choose the best. Such as the Marianna: It concentrates everything one would seek in a stroller and more." The "and more" signals the
marketing team's recognition that a mother's consumer decisions are cal-

culated to benefit not only the child but also the woman herself. Therefore, the good consumer-mother is assured that the Marianna "concentrates" not only elegance, comfort, security, and easy use but also the possibility of choice: "From an extensive series of styles and designs, you can choose 'your' stroller." The stroller might be "for" a child, but it belongs to, and reflects back on, the mother-consumer. The ad thus suggests that a good consumer is a good mother. She demonstrates that she wants "the best" for her child, and that she recognizes quality when she sees it.

Presenting aesthetic technologies of motherhood available for women's consumption, in the middle 1990s Greek women's magazines followed an American trend to glamorize pregnancy that was established with the *Vanity Fair* cover shot of Demi Moore and her advanced state of pregnancy (a shot that was itself reprinted in Greek media; see for example Sekerli 1994). The May 1994 issue of *Yinéka* contained at least three full-page ads for high-end maternity wear boutiques with addresses in the posh center-city shopping district of Kolonaki, which sported English names such as Mama Chic, babyboom, and Mother Land. These ads are, as a rule, simple: we see a beautiful, poised, elegantly dressed and obviously pregnant woman accompanied by the name and address of the shop. The fashion styles vary considerably, from storybook innocence conveyed by a straw hat and lace collar, to a competent urban style achieved with linen slacks and vest, to a dissonant coquettishness suggested by the "baby doll" look that was then popular on both sides of the Atlantic (see figure 4). The women themselves all appear calm, even aloof, without even a trace of stress. An earlier issue of *Yinéka* given to me, dated 1987, features only one ad for a maternity-wear shop, Mama Chic; it covers just half a page and the model looks rather like an overgrown grade school student. Motherhood, ever a responsibility, has not always been glamorous.

And perhaps pregnancy's symbolic capital as a fashion accessory of the modern woman has not withstood deflation. The August 1998 issue of *Yinéka* I picked up on a subsequent trip is notable for its absence of advertisements for maternity wear and home pregnancy tests, another maternal product popularly advertised in the early nineties. The most heavily advertised product in this later issue was another kind of prophylactic: foreign name-brand sun protection creams. I notice a general trend toward marketing products for women's personal use, including imported perfumes and cosmetics (although arguably these may be marketed for women's use and men's enjoyment), three brands of cigarettes, and something I had never before seen in a Greek woman's magazine: automobile ads. However, several of the sunscreen ads featured photographs of smiling women pro-

Figure 4. Advertisement for Mama Chic maternity wear shop in Kolonaki, Athens. *Yinéka* magazine, May 1994, p. 123.

tecting small children from harmful ultraviolet rays. As Anthi Doxiadi-Trip anticipated in her 1993 popular piece on prophylactics, modern mothers are made in part by assuming responsibility for instilling an imported ethic of well-being in very young children.

A final advertisement exploits the moral value and social institution of motherhood to sell a credit card (see figure 5). Also from *Yinéka* magazine (1993), this advertisement by Commercial Bank shows a small girl wearing a white dress, her hair pulled back in a bow, watching over a gauze-draped bassinet in which a shiny plastic doll appears to be feeding from a bottle. In

Figure 5. Advertisement for "EMPOROKARTA"—credit card of Commercial Bank of Greece S.A. The caption reads: "We grew up . . . and our desires became needs." *Yinéka* magazine, May 1993, pp. 76–77. Reproduced with permission of ABC ADVERTISING SA, Athens, Greece.

the distance, a row of bobby-socked, plaid-skirted girls' legs suggests that this girl is not alone: she is an icon of girlhood. Along the top of the facing page we read, "We grew up . . . and our desires became needs." When a girl grows up, her assumed desire to have babies turns out to cost a lot of money. As in the FPAG pamphlet *What Do You Know about Contraception?* desire to mother becomes a "need"—it is socially expected of a woman—but here the desire itself "needs" bank credit. Naturalized desire generates naturalized need for financial flexibility. The credit card ad uses the iconicity of motherhood—an unquestioned "good" that has become inextricable from modern financial concerns—to naturalize advanced capitalism. Motherhood, long fetishized in Greece through the pervasive icon of the Panayía Vrefokratoúsa, is now made a tool of commodity fetishism. And by invoking the plight of women hoping to fulfill childhood expectations for motherhood, credit cards are made to seem not only desirable but also moral. By extension, the women who wield the very modern financial flexibility afforded by credit cards are depicted as doing so not out of egotistical self-indulgence but out of a self-sacrificing maternal impulse. If to be good at being a woman today entails being a good consumer, the sug-

gestion that consumption fundamentally incorporates modern motherhood again reassures all that these consumers are also good (virtuous)
women.

The extent to which modern motherhood is fetishized in these advertisements becomes all the more significant when juxtaposed with a complete absence of fetishized *fetal* imagery. Donna Haraway writes, "In many
domains in contemporary European and U.S. cultures, the fetus functions
as a kind of metonym, seed crystal, or icon for configurations of person,
family, nation, origin, choice, life, and future" (1997, 175). This, Haraway
explains in the Strathernian terms (1992a,b) of how modern Euro-American kinship anticipates personhood: individuality (a person's place in the
kinship-social system) is prior to personhood, but personhood is anticipated by reference to the physical presence of a discrete individual.[15]
Strathern has joined others in arguing that ultrasound technology and
public displays of fetal sonogram images—advertising campaigns have
used fetal imagery to sell products, for example (Petchesky 1990; Taylor
1992, 1998; Duden 1993; Newman 1996; Haraway 1997)—are pushing
back the moment of discreteness to before childbirth. In such ways the
fetus has come to anticipate the person and, in effect, itself gain personhood (Morgan and Michaels 1999). But in Greece, although ultrasound imaging has been quite routinized in prenatal care (Georges 1996b; Mitchell
and Georges 1997), fetuses (or rather, fetal images) do not sell cars, nor do
they advertise long-distance telephone service.[16] If the unbaptized infant is
not awarded full social personhood, then surely neither is the fetus.

But does the reverse logic hold? Is the unbaptized infant no more a person than the fetus is? Eva and Richard Blum report that Greek villagers
they lived among in the 1950s made little linguistic or practical distinction
between "nine-month abortions," stillbirths, and infanticide (1965, 73). As
discussed in chapter 2, however, stories of maternal infanticide have recently been paraded in the media for public scrutiny. More than one
woman I spoke with offered the idea that, on a relative and progressive
scale, abortion is a moral improvement over infanticide. The traditional
underpinnings of fetal and infant liminality may be giving way to Western
secularizing (or "Protestantizing") trends, of which market logic is just one
aspect. After all, in this era of Greece's *ipoyenitikótita* (underfertility), the
fetus has become a baby for pronatal nationalists. True to form, pronatal
and pro-life groups such as the Panhellenic Association for the Protection
of the Unborn Child and the Panhellenic Union of Friends of the Polytéknon have over the past decade or two disseminated fetal images designed
to deter women from abortions (e.g., Psaroudhaki 1992). That fetal images

are being used to "sell" nationalism suggests a creeping fetishization of the fetus that may yet have implications for abortion rights. It certainly signals a remix of liberal and Christian versions of modernity that edges Greece closer to its Western counterparts. It could well be that, in the future, Greeks too will anticipate social personhood in fetuses. The repercussions this will surely have for modern women's reproductive accountability is an active concern among Athenian feminists.

OUR MODERNITIES, OUR SELVES?

If fetal ontology is being rethought in Athens, more durable and morally potent is the connection between womanhood and motherhood exploited by the bank credit card advertisement. Speaking of this connection, Koralia, an unmarried heterosexual woman who participates in an ancient matriarchy study group, articulated its dual origins in nature and society as well as its ideological repercussions:

> It comes from nature, to start with. It's an ability that women have. They either want it or they don't want it, but it's a natural ability—I think that motherhood is the key point which has influenced women's position in society over all the years. It has been a positive influence in some years, in the years of matriarchy, as I believe existed. And in our society, now in patriarchy, motherhood is now the key question of women's oppression. And the real key lies in contraception, in abortion, in childbirth—this is where the power game is played—including infertility, of course.

As Koralia speaks, the separation between natural and social factors that she set out to delineate becomes blurred, revealing that however strong the connection between womanhood and motherhood, it is also exceptionally flexible. (Koralia would say, too, that an affirmative link between womanhood and motherhood is ancient, and that it once supported matriarchy, a social formation that functions in her argument similarly to the way "tradition" does when it is invoked as a necessary, and retrospectively imagined, contrast to "modernity." In contrasting matriarchy and patriarchy, she moves the strategic comparison of tradition and modernity from a historical to a prehistorical register in order to denaturalize patriarchal tradition.) In her attempts to separate social and natural aspects of experience, Koralia appeals to a radical feminist version of an ethic of choice that is clearly, significantly gendered: motherhood is a choice women experience differently from how men experience parental choice ("even the very good, compassionate men who are good husbands") because, to return to her words in this chapter's epigraph, for women "the experience of motherhood passes through their bodies."

What I find most significant is Koralia's sense that women embody an experience of motherhood *regardless* of whether they actually become pregnant and birth a child. In order to fully grasp this possibility—that is, in order to take seriously women's experiences in assessing the social impact of fertility control technologies—we must follow through on my contention that women's embodiment of gender and kinship in Greece happens through socially realized nature. We must not fall back on materialist assumptions about a "real nature" in searching for a biological truth about whether a woman "actually" became pregnant and gave birth (or, for that matter, whether a certain man's sperm "actually" was used in IVF). As Koralia said, women "have to consider" motherhood, one way or another. What is more, women can and do experience motherhood *in their bodies* without going through the seemingly definitive physiological events of pregnancy and childbirth. To see how this happens, consider the question posed at the beginning of this book: Why it is that Phoebe and Niki, both childless well into their reproductive years, view motherhood as being "within the nature" of a woman and yet as that which must be achieved in order to "complete" a woman?

If a woman has motherhood "inside her" even without birthing, then today, when the event of motherhood does more to differentiate gender (young women and men have similar opportunities and responsibilities before confronting parenting roles) than to differentiate women from maidens (as Dina saw it), then childless women such as Phoebe and Niki can recuperate a fully gendered identity. In Greek cultural life, perfection (i.e., nature) is not expected in gender performance; it is approximated. Skilled actors use the appearance of gender's rigidity (e.g., it is "in the nature" of a woman to suffer for her children) to play personal and systemic imperfections to strategic advantage. For Phoebe, the realization of woman's maternal nature does not require childbirth:

> I believe that within a woman exists feelings of motherhood. And you
> will see this even in women who haven't had a child: it comes out in
> their behavior toward an animal, let's say, a dog, or a cat. It's a special
> behavior that seems somewhat like the feeling of motherhood.

Similarly, it is no coincidence to Artemis that, after suffering four miscarriages and never having a child, she has devoted her adult life to teaching children. If motherhood completes a woman, as both Phoebe and Niki expressed to me, the fact that motherhood is "inside" them anyway lets them off the hook for failing to "make" children by this point in their middle-aged lives. That childless women make such claims is particularly interesting when psychologists Aliki Andoniou and Vaso Skopeta agree they have a hard time convincing women who are mothers, and who compromise their adult autonomy and even comfort to give their children "the best," that, in Andoniou's words, "the gift of motherhood is there anyway," even when women feel inadequate in the material support they can offer their children.

"Motherhood completes a woman" is a performative statement that momentarily mediates the contradictions between a modern woman's ideal expectations for being a woman (which should include being a mother) and her lived reality. Underemployed Niki and her husband, recall, do not have enough money to raise children as they would like. When Phoebe continued working after marriage, she and her husband fought too much to want to bring a child into their lives. It may be paradoxical, but it is *not* inconsistent that Niki, after insisting that she is "not complete as a woman" shrugged off her childlessness by concluding, "What can I do?" In making a statement that appears at first glance to evoke essentialist rhetoric but actually refers us to everyday practice, childless Athenian women demonstrate what I have called gender proficiency. By expressing a "natural" desire that all women (should) wish to become mothers, they signal moral approval of motherhood and, in so doing, are being good at being women as well as being "good" women.

Thus when women confront decisions regarding motherhood, they (unlike male politicians and policy makers) never pose these as yes or no, "do I?" or "do I not?" questions. In describing this, Koralia also underscores what I have argued about the construction of motherhood in urban Greece, that it fundamentally concerns the potential *quality* of mothering: "Women who have to decide about motherhood come up with questions like, 'How do I bring a child into this world with wars and with pollution, and with starvation and drugs?'" Continuing, Koralia speaks of the socially realized nature of motherhood in terms that remind me of Vaso Skopeta's "compassion circle" described in the opening chapter; here again, a socially experienced natural relationship of women to motherhood obtains regardless of whether they actually give birth to and raise children:

> So through the question of motherhood, women share their existence with other beings, whether with their children or their imaginary children, or the children they have aborted, or the children they have decided not to do. It always comes in. This is the personal part. And then

of course there is the social part, because motherhood nowadays, in my opinion, most of the time it's a trap. Even if it's very conscious and desired and so on. Once you have the baby, it's always there. And it's very hard to resist getting into the social role of "the mother," which means washing, feeding, loving, getting it to school, thinking of its future. This I find very hard. And I think that 99 percent of women get into that trap, because there is no other model at the moment. One would have to change the whole model—for example, how children are raised, if the children were raised collectively or by the whole society. But now the child is raised by the mother. And the other people, if there are good people around, they can help a little bit. But it's the mother's sole responsibility. I don't find this right, but this is how it works now.

I have argued that gender in Greece entails a personal responsibility to behave in a morally proper manner. As Koralia's words attest, the moral problem facing women today is that the nature they must realize through appropriate action is inherently contradictory. To be good women they are required to emulate, if not enact, motherhood by subordinating their interests to those of others; to be good (i.e. modern) adults, they are required to strive for independence, calculate their actions to further their own well-being, and be always in control of their lives. The two sets of expectations are incompatible, in Greece as elsewhere (Collier 1986; Ginsburg 1989; Rapp 1999).

But as I have tried to emphasize, even the most pervasive features of modernity are recast and retooled in local settings. What was striking to me about this gender-kinship formulation in Athens was how clearly many middle-class Athenian women *recognized* and could articulate contradictions between being a woman and being a mother. When I pushed Koralia to describe how she herself came to the decision not to have children (which she had announced to me in a previous discussion), she replied:

This decision is becoming more conscious as the years pass. When I first decided, it was after I had a delay in my menstruation and some symptoms [which led her to believe] I might be pregnant. I was quite young at the time, and I was horrified. I was panicked. But it had two sides, I have to admit now. On the one side it was a very exciting time. Just like that, to have a baby! And with this particular boy, with whom I was in love. And on the other side, there was a very negative feeling: There I am, the baby at the breast, the boyfriend at the side—*if* he would stay by my side—and finished with all my plans for everything. And doing what? Looking after my baby. Oooh! I could not do that. And that was when I made the decision. I wasn't pregnant in the end, but before I found out, the decision had been made. . . . I am not so interested in being a mother. If you have this experience, you have to balance it with a hundred different ones. It's an experience that defines your lifestyle, your plans, your job, the way you make your living, the money you earn. Everything. Even the friends you meet—you can't have your babies running around when you visit your friend, because they will break everything in the house. You cannot oppress your babies, and you cannot oppress your friends. So it's a thing that would define too much for me, and I am an adventurous person. . . . This is how I came to the decision: I preferred a different lifestyle. Of course, I would have liked to have babies too, but you can't have everything; and if you have to choose, it's very conscious for me to choose that. As the years pass and I'm growing older, I don't regret it. In fact many times I have blessed myself for making this decision in time.

Not only is Nature not fixed, but Culture is conceptually inconsistent, inherently contradictory. This is because culture is not a rational system but a power structure in which even moral systems contribute to the maintenance of relational inequalities.

While Athenian women continue to view motherhood and womanhood as self-evident in their own right, the relationship between these is being recast through the reconstitution of women's ethical subjectivity. Today, as condom ads pitched to women frequently proclaim, being good at being a woman means "looking out for yourself" as well as for your loved ones. At the same time, being a good mother still means looking out first and foremost for your loved ones, sometimes by subordinating personal desires (for example, to have a quiet chat with a friend) to the interests of children ("you can't oppress your babies").

Women's internalized ethical conflict produces a counterhegemonic claim that motherhood no longer epitomizes proper womanhood: indeed, this discourse suggests a mother *loses* her identity as a woman. A physiotherapist who returned an IVF survey, apologizing at the end, writing that she had no time to do an interview (I had asked willing persons to list their name and telephone number), put this in terms of gender difference, implying that modern women (like herself) are becoming "more like men." In response to my query "How do you perceive the general relationship between motherhood and being a woman, and fatherhood and being a man," she wrote, "I think there's no relation. Motherhood is one thing, woman is another. The one is in battle with the other. The same with manhood and fatherhood." Ariadne, who also so wanted a child that she did IVF, voiced skepticism of modern women's "liberation," not as compared to the freedom enjoyed by men but to that of women of her mother's generation. While admitting that she has more mobility now than "as an eighteen-year-old girl, [when] I had many restrictions (I couldn't go out late, I had to return home by midnight)," she compared her expectations for motherhood with those of her own mother: "My mother used to tell me, 'Look, when you become married, then you can do what you want.' And I used to tell her that, when I become married, I would not be able to do what I want. From then on you 'do' a family. You do what you want when you are single." Now that women's moral worth is more carefully evaluated in terms of their maternal behavior than their sexual comportment, motherhood does not signal a woman's freedom so much as the *loss* of it: "From then on you 'do' a family."

Such statements reveal the paradox of modern motherhood in urban Greece: women as mothers should be both self-actualizing and self-sacrificing. This is not the same paradox that white, middle-class American women face, which Rapp characterizes as a "running battle over the question of self-ishness and self-actualization" (1999, 138). What is more, when Athenian women talk about changes in the material conditions of motherhood over the past decades that have happened throughout the capitalist world, they narrate these changes at the level of subjectivity. Maro said to me, "I think the role of a mother is very important—it doesn't matter that I don't want to have a child myself. It changes her frame of mind, *she becomes another person*" (emphasis added). Women see their very selves as changing, historically as well as over the life course. Some of these changes undermine forms of agency available to women under the now traditional ethic of service—for instance, in avoiding the burden of undue reproductive accountability. Ethics provides a sanctioned vocabulary for articulating cultural critique.

In using fertility control practices as a window onto wider social and conceptual changes in everyday middle-class urban Greek life and thought, my ethnography is indebted to recent feminist transformations of what can count as proper anthropology by moving "reproduction to the center of social theory" and establishing that reproductive practices constitute an entirely adequate frame for examining individual and group identities, local and global inequalities, and national and international politics (Ginsburg and Rapp 1995, 15; Gal and Kligman 2000). Because reproductive issues condense nested meanings of personal, social, and national identity (Kligman 1998, 5), attitudes about contraception, abortion, and IVF bring cultural tensions into focus and "reveal the workings of social relations" (Ginsburg and Rapp 1995, 6). Looking through this window primarily from the perspective of middle-class Athenian women, I have taken seriously these women's situated knowledges (Haraway 1991) in developing my own analysis of modern Greek subjectivity and sociality. Careful ethnography can build responsible ethnology.

In this regard, my work has been in dialogue with Rapp's New York City study centered on the moral positioning of women confronting new reproductive technologies. Rapp writes of amniocentesis:

> It is my contention that the construction and routinization of this technology is turning the women to whom it is offered into *moral pioneers:* Situated on a research frontier of the expanding capacity for prenatal genetic diagnosis, they are forced to judge the quality of their own fetuses, making concrete and embodied decisions about the standards for entry into the human community. (1999, 3, emphasis added)

In urban Greece, where gender and virtue are simultaneously embodied through a notion of realized nature, women who confront imported contraceptive and fertility technologies in the context of new material conditions of motherhood do not see themselves as "moral pioneers" so much as pioneers of modernity. Many of the women I met and whose narratives give form to this book perceive the social and conceptual changes depicted as a progressive move toward a more liberated and Western future. In their everyday efforts to do the right thing, these women see themselves as challenging the culture in which they live and the culture that lives in them (McCaughey 1997, xi; see also Becker 2000, 102).

But are we to take at face value their progress narrative? As Lila Abu-Lughod has noted, the "tricky task" is "to be skeptical of modernity's progressive claims of emancipation and critical of its social and cultural operations and yet appreciate the forms of energy, possibility, even power that aspects of it might [enable], especially for women" (1998, 12). Greek politicians, family planning workers, social scientists, and middle-class Athenians agree that women are more likely than men to accept the promises and program of family planning, and they thereby recognize women as the vanguard of this "means of modernity" (Appadurai 1996). However, the moral and political evaluations and aspirations they draw from this diverge significantly. While (predominantly male) politicians try to marshal ideational and material change into a "freely chosen" maternal citizenship that holds women responsible for the nation's demographic well-being, many women see wider social egalitarianism emerging through their everyday, often domestic negotiations with men. At the localized junctions of political history and mythmaking, "gender serves as one of the central modalities through which modernity is imagined and desired" (Rofel 1999,

19), but it does more than this. Neither gender nor modernity is singular. Middle-class urban Greeks frequently perceive the modernity they are producing and inhabiting to be increasingly "like" that of western Europe and the United States; nevertheless, Athenian discussions of what it means to be modern continuously bump up against what it means to be Greek in the contemporary world. A women-centered analysis of social change demonstrates how gender is constitutive of modernities—encompassing understandings of how emotion, morality, and reasoned action inform one another—that may simultaneously forward and undermine local struggles for self-determination, equity, and justice.

Seeing nature as realized through ethical action allows us to understand how Athenian women, regardless of whether they have children, perceive and inhabit motherhood and womanhood as kinds of technologies—that is, as tools with which they craft ethical selves and social relations. Viewing gender as a system of virtues reveals what sex/gender obscures: Agency is neither a matter of free will nor of resistance to the imperatives of a fixed nature or a constraining culture, but emerges in ways that simultaneously reproduce and reconfigure social relations. Such an approach also sidesteps the question of whether specific persons, practices, or mentalities are either traditional or modern, at the same time that it takes seriously people's invocations of these terms in comprehending how their experiences articulate with the larger imperatives of such entities as nation-states and legislative bodies. Modern mothers are women in the making and remaking who endeavor to be responsible to themselves, to their loved ones, and to the past, present, and future of their social worlds.

Total Fertility Rates, European Union Countries, 1960–2000

Total Fertility Rates: Children per Woman Age 15–49

	1960	1970	1980	1990	2000
European 12 (in 2000, 15)	2.61	2.40	1.82	1.54	1.48*
Italy	2.41	2.42	1.64	1.26	1.24*
Spain	2.86	2.90	2.20	1.33	1.23*
Greece	2.28	2.39	2.21	1.42	1.29*
(West) Germany	2.37	2.03	1.56	1.45	1.36*
Portugal	3.10	2.83	2.18	1.50	1.52
Luxembourg	2.28	1.98	1.49	1.60	1.80
Belgium	2.56	2.25	1.68	1.62	1.66
Denmark	2.57	1.95	1.55	1.67	1.77
France	2.73	2.47	1.95	1.78	1.88*
Netherlands	3.12	2.57	1.60	1.62	1.72
United Kingdom	2.72	2.43	1.90	1.84	1.64
Ireland	3.76	3.93	3.23	2.19	1.89*

SOURCE: Eurostat, *Eurostat Demographic Statistics* (Brussels: Eurostat, 2003).
*Figures are provisional.

Legislation of the Greek State Pertaining to Gender Equality, Marriage, Family, and Reproduction

PASOK reforms are those dated from 1982 to 1989. New Democracy Party bills are those dated prior to 1982 and between 1990 and 1993.

MARRIAGE AND FAMILY

Law 1250/82 established civil weddings as being equal to religious ones.

Law 1329/83 reformed the Family Law and accommodated it by constitutional order to the equality of the sexes. It abolished

- the concept of the patriarchal family and replaced it with the "family of equality";
- the institution of the dowry—both spouses are required to contribute in accordance with their ability to the needs of a family.

It ordered

- that a woman keep her family name after marriage;
- that those about to be married be allowed, before the wedding, to select the surname that will be given to all their children; this can be the family name of either spouse, or it can combine the two;
- that eighteen be the minimum age of marriage for both sexes;
- that children's upbringing and education must ensue without regard for sex;
- that both spouses be entitled to file a "claim of participant" in the case of property that is obtained throughout the duration of the marriage;
- that divorce by consent be institutionalized;

- that there be absolute compatibility between the rights of children born out of marriage and the rights of children born within marriage, as well as legal reinforcement of the position of the unwed mother.

WORKING MOTHERS

Law 549/77 made possible the allocation of pregnancy and motherhood allowances paid to working mothers by the Social Insurance Agency (IKA).

Law 825/78 ordered IKA not only to provide medical care to pregnant workers but also to assist with childbirth and nursing expenses by giving payments to the obstetrician of the pregnant woman's preference.

Law 1082/80 forbade the dismissal of a pregnant woman from her employment.

Law 1302/83 ratified International Convention 103, which seeks the "protection of motherhood" and makes provisions for women (regardless of age, race, religion, or marital status) to have

- minimum maternity leave of twelve weeks and monetary allowances throughout the leave;
- the right to interrupt work for breast-feeding;
- employment protection during maternity leave;
- allocations for a satisfactory standard of living for six weeks before and six weeks after childbirth (this is for women who do not have the right to monetary compensation from insurance).

Law 1483/84, or the Greek Parental Leave Act (for the "protection and assistance of workers with family obligations—modifications and improvements of employment laws") provided for, among other things,

- parental leave without emoluments for the upbringing of a child amounting to three months for each parent (including adoptive parents), to be completed in the space of time from the end of maternal leave until the child completes the age of two and a half years; the single mother (i.e., single because of divorce, separation, widowhood, unwed birth) is entitled to parental leave of up to six months;
- leave without emoluments for up to six working days a year, in the case of child illness or illness of other family members;

- leave with emoluments to attend a child's school presentations in elementary school for up to four days a year;
- space for the operation of infant care centers—to be provided by public- and private-sector industrial enterprise services that employ more than three hundred persons—to attend to the needs of the personnel.

Law 1539/85 increased maternity leave in the private sector from twelve to fourteen weeks and, in the public sector, sixteen weeks.

Law 1541/85 provided postpartum allowance after childbirth for workers insured by OGA.

Law 1563/85 provided tax deductions for working mothers for the cost of the upkeep of children until the age of six.

Law 1576/85 ratified the International Convention of Employment 156 for the equal opportunity and equal treatment of workers and of the two sexes, especially in the case of workers with family obligations.

Presidential Order 193/88 extended the provisions of law 1483/84 to provide assistance to workers in the public sector with family obligations, and included parental leave, absentee leave for illness or disability of dependant members, reduced hours, and so on.

Law 1849/89 ensured maternity leave of fifteen weeks in the private sector and provisioned "married income" to unwed, widowed, and divorced parents.

Law 2085/92 provisioned leave without emoluments for up to two years for professional mothers in the public sector with children under six years of age; also provisioned pregnancy leave with half emoluments for city employees who have special need for family therapy.

1993 Joint Convention of Workers made provisions—following the proposal of the General Secretariat for Equality, relating to the equal treatment of men and women—for equal compensation for the same work, parental leave of up to three and a half months for each parent, total maternal leave of sixteen weeks, and breast-feeding and child care leave (which alternatively can be requested by the husband provided that the working mother does not use it), as well as regulations relating to the nighttime work of pregnant women, in agreement with a new International Employment Convention, article 17 1.

UNWED MOTHERS

Law 1329/83 (the reformation of the Family Law) gave the unwed mother legal status comparable to that of the married mother regarding the matter of rights and obligations, and gave her children legal status comparable to that of the children of the married mother.

Law 1473/84 reduced income tax of unwed mothers and provided the working unwed mother with lightened taxation for the care of her child until the age of six years.

Law 1483/84 provided parental leave for the upbringing of the child for six months, and, for the unwed mother, provided leave until the child completes two and a half years.

Law 1849/89 provided income for the unwed mother.

POLÝTEKNES MOTHERS

Law 1892/90 (article 63) provided the *polýtekni* mother—that is, the mother of three or more children—with a monthly allowance equivalent to one and a half times the daily wage of an unspecialized worker, multiplied by the number of her unwed children up to the age of twenty-five. This allowance is paid until the *polýtekni* ceases to have unwed children under the age of twenty-five. In addition, a lifelong pension is provisioned to the mother who is no longer entitled to the above allowance, equivalent to a quarter of the daily wage of an unskilled worker. The above allowance is paid to the mother independently of any other allowance, salary, pension, compensation, and so on.

FAMILY PLANNING AND ABORTION

Law 821/78 reformed the abortion law, allowing abortion up to the twentieth week of pregnancy for eugenic reasons—that is, in the case of serious genetic abnormalities in the fetus—and up to the twelfth week in the case of severe mental health disturbances of the pregnant woman, certified by a state hospital psychiatrist.

Law 1036/80 institutionalized family planning in Greece and made provisions for the establishment of Family Planning Centers throughout the state.

Law 1397/83, article 15 included family planning in the scope of the National Health System; in effect, the letter of the law restricted family planning services to state centers.

Law 1609/86 legalized the "technical interruption of pregnancy" on request before the completion of the twelfth week of pregnancy, except when the operation can take place up to the nineteenth week—in the case of rape, seduction of a minor, incest, or abuse of a disabled woman—and up to the twenty-fourth week in the case of a genetic defect of the fetus or severe danger to the woman's physical or mental health. If the pregnant woman is underage (less than age sixteen), the consent of one of her parents or a guardian is required. The costs of the treatment fall on the insurance carrier (state or private) of the pregnant woman, so long as the abortion takes place in a state hospital.

PROSTITUTION AND TRADE OF WOMEN

In Greek law, prostitution is not punishable. Laws that relate to prostitution presuppose its exercise.

Law 1193/81 pertains to issues relevant to the protection against and regulation of sexual diseases and includes a series of related stipulations that specify conditions for the practice of prostitution.

Sources: Margaritidou and Mesteneos 1991; General Secretariat for Equality 1993; Comninos 1988.

Birthrates, Greece, 1934–1999

YEAR	BIRTHRATE
1934	16.1
1935	13.3
1936	12.7
1937	11.1
1938	12.7
1939	10.9
1940	11.7
1954	12.2
1955	12.5
1956	12.3
1957	11.6
1958	11.9
1959	12.0
1960	11.6
1961	10.3
1962	10.1
1963	9.6
1964	9.8
1965	9.8
1966	10.1

Birthrates, Greece, 1934–1999 *(continued)*

YEAR	BIRTHRATE
1967	10.4
1968	9.9
1969	9.3
1970	8.1
1971	7.6
1972	7.2
1973	6.7
1974	7.6
1975	6.7
1976	7.1
1977	6.5
1978	6.9
1979	7.0
1980	6.3
1981	5.6
1982	5.2
1983	4.3
1984	3.8
1985	2.4
1986	2.1
1987	1.1
1988	1.5
1989	.89
1990	.87
1991	.70
1998	−.20
1999	−.20

Sources: NSSG 1992, 2002.

Notes

1. All statements quoted from interviews are my translations from the Greek unless otherwise noted.

2. See du Boulay 1974, 1986; Hirschon 1978; Iossifides 1991; Dubisch 1993.

3. In the early 1990s, only 1.2 to 2 percent of the female population of reproductive age nationwide used the contraceptive pill; among the urban middle classes, this rate ran higher, somewhere between 7 and 12 percent. But even this figure is low compared to the average in the European Union, which since the early 1990s has stayed at about 35 percent. The Fifth Panhellenic Conference on AIDS and Sexually Transmitted Diseases, Caravel Hotel, Athens, 11–13 February 1994.

4. See Jordan 1993; Rich 1980, 1986; Delaney 1986; Rothman 1986, 1989; Martin 1987; Yanagisako and Collier 1987; Davis-Floyd 1992; Stolcke 1988, 1993; Rapp 1988, 1999; Ginsburg 1989; Ginsburg and Rapp 1991, 1995; Treichler 1990; Strathern 1992a,b; Franklin 1993, 1997; Ragoné 1994; Inhorn 1994, 1996; Harcourt 1997; Franklin and Ragoné 1998; Ram and Jolly 1998; Becker 2000; Russell, Sobo, and Thompson 2000; Ragoné and Twine 2000; Kahn 2000; Oaks 2001.

5. For feminist accounts of this transition, see Sutton 1986; Stamiris 1986; Chronaki 1992.

6. This seminar, held in Athens, 19–21 November 1993, was sponsored and organized by the privately run Foundation for Research on Childhood.

7. For an anthropological analysis of Sikaki-Douka's text, see Georges and Mitchell 2000.

8. The name Vaso Skopeta is a pseudonym. Our interview was conducted primarily in English.

9. The linguistic distinction that Anglophone and Francophone societies make between sex and gender does not obtain in Greek. Contrary to the implications of the sex/gender system, in Greece men's relationship to masculinity is

not structurally equivalent to women's relationship to femininity. The word *thilikótita* and its derivations encompass "female" sex difference (applicable to all female animals), as well as behavioral characteristics and virtues associated with human females, while male *(arsenikó)* humans get to express not merely their maleness but also, more important, their distinctly human manliness *(andrismós)*. Manliness and femininity are not structurally equivalent. This inequivalency is found too in Aristotelian thought, in his philosophy of anatomy that portrayed women as "deformed males" (*Generation of Animals,* Loeb Classical Library Edition [Cambridge: Harvard University Press, 1979], 175).

10. Foucault, for his part, was content to draw from Aristotle an "ethics of [free] men made for [free] men" that is only partially applicable to women (1990b, 83).

11. This was not the case, of course, for Aristotle, who claimed that women, in comparison to men, were naturally deficient in moral virtues such as temperance and self-mastery, owing to their "deformed" soul, "inadequate vital heat," and resultant lack of facility to reason properly (Lange 1983; Spelman 1983). Here we see evidence of the hybridization of ancient Greek and Orthodox Christian notions of nature. While Aquinas introduced misogynist elements of Aristotelian biology into Western Christianity, Byzantine Orthodoxy has been influenced more strongly by Plato and the neoplatonist philosophers (some of whom were women), who held more egalitarian views of women and men (and slaves, for that matter) than did Aristotle (see Meyendorff 1974).

12. To argue that the personal agency entailed in ethical subjectivity can well be politicized and extended into social movement, let me briefly address the hesitation among some cultural critics to take seriously people's moral claims. Much of the current scholarly attention to ethics is inspired by Foucault's later work (1990b), in which ethical subjectivity figured centrally in his move away from theorizing humans as "docile bodies" inscribed by power, and toward contemplating the agency in what he called "techniques of self." According to Jeffrey Weeks, Foucault hoped to forward the idea that contemporary Western society might learn from the ancients' "aesthetics of existence in which autonomous individuals become the artists of their own lives, in which the body and its pleasures become the focus for transcending the limits of the existing apparatus of sexuality" (1995, 69). Foucault's celebration of the individual self-fashioning encouraged by the ethically moderated "use of pleasures" depicted in classical Greek texts is understandable in comparison (as Foucault drew it) to Western Christianity's imposition of a single, rigid set of moral codes on all persons. Yet it is precisely this "aestheticization of ethics" that has drawn criticism for being apolitical and blind to constraints on autonomy, especially for women (McNay 1992, 2000; Grimshaw 1993, 60). Similarly, Herzfeld has critiqued his own earlier depiction of a "poetics of manhood" as an "aestheticization" of performance which risks masking the relations of power that help set the scene and dictate the appropriateness of public acts. In steering away from absolutist prescriptions for static identities, he rightly warns that we must not leap to embrace libertarian notions of cre-

ative self-invention, strategic or otherwise, for this may obscure the workings of power and inequality (1997a, 22). Furthermore, as Weeks cautions us about Foucault's later work, attending to the "care of the self" begs the ethical question of the care of the Other. However, the response to such criticism is not to turn away from ethics but to fully attend to already existing articulations between virtue, gender, sexuality, selfhood, inequality, and community. The challenge for such a project in richly multicultural societies is readily apparent (Bhabha 2000).

13. This is where I part company with Susan Parson, who recently reformulated "the ethics of gender" (2002). Parsons, writing within a theological framework, thinks ethics through gender and seeks to rescue a universalistic ethical project for Christian thought that is attentive to feminist theory. My attempt here is the reverse: I think gender through ethnographic attention to ethical action. While I agree with Parsons that ethics is a discourse concerning good, I am most interested in how good is itself made in particular, locally meaningful practices.

14. Orthodox theology colludes in this by regarding persons as inherent members of aggregate communities: the social family mirrors the Holy Family, and people come to know their human and divine natures through direct experience of these relationships (du Boulay 1974, 1986; Dubisch 1995).

15. According to an *Athens News* report dated 9 April 1997, the Ministry of the Interior, bowing to pressure from international human rights groups, planned to remove the category of religion from *taftótita* (identification cards). This followed years of struggle between politicians and priests. In 1993, New Democracy, then as now the opposition party, had made motions toward abolishing religion from *taftótita*, inciting incendiary sermons from priests across the country. An editorial in a June 1993 edition of the Sunday *Eleftherotipía*—given to me as a handout in my advanced Greek class—argued against the mandatory reporting of religious persuasion: "Religious belief is a personal entity, it springs from the free will of someone, it is not ordered or certified on public paper, such as *taftótita*." Politicians have been hesitant to cross the will of a priestly majority, since priests exercise significant influence over voters.

16. I agree with Charles Piot, an anthropologist who has grappled with similar issues in writing about West African society, in wanting to "challenge orientalism's polarized and hierarchical conceptions not by showing how individualistic Others are—one of the strategies of orientalism's critics—but instead by pointing out how non-individualistic (non-'Western') Westerners are" (1999, 20).

17. Unless otherwise indicated, all interviews were conducted in Greek and, with the written permission of the interviewee, tape-recorded. Occasionally, women would hit the pause button on the machine to clarify a question or to make a remark off the record.

18. It also proved far easier for me to meet women in a professional manner than to meet men. A few early experiences interviewing men professionally involved with reproductive issues reinforced my decision not to pursue

more personal interviews with men unknown to myself (see also Inhorn 1994). To give just one example, during an interview I conducted in the hospital office of a noted physician, a male assistant to the doctor who sat in on our discussion spent much of the hour silently staring at my chest, a smirk plastered on his young face. These were by no means serious incidents in their own right, and I do not intend to suggest that it was especially difficult or uncomfortable being a foreign woman in Greece (I quickly learned how to deal, quite effectively and not impolitely, with catcalls on the street), but I admit that the accumulated experience injured my professional confidence.

19. In 1994, the purchase price of an apartment in Pangrati was, on average, 200,000–280,000 drachmes (U.S.$1,480–$2,074) per square meter, compared with the city mean of 250,000–300,000 drachmes in such areas as Nikia, Nea Smyrni, Marousi, Halandri, and Glyfadha, which are not so centrally located. Kypseli offered the cheapest prices (150,000–200,000 drachmes), while prices in the tree-lined suburb of Kifisia ranged from 300,000 to 800,000 drachmes per square meter (*Ta Nea*, 1 April 1994).

20. Angelo Saporiti (1989) approaches what I have in mind in theorizing that a fertility decline emerges out of a shift from uncontrolled to controlled fertility, when the source of fertility control is wrested away from social institutions, such as the church (or even from God—i.e., from supernatural forces), and handed over to individual couples making their (supposedly) private choice. In order to account for why high fertility is associated with traditional sensibilities and lower fertility with modern sensibilities, Saporiti moves to a smaller unit of analysis and considers the family as a social structure that can effect change and not just be the passive recipient of change. Adopting Pierre Bourdieu's notion of "family strategy" (1976), Saporiti considers how reproductive decision making is guided at the familial level by maintaining or improving social position. This framework, at the surface, articulates what middle-class Athenians related to me of their experiences. Inheritance, socialization, education, choice of spouse, labor participation, labor migration, and reproduction are all entwined, says Bourdieu, and this allows us, adds Saporiti, to understand how microlevel practices are tied to, but not subsumed by, collective interests and cultural standards for behavior. While I applaud the attempt to grant individuals credit for their ingenuity in applying the faculty of reason, in the end both Bourdieu and Saporiti rely on the assumption that, when individuals are granted more agency in reproduction, they will choose to have fewer children. This is not the argument I make.

21. On female chastity codes, see Friedl 1967; Schneider 1971; Hirschon 1978; Herzfeld 1983; du Boulay 1986. On equating sex with procreation, see Hirschon 1978; Loizos and Papataxiarchis 1991a. On birthing as the legitimation of female sexuality, see du Boulay 1974, 1986.

22. For related critiques of the gender neutrality of rational models embedded in structural adjustment programs, see Owoh 1995; in AIDS-prevention campaigns in Africa, Schoepf 1997.

CHAPTER 2

1. Metaxas was appointed prime minister in 1936 by King George II in an effort to stabilize loyalty to the Crown. In 1924, following bitter defeat in the Greek-Turkey War (1919–1922), Greece declared itself a republican monarchy. That early republic lasted a total of twelve years, during which time it witnessed eleven changes in government and two coups as it waxed and waned under enduring conflict between staunch monarchists and idealist republicans. Popular memory of that time overlooks the domestic difficulties, so great is Metaxas's reputation for his patriotic defiance of Italian fascism. In 1940, with Italian and Greek troops poised in stalemate at the Albanian border, Mussolini issued Greece an infamous ultimatum to capitulate. Metaxas's reply, a thundering "No!," is memorialized today by a national holiday on the 28th of October to celebrate Greek self-determination. The Italians retreated, and Greece delayed, at least for a short time, its engagement in World War II.

2. Drawing on ethnographic depictions of village life from the 1950s and 1960s, and following the tendency of middle-class Athenians, my discussion here edges toward oversimplifying regional differences (in inheritance and residency patterns, for instance) of rural Greece.

3. Writing of the early 1980s, du Boulay notes that girls, "although they have so much to lose from this situation, apparently believe that a man who does not attempt to sleep with them within a very few days of their first going out together must be a homosexual" (1986, 151).

4. By *substance* I mean only that which counts as nature, and which people must endeavor to control in order to demonstrate virtue (I contrast sexual impulse and behavior with fertilization of egg and sperm); this should not be confused with the very particular meaning of *substance* in Aristotelian philosophy, which is not relevant to this discussion.

5. Greek sexuality is centrally categorized not by heterosexual (opposite-sex) and homosexual (same-sex) desire, but by active and passive sexual orientations (Hirschon 1978; Faubion 1993).

6. Merely by being in the wrong place at the wrong time, a woman provided cause to doubt her propriety. In the past, a woman who did not belong to a "house" (read: to the patriarch of a house) as daughter, wife, or *yerontokóri* all too frequently became, by implication, a "woman of the road" (Hirschon 1978). Young widows living alone were especially vulnerable to nighttime visitation by village men and to daytime ostracization by the wives of these men.

7. During the Orthodox wedding ceremony, as the priest crosses the ceremonial wedding crowns *(stéfana)* three times over the heads of the bride and groom, he chants, "Unite them in one mind; Crown them into one flesh" (Stewart 1991, 68).

8. Delaney argues that, from the cultural understanding that men are seen to create human life through "sowing" their generative "seed," they have taken license to control the human lives they create—and they begin by controlling the sexuality of women, a precursor to determining which children are

generated from which men's seed (1986, 1991, 1998; see also Schneider 1971; du Boulay 1974; Hirschon 1978). The symbolic and practical basis of patriarchy is, according to Delaney, known paternity.

9. An Athenian anthropologist once remarked to me that in Athens still today, regardless of socioeconomic class, relatives and family friends keep a close eye on the belly of a recently wed woman, watching for signs of gestation.

10. The loss of a child through miscarriage, stillbirth, or infant mortality has been blamed on *ksotiká*, on the Nereids, fairies, and demons (fallen angels) that lurk in unrouted territories and pop up during liminal periods in daily or calendrical cycles and during gestation (Stewart 1991). When miscarriage, still-birth, and infant mortality are attributed to the trespass of demons, a woman is not held ultimately responsible for the outcome of her pregnancy but is pitied for having this gift of God taken away from her by forces beyond her control.

11. Her eyes shining with admiration, Eleni told me several stories about this woman. Once she was called to a delivery, a complicated one where the woman almost died, while the husband was off at the *kafenío*. This *maía* (mid-wife) stormed down the street with two pistols at her waist, marched into the *kafenío*, fired two shots into the ground, and yelled, "Man! Get home to your woman. She almost died birthing your son!" The street had cleared out for her to pass.

12. Roland Moore (personal communication), who conducted ethnographic research in the 1980s in a village not far from Athens, confirms this speculation based on his conversations with Greek men.

13. This figure corresponds with a still-low abortion rate (Comninos 1988).

14. Writing of marriage two decades ago in Viotia, du Boulay remarks, "The sexual relationship between men and women is, basically, one in which the strength and the desire of the man is the dominant feature, and in which, as in the matter of outright physical violence, there is an unquestionably ex-ploitative element. Women are taken, so they say, whether they are well or ill, 'wanting or not wanting' *(thelontas, de thelontas),* whether they are tired or not, resisting only at the risk of blows" (1986, 150).

15. An anthropologist from Salonika shared with me a saying among her grandmother's friends regarding appropriate family size: "Four—many, three—good, two—few, one—nobody" *(téssara pollá, tría kalá, dhío lígha, éna kanéna).*

16. Throughout the 1920s and 1930s, at least one-tenth of all children died within a year of birth; the infant mortality rate gradually fell to 40 in 1,000 by 1960, and 14 in 1,000 by 1985 (NSSG 1993). One young woman noted that, "in the past, most people had about four kids and would say *'dhío tou theoú'"* (two of God) because so many children were lost in infancy or early childhood. Still today, it is common practice—"from when there were a lot of kids dying in in-fancy," as another young mother explained to me—to wish a newly birthed mother *"Na zísi"* or *"Na sou zísi"* ("May it live" or "May it live for you").

17. Sexual relations among women seem, according to the ethnographic literature, to have been rare; if so, this is not the result of prohibition so much

as because sexual liaisons between women have been unspeakable and virtually unthinkable. The church, lacking scriptural cues, does not say anything on
the matter (Faubion 1993, 221). Although some ethnographers point here to an
equation between female sexuality and procreation (Loizos and Papataxiarchis
1991a, 229), I reject this explanation in favor of one forwarded by James
Faubion, drawing on the analysis that Greek sexuality is categorized not by
"male" and "female," but by "active" and "passive" roles (see also Hirschon
1978): "Women may perhaps 'play' with one another. But they are without the
single, crucial implement that could lend to their sexual play genuine political
import. Of no political consequence, sexual liaisons between women are traditionally not of any particular categorical consequence either" (Faubion 1993,
221). That sexual intimacy between women has not counted culturally, and
therefore politically, has allowed a subcultural, intellectually vibrant lesbian
community to flourish in Greece's cities (and vacation on the isle of Lesvos).

Nevertheless, over at least the past decade, lesbian sex acts have been graph-
ically depicted in popular magazines (Panopoulos 1994), and the label *lesbian*
is entering into everyday discourse. Eleni told me of a recent visit to her family village in the Peloponnese, where she spoke with the daughter of a friend
who is in her early twenties, asking how life was in the village these days. The
young woman replied, "I was happy when I was a teenager; I didn't have a
boyfriend and didn't want to and so everybody said that I was a lesbian."
Eleni's eyes widened in astonishment as she reported this. "That's a nonword,
I didn't expect it," she told me. The young woman is not lesbian; today she lives
with her boyfriend. But Eleni was favorably impressed that the idea of women
loving other women sexually if not romantically was both acknowledged and
named in this village in the 1990s, and that her young friend benefited from
the label because it took pressure off her to go with a high school boy.

18. The original title of the book translates as *Life and Social World of
Alexis Zorbas*. Kazantzakis's Zorbas embodies a masculine national character
that has been codified by its English title, in both the book and the film, as
Zorba the Greek (Herzfeld 1997a, 97).

19. In areas of northern Greece, one marriage custom has the bride's father
walk beside her as she leaves his house for the wedding. The father carries a
large knife and with it cuts into the ground beneath her foot each time she
takes a step, vividly symbolizing the severing of her roots to her natal household. From here on, the woman is largely on her own in a potentially hostile
environment—at least until she has children of her own.

20. Although before his death General Metaxas successfully resisted Italian occupation of the mainland, his successor welcomed British troops into
Athens, which, true to Metaxas's predictions, provoked Hitler to invade.
Shamed by the outcome of his request for foreign aid, the fledgling prime minister committed suicide, leaving the nation leaderless and occupied. In the
rugged isolation of the mountains, Communist activists consolidated the National Liberation Front to organize resistance against Nazi Germans. Motivated by the desire to feed themselves and their families, and perhaps spying

an opportunity to break free from patriarchal strictures, large numbers of women fought alongside men in the resistance (McNeill 1978; Fourtouni 1986; Hart 1996). When the war ended, Greece found itself under British governance as part of a deal struck between Churchill and Stalin. Britain denied much of the triumph to the Resistance, and Communists were heavily underrepresented in reconstruction efforts. Between October 1944 and November 1945, the government changed hands six times, without elections, as prime ministers were appointed and reappointed by U.S. and British embassies. Political instability and disenfranchisement led to civil war. Having no chance to recover from the ravages of occupation, Greeks found themselves again facing food shortages and fear of raiding, again sending children, spouses, and siblings into guerrilla-style skirmishes. War dragged on until 1949, when the newly thrown-together Greek National Army eventually quashed the insurgent uprising, owing in no small measure to emergency aid supplied by the Truman Doctrine to the "free" peoples of Greece in the form of U.S. guns and CIA training to combat internal Communist subversion (McNeill 1978; Fourtouni 1986; Clogg 1992). U.S. and British fears of Communism benefited the right-wing national army and not only decided the outcome of civil war but also contributed to rifts in Greek politics that would lead to another military dictatorship in the 1970s. During the civil war, one-tenth of the population was forced out of the mountains (where residents provided a resource base for the rebels) and into refugee camps built with Marshall Plan money around the outskirts of Athens. Today in the remote mountains of the Peloponnese, travelers still encounter the ghostly shells of villages, accessible only by mule (and not army vehicles), which the state forbade people to repopulate (McNeill 1978).

21. As housing became a key investment strategy for the postwar middle class, land speculation and construction created the apartment blocks that constitute today's urban sprawl. Here, urban dwellers of all social and class backgrounds found themselves integrated not only in the same neighborhoods but also living together in the same buildings. Such proximity has contributed to a continuity in social expectations and perceptions among people across the middle-class spectrum (Prevelakis 1989, 22–24). The legal system of land speculation and development that took off in the 1950s is called *antiparochí*, or "in exchange for." In exchange for the plot of land on which, most often, his or her family's house stood, the original landowner received a promise from the developer that, once the new apartment building was completed, the family would own part of it, a part at least equal in size to the house demolished. Each apartment is owned by a personal interest who may either occupy or let it. Usually the original landowner was assured of a minimum of two apartments in the new building, one to live in and the other to rent out—at least until it was needed as dowry. Apartments dowered in this way provided the structural possibility that urban migration would not disrupt the custom of matrilocal (or, if the apartment is given as a wedding gift to the groom by his parents, patrilocal) residence patterns. It is common today to see the same surname appear two or three times on the rows of nameplates outside an apartment building's

front entrance. The "eventual dowry" apartment I rented in Pangrati was owned by a teenager who lived with her parents on the island of Chios. I paid my rent each month, in cash, to the girl's cousins who lived on the first floor.

22. My own parents recall walking the streets of Athens in 1975, two small children in tow and my mother visibly pregnant with a third, and being stopped more than once by an outraged (but also envious?) Greek demanding, "What are you doing having such a large family? What are you going to do when the [next] war comes!"

23. In 1937 Archbishop Chrysostomos and fifty-five metropolitans issued a letter strongly opposing every contraceptive device and the act of abortion, "viewing them as threats to family life and as evil acts against God's will and rebellion against His laws" (Comninos 1988, 208). The present patriarch of Constantinople, while condemning abortion, recognizes the practical need to protect against unwanted pregnancy and the sexual transmission of disease.

24. Born in western Canada, where she was raised by recently immigrated parents in a strongly Greek community, Katherine moved to Athens in her early twenties. In 1967 she relocated to Canada and, soon thereafter, divorced. She raised her sons in Canada, as Canadians, but had since moved back to Athens (as had her younger son, even though that meant serving a stint in the Greek army). That Katherine is Greek Canadian may contribute to her candidness; she has adopted what I think of as a North American penchant for "the confession," that willingness, even need, that leads many to divulge their inner secrets and past experiences to near strangers in an effort to control the self-image being presented and to ensure that others know who they "really" are. This reflects a very different strategy of presentation than called for by the Greek sense that "one learns to know oneself primarily by contrast with others" (Friedl 1962, 76). In Athens, Katherine and I came to be neighbors and great friends. My vast balcony faced her living room window, and we delighted in calling to each other across the gap between our buildings. We met often to drink coffee and talk about feminism and writing and Greece and my love life and her love life and the love lives of mutual friends.

25. The pill was introduced in Greece in 1963, but could be sold only by doctor's prescription for regulation of the menstrual cycle (Siampos 1975, 343). In the United States at that time, only married women had access to oral contraceptives.

26. In the midst of writing the first draft of this text, I returned to Athens for a brief visit in 1996 and slept on Katherine's sofa, which had moved with her to an apartment on the slope of Mount Lykavitos. We sat together with a chapter draft I had previously mailed her. Two years had passed since our initial interviews and, even in that relatively short span of time, her take on some of the issues had changed. In 1996 she was more definitive in her words. She edited out qualifiers. She asked me to use her real name.

27. The name Ourania Katsigianni is a pseudonym. Our interview was conducted primarily in English.

28. Abortion rates in Catholic southern European countries are also high relative to the rest of western Europe. Italian and Spanish Catholic women apply a similar kind of relative ethics, based in a moral commitment to being good mothers, to reconcile abortion use as a means of family limitation when men do not cooperate with withdrawal and abstinence (for a supporting argument concerning abortion practice under Italian fascism, see De Grazia 1993, 51–52).

29. The Latin word *dispenatio* is canonically used in biblical translations of *ikonomía*. The Roman Catholic notion of dispensation has acquired the strict meaning of "exception to the law granted by the proper authority."

30. To provide an example of how *ikonomía* is used, both Meyendorff and Timothy Ware (1963) turn to marriage law. Marriage in the Orthodox tradition is not simply a contract drawn between two consenting adults under God's blessing; Orthodox marriage is upheld as a unique and eternal relationship through which "human love is being projected into the eternal Kingdom of God" (Meyendorff 1974, 197). Under the direction of *ikonomía*, however, second or third marriage is tolerated, regardless of whether the first ended by death or divorce. The idea is that, if a person failed in his or her first attempt at union, but desires to try again, then remarriage is considered a lesser evil than solitude: "Byzantine tradition accepts the possibility of an initial mistake, as well as the fact that single life, in cases of death or the simple absence of the partner, is a greater evil than remarriage for those who cannot 'bear' it" (197). A second marriage is, however, distinguished from the first, sacral marriage; the ceremony is altered, the crowning is omitted, and rites of penance are introduced: "Byzantine tradition approaches the problem of remarriage—after widowhood or divorce—in terms of penitential discipline" (197).

31. The overall drop may be primarily attributable to rural areas where women may be less inclined to report agricultural work as labor. Peter Allen, who also cites this curious statistic, calls attention to the fact that Greek census data depend on responses to questionnaires, and he notes that rural women would be likely not to consider the work they do in orchards and fields as "outside employment" (1986, 9). I wonder further whether women would be hesitant to admit to being paid for menial labor, a clear form of outside employment, because this work is denigrated, particularly so during this era (if the housewife was upheld as the ideal woman, as Stamiris [1986] suggests), and because she would want to obscure the receipt of income on which she was not paying taxes.

32. Pleased by its zero tolerance policy toward Communism, the United States and other Western powers allowed the junta to flourish. Spiro Agnew, a U.S. vice president and second-generation Greek American, visited Athens in 1971 to lend his support to the anti-Communist regime.

33. In the autumn of 1973, student dissidents driven by a Marxist political ideology occupied the law school and, on the 14th of November, overtook the Athens Polytechnic University. On November 17, military troops and police stormed the school. Over thirty persons were killed. This bloody event soon

led to Papadopoulos's overthrow. The event is commemorated by the autonymic anarchist-terrorist group November 17.

34. Nationwide, the majority of women work in pink collar sectors of the economy; in 1981, 40 percent of waged and salaried women workers were located in the social services, followed by manufacturing, trade, finance, and agriculture (Tzannatos 1989, 157). Salaried employees, primarily of the government, accounted for only 29.2 percent of female employment overall (the vast majority of women working in urban areas, however, are salaried employees); 68.6 percent of working women worked as unpaid family members on farms and in fields, as well as in family-owned shops, restaurants, and other small businesses. Much of this nonsalaried work has entailed the marketing of domestic services that women have already been trained to do (see also Gal and Kligman 2000, 59). For example, women throughout Greece earn money by renting rooms to tourists as part of an informal system only partially overseen by the Ministry of Tourism. Almost the exclusive business domain of women, these *dhomátia* (let rooms) range from a spare room in someone's home to a wing added to a house that provides as many as a half dozen rooms with or without private baths. It is far more difficult in cities for women to establish their own business enterprises.

35. Jill Dubisch has noted that people on the island of Tinos have a saying that espouses this view: "Many children are poverty" (1986, 33).

36. See also Denich 1974 on Montenegro; Collier 1986 on Andalusia; and Kligman 1998 on Romania.

37. This interview was conducted primarily in English.

38. The president of the Greek Housewives Union, a woman I interviewed and refer to by a pseudonym, was quoted in the newspapers as saying, "We provide child-care and look after the elderly, thus relieving the state from the burden of providing these services. The value of this free work does not appear in the [state's] budget" (*Athens News,* 20 June 1995). This story reports an opinion survey conducted among registered voters in the greater Athens area for the Athenian daily *Ta Nea:* 86 percent surveyed agreed with the idea that housewives should receive a state pension, while only 9.5 percent disagreed.

39. According to the *Statistical Yearbook of Greece,* 21.8 percent of all births in 1989 occurred within the first year of a marriage (NSSG 1992).

40. This interview was conducted primarily in English.

41. "Babies Killed and Sold in Parents' Desperation," *Athens News,* 11 November 1993, p. 2.

42. "Stavroula Looks at Life," *To Víma,* 19 September 1993.

43. The name Aliki Andoniou is a pseudonym.

44. Contrasting examples can be found in the modernism of industrial societies under socialist paternalism, most notably Ceausescu's Romania (Kligman 1998), in which the paternal state assumes many "parental" responsibilities for raising and training the "children" of the nation.

45. In 1998, Eva married a man from her village; soon after, she birthed a baby. The family lives in Athens.

46. The woman who helped me with transcribing and translating this interview—who is the same age as these three, holds a master's degree, and was working as a secretary—added the following comment to my notes: "My grandmother used to cut off the tops off my winter shoes to make them summer shoes; this is 1968–70, and it's not that we didn't have the money [her father works in shipping], but that is how she was."

47. This price would fetch a one- or perhaps two-bedroom flat, depending on the size, the floor (ground floor versus a higher one, possibly with a view), and the neighborhood.

48. The word Athena used here is *faghitó*, the general word for "food"; but my assistant who transcribed this tape translated it as "meat" *(kréas)*. In her view, "regular food" means meat, so if parents are skimping for economy's sake, meat is what they would skip. I tried to imagine this happening among middle-class families in the United States and could think only of parents (such as those for whom I have baby-sat) who feed their children at 5 P.M., get them to bed by 7 P.M., and sit down to a child-free dinner after 8 P.M.

49. In U.S. dollars in 1994, these translate to $174 and $43. It is important to keep in mind that, relative to U.S. cities, rent in Athens is inexpensive and material goods are exorbitant. A standard cotton blouse in a downtown Athens clothing store that year cost between $45 and $60.

50. Between 1963 and 1981, female hourly earnings in manufacturing consistently averaged 67 percent of male earnings (Tzannatos 1989, 157). However, on assuming full EEC membership, Greece has been required to provide equal pay, treatment, and opportunity for women in the labor force. Between 1981 and 1982, the average female wage in manufacturing industries, which employ one-third of all paid women workers, increased relative to the average male wage by 9 percent (from 67.2 percent to 73.1 percent), rising to 73.9 percent in 1983 (Tzannatos 1989, 158).

51. More than one woman mentioned proudly to me that Greek Orthodoxy is less oppressive to women than is Islam; Orthodox women, for instance, most frequently act as their family's intercessor with the Divine (see Dubisch 1986, 1995; although see Inhorn 1994 on Egyptian Muslim women's domestic religion). Athenians also say it is easier for women to walk the streets of Greek cities than Turkish ones.

52. In another act of gendered intimacy, some Athenians have invented a new wedding custom: when the priest chants about a woman "fearing her husband," a bride will step on her husband's foot as if to say, "Enjoy this while you can, because we know who's *really* going to be in charge of things." The "appearance of prestige" and the "reality of power" seem so often to coexist without their contradictions causing chaos (Friedl 1967; Bourdieu 1977). Greek women I have met (and have read about) take the stance that, as long as you let the men think they are in charge, they will pay no attention to what is really going on behind the scenes. This cultural tendency emerges from a patriarchal society in which ethics has been organized around the maintenance of conventional appearance.

53. A *koumbáros* is a friend or relative of the bride and groom who, as part of the wedding ceremony, assumes spiritual responsibility to the married couple. This person is somewhat analogous to a godparent who, during baptism, assumes spiritual responsibility to the child.

54. At Mitera Hospital, the prestigious private maternity hospital in Athens that is computer-linked with the Boston Lying-In Hospital, a delivery in 1994 cost about U.S.$4,000, when the average Athenian income was between $770 and $1,150 a month. An office visit with an obstetrician-gynecologist averaged 5,000–11,000 drachmes (U.S.$22–$48) per visit, a visit to a pediatrician a bit less.

55. In 1993, the Greek consumer price inflation rate fell to 12.1 percent, down from 14.4 percent the previous year. The 12 percent rate was about three times the EU average in 1993 (*Athens News,* 8 January 1994, p. 6).

56. The significance of providing education as an obligation of *teknopiía* emerged during a 1997 public inheritance battle between the widow and children (by a former wife) of Prime Minister Andreas Papandreou, which was complicated by the discovery of Papandreou's mother's handwritten will, dated 1 May 1964. In her will, published in the newspapers, Sophia Mineiko left exclusively to her granddaughter, Sophia, the family home in Paleo Psychiko (an Athens suburb). "As for my other grandchildren—George, Nicholas and Andrikos, whom I loved equally—I have no other property to leave to them. And the above-mentioned property would lose value if it were to be divided up. For this reason, I wish them every success and progress. Taking into account that my other grandchildren are all males, their financial struggle in life will be an easier one." Sophia's equitable reasoning extended to her most famous son. "Regarding my beloved son Andreas, I have devoted my life to his upbringing and education. [Two properties] were sold to finance his studies at Minneapolis in the United States and then his postgraduate studies at Berkeley, California. Thus I have my conscience clear that I have fulfilled my duty toward my beloved son Andreas."

57. Greeks speak passionately about education in general. Such feeling may have been spurred initially by a patriotic desire to be free of Turkish "corruption"; according to the Constitution of 1952 (instituted following the civil war), education should enable "development of the national consciousness of the youth on the basis of the ideological directions of Hellenochristian civilization" (quoted in Augustinos 1995, 190). In 1890 the first woman was admitted to the University of Athens, and by 1981, 4 percent of the entire population (age ten and above) held an advanced degree (69 percent of these were male). In relation to GNP, in the 1980s twice as many Greek students as Americans pursued higher education (Cowan 1988, 82). The nationwide literacy rate for individuals above the age of ten in 1981 was 91.4 percent (97 percent of those illiterate were female; NSSG 1993).

58. Between 120,000 and 130,000 students take the exam each year, competing for 35,000 admissions.

59. The name Galena Skiatha is a pseudonym.

60. Eleni argued, "I don't think the dowry is so humiliating for women as the American culture or the western European culture thinks. It was a burden for the whole family, and especially for the men of the family," who were obliged to help marry off their sisters before they could get married. "A friend of mine was in love with a boy; she was working—she had a clothing shop—and in the next village was this man with four sisters. And he said he couldn't get married because of the four sisters. That was twenty years ago. And of course they never got married."

61. Interview with Aliki Andoniou, 28 March 1994.

62. There is a saying in Greece that "everything is illegal, yet anything is allowed" (*óla apaghorévonte allá óla epitréponte*). On several occasions I heard Athenians philosophize that the illicit nature of something (drugs, sex) is what makes it more appealing; in illustration, they raised the problem of alcoholism in America, where the legal drinking age is twenty-one—in their minds an absurdly advanced age.

63. I caught part of one such show that aired during prime-time evening hours on a private television station (there is no governmental regulation of the airwaves). This was a 1970s U.S. how-to sexual relationship video of a new-age genre that is apparently a popular rental item in Britain. I watched a naked, white, heterosexual couple sitting cross-legged, facing one another, palms out and nearly touching as they circled their hands in slow, synchronized motions intended to unite their energies, or something like that. A hypnotic male voice-over provided running commentary. I found it instructive on European stereotypes of Americans.

64. Nia, the anthropology student whose female relatives live in the village where her parents were raised, shared with me many of that region's myths (as she called them) surrounding the female body, including those "to do with the women's internal system, about the strength [*dhínami*] that the placenta holds and the magical abilities of the umbilical cord." In her matrilocal village, a piece of his own dried umbilical cord is given to a male child "as a good luck charm." Girls are seen not to need such a charm, since "the relationship of the mother and the daughter is of the same sex, and is very close." In this region, mothers and daughters remain proximately close to one another; there is no need for a symbolic tie. A boy, on the other hand, "after the age of fifteen leaves the home environment and goes with the men." By symbolically retaining the in utero bond between mother and son, "the umbilical cord connects the house with the society." Here, a woman *as mother* is "the house" and her sons are "the society" (du Boulay 1974, 1986).

65. For similar arguments regarding men's activities, see Herzfeld 1985; Papataxiarchis 1991.

66. While it may at first glance seem trivial, the adoption of timesaving devices and prepared food items further signals a shift in cultural emphasis from women's sexual activities to their production of successful children. In her 1978 article "Open Body/Closed Space," Renée Hirschon writes that women's status is measured in accordance with the extent to which she demonstrates re-

straint or self-control externally, through social convention, and internally, through moral force. A woman is expected to show restraint in the four most important areas of her life: her sexuality, her access to the world beyond her home, her speech, and her use of time. Traditional Greek foods, Hirschon says, involved long preparation times in order to keep women out of trouble. Foods easily thrown together are referred to as "prostitute's food" (like the Italian pasta putanesca). Thus timesaving devices challenge notions of women's appropriate occupation. These days, however, when a woman's status is based more on who her children are and what they do, and less on her sex life, prepared foods can be morally appropriate in that they let her spend more quality time with her children.

CHAPTER 3

1. The Fifth Panhellenic Conference on AIDS and Sexually Transmitted Diseases, Caravel Hotel, Athens, 11–13 February 1994. George Creatsas, a professor of adolescent gynecology, reiterated these statistics, which I first heard in 1994, when speaking to reporters in anticipation of the Second National Family Planning Conference, held at the War Museum of Athens, 18–20 February 2000. As stated by a headline in the Athens newspaper *Kathimerini*, "Abortions Equal Number of Births: Greek Rate Highest in European Union," 16 February 2000 (on-line English edition, http://www.ekathimerini.com; accessed July 2000).

2. These Athens conferences include "Birth and the Future: European Program of Educating Educators," a three-day professional seminar run by the Foundation for Research on Childhood, 19 November 1993; "Contemporary Demographic Trends and Family Planning in Greece," a public symposium sponsored by the Family Planning Association of Greece, 21 January 1994; "Woman and AIDS," a panel at the Fifth Panhellenic Conference on AIDS and Sexually Transmitted Diseases, at the Caravel Hotel, 11–13 February 1994; and the Family Planning Association's fourth "Sexual Education and Health" seminar, War Museum, 3–5 November 1994.

3. A 1994 article published in the progressive youth magazine *01* (Lykouropoulos 1994) reported that many Greek companies that package foreign-manufactured condoms do so without sterilizing the imported product, which has never been tested for tears or other damage. Indeed, in March 1998 seven brands of imported condoms were removed from the Greek market after they were found to be defective. Included among these were models of the top-selling brand DUO, manufactured in Malaysia and packaged in Greece under the German-based multinational corporation Beiersdorf (*Athens News*, 12 March 1998).

4. Surveying male and female Athenians (ages sixteen to sixty-four), this study found that, while 79.7 percent were "aware of" the pill, only 6.8 percent of the women respondents had used it.

5. Women in Greece are generally advised to have a Pap test once a year, as in the United States. In Britain, in contrast, women are told they need it just once every three years, probably owing to financial issues. Both the United Kingdom and Greece offer comprehensive national health care, but it is less extensively used in Greece.

6. Feminine pads and panty liners certainly outnumber tampons on supermarket shelves, and yet nonapplicator tampons dominate this market in urban Greece.

7. The name George Kakoyanis is a pseudonym.

8. In 1988, 27.3 abortions per 1,000 women age fifteen to forty-four were performed in the United States. Statistics from the U.S. Centers for Disease Control and Prevention, *Abortion Surveillance—United States, 1996.* 30 July 1999.

9. Interview with Kakoyanis conducted in English.

10. Consciousness-raising, as Sara Evans has noted, is founded on the belief that people instigate social change "through a process of talking together, discovering common problems, and thereby understanding the need for collective action" (1979, 134). In these words can be recognized a committed belief in human rationality: given certain knowledge, given the opportunity to reflect on one's experiences, and using the tools of socialist principles, people will naturally be led to rethink their position in the world and will cease capitulating to previously unexamined forms of oppression. Fertility control issues have been central to feminist consciousness-raising.

11. The following chapter discusses why and how the FPAG's initial and ongoing task has been to confront this stereotype and to convince the public and the government that family planning can and does extend to concerns other than population limitation.

12. Many Greek family planning volunteers have trained at the Margaret Sanger Center in New York. The FPAG recently inaugurated training centers throughout the country, where people who have been to the New York program train others who will eventually replace them. In addition, FPAG members attend numerous conferences abroad to keep abreast of ongoing developments in contraceptive and fertility technologies.

13. The organization was established in 1962 to provide general social welfare services for mothers and infants, including supplemental nutritional support, medical services, and emergency services following natural disasters. It also organized research into problems associated with maternity and childhood (Siampos 1975, 348–49).

14. Biological and sociocultural anthropologists have, however, demonstrated that the twenty-eight-day cycle is not a cultural universal. Based on a sedentary European housewife's life, this so-called normal cycle is not normal for women whose everyday activities are much more or less active and energy intensive.

15. The text reads: "During the sexual act the sperm passes from the male genital organ (penis) inside the female genital organ (vagina). The spermatozöa move about very quickly and enter through the vagina into the uterus,

passing through a narrow opening called the cervix. Every month regularly an ovum ripens and is freed (ovulation) from an ovary and passes inside the fallopian tubes toward the uterus. If a spermatozöon meets the ovum inside a fallopian tube, they are joined—that is, fertilization occurs—and the now fertilized ovum descends toward the uterus. AND . . . a baby begins to develop inside the uterus of the mother."

16. The fourth "Sexual Education and Health" seminar was held by the FPAG with support by IPPF, at the War Museum of Athens, 3–5 November 1994. This speaker, George Kindis, a leading researcher, did stress that the content of the pill is changing, and that the levels of hormones such as progesterone have been significantly reduced. However, George Creatsas, who convened this roundtable, "Sexual Relations among Adolescents," agreed that the pill in particular is largely misunderstood by Greek women. He further commented that "we have to get beyond the era when a woman goes to her doctor and says, 'Give me anything but hormones.' "

17. A thirty-eight-year-old resident of Rhodes, who birthed her first baby in 1961, told the anthropologist Mary Lefkarites in the late 1970s, "I thought of birth as so dangerous, so frightening, that I did not feel anyone [at home] could help me except for the physician. [He is] like God. Especially if he gives you a little encouragement. You feel that he is the reason [for nothing bad happening]" (1992, 404).

18. Distribution and frequency of family planning services ($n = 20$), adapted from Margaritidou and Mesteneos 1992, 28:

TYPE OF SERVICE	VERY FREQUENT	FREQUENT	RARE	NEVER
Family planning counseling	4	6	–	–
Contraception	9	9	2	–
Abortion information	6	5	7	1
Genetic counseling	6	3	6	3
Prenatal checkup	5	4	7	3
Infertility advice	4	4	9	–
Sex education	4	12	2	–
STD or AIDS information	3	10	5	–
Gynecological illness	12	4	2	–
Pap test	18	–	–	–
Breast examination	13	5	–	–

19. An extreme example of this same modern faith in rational action can be found in *Private Choices and Public Health: The AIDS Epidemic in an Economic Perspective* (Philipson and Posner 1993). In his review for the *Times Higher Education Supplement* (London), Keith Tolley (1994) writes, "The premise [of the book] is that individuals prefer sex without a condom. When, because infected numbers are low, the probability of experiencing a sexual trade with an infected person is low, the extra satisfaction (i.e., gain in utility) that risky sex provides over safe sex, is likely to exceed the perceived cost (i.e., loss of utility) associated with a higher risk of infection. Basic economic theory of trading under conditions of uncertainty means that as the incidence of Aids [sic] in a population increases, the probability of experiencing a sexual trade with an infected person also increases, resulting in a rise in the price (i.e., the expected cost) of risky sex and a fall in demand. As there is a reasonably close substitute available, i.e., sex with a condom, the individual wishing to maximise utility, has an incentive to switch to this activity. The economic model thus predicts a natural limit on the growth in Aids [sic] cases." Tolley goes on to note, "The existence of 'irrational behaviour,' a distinct possibility in actual sexual behaviour, is not considered."

20. Several feminist anthropologists have leveled similar critiques of the implementation of national and international, public and private, family planning programs throughout the developing world. See, for example, Morsy 1995; Pearce 1995; Van Eeuwijk and Mlangwa 1997; Kligman 1998; Rivkin-Fish 1999, 2000; Stark 2000; Thompson 2000.

21. For some of the pro-lifers in Ginsburg's account, however, abortion is so unnatural to womanhood that they describe it as imbued with male sexual violence and destruction.

22. In Greece, maternity and motherhood are lauded without creating the kinds of conceptualizations that bestow independent personhood on a fetus and lend credence to the application of individual rights discourse to a fetus in abortion cases. The ontological indeterminacy of the fetus, credited with human life but not human personhood, was brought to attention in a story in the *Athens News* (3 August 1995, p. 3) about a controversy in a Thessaloniki hospital exposed for cremating babies born dead—a violation of the dictates of the Orthodox Church. "Ippocration Hospital placed dead babies and embryos in the infirmary's incinerator, normally used for the destruction of amputated body parts and tissue removed during surgery," it was reported. Cremation is forbidden by law in Greece with the exception of aborted fetuses that are less than six months old. This law, then, makes an ontological distinction between early- and late-term fetuses by applying the burial law only to late-term fetuses. Hospital officials, insisting that the parents of stillborn babies were given the choice of hospital cremation or a proper burial, stated that many poor families did not claim their dead infants' bodies for they could not afford to pay the funeral expenses. They furthermore denied charges of wrongdoing on the claim that "there were 'gaps in the law' concerning the burial of newborns,"

presumably relating to the question of baptism. Clearly, the status of both fetus and newborn infant is open to contestation.

23. To guard against the mischief and misfortune of *ksotiká*, many restrictions have been placed on pregnant and menstruating women; they are not allowed to venerate (kiss) church icons or prepare the *kóliva*, a ritual funerary food. As Nia explained, "In the whole of Greece, women [when they are menstruating] are not allowed to take communion *[na metalávi]* because, through the blood you are losing you also lose the blood of Christ, which you take."

24. Krengel and Greifeld make a similar point about family planning in Uzbekistan (2000, 209).

25. See Jonathan Ned Katz's "The Invention of Heterosexuality" (1990) on the invention of this modern value in nineteenth-century western Europe.

26. That abortion rates are also high in Catholic southern European countries facing economic conditions similar to those in Greece suggests that "the Catholic Church"—or rather, Italian and Spanish Catholicism—is "more flexible" in everyday practice than Greeks often assume.

27. In the first draft of a medical report on local knowledge, attitudes, and practices in relation to HIV and AIDS in Athens, the authors write, "Abortion is not a moral issue of any dimension in Greece, and . . . there is a general lack of guilt about the subject" (Agrafiotis et al. 1990a, 38). Like Naziri's article, this is evocative of Edward Banfield's 1958 ethnography of southern Italian village life, *The Moral Basis of a Backward Society*. In this work, Banfield explicates what he sees as a problematic lack of " 'enlightened' self-interest" (11) in the villagers he lived among, faulting poverty, ignorance ("the peasant is as ignorant as his donkey" [35]), desire for status quo (blind adherence to convention), and a history of oppression that breeds despairing fatalism. Banfield concludes that the villagers are unable "to act together for their common good or, indeed, for any end transcending the immediate, material interest of the nuclear family" (10). While much of Banfield's language reads today as orientalizing and dated, his concern that a "family-centered ethos" (155) impedes productive "public spiritedness" resonates with the family planning notion that a family-centered ethos gets in the way of women's liberating self-interest. In both cases, peasant-minded lack of proper knowledge and the subordination of self-interest to the family unit are seen as stumbling blocks to the exercise of modern rationality.

28. On similar trends in post–Soviet Russia, see Rivkin-Fish 1999.

29. The difference between having sex and making love, or between modern and traditional sexual practices, may be one of semantics only. People may now simply be talking about a variety of sexual practices in which others have been happily (or in resignation) engaging, quietly, for generations. One friend told me that she heard older women in her husband's village giggling one day in the fields, telling dirty jokes. The women started saying, "Oh, you know sex, it's really good" (not the attitude she expected them to convey). "And you know, if you don't want children, you do it from behind!" My friend, a Greek-American, was aghast. "No, really," a woman of her grandmother's generation

assured her, "how else are you going to do it and have a good time—you just do it from behind!" The correlation between anal sex and contraceptively safe sex has been noted in other areas of the Mediterranean (Delaney 1991, 50–51).

30. In 1989, an estimated 8,000 persons had tested HIV positive in Greece (Agrafiotis et al. 1990a, 1). In 1993, the Greek Ministry of Health and Welfare reported for Greece a total of 845 known AIDS cases, which resulted in 323 deaths through September of that year (*Athens News*, Sunday, 28 November 1993). These numbers are low in comparison with other European countries. In 1993, 22,939 cases were reported in France, 17,029 in Spain, 15,780 in Italy, and in the United Kingdom 6,929 (Hellenic Archives of AIDS 1993, 141, cited in Tsalicoglou 1995, 95). But as Tsalicoglou points out, the relatively small numbers in Greece should be considered in light of an increasing rate of occurrence (1995, 85). In 1992, she notes, there were thirty times more new cases (162) than in 1984. By early 1994, 871 persons reportedly were living with AIDS in Greece; of these 779 were men and 92 were women (35.2 percent of the women were infected by their husbands) ("Woman and AIDS" panel at the Fifth Panhellenic Conference on AIDS and Sexually Transmitted Diseases, Caravel Hotel, 11–13 February 1994).

31. Greek Ministry of Health and Welfare statistics on means of infection do not quite match up with the common *noötropía:* 58 percent of AIDS cases were linked to homosexual contact, and only 4 percent to intravenous drug use. Ten percent were reportedly due to blood transfusion (despite a KEEL pamphlet's assurance that you can get a blood transfusion without fear of contracting HIV); 15 percent were from heterosexual contact, and 11 percent were linked to an "unknown source" (*Athens News*, Sunday, 28 November 1993).

32. Indeed, traumatic images of AIDS victims from around the world, but particularly Africa, had instilled a fear among Greeks in the 1990s that bordered on paranoia (for a critique of such images, see Patton 1992). A German man working at a small inn in Mytilene, Lesvos, complained to me in 1992 that, over the last couple of years, Greek tourists had begun to grumble noisily about having to share a bathroom with "other" (meaning foreign) guests; they purportedly feared they would "catch AIDS" from the toilet seat. In early 1994 a health clinic–social center opened in a working-class neighborhood near Piraeus, a place where people living with AIDS or with HIV could come for support, care, and counseling. According to newspapers, kids at a nearby elementary school staged a strike, claiming that the "air was bad," while a neighboring restauranteur complained that his business had suffered since the clinic's opening. So widespread are the misperceptions of how one can contract HIV that a KEEL pamphlet goes through a list of thirteen things you can do and *not* be in danger: embrace someone; shake hands; give a simple kiss; be near someone who sneezes; use someone else's books or pencils; use a "foreign" toilet, shower, or towel; swim in a pool; eat in a restaurant; handle foreign plates or glasses; be stung by mosquitoes; fall with an open wound; give blood; and get a blood transfusion. The quotes are from the FPAG leaflets "AIDS: The Known

'Unknown': Knowledge without Prejudices" and "AIDS and Otherwise . . . Prophylactic!"

33. From the FPAG leaflet "AIDS: The Known 'Unknown': Knowledge without Prejudices."

34. The Greek word here is *asfalós,* and surely the copywriters are playing on the double signification of the word, meaning not only "certainly" but also "safely."

35. While I was in Athens, Eftyhia Leontidou requested that I use her real name in my book. She has kindly read and approved all passages in which her name appears. Our interviews were conducted in English.

36. Not only is more tobacco consumed per capita in Greece than in nearly any other country in the world, but its rate of use is still increasing (Tsalicoglou 1995, 92).

37. At the same FPAG seminar, George Kakoyanis, to his credit, hinted that women's sexual behavior carries with it moral implications that family planners should address. He suggested that the pill's purported link with cancer suppressed its uptake in Greece not merely owing to the health risk but also because it exacerbated the association of women's pill use with a loose sexual morality—a woman taking pills could be seen by "others" to have "a certain attitude," an overly developed enthusiasm toward sex because she was willing to risk cancer for it. Family planners frequently respond to this kind of observation, however, by reducing gender roles to some realm of culture that rational action can and should overcome.

38. Several professionals I interviewed mentioned this; see also Emke-Poulopoulou 1994.

39. The claim was based on surveys of Greek army men, aged eighteen to twenty-four and from urban areas, in 424 general military hospitals, presented at the Ninth Northern Greek Medical Conference in Thessaloniki, 6–10 April 1994, and reported in "They Know Only the Prophylactic," 1 April 1994.

40. Interview conducted in English.

41. Valaoras and Trichopoulos, in separate publications, claim that induced abortions account for 40 percent of the reduction of the birthrate since World War II (see Comninos 1988). Their study of 1,000 women with secondary sterility found that in 475 of these cases the infertility was directly related to anatomical damage to the reproductive organs following induced abortion.

42. The FPAG publishes a leaflet on abortion titled "Do You Know? It Could Happen to You . . . Abortion: Procedure, Repercussions, Legality, Prevention." After explaining the options available to a woman facing an "undesirable" *(anepithímiti)* pregnancy, and after going into procedural detail about the aspiration method of abortion and the letter of the law on legal abortion, the text asks, "Is abortion dangerous?" The unequivocal answer given is "Yes." "Even if abortion is considered a relatively simple and safe surgical procedure," it warns, "all the same there are dangers caused by the drugs or this procedure itself." The pamphlet lists as dangers: allergic reaction to anesthetic drugs, hemorrhage, perforation of the uterus, damage to the neck or interior of the

uterus, inflammation, fever, endometriosis, and salpingitus, which increase the danger of ectopic pregnancy or sterility.

At a small, in-house seminar on family planning that I sat in on at Evangelismos (state) Hospital (12–13 February 1995), researchers presented statistical figures on complications resulting from abortions, following research conducted in New York. Uterine perforation was said to have an occurrence rate of just 1:10,625, or 0.009 percent. Since sterility can result from the scraping method of abortion (*apóksesi*, or in English a dilation and curettage or D and C), the aspiration method was recommended. The vast majority of abortions performed in Greece are by the aspiration method. In light of these developments, the language of the family planning campaign sounds harsh to my liberal American ears and closely resembles reactionary scare tactics (see also Rivkin-Fish 1999).

43. Since many Athenians are well aware of the pro-life political climate in the United States, I assumed that women I interviewed might suspect me of such judgment. In part for this reason, I never asked a woman outright whether she had had an abortion.

44. In 1996, the *Athens News* reported from a survey by the Greek Institute of Sexology among twenty- to twenty-five-year-old Athenians that "a large percentage . . . were not impressed the first time they had sex. For example, 61.6% of women said that the attempt had failed and 47.7% of men said they were not able to carry out the act" ("Youths Turning Backs on Sex," 20 January). This suggests that Greek sexologists, too, define sex as male-initiated heterosexual intercourse.

45. British feminist Scarlet Pollock writes, "Contraceptive research and the distribution of contraceptive methods are based upon [a] male-centered version of sex. Of central concern is how to prevent pregnancy and thus control the birth rate. It is *not* to question why it is women who bear the consequences of 'normal' sex; nor is it to ask what is so sacred about this male-oriented form of sexuality. The goal of government, pharmaceutical and medical organisations is to develop and distribute contraceptives which are most likely to prevent pregnancy while least likely to interfere with men's enjoyment of heterosexual intercourse" (1984, 138–39).

46. In "The Struggle for Reproductive Freedom," Gordon concluded in the late 1970s that, "for women, therefore, heterosexual relations are always intense, frightening, high-risk situations which ought, if a woman has any sense of self-preservation, to be carefully calculated. These calculations call for weapons of resistance, which may include sexual denial . . . [and] pregnancy itself" (1979, 127). The liberating promise of rational calculation is hard to ignore in Enlightenment-based societies.

47. The association between condoms and infidelity has been noted in regard to a variety of cultural settings; for example, concerning Ethiopian Jews in Israel, see Davids 2000, 152.

48. This conversation was held primarily in English.

49. "One of Six Greek Girls Are Sexually Abused, Study Reveals," *Athens News*, 16 April 1994, p. 2.

50. Young writers are addressing issues of domestic violence and sexual abuse in Greek literature. Eugenia Fakinou's lyrical novel *Astradeni* (1991) tells the story of eleven-year-old Astradeni, whose family leaves the small island of Symi, near Rhodes, to seek economic refuge in the capital city of Athens. Beneath the grace of the young girl's narratives and her longing for their island home, the reader is fed biting commentary on the cultural violence inherent in social change and urbanization. The concluding lines of the book echo and reverberate painfully with Astradeni's cries of protest as she beats her small fists against the hairy chest of their "smelly" neighbor as he rapes her: "No, not my dress. Don't lift my dress. No, not my dress, my tunic. No, not my tunic—not my tunic. No!" (231).

51. Male perpetrators of extrafamilial rape, which entails no blood taboo, have also been protected. In 1980, a Greek woman who wounded a man attempting to rape her was arrested and imprisoned for three years; her attacker was handed a mere five-and-a-half-month sentence (reported in Morgan 1984, 266).

52. From the FPAG leaflet, "AIDS and Otherwise . . . Prophylactic!"

CHAPTER 4

1. Although in other contexts I prefer to designate the political position that this phrase glosses as "antichoice," I take Faye Ginsburg's anthropological lead here in using the term by which proponents call themselves (1989).

2. The fact that those of us who study contemporary Greece are frequently compelled to preface our area of study with the word *modern*, since otherwise people assume we are talking about ancient peoples, is telling (Herzfeld 1987; Clogg 1996).

3. Rousseau further stipulated that this organic, state-ready nation is also "that which has neither customs nor superstitions firmly rooted; that which has no fear of being overwhelmed by a sudden invasion, but which, without entering into the disputes of its neighbors, can single-handed resist either of them, or aid one in repelling the other, that in which every member can be known by all, and in which there is no necessity to lay on a man a greater burden than a man can bear; that which can subsist without other nations, and without which every other nation can subsist, that which is neither rich nor poor and is self-sufficing; lastly, that which combines the stability of an old nation with the docility of a new one" ([1762] 1967, 53–54). He could think of but one likely candidate: Corsica.

4. "Editorial: National Threat." *Kathimerini*, Monday, 2 March 2000 (online English edition, http://www.ekathimerini.com; accessed July 2000).

5. Andreas Papandreou, "Eksoterikí Politikí ke Ethnikí Anayénisi," in *Dhimokratía ke Ethnikí Anayénisi* (1966, 72–79), translated and quoted in Augustinos 1995 (168).

6. The Fifth Panhellenic Conference on AIDS and Sexually Transmitted Diseases, Caravel Hotel, Athens, 11–13 February 1994.

7. Interview with George Siampos, 4 March 1994.

8. Held 11–13 April 1997, in Iraklio, Crete.

9. It would be worthwhile to explore comparatively the connections of race-nation-citizen as they obtain with the contemporary nation-state, the ancient city-state of Pericles, and the diasporic nation under Alexander. Not only is the nation-state a modern invention, but the reliance on blood metaphors seems to be as well. Alexander, for instance, is reputed to have addressed his conquered peoples thusly:

> Consider the world as your country, with laws common to all and where the best will govern, irrespective of tribe. I do not distinguish among men, as the narrow-minded do, both among Greeks and barbarians. I am not interested in the descent of the citizens, or their racial origins. I classify them using only one criterion: virtue. For me every virtuous foreigner is a Greek, and every evil Greek worse than a barbarian. . . . On my part, I shall consider you all equal, whites or blacks, and I wish you would be not only subjects of the commonwealth, but participants and partners.

This passage is quoted by Nicolaos Martis in his polemical text *The Falsification of Macedonian History*, which has been translated into several languages and conveniently made available to tourists at major Greek archaeological sites (1984, 69). He quotes this passage from a 1971 book, written in Greek by Christos Zalokosta, entitled *Alexander the Great, Precursor of Christ*.

The Periclean polis had as citizens only free men—women and slaves were categorically excluded. So the Greek city-state, unlike the Greek nation-state, did not rely on metaphors of kinship; one was not born into state citizenship. To the contrary, the city-state was supposed to be transcendent of blood relations and for this reason did not demand direct contributions of women (Pateman 1988).

10. This claim is not entirely factual; many African refugees in Greece come from Ethiopia, a historically Christian nation. This reveals the dubious, thin line between cultural and biological racism.

11. Unstated here is that the greater number of Balkan and African immigrants in Greece are undocumented economic or political refugees or both. Legally registered immigrants, according to NSSG (1992) figures, account for just 2.4 percent of the population.

12. This trend may be changing. See "A New, Multiethnic Greece: Research Shows That 43 Percent of Migrants from 120 Countries Want to Stay On," *Athens News*, Wednesday, 1 December 1999 (on-line edition, http://www.athensnews.gr; accessed July 2000).

13. For example, in a 1997 report on Greek demographics, it was reported that "the proportion of mothers who have one child has increased in the past two decades, while the rate of women with two has remained stable at 38–39 percent. The proportion of mothers with three children has decreased from 13.4 to 12 percent and those with four from 7.1 to 4.8 percent. An estimated

100,000 births are recorded every year in the country, while the number of abortions exceeds 300,000 annually" ("Birth Rate Needs Boost, Says Scientist," *Athens News*, 9 April 1997, on-line edition, http://www.athensnews.gr; accessed July 2000).

14. The following modest tax exemptions for families were announced: 20,000 drachmes (U.S.$88) per child for families with two children; 30,000 drachmes (U.S.$132) per child for families with three children; 40,000 drachmes (U.S.$176) per child for families with four or more children; plus exemptions for these children for medical expenses. Reported in *Ta Nea*, Saturday, 4 December 1993.

15. *See* Drettakis 2000.

16. Phoebos Ioannides was then the PASOK undersecretary of health.

17. During the 1990s, "the Greek family" was subject to numerous scholarly and public discussions. For example, on 23 March 1994, I attended a public roundtable titled "The Greek Family: Myth and Reality," sponsored by the Ministry of Culture and the Museum of Greek Folk Art as part of a series to recognize the international Year of the Family. Significantly, it was held at the Museum of Greek Folk Art in Plaka, at the foot of the ancient Acropolis, where one of the permanent cultural displays is a photo story on male-dominated coffeehouses. All speakers were from the Research Center of Greek Society at the Academy of Athens.

18. The name Sotiris Angelopoulos is a pseudonym. This interview was conducted in English.

19. Although I am convinced by Angelopoulos that politics is generally more determining of policy in Greece than religious ideology is, it should be noted that in 1985, when Darwinian evolution was included in Greek textbooks under the PASOK government, five thousand priests took to the streets to protest (Kaplan 1992, 225).

20. To give one example from 1999, following President Bill Clinton's hostile public reception in Athens—his visit was poorly timed to nearly coincide with the anniversary of the violent suppression of the student uprising against the United States–backed junta in 1974—a Greek journalist wrote in *New Republic*, "Though Greek police kept the protestors far away from the president, nothing could shield Clinton, or anyone watching in the West, from their message: Greece may be a member of NATO and the European Union, but it is not part of the West. . . . Today 'Western' implies a consciousness of the universality of human rights, and in Greece that is very hard to find" (Michas 1999, 12).

21. In 1985, over 95 percent of Greek members of Parliament were men (Kaplan 1992, 47).

CHAPTER 5

1. By Euro-American, Strathern refers to "middle-class consciousness and enquiry" that is "recognisable across Northern European and North American cultures" (1992b, 15). Euro-American, then, is an ideal typic model and not an

empirically derived classification that purports to describe an actual, uniform, bounded population. Greeks do not fit the Euro-American model, although they may aspire to and may adopt certain of its characteristic views.

2. Male homophobia in Athens must also be connected to the burden of foreign perceptions deriving from an understanding that contemporary Greeks are heir to classical Greek culture. Contemporary Athenians are quite aware of foreign stereotypes of "Greek" homosexuality and homosociality based on ancient examples, and often go to great lengths to repudiate them. In 1994, one of the major cinemas along Kifisias Avenue showed Woody Allen's classic film *Love and Death*, set in eighteenth-century Russia. The climax of the movie finds the characters played by Woody Allen and Diane Keaton traveling to Moscow with the plan of assassinating Napoleon. Allen's character has second thoughts as the time for action approaches. In a close-focus monologue, he appeals to Western philosophical fathers for ethical advice, asking, "What would Socrates do?" "All those Greeks were homosexuals," he muses distractedly. "Boy, they must have had some wild parties!" He turns to deductive reason: "(A) Socrates was a man. (B) All men are moral. (C) All men are Socrates. That means all men are homosexuals. But I'm not homosexual. . . ." He concludes that he must be "too logical" and never manages to kill Napoleon. At this Athenian cinema, the Greek subtitles for the dialogue about "all those Greeks" and homosexuality were scrambled so as to be illegible. Of course many audience members understood the English soundtrack, but it is telling that the theater saw fit to edit the tongue-in-cheek lines linking Greek men and homosexuality.

3. The name Michalis Stamatis is a pseudonym.

4. In 1994, the Ekso clinic had been in business for six and a half years, had seen three thousand women, and reported an impressive 25 percent pregnancy rate for all ages (although not all pregnancies were carried to term). In Athens at that time, a cycle of IVF cost around U.S.$2,000 inclusive of the injectable hormones, and while this amount is certainly significant, it compared favorably to $10,000 per cycle in the United States or around $6,000 elsewhere in Europe. Use of IVF is not restricted to Athens's professional class. The Ekso clinic's lead obstetrician-gynecologist, Dr. Michalis Stamatis, first worked in IVF in Virginia; Zoë, one of the biologists whom I came to know socially, trained in England under Dr. Patrick Steptoe, the in vitro pioneer.

5. Angeliki, who gets national health insurance through her job at the state electric company (DEH), called her coverage "a joke," while acknowledging it helps. The hormones she takes to superovulate, for instance, would cost 100,000 drachmes (about U.S.$440) a month without any insurance, but with insurance she pays 25,000 per cycle (U.S.$110). The IVF itself costs 300,000 per attempt (U.S.$1,300); DEH will give her 120,000 per year for IVF. If she makes more than one attempt in a year, she and her husband must pay for it on their own. She says, "It's a lot of money. Because of this, most of them tell you, I'll go to the gynecologist, not IVF. I'll pay 10,000 (U.S.$45) for an office visit—10 thousand rather than 300,000 drachmes. There's a difference."

6. Because few babies are available for legal adoption, prospective parents must pay exorbitant fees (far more than to pursue IVF), frequently even bribe doctors and bureaucrats, and expect to wait four years for a daughter, six years for a son. A regular feature in Greek news media has been the police discovery of baby selling. In October 1993, police busted a child-smuggling ring allegedly involving thirty-five people, including lawyers, doctors, and social workers ("Police Arrests Blow Open Problem of Child-Smuggling," *Athens News,* 19 October 1993, p. 3). In this and other such rings, babies and small children were taken from their parents (mainly by "gypsies," it is reported) in northern parts of Greece and brought to Athens, where they are sold to childless couples for between 3 and 3.5 million drachmes (roughly U.S.$12,750 to $15,000). According to this same story, between 1989 and 1993, Greeks adopted more than forty-five hundred children (most illegally) from Romania alone.

7. For a fascinating discussion of how blood and genes are strategically, and variously, called on to designate parenthood in cases of IVF using donor egg and sperm in the United States, see Cussins 1998.

8. The word *pelátis* encompasses the meanings in English of both "customer" or "client" and "patient," at once obscuring and emphasizing the simultaneous commodification and pathologization of infertility problems and treatments. In Greece, though, the emphasis falls more on client as patient than as customer; when speaking with me in English, for example, staff at the Ekso clinic consistently referred to the women they see as "patients" rather than "clients," the standard appellation in British and U.S. IVF practice.

9. In her study of amniocentesis in New York, Rayna Rapp demonstrates that among "Americans," demands for statistical information and a "sense of entitlement to the best scientific data" must be understood not merely in terms of "American culture," but as a "class-based response to anxiety" (1999, 110). Because IVF is relatively more expensive and less extensively covered by health insurance in the United States than in Greece, the American "clients" Zoë encountered in her IVF work were most likely to belong to the professional class that Rapp reports seeks comfort in numbers.

10. The Orthodox Church, for instance, does not join the Catholic Church in accepting the doctrine of immaculate conception. This goes back to the difference between the two churches on original sin. For Catholicism, the human legacy of Adam's fall is guilt relating to sensuality; the doctrine of immaculate conception frees Mary from being tainted with that guilt. For Orthodoxy, the human legacy of Adam's fall is mortality (sensuality, as previously discussed, is not seen as an occasion for guilt, precisely because it is given to us not as a matter of our choosing). Because Mary was indisputably human, and therefore mortal, there is no theological need for her immaculate conception.

11. Church leaders do apparently distinguish between "AIH" and "AID" more generally—that is, means of artificial insemination using the sperm of husbands to complete the family form are fine, while artificial insemination with donor sperm potentially disrupts family unity based on the union of blood. But there is no official pronouncement on the matter.

12. According to an article published in the 27 April 2000 on-line English edition of the newspaper *Kathimerini,* surrogacy for hire has recently been practiced in northern Greece, where Greek pronatalism is propagated more strongly and immigrant Balkan women are more numerous ("Rent-a-Mother Probe: Doctors Claim Foreign Women Paid to Bear Babies for Childless Greeks," at http://www.ekathimerini.com; accessed July 2000). The public prosecutor in Thessaloniki instigated an investigation into accusations that foreign women are being employed to undergo "artificial fertilization," gestate, and birth babies on behalf of childless Greek couples. The case of a young Bulgarian woman who had been paid "a few million drachmes" (or a few thousand dollars) to act as a surrogate mother became known to the public after she "reportedly gave birth prematurely to a child with health problems, resulting in a disagreement between the two sides." Local doctors admitted to journalists following this incident that "many women have given birth for payment in a private clinic over the last five years."

13. A child conceived through incest, for instance, would be considered abnormal because the "mixed blood" (which is the literal rendering of the Greek word for "incest") constituting the child is "returned" to the family, rather than allowed to properly extend and rejuvenate the lineage (du Boulay 1984).

14. "I prótes yennísis me mikroghonimopíisi" [The first births with microfertilization], *To Víma,* 7 November 1993.

15. Strathern (1992a,b) has demonstrated that Euro-American persons are always not only members of a society that they help create but also autonomous individuals with needs and desires of their own. People are both greater than and less than society; they are of a different order than the kinship that connects them. People are greater than society as persons, with distinct personalities and subjective desires. And they are less than society as individuals, placeholders in the kinship system that both connects and generates new people. What happens then, as we have seen, is that one dimension, the latter one associated with Nature, acts as the grounding and reference point for the other, what Euro-Americans consider to be society.

16. Eleni, stalwart among Greece's first-wave feminists, was one woman I interviewed who voiced skepticism of compulsory ultrasound imaging, in vitro fertilization, and other reproductive technologies; she regards these as additional means by which male doctors can profit from female reproductive events. She went on, however, to acknowledge that there may be an unintended benefit from fetal sonogram technology. The husband of her daughter's friend, she told me, had something of a revelatory experience seeing the sonogram of his wife's womb: "Because men, they don't feel the pregnancy, they don't have this feeling that women have. And for him, I think he became a father the minute he saw this screen. He was like that [she opens wide her mouth and eyes, mimicking astonishment]. He couldn't speak. That's good. That's very positive. I think this is good for men, for fathers." Sonogram images may move men to take more interest in the impending birth of a child, and this, she hopes, might encourage men to take a more active role in early child care,

something that has been left almost entirely to women or, in a pinch, to grand-fathers.

Let me emphasize, however, that the visualization of a fetus is not deemed necessary to *maternal* bonding. Chloe, a young woman with an eight-month-old son, was not particularly impressed by the ultrasound images of her fetus:

> They are vague. They are very—to doctors, you know, they can actually see. But you, you can't really. You have to be directed, and then it leaves a lot for your imagination. But the most important thing is—you have anxiety about whether the kid is all right, and by seeing this and by having the doctor explain that he has all five toes, this anxiety is less-ened. That was all. Otherwise I didn't need to see a picture to know that there was something growing inside me. I could feel it. But it's the re-assurance that it was growing in the normal way. That was it.

References

Abelove, Henry

    1992   Some speculations on the history of "sexual intercourse" during the "long eighteenth century" in England. In *Nationalisms and Sexualities*, ed. Andrew Parker, Mary Russo, Doris Sommer, and Patricia Yaeger, pp. 335–42. New York: Routledge.

Abu-Lughod, Lila

    1986   *Veiled Sentiments: Honor and Poetry in a Bedouin Society.* Berkeley: University of California Press.

    1990   The romance of resistance: Tracing transformations of power through Bedouin women. *American Ethnologist* 17, no. 1:41–55.

    1998   Feminist longings and postcolonial conditions. In *Remaking Women: Feminism and Modernity in the Middle East*, pp. 3–31. Princeton: Princeton University Press.

Afxendiou, Georgia

    1996   Paper presented at the Ninety-fifth Annual Meeting of the American Anthropological Association, San Francisco, 20–24 November.

Agrafiotis, Dimosthenis, P. Pantzou, E. Ioannidis, A. Doumas, Ch. Tselepi, and A. Antonopoulou

    1990a   Knowledge, attitudes, beliefs, and practices in relation to HIV infection and AIDS: The case of the city of Athens, Greece. Athens School of Public Health, Department of Sociology. First draft.

    1990b   *AIDS: Knowledge, Attitudes, Beliefs, and Practices of Young People.* Athens School of Public Health, Department of Sociology, Research Monograph no. 2. Athens: Sociology of Health and Illness.

Alexander, Katherine

    1987   *Children of Byzantium.* Ontario: Cormorant Books.

Allen, Peter S.

1986　　　　Female inheritance, housing, and urbanization in Greece. *Anthropology* 10, no. 1:1–17.

Alpern, Kenneth D., ed.

1992　　　　*The Ethics of Reproductive Technology.* Oxford: Oxford University Press.

Althusser, Louis

1971　　　　Ideology and ideological state apparatuses: Notes toward an investigation. In *Lenin and Philosophy and the Other Essays,* pp. 121–73. Trans. from the French by Ben Brewster. London: New Left Books.

Anderson, Bridget

2000　　　　*Doing the Dirty Work? The Global Politics of Domestic Labour.* London: Zed Books.

Anthias, Floya, and Gabriella Lazaridis, eds.

2000　　　　*Gender and Migration in Southern Europe: Women on the Move.* Oxford: Berg.

Anthias, Floya, and Nira Yuval-Davis

1992　　　　*Racialized Boundaries: Race, Nation, Gender, Colour, and Class and the Anti-racist Struggle.* London: Routledge.

Anthias, Floya, and Nira Yuval-Davis, eds.

1989　　　　*Woman-Nation-State.* New York: St. Martin's Press.

Apostolopoulou, Sophia

1994　　　　Population policy and low birth rate in Greece. *Planned Parenthood in Europe* 23, no. 2:14.

Appadurai, Arjun

1996　　　　*Modernity at Large: Cultural Dimensions of Globalization.* Minneapolis: University of Minnesota Press.

Arditti, Rita, Renate Klein, and Shelley Minden, eds.

1984　　　　*Test-Tube Women: What Future for Motherhood?* London: Pandora Press.

Aristotle

1947　　　　Nicomachean ethics. Trans. from the ancient Greek by W. D. Ross. In *Introduction to Aristotle,* ed. Richard McKeon, pp. 308–543. New York: Modern Library.

Arnold, Marlene Sue

1985　　　　Childbirth among rural Greek women in Crete: Use of popular, folk, and cosmopolitan medical systems. Ph.D. diss., Department of Anthropology, University of Pennsylvania.

Astrinaki, Ourania

1994　　　　Presentation of current research to the Department of Anthropology, Panteion University, Athens, March.

Athanasiou, Athena

1999   Crafting timeless time: The quest for future [sic] in construc-
            tions of demographic dystopias. Paper presented at the Ninety-
            eighth Annual Meeting of the American Anthropological Asso-
            ciation, Chicago, 17–21 November.

Augustinos, Gerasimos

1977   *Consciousness and History: Nationalist Critics of Greek Soci-
            ety, 1897–1914.* East European Monographs 32. New York: Co-
            lumbia University Press.

1995   Hellenism and the modern Greeks. In *Eastern European Na-
            tionalism in the Twentieth Century,* ed. Peter Sugar, pp.
            163–204. Washington, D.C.: American University Press.

Bakalaki, Alexandra

1993   Review of *Contested Identities,* ed. Peter Loizos and Evthymios
            Papataxiarchis, *Journal of Modern Greek Studies* 11, no. 1:160.

Banfield, Edward

1958   *The Moral Basis of a Backward Society.* Glencoe, Ill.: Free
            Press.

Becker, Gay

2000   *The Elusive Embryo: How Women and Men Approach New
            Reproductive Technologies.* Berkeley: University of California
            Press.

Bhabha, Homi K.

2000   On cultural choice. In *The Turn to Ethics,* ed. Marjorie Garber,
            Beatrice Hanssen, and Rebecca L. Walkowitz, pp. 181–200. New
            York: Routledge.

Blum, Richard, and Eva Blum

1965   *Health and Healing in Rural Greece: A Study of Three Com-
            munities.* Stanford: Stanford University Press.

1970   *The Dangerous Hour: The Lore and Culture of Crisis and Mys-
            tery in Rural Greece.* London: Chatto and Windus.

Bonio, Vasili

1996   O érotas sta chroniá tis choléras [Love in the time of cholera].
            Colt, no. 2:59–67.

Bordo, Susan

1986   The Cartesian masculinization of thought. *Signs: Journal of
            Women in Culture and Society* 11, no. 3:439–56.

Borgeois-Pichat, J.

1983   The demographic transition in Europe. In *Proceedings of the
            European Population Conference, 1982, Strasbourg, 21–24
            September 1982.* Strasbourg: Council of Europe.

Bourdieu, Pierre

1976   Marriage strategies as strategies of reproduction. Trans. from
            the French by Elborg Forster and Patricia Ranum. In *Family
            and Society,* ed. Robert Forster and Orest Ranum, pp. 117–44.
            Baltimore: John Hopkins University Press.

1977   *Outline of a Theory of Practice.* Trans. from the French by Richard Nice. Switzerland: Librairie Droz S.A., 1972. Reprint, Cambridge: Cambridge University Press.

Burton, Barbara

1997   The nature and culture of incest: Civilizing sexual abuse for anthropology. Paper presented at the American Ethnological Society Meetings, Seattle, 6–9 March.

Butler, Judith

1989   *Gender Trouble: Feminism and the Subversion of Identity.* New York: Routledge.

1993   *Bodies That Matter: On the Discursive Limits of "Sex."* New York: Routledge.

Campbell, John K.

1964   *Honour, Family, and Patronage: A Study of Institutions and Moral Values in a Greek Mountain Community.* Oxford: Oxford University Press.

Carter, Anthony

1995   Agency and fertility: For an ethnography of practice. In *Situating Fertility: Anthropology and Demographic Inquiry,* ed. Susan Greenhalgh, pp. 55–85. Cambridge: Cambridge University Press.

Chronaki, Zogia

1992   I yinéka anámesa stin ikoyénia ke tin ergasía [The woman between the family and work]. *Katina* (Athens), no. 7:10–13.

Clogg, Richard

1992   *A Concise History of Greece.* Cambridge: Cambridge University Press.

1996   Captive to history: Will Greece ever stop relying on its past? *Odyssey* 3, no. 7:29–32, 74–75.

Cole, Sally

1991   *Women of the Praia: Work and Lives in a Portuguese Coastal Community.* Princeton: Princeton University Press.

Collier, Jane F.

1986   From Mary to modern woman. *American Ethnologist* 13, no. 1:100–107.

1997   *From Duty to Desire: Remaking Families in a Spanish Village.* Princeton: Princeton University Press.

Collier, Jane, and Sylvia Yanagisako

1989   Theory in anthropology since feminist practice. *Critique of Anthropology* 9, no. 2:27–39.

Comninos, Anthony C.

1988   Greece. In *International Handbook on Abortion,* ed. Paul Sachdev, pp. 207–15. New York: Greenport Press.

Coombe, Rosemary

1990   Barren ground: Re-conceiving honour and shame in the field of Mediterranean ethnography. *Anthropologica* 32:221–38.

Corea, Gena
1985   *The Mother Machine: Reproductive Technologies from Artificial Insemination to Artificial Wombs*. New York: Harper and Row.
Cornell, Drucilla
1995   What is ethical feminism? In *Feminist Contentions: A Philosophical Exchange*, ed. Linda Nicholson, pp. 75–106. New York: Routledge.
Council of Europe
2001   *Demographic Yearbook*. Strasbourg: Council of Europe.
Cowan, Jane
1988   The Greek way of life. In *Insight Guide to Greece*, ed. Karen Van Dyck, pp. 61–83. Singapore: APA Productions.
1990   *Dance and the Body Politic in Northern Greece*. Princeton: Princeton University Press.
Cussins, Charis
1998   Producing reproduction: Techniques of normalization and naturalization in infertility clinics. In *Reproducing Reproduction: Kinship, Power, and Technological Innovation*, ed. Sarah Franklin and Helena Ragoné, pp. 66–101. Philadelphia: University of Pennsylvania Press.
Danforth, Loring
1982   *The Death Rituals of Rural Greece*. Princeton: Princeton University Press.
Daoudaki, Nana
1994   Klimákosi stin asfálisi [Escalation in insurance]. *Ta Nea*, Friday, 1 April, p. 15.
Davids, Jennifer Phillips
2000   "Weak blood" and "crowded bellies": Cultural influences on contraceptive use among Ethiopian Jewish immigrants in Israel. In *Contraception across Cultures: Technologies, Choices, Constraints*, ed. Andrew Russell, Elisa J. Sobo, and Mary S. Thompson, pp. 129–60. Oxford: Berg.
Davis, Angela
1998   Surrogates and outcast mothers: Racism and reproductive politics in the nineties. In *The Angela Y. Davis Reader*, ed. Joy James, pp. 210–21. Malden, Mass.: Blackwell.
Davis-Floyd, Robbie E.
1992   *Birth as an American Rite of Passage*. Berkeley: University of California Press.
De Grazia, Victoria
1993   *How Fascism Ruled Women: Italy, 1922–1945*. Berkeley: University of California Press.
de Lauretis, Teresa
1987   *Technologies of Gender: Essays on Theory, Film, and Fiction*. Bloomington: Indiana University Press.

Delaney, Carol

1986   The meaning of paternity and the virgin birth debate. *Man* 21, no. 3:494–513.

1987   Seeds of honor, fields of shame. In *Honor and Shame and the Unity of the Mediterranean*, ed. David Gilmore, pp. 35–48. Washington, D.C.: American Anthropological Association.

1991   *The Seed and the Soil: Gender and Cosmology in Turkish Village Society.* Berkeley: University of California Press.

1995   Father state, motherland, and the birth of Modern Turkey. In *Naturalizing Power: Essays in Feminist Cultural Analysis*, ed. Sylvia Yanagisako and Carol Delaney, pp. 177–99. New York: Routledge.

1998   *Abraham on Trial: The Social Legacy of Biblical Myth.* Princeton: Princeton University Press.

Delidhaki, Eva

1991   Epídhoma stin polýtekni mitéra [Many-birthed mother's allowance]. *Gonís*, no. 183 (March): 21–22.

Delphy, Christine, and Diana Leonard

1992   *Familiar Exploitation: A New Analysis of Marriage in Contemporary Western Societies.* Cambridge, U.K.: Polity Press.

Denich, Bette

1974   Sex and power in the Balkans. In *Woman, Culture, and Society*, ed. Michelle Zimbalist Rosaldo and Louise Lamphere, pp. 243–62. Stanford: Stanford University Press.

Dheligianni, I., and C. Kousoula

1984   *Ikoyeniakó dhíkeo* [Family law]. Thessaloniki: Sakkoula.

Diamandouros, P. Nikiforos

1993   Politics and culture in Greece, 1974–91: An interpretation. In *Greece, 1981–1989: The Populist Decade*, ed. Richard Clogg, pp. 1–25. New York: St. Martin's Press.

Dimen, Muriel

1986   Servants and sentries: Women, power, and social reproduction in Kriovrisi. In *Gender and Power in Rural Greece*, ed. Jill Dubisch, pp. 53–67. Princeton: Princeton University Press.

Dirks, Nicholas B.

1990   History as a sign of the modern. *Public Culture* 2, no. 2:25–32.

Donzelot, Jacques

1979   *The Policing of Families.* Trans. from the French by Robert Hurley. New York: Pantheon Books.

Dorkofiki, Irini

1985   *Amvlosis: o afanismos tou yenous* [Abortion: The annihilation of the race]. Athens: Ellinikí Evroëkdhotikí.

Doumanis, Mariella

1983   *Mothering in Greece: From Collectivism to Individualism.* London: Academic Press.

Doxiadi-Trip, Anthi
1993   Pro-profilaktiká [Pro-prophylactics]. *Yinéka* (May): 320–21.
Drettakis, Manolis G.
2000   Few births, many deaths: Demographic time bomb is ticking while governments are fiddling. *Kathimerini*, 13 December (on-line English edition, http://www.ekathimerini.com).
du Boulay, Juliet
1974   *Portrait of a Greek Mountain Village*. Oxford: Clarendon Press.
1983   The meaning of dowry: Changing values in rural Greece. *Journal of Modern Greek Studies* 1, no. 1:243–70.
1984   The blood: Symbolic relationships between descent, marriage, incest prohibitions, and spiritual kinship in Greece. *Man* 19, no. 14:533–56.
1986   Women: Images of their nature and destiny in rural Greece. In *Gender and Power in Rural Greece*, ed. Jill Dubisch, pp. 139–68. Princeton: Princeton University Press.
Dubisch, Jill
1986   Introduction to *Gender and Power in Rural Greece*, ed. Jill Dubisch, pp. 3–41. Princeton: Princeton University Press.
1993   "Foreign chickens" and other outsiders: Gender and community in Greece. *American Ethnologist* 20, no. 2:272–87.
1995   *In a Different Place: Pilgrimage, Gender, and Politics at a Greek Island Shrine*. Princeton: Princeton University Press.
Duden, Barbara
1993   *Disembodying Women: Perspectives on Pregnancy and the Unborn*. Cambridge: Harvard University Press.
Dworkin, Andrea
1983   *Right-Wing Women*. New York: Perigee Books.
Emke-Poulopoulou, Ira
1994   *To dhimoghrafikó* [Demographics]. Athens: Ellin.
Evans, Sara
1979   *Personal Politics: The Roots of Women's Liberation in the Civil Rights Movement and the New Left*. New York: Vintage Books.
Evert, Miltiadhes
1994   Yia tin isótita ton anthrópon ke tin mia kinonía [For the equality of humans in a society]. *Yinéka* (May): 132–33.
Evropaïkó Fórum Aristerón Feministrión, Ellinikó Tmíma [European Forum of Left Feminists, Greek Chapter].
1993   Dhimoghrafikó: I yinékes ke páli énohes [Demographics: Women are again to blame]. *Eleftherotipía*, 12 December, p. 44.
Fakinou, Eugenia
1991   *Astradeni*. Trans. from the Greek by H. E. Criton. Athens: Kedros.
Faubion, James D.
1993   *Modern Greek Lessons: A Primer in Historical Constructivism*. Princeton: Princeton University Press.

Fletcher, Ruth

1995   Silences: Irish women and abortion. *Feminist Review* 50:44–66.

Foucault, Michel

1990a   *History of Sexuality.* Vol. 1. Trans. from the French by Robert Hurley. New York: Vintage Books. Originally published by Editions Gallimard in France in 1976. First American edition published by Random House in 1978.

1990b   *The Use of Pleasure: The History of Sexuality.* Vol. 2. Trans. from the French by Robert Hurley. New York: Vintage Books. Originally published by Editions Gallimard in France in 1984. First American edition published by Random House in 1985.

Fourtouni, Eleni

1986   *Greek Women in Resistance.* New Haven: Thelphini Press.

Franklin, Sarah

1993   Postmodern procreation: Representing reproductive practice. *Science as Culture* 3, no. 4:522–61.

1997   *Embodied Progress: A Cultural Account of Assisted Conception.* London: Routledge.

Franklin, Sarah, and Helena Ragoné, eds.

1998   *Reproducing Reproduction: Kinship, Power, and Technological Innovation.* Philadelphia: University of Pennsylvania Press.

Friedl, Ernestine

1962   *Vasilika: A Village in Modern Greece.* New York: Holt, Rinehart, and Winston.

1967   The position of women: Appearance and reality. *Anthropological Quarterly* 40, no. 3:97–108.

Fuss, Diana

1989   *Essentially Speaking: Feminism, Nature, and Difference.* New York: Routledge.

Gal, Susan, and Gail Kligman

2000   *The Politics of Gender after Socialism.* Princeton: Princeton University Press.

Garber, Marjorie, Beatrice Hanssen, and Rebecca L. Walkowitz, eds.

2000   *The Turn to Ethics.* New York: Routledge.

Gatens, Moira

1996   *Imaginary Bodies: Ethics, Power, and Corporeality.* London: Routledge.

Gefou-Madianou, Dimitra

1992   Exclusion and unity, retsina and sweet wine: Commensality and gender in a Greek agrotown. In *Alcohol, Gender, and Culture,* ed. Dimitra Gefou-Madianou, pp. 109–35. London: Routledge.

1999   Cultural polyphony and identity formation: Negotiating tradition in Attica. *American Ethnologist* 26, no. 2:412–39.

General Secretariat for Equality

1993   *Ethnikí ke Evropaïkí nomothesía yia tin sýchroni ellinídha* [National and European laws for the contemporary Greek woman]. Athens: Ethnikó Tipoghrafío.

Georges, Eugenia

1996a   Abortion policy and practice in Greece. *Social Science and Medicine* 42, no. 4:509–19.

1996b   Fetal ultrasound imaging and the production of authoritative knowledge in Greece. *Medical Anthropology Quarterly* 10, no. 2:157–75.

Georges, Eugenia, and Lisa Mitchell

2000   Baby talk: Rhetorical constructions of women and the fetus in Greek and Canadian pregnancy guidebooks. In *Writing and Speaking the Body: Feminist and Rhetorical Studies of Reproductive Sciences and Technologies,* ed. Mary Lay and Helen Longino, pp. 184–206. Madison: University of Wisconsin Press.

Giddens, Anthony

1991   *Modernity and Self-Identity: Self and Society in the Late Modern Age.* Stanford: Stanford University Press.

Gilligan, Carol

1982   *In a Different Voice: Psychological Theory and Women's Development.* Cambridge: Harvard University Press.

Gilmore, David, ed.

1987   *Honor and Shame and the Unity of the Mediterranean.* Washington, D.C.: American Anthropological Association.

Gilroy, Paul

1993   *The Black Atlantic: Modernity and Double Consciousness.* Cambridge: Harvard University Press.

Ginsburg, Faye D.

1989   *Contested Lives: The Abortion Debate in an American Community.* Berkeley: University of California Press.

1990   The "word-made" flesh: The disembodiment of gender in the abortion debate. In *Uncertain Terms: Negotiating Gender in American Culture,* ed. Faye Ginsburg and Anna Lowenhaupt Tsing, pp. 59–75. Boston: Beacon Press.

Ginsburg, Faye, and Rayna Rapp

1991   The politics of reproduction. *Annual Review of Anthropology* 20:311–43.

1995   Introduction to *Conceiving the New World Order: The Global Politics of Reproduction,* ed. Faye Ginsburg and Rayna Rapp, pp. 1–17. Berkeley: University of California Press.

Glendon, Mary Ann

1987   *Abortion and Divorce in Western Law.* Cambridge: Harvard University Press.

Goodale, Jane C.

1980   Gender, sexuality, and marriage: A Kaulong model of nature and culture. In *Nature, Culture, and Gender,* ed. Carol Mac-Cormack and Marilyn Strathern, pp. 119–42. Cambridge: Cambridge University Press.

Gordon, Linda

1979   The struggle for reproductive freedom: Three stages of feminism. In *Capitalist Patriarchy and the Case for Socialist Feminism,* ed. Zillah Eisenstein, pp. 107–32. New York: Monthly Review Press.

Greenhalgh, Susan

1995   Anthropology theorizes reproduction: Integrating practice, political economic, and feminist perspectives. In *Situating Fertility: Anthropology and Demographic Inquiry,* ed. Susan Greenhalgh, pp. 3–28. Cambridge: Cambridge University Press.

Greer, Germaine

1984   *Sex and Destiny: The Politics of Human Fertility.* London: Secker and Warburg.

Grimshaw, Jean

1993   Practices of freedom. In *Up against Foucault: Explorations of Some Tensions between Foucault and Feminism,* ed. Caroline Ramazanoglu, pp. 51–72 London: Routledge.

Hacking, Ian

1982   Biopower and the avalanche of printed numbers. *Humanities in Society* 5:279–95.

Halkias, Alexandra

1998   Give birth for Greece! Abortion and nation in letters to the editor of the mainstream Greek press. *Journal of Modern Greek Studies* 16, no. 1:111–38.

Haraway, Donna

1991   *Simians, Cyborgs, and Women: The Reinvention of Nature.* New York: Routledge.

1997   Fetus: The virtual speculum in the new world order. In *Modest_witness@second_millennium: FemaleMan©_meets_OncoMouse™,* pp. 173–212. New York: Routledge.

Harcourt, Wendy

1997   An analysis of reproductive health: Myths, resistance, and new knowledge. In *Power, Reproduction, and Gender: The Intergenerational Transfer of Knowledge,* ed. Wendy Harcourt, pp. 8–34. London: Zed Books.

Hart, Janet

1996   *New Voices in the Nation: Women and the Greek Resistance, 1941–1964.* Ithaca: Cornell University Press.

Hart, Laurie Kain

1992   *Time, Religion, and Social Experience in Rural Greece.* Lanham, Md.: Rowman and Littlefield.

Helmreich, Stefan
 1992   Kinship, nation, and Paul Gilroy's concept of diaspora. *Dias-pora* 2, no. 2:243–49.
Heng, Geraldine, and Janadas Devan
 1992   State fatherhood: The politics of nationalism, sexuality, and race in Singapore. In *Nationalisms and Sexualities,* ed. Andrew Parker, Mary Russo, Doris Sommer, and Patricia Yaeger, pp. 343–64. New York: Routledge.
Herzfeld, Michael
 1982   *Ours Once More: Folklore, Ideology, and the Making of Modern Greece.* Austin: University of Texas Press.
 1983   Semantic slippage and moral fall: The rhetoric of chastity in rural Greek society. *Journal of Modern Greek Studies* 1, no. 1:161–72.
 1985   *The Poetics of Manhood: Contest and Identity in a Cretan Mountain Village.* Princeton: Princeton University Press.
 1986   Within and without: The category of "female" in the ethnography of modern Greece. In *Gender and Power in Rural Greece,* ed. Jill Dubisch, pp. 215–34. Princeton: Princeton University Press.
 1987   *Anthropology through the Looking-Glass.* Cambridge: Cambridge University Press.
 1991   Silence, submission, and subversion: Toward a poetics of womanhood. In *Contested Identities: Gender and Kinship in Modern Greece,* ed. Peter Loizos and Evthymios Papataxiarchis, pp. 79–97. Princeton: Princeton University Press.
 1992   *The Social Production of Indifference: Exploring the Symbolic Roots of Western Bureaucracy.* Chicago: University of Chicago Press.
 1997a   *Cultural Intimacy: Social Poetics in the Nation-State.* New York: Routledge.
 1997b   *Portrait of a Greek Imagination: An Ethnographic Biography of Andreas Nenedakis.* Chicago: University of Chicago Press.
Hewlett, Sylvia Ann
 1986   *A Lesser Life: The Myth of Women's Liberation in America.* New York: Warner Books.
Hillmann, Verena, and Therese Vögeli Sörensen
 1997   Motherhood in Switzerland: A rational and responsible choice? In *Power, Reproduction, and Gender: The Intergenerational Transfer of Knowledge,* ed. Wendy Harcourt, pp. 165–83. London: Zed Books.
Hirschon, Renée
 1978   Open body/closed space: The transformation of female sexuality. In *Defining Females: The Nature of Women in Society,* ed. Shirley Ardener, pp. 66–88. New York: John Wiley and Sons.

1989   *Heirs of the Greek Catastrophe: The Social Life of Asia Minor Refugees in Piraeus.* Oxford: Clarendon Press.

Horn, David

1994   *Social Bodies: Science, Reproduction, and Italian Modernity.* Princeton: Princeton University Press.

Hochschild, Arlie

1989   *The Second Shift: Working Parents and the Revolution at Home.* New York: Viking.

Inhorn, Marcia C.

1994   *The Quest for Conception: Gender, Infertility, and Egyptian Medical Traditions.* Philadelphia: University of Pennsylvania Press.

1996   *Infertility and Patriarchy: The Cultural Politics of Gender and Family Life in Egypt.* Philadelphia: University of Pennsylvania Press.

2000   Missing motherhood: Infertility, technology, and poverty in Egyptian women's lives. In *Ideologies and Technologies of Motherhood: Race, Class, Sexuality, Nationalism,* ed. Heléna Ragoné and France Winddance Twine, pp. 139–68. New York: Routledge.

Iordanidou, Dosi

1992   Profilaktiká [Prophylactics]. *Diva,* no. 22:130–34.

Iossifides, Marina

1991   Sisters in Christ: Metaphors of kinship among Greek nuns. In *Contested Identities: Gender and Kinship in Modern Greece,* ed. Peter Loizos and Evthymios Papataxiarchis, pp. 135–55. Princeton: Princeton University Press.

Ivy, Marilyn

1995   *Discourses of the Vanishing: Modernity, Phantasm, Japan.* Chicago: University of Chicago Press.

Jaggar, Alison

1989   Love and knowledge: Emotion in feminist epistemology. In *Gender/Body/Knowledge: Feminist Reconstructions of Being and Knowing,* ed. Alison Jaggar and Susan Bordo, pp. 145–71. New Brunswick: Rutgers University Press.

2000   Feminist ethics. In *The Blackwell Guide to Ethical Theory,* ed. Hugh LaFollette, pp. 348–74. Oxford: Blackwell.

Jordan, Brigitte

1993   *Birth in Four Cultures: A Cross-Cultural Investigation of Childbirth in Yucatan, Holland, Sweden, and the United States.* 4th ed. Montreal: Eden Press, 1978. Reprint, Prospect Heights, Ill.: Waveland Press.

Jowkar, Forouz

1986   Honor and shame: A feminist view from within. *Feminist Studies* 6, no. 1:45–65.

Jusdanis, Gregory
1991   Greek Americans and the diaspora. *Diaspora* 1, no. 2:209–24.
Just, Roger
1988   Anti-clericalism and national identity: Attitudes toward the Orthodox Church in Greece. In *Vernacular Christianity: Essays in the Social Anthropology of Religion in Godfrey Lienhardt*, ed. Wendy James and Douglas H. Johnson, pp. 15–30. New York: Lilian Barber Press.
1989   Triumph of the ethnos. In *History and Ethnicity*, ed. Elizabeth Tonkin, Malcolm Chapman, and Maryon McDonald, pp. 71–88. London: Routledge.
Kahn, Susan Martha
2000   *Reproducing Jews: A Cultural Account of Assisted Conception in Israel*. Durham: Duke University Press.
Kanaaneh, Rhoda A.
1997   Conceiving difference: Birthing the Palestinian nation in the Galilee. *Critical Public Health* 7, no. 3 and 4:64–79.
2000   New reproductive rights and wrongs in the Galilee. In *Contraception across Cultures: Technologies, Choices, Constraints*, ed. Andrew Russell, Elisa J. Sobo, and Mary S. Thompson, pp. 161–77. Oxford: Berg.
Kaplan, Gisela
1992   *Contemporary Western European Feminism*. New York: New York University Press.
Karakasidou, Anastasia N.
1997   *Fields of Wheat, Hills of Blood: Passages to Nationhood in Greek Macedonia, 1870–1990*. Chicago: University of Chicago Press.
Katsillis, John, and Richard Rubinson
1990   Cultural capital, student achievement, and educational reproduction: The case of Greece. *American Sociological Review* 55, no. 2:270–79.
Katz, Jonathan Ned
1990   The invention of heterosexuality. *Socialist Review* 20, no. 1:7–33.
Kazantzakis, Nikos
1952   *Zorba the Greek*. Trans. from the Greek by Carl Wildman. New York: Simon and Schuster.
Kennedy, Robinette
1986   Women's friendships on Crete: A psychological perspective. In *Gender and Power in Rural Greece*, ed. Jill Dubisch, pp. 121–38. Princeton: Princeton University Press.
Kertzer, David
1993   *Sacrificed for Honor: Italian Infant Abandonment and the Politics of Reproductive Control*. Boston: Beacon Press.

Ketting, Evert
1995   Editorial: Infertility is our concern. *Planned Parenthood in Europe* 24, no. 1:1.

Kittay, Eva Feder
1999   *Love's Labor: Essays on Women, Equality, and Dependency.* New York: Routledge.

Kligman, Gail
1998   *The Politics of Duplicity: Controlling Reproduction in Ceausescu's Romania.* Berkeley: University of California Press.

Koukiou, Vaso
1995   Save safe sex. *Flash*, no. 41:72–73.

Koumantou, Georgos
1985   *Paradhósis ikoyeniakoú dhikéou* [Traditions of family law]. 4th ed. Athens: Sakkoula.
1988   *Ikoyeniakó dhíkeo* [Family law]. Vol. 1. Athens: Sakkoula.

Krengel, Monika, and Katarina Greifeld
2000   Uzbekistan in Transition—Changing Concepts in family planning and reproductive health. In *Contraception across Cultures: Technologies, Choices, Constraints*, ed. Andrew Russell, Elisa J. Sobo, and Mary S. Thompson, pp. 199–220. Oxford: Berg.

Landsman, Gail
2000   "Real motherhood," class, and children with disabilities. In *Ideologies and Technologies of Motherhood: Race, Class, Sexuality, Nationalism*, ed. Heléna Ragoné and France Winddance Twine, pp. 169–87. New York: Routledge.

Lange, Lynda
1983   Woman is not a rational animal: On Aristotle's biology of reproduction. In *Discovering Reality: Feminist Perspectives on Epistemology, Metaphysics, Methodology, and Philosophy of Science*, ed. Sandra Harding and Merrill B. Hintikka, pp. 1–15. Dordrecht, Holland: D. Reidel.

Latour, Bruno
1993   *We Have Never Been Modern.* Trans. from the French by Catherine Porter. Paris: La Découverte, 1991. Reprint: Cambridge: Harvard University Press.

Layne, Linda, ed.
1999   *Transformative Motherhood: On Giving and Getting in Consumer Society.* New York: New York University Press.

Lazaridis, Gabriella
2000   Filipino and Albanian women migrant workers in Greece: Multiple layers of oppression. In *Gender and Migration in Southern Europe: Women on the Move*, ed. Floya Anthias and Gabriella Lazaridis, pp. 49–79. Oxford: Berg.

Lefkarites, Mary P.
1992   The sociocultural implications of modernizing childbirth among Greek women on the island of Rhodes. *Medical Anthropology* 13:385–412.
Lévi-Strauss, Claude
[1949] 1969   *The Elementary Structures of Kinship.* Trans. from the French by James Harle Bell, and John Richard von Sturmer. Ed. Rodney Needham. Boston: Beacon Press.
Light, Donald
1994   Comparative models of "health care" systems. In *The Sociology of Health and Illness,* ed. Peter Conrad and Rochelle Kern, pp. 455–70. New York: St. Martin's Press.
Linke, Ule
1999   *German Bodies: Race and Representation after Hitler.* New York: Routledge.
Loizos, Peter, and Evthymios Papataxiarchis
1991a   Gender, sexuality, and the person in Greek culture. In *Contested Identities: Gender and Kinship in Modern Greece,* ed. Peter Loizos and Evthymios Papataxiarchis, pp. 221–34. Princeton: Princeton University Press.
1991b   Introduction: Gender and kinship in marriage and alternative contexts. In *Contested Identities: Gender and Kinship in Modern Greece,* ed. Peter Loizos and Evthymios Papataxiarchis, pp. 3–25. Princeton: Princeton University Press.
Luker, Kristen
1975   *Taking Chances: Abortion and the Decision Not to Contracept.* Berkeley: University of California Press.
1984   *Abortion and the Politics of Motherhood.* Berkeley: University of California Press.
Lykouropoulos, Giorgos
1994   To toúnel tis aghápis [The tunnel of love]. *01,* no. 5:72–74.
MacCormack, Carol P.
1980   Nature, culture, and gender: A critique. In *Nature, Culture, and Gender,* ed. Carol MacCormack and Marilyn Strathern, pp. 1–24. Cambridge: Cambridge University Press.
MacLeod, Arlene Elowe
1996   Transforming women's identity: The intersection of household and workplace in Cairo. In *Development, Change, and Gender in Cairo,* ed. Diane Singerman and Homa Hoodfar, pp. 27–50. Bloomington: University of Indiana Press.
Mahmood, Saba
2001   Feminist theory, embodiment, and the docile agent: Some reflections on the Egyptian Islamic revival. *Cultural Anthropology* 6, no. 2:202–36.

Malaby, Thomas
2001   The future of class? The role of temporality in class identity in Greece. *Journal of the Society for the Anthropology of Europe* 1, no. 1:4–8.

Margaritidou, Vaso, and Elizabeth Mesteneos
1991   *Aksiologhísi ton Ipiresíon Ikoyeniakoú Programmatismoú* [Evaluation of family planning services]. Athens: Etería Ikoyeniakoú Programmatismoú.
1992   The family planning centers in Greece. *International Journal of Health Sciences* 3, no. 1:25–31.

Martin, Emily
1987   *The Woman in the Body: A Cultural Analysis of Reproduction.* Boston: Beacon Press.

Martis, Nicolaos
1984   *The Falsification of Macedonian History.* Trans. from the Greek by Philip Smith. Athens: Ikaros.

McCaughey, Martha
1997   *Real Knockouts: The Physical Feminism of Women's Self-Defense.* New York: New York University Press.

McKinnon, Susan
1995   American kinship/American incest: Asymmetries in a scientific discourse. In *Naturalizing Power: Essays in Feminist Cultural Analysis,* ed. Sylvia Yanagisako and Carol Delaney, pp. 25–46. New York: Routledge.

McLaren, Angus
1984   *Reproductive Rituals: The Perception of Fertility in England from the Sixteenth Century to the Nineteenth Century.* London: Methuen.

McNay, Lois
1992   *Foucault and Feminism: Power, Gender, and the Self.* Boston: Northeastern University Press.
2000   *Gender and Agency: Reconfiguring the Subject in Feminist and Social Theory.* Cambridge, U.K.: Polity Press.

McNeill, William Hardy
1978   *The Metamorphosis of Greece since World War II.* Chicago: University of Chicago Press.

Meyendorff, John
1974   *Byzantine Theology.* London: Mowbray's.
Michas, Takis
1999   Athens dispatch: Modern Orthodox Greece leaves the West. *New Republic,* no. 4430 (3 December): 12–13.

Mitchell, Juliet
1971   *Women's Estate.* New York: Vintage Books.
Mitchell, Lisa, and Eugenia Georges
1997   Cross-cultural cyborgs: Greek and Canadian women's discourses on fetal ultrasound. *Feminist Studies* 23, no. 2:373–401.

Moore, Henrietta
1993   The differences within and the differences between. In *Gendered Anthropology*, ed. Teresa del Valle, pp. 193–204. London: Routledge.
Morgan, Lynn, and Meredith W. Michaels, eds.
1999   *Fetal Subjects, Feminist Positions*. Philadelphia: University of Pennsylvania Press.
Morgan, Robin, ed.
1984   *Sisterhood Is Global*. Garden City, N.Y.: Anchor Press.
Morsy, Soheir A.
1995   Deadly reproduction among Egyptian women: Maternal mortality and the medicalization of population control. In *Conceiving the New World Order: The Global Politics of Reproduction*, ed. Faye D. Ginsburg and Rayna Rapp, pp. 162–76. Berkeley: University of California Press.
Moschou-Sakorafou, Sasha
1988   Epiptósis stin ikoyénia apó tis metarithmísis tou ikoyeniakoú nomoú (1329/83) [The effects on the family as a result of the reforms of the family law]. *O Aghónas tis Yinékas* 39:19, 26–30.
Mourselas, Kostas
1992   *Red Dyed Hair*. Trans. from the Greek by Fred Reed. Athens: Kedros.
National Statistics Service of Greece (NSSG) [Ethnikí Statistikí Ypiresía Elládhos]
1992   *Statistical Yearbook of Greece, 1989*. Athens: NSSG.
1993   *Statistikí tis fisikís kiníseos tou plithismoú tis Elládhos, 1986* [Statistics on the natural movement of the population of Greece, 1986]. Athens: NSSG.
2002   *Greece in Figures, 2002*. Athens: NSSG.
Naziri, Despina
1989   I ellinídha ke i éktrosi: kinoniko-psychologhikí meléti tou fenoménou tis epanalamvanómeni prosfighís stin éktrosi [The Greek woman and abortion: Psychosocial study of repeated recourse to abortion]. *Psychologhiká Thémata* 2, no. 1:18–32.
1990   Le recours répétitif à l'avortement en Grèce: Comportement "marginal" ou étape du devenir-femme? *Sciences Sociales et Santé* 8, no. 3:86–106.
1991   The triviality of abortion in Greece. *Planned Parenthood in Europe* 20, no. 2:12–14.
Nelson, Diane
1999   *A Finger in the Wound: Body Politics in Quincentennial Guatemala*. Berkeley: University of California Press.
Neta, Sofia, and Anna Sterghiou
1995   I pio megháli mamá stin Elládha [The oldest mom in Greece]. *Eleftherotipía*, Tuesday, 18 July, p. 17.

Newman, Karen
1996   *Fetal Positions: Individualism, Science, Visuality.* Stanford: Stanford University Press.

Noddings, Nel
1984   *Caring: A Feminine Approach to Ethics and Moral Education.* Berkeley: University of California Press.

Oaks, Laury
2001   *Smoking and Pregnancy: The Politics of Fetal Protection.* New Brunswick: Rutgers University Press.

Ong, Aihwa
1996   Anthropology, China, and modernities: The geopolitics of cultural knowledge. In *The Future of Anthropological Knowledge,* ed. Henrietta Moore, pp. 60–92. London: Routledge.

Ortner, Sherry
1984   Theory in anthropology since the sixties. *Comparative Studies in Society and History* 26, no. 1:126–66.

Owoh, Kenna
1995   Gender and health in Nigerian structural adjustment: Locating room to maneuver. In *enGENDERing Wealth and Well-Being: Empowerment for Global Change,* ed. Rae Lesser Blumberg, Cathy A. Rakowski, Irene Tinker, and Michael Monteón, pp. 181–94. Boulder: Westview Press.

Panopoulos, Yiorgos
1994   Lipstick lesbians (in Greek). *Klik,* no. 83:64–69.

Panourgia, Neni
1995   *Fragments of Death, Fables of Identity: An Athenian Anthropography.* Madison: University of Wisconsin Press.

Papadopoulos, Theodoros N.
1998   Greek family policy from a comparative perspective. In *Women, Work, and the Family in Europe,* ed. Eileen Drew, Ruth Emerek, and Evelyn Mahon, pp. 47–57. London: Routledge.

Papagaroufali, Eleni, and Eugenia Georges
1993   Greek women in the Europe of 1992: Brokers of European cargoes and the logic of the west. In *Perilous States: Conversations on Culture, Politics, and Nation,* ed. George Marcus, pp. 235–54. Chicago: University of Chicago Press.

Papandreou, Margaret
1984   Greece: A village sisterhood. In *Sisterhood Is Global,* ed. Robin Morgan, pp. 272–77. Garden City, N.Y.: Anchor Press.

Papataxiarchis, Evthymios
1991   Friends of the heart: Male commensal solidarity, gender, and kinship in Aegean Greece. In *Contested Identities: Gender and Kinship in Modern Greece,* ed. Peter Loizos and Evthymios Papataxiarchis, pp. 156–79. Princeton: Princeton University Press.

Parker, Andrew, Mary Russo, Doris Sommer, and Patricia Yaeger
1992   Introduction to *Nationalisms and Sexualities,* ed. Andrew
              Parker, Mary Russo, Doris Sommer, and Patricia Yaeger, pp.
              1–18. New York: Routledge.
Parliament of Greece
1986   Transcript, sessions debating the legalizing of abortion. Athens.
1993   Pórisma, yia ti meléti tou dhimoghrafikoú provlímatos tis
              hóras ke dhiatíposi protáseon yia tin apotelesmatikí an-
              timetópisí tou [Findings, for the study of the demographic
              problem of the country and the formulation of recommenda-
              tions for its effective confrontation]. February. Athens.
Parsons, Susan F.
1987   Feminism and the logic of morality: A consideration of alterna-
              tives. In *Ethics: A Feminist Reader,* ed. Elizabeth Frazer, Jen-
              nifer Hornsby, and Sabina Lovibond, pp. 380–412. Oxford:
              Blackwell.
2002   *The Ethics of Gender.* Oxford: Blackwell.
Pateman, Carole
1988   *The Sexual Contract.* Stanford: Stanford University Press.
Patton, Cindy
1992   From nation to family: Containing "African AIDS." In *Nation-
              alisms and Sexualities,* ed. Andrew Parker, Mary Russo, Doris
              Sommer, and Patricia Yaeger, pp. 218–34. New York: Routledge.
Paxson, Heather
1997   Demographics and diaspora, gender and genealogy: Anthropo-
              logical notes on Greek population policy. *South European Soci-
              ety and Politics* 2, no. 2:34–56.
2002   Rationalizing sex: Family planning and the making of modern
              lovers in urban Greece. *American Ethnologist* 29, no. 2:1–28.
Pearce, Tola Olu
1995   Women's reproductive practices and biomedicine: Cultural
              conflicts and transformations in Nigeria. In *Conceiving the
              New World Order: The Global Politics of Reproduction,* ed.
              Faye D. Ginsburg and Rayna Rapp, pp. 195–208. Berkeley: Uni-
              versity of California Press.
Peristiany, John G., ed.
1966   *Honour and Shame: The Values of Mediterranean Society.*
              Chicago: University of Chicago Press.
Petchesky, Rosalind
1987   Fetal images: The power of visual culture in the politics of re-
              production. *Feminist Studies* 13, no. 2:263–92.
1990   *Abortion and Woman's Choice: The State, Sexuality, and Re-
              productive Freedom.* Rev. ed. Boston: Northeastern University
              Press.
1995   The body as property: A feminist re-vision. In *Conceiving the
              New World Order: The Global Politics of Reproduction,* ed.

Faye Ginsburg and Rayna Rapp, pp. 387–406. Berkeley: University of California Press.

Pfeffer, Naomi

1993   *The Stork and the Syringe: A Political History of Reproductive Medicine.* Cambridge, U.K.: Polity Press.

Philipson, Tomas J., and Richard A. Posner

1993   *Private Choices and Public Health: The AIDS Epidemic in an Economic Perspective.* Cambridge: Harvard University Press.

Piot, Charles

1999   *Remotely Global: Village Modernity in West Africa.* Chicago: University of Chicago Press.

Pitch, Tamar

1992   Decriminalization or legalization? The abortion debate in Italy. In *The Criminalization of a Woman's Body,* ed. Clarice Feinman, pp. 27–40. Binghamton, N.Y.: Harrington Park Press.

Pitt-Rivers, Julian

1966   Honour and social status. In *Honour and Shame: The Values of Mediterranean Society,* ed. John G. Peristiany, pp. 19–77. Chicago: University of Chicago Press.

Pollack, Scarlet

1984   Refusing to take women seriously: "Side effects" and the politics of contraception. In *Test-Tube Women: What Future for Motherhood?* ed. Rita Arditti, Renate Klein, and Shelley Minden, pp. 138–52. London: Pandora Press.

Pollis, Adamantia

1992   Greek national identity: Religious minorities, rights, and European norms. *Journal of Modern Greek Studies* 10, no. 2:171–95.

Prevelakis, George

1989   Culture, politics, and the urban crisis: The case of modern Athens. *Modern Greek Yearbook* 5:1–31.

Prokhovnik, Raia

1998   Public and private citizenship: From gender invisibility to feminist inclusiveness. *Feminist Review* 60:84–104.

Psaroudhaki, Nikolaou

1992   *Thélo na zíso* [I want to live]. Athens: Ekdhosis Oriothetísi.

Rabinow, Paul

1989   *French Modern: Norms and Forms of the Social Environment.* Cambridge: MIT Press.

Ragoné, Helena

1994   *Surrogate Motherhood: Conception in the Heart.* Boulder: Westview.

2000   Of likeness and difference: How race is being transfigured by gestational surrogacy. In *Ideologies and Technologies of Motherhood: Race, Class, Sexuality, Nationalism,* ed. Heléna Ragoné and France Winddance Twine, pp. 56–75. New York: Routledge.

Ragoné, Heléna, and France Winddance Twine, eds.
2000   *Ideologies and Technologies of Motherhood: Race, Class, Sexuality, Nationalism.* New York: Routledge.

Ram, Kalpana, and Margaret Jolly, eds.
1998   *Maternities and Modernities: Colonial and Postcolonial Experiences in Asia and the Pacific.* Cambridge: Cambridge University Press.

Rapp, Rayna
1982   Family and class in contemporary America: Notes toward an understanding of ideology. In *Rethinking the Family: Some Feminist Questions,* ed. Barrie Thorne and Marilyn Yalom, pp. 25–39. New York: Longman.

1988   The power of positive diagnosis: Medical and maternal discourses on amniocentesis. In *Childbirth in America,* ed. Karen Michaelson, pp. 103–16. South Hadley, Mass.: Bergin and Garvey.

1991   Moral pioneers: Women, men, and fetuses on a frontier of reproductive technology. In *Gender at the Crossroads of Knowledge,* ed. Micaela di Leonardo, pp. 383–95. Berkeley: University of California Press.

1999   *Testing Women, Testing the Fetus: The Social Impact of Amniocentesis in America.* New York: Routledge.

Raymond, Janice
1993   *Women as Wombs: Reproductive Technologies and the Battle over Women's Freedom.* New York: HarperCollins.

Renan, Ernest
[1882] 1990 What is a nation? In *Nation and Narration,* ed. Homi Bhabha, pp. 8–22. London: Routledge.

Rich, Adrienne
1980   Compulsory heterosexuality and the lesbian continuum. In *Women: Sex and Sexuality,* ed. Catharine Stimpson and Ethel Spector Person, pp. 62–91. Chicago: University of Chicago Press.

1986   *Of Woman Born: Motherhood in Experience and Institution.* New York: W. W. Norton and Company.

Riddle, John M.
1992   *Contraception and Abortion from the Ancient World to the Renaissance.* Cambridge: Harvard University Press.

Rivkin-Fish, Michele
1999   Sexuality education in Russia: Defining pleasure and danger for a fledgling democratic society. *Social Science and Medicine* 49, no. 6:801–14.

2000   Health development meets the end of state socialism: Visions of democratization, women's health, and social well-being for contemporary Russia. *Culture, Medicine, and Psychiatry* 24:77–100.

Rofel, Lisa
1999   *Other Modernities: Gendered Yearnings in China after Social-
            ism.* Berkeley: University of California Press.
Rothman, Barbara Katz
1984   The meanings of choice in reproductive technology. In *Test-
            Tube Women: What Future for Motherhood?* ed. Rita Arditti,
            Renate Klein, and Shelley Minden, pp. 23–33. London: Pandora
            Press.
1986   *The Tentative Pregnancy: Prenatal Diagnosis and the Future of
            Motherhood.* New York: Viking.
1989   *Recreating Motherhood: Ideology and Technology in a Patriar-
            chal Society.* New York: W. W. Norton and Company.
Rousseau, Jean-Jacques
[1762] 1967 *The Social Contract and Discourse on the Origin of Inequality.*
            Edited by Lester G. Crocker. New York: Washington Square
            Press.
Rubin, Gayle
1975   The traffic in women: Notes on the political economy of sex. In
            Toward an Anthropology of Women, ed. Rayna Reiter Rapp,
            pp. 157–210. New York: Monthly Review Press.
Russell, Andrew, Elisa J. Sobo, and Mary S. Thompson, eds.
2000   *Contraception across Cultures: Technologies, Choices, Con-
            straints.* Oxford: Berg.
Said, Edward
1978   *Orientalism.* New York: Pantheon Books.
Salamone, S. D., and J. B. Stanton
1986   Introducing the nikokyra: Ideality and reality in social process.
            In *Gender and Power in Rural Greece,* ed. Jill Dubisch, pp.
            97–120. Princeton: Princeton University Press.
Saporiti, Angelo
1989   Historical changes in the family's reproductive patterns. In
            *Changing Patterns of European Family Life: A Comparative
            Analysis of Fourteen European Countries,* ed. Katja Boh,
            Maren Bak, and Cristine Clason, pp. 191–215. London: Rout-
            ledge.
Schein, Louisa
1999   Performing modernity. *Cultural Anthropology* 14, no.
            3:361–95.
Scheper-Hughes, Nancy, and Margaret Lock
1991   The message in the bottle: Illness and the micropolitics of re-
            sistance. *Journal of Psychohistory* 18, no. 14:409–31.
Schneider, David
1968   *American Kinship: A Cultural Account.* Chicago: Chicago Uni-
            versity Press.
1969   Kinship, nationality, and religion in American culture. In *Sym-
            bolic Action,* ed. Victor Turner, pp. 116–25. Tulane: American
            Ethnological Society.

1976   The meaning of incest. *Journal of Polynesian Society* 85, no. 2:149–69.

Schneider, Jane
1971   Of vigilance and virgins: Honor, shame, and access to resources in Mediterranean societies. *Ethnology* 10, no. 1:1–24.

Schneider, Jane, and Peter Schneider
1995   Coitus interruptus and family respectability in Catholic Europe. In *Conceiving the New World Order: The Global Politics of Reproduction*, ed. Faye D. Ginsburg and Rayna Rapp, pp. 177–94. Berkeley: University of California Press.

Schoepf, Brooke Grundfest
1997   AIDS, gender, and sexuality during Africa's economic crisis. In *African Feminism: The Politics of Survival in Sub-Saharan Africa*, ed. Gwendolyn Mikell, pp. 310–32. Philadelphia: University of Pennsylvania Press.

Scott, James C.
1987   *Weapons of the Weak: Everyday Forms of Peasant Resistance.* New Haven: Yale University Press.

Segura, Denise A.
1994   Working at motherhood: Chicana and Mexican immigrant mothers and employment. In *Mothering: Ideology, Experience, and Agency*, ed. Evelyn Nakano Glenn, Grace Chang, and Linda Rennie Forcey, pp. 211–33. New York: Routledge.

Sekerli, Lena
1994   Eghkimosíni me omorfía [Pregnancy with beauty]. *Yinéka*, no. 1105:176–79.

Seremetakis, C. Nadia
1991   *The Last Word: Women, Death, and Divination in Inner Mani.* Chicago: University of Chicago Press.
1996   In search of the barbarians: Borders in pain. *American Anthropologist* 98, no. 3:487–511.

Shorter, Edward
1975   *The Making of the Modern Family.* New York: Basic Books.

Siampos, George
1975   Law and fertility in Greece. In *Law and Fertility in Europe.* Vol. 2, ed. M. Kirk, M. Bacci, and E. Szabady. Brussels: Dolhain.

Sikaki-Douka, Aleka
1993   *O toketós íne aghápi* [Childbirth is love]. 4th ed. Athens, n.p.

Skilogianis, Joanna
1997   Negotiating fertility in urban Greece: Traditional methods and modern ideas. Paper presented at the American Ethnological Society Meetings as part of the panel "New Technologies, New Ethnographies: Cultural and Canonical Changes in the Study of Reproduction in Greece," Seattle, 6–9 March.

Spallone, Patricia
1989   *Beyond Conception: The New Politics of Reproduction.* Cambridge: Bergin and Garvey Publishers.

Spanidou, Irini
1987   God's Snake. New York: W. W. Norton, 1986. Reprint, New
                York: Viking Penguin.
Spelman, Elizabeth
1983   Aristotle and the politization of the soul. In Discovering Real-
                ity: Feminist Perspectives on Epistemology, Metaphysics,
                Methodology, and Philosophy of Science, ed. Sandra Harding
                and Merrill B. Hintikka, pp. 17–30. Dordrecht, Holland: D. Rei-
                del.
St. Clair, William
1972   That Greece Might Still Be Free: The Philhellenes in the War of
                Independence. London: Oxford University Press.
Stamiris, Eleni
1986   The women's movement in Greece. New Left Review
                158:98–112.
Stark, Nancy
2000   My body, my problem: Contraceptive decision-making among
                rural Bangladeshi women. In Contraception across Cultures:
                Technologies, Choices, Constraints, ed. Andrew Russell, Elisa J.
                Sobo, and Mary S. Thompson, pp. 179–196. Oxford: Berg.
Stewart, Charles
1991   Demons and the Devil: Moral Imagination in Modern Greek
                Culture. Princeton: Princeton University Press.
Stivens, Maila
1998   Modernizing the Malay mother. In Maternities and Moderni-
                ties: Colonial and Postcolonial Experiences in Asia and the Pa-
                cific, ed. Kalpana Ram and Margaret Jolly, pp. 50–80. Cam-
                bridge: Cambridge University Press.
Stolcke, Verena
1988   New reproductive technologies: The old quest for fatherhood.
                Reproductive and Genetic Engineering 1, no. 1:5–19.
1993   Is sex to gender as race is to ethnicity? In Gendered Anthropol-
                ogy, ed. Teresa del Valle, pp. 17–37. London: Routledge.
Strathern, Marilyn
1980   No nature, no culture: The Hagen case. In Nature, Culture, and
                Gender, ed. Carol MacCormack and Marilyn Strathern, pp.
                174–222. Cambridge: Cambridge University Press.
1988   The Gender of the Gift. Berkeley: University of California
                Press.
1992a   After Nature: English Kinship in the Late Twentieth Century.
                Cambridge: Cambridge University Press.
1992b   Reproducing the Future: Anthropology, Kinship, and the New
                Reproductive Technologies. New York: Routledge.

Sutton, David

1994   "Tradition and modernity": Kalymnian constructions of identity and otherness. *Journal of Modern Greek Studies* 12, no. 2:239–60.

1997   Local names, foreign claims: Family inheritance and national heritage on a Greek island. *American Ethnologist* 24, no. 2:415–37.

Sutton, Susan Buck

1986   Family and work: New patterns for village women in Athens. *Journal of Modern Greek Studies* 4, no. 1:33–49.

Symeonidou, Haris

1990   *Apaschólisi ke gonimótita ton yinekón stin periohí tis protévousas* [Occupation and fertility of women in greater Athens]. Athens: Ethnikó Kéntro Kinonikón Erevnón.

1994   Fertility: Trends and projections. Paper presented at the public symposium, "Contemporary Demographic Trends and Family Planning in Greece," sponsored by the Family Planning Association of Greece, Athens, 21 January.

Tabet, Paola

1987   Imposed reproduction: Maimed sexuality. *Feminist Issues* 7, no. 2:3–32.

Taylor, Janelle S.

1992   The public fetus and the family car: From abortion politics to a Volvo advertisement. *Public Culture* 4, no. 2:67–80.

1998   Image of contradiction: Obstetrical ultrasound in American culture. In *Reproducing Reproduction: Kinship, Power, and Technological Innovation*, ed. Sarah Franklin and Helena Ragoné, pp. 15–45. Philadelphia: University of Pennsylvania Press.

Thompson, Mary S.

2000   Family planning or reproductive health? Interpreting policy and providing family planning services in highland Chiapas, Mexico. In *Contraception across Cultures: Technologies, Choices, Constraints*, ed. Andrew Russell, Elisa J. Sobo, and Mary S. Thompson, pp. 221–43. Oxford: Berg.

Tolley, Keith

1994   Risky sex and economic reason: Review of *Private Choices and Public Health: The AIDS Epidemic in an Economic Perspective*, by Tomas J. Philipson and Richard A. Posner. *The Times Higher Education Supplement* (London), 1 July.

Treichler, Paula

1990   Feminism, medicine, and the meaning of childbirth. In *Body/Politics: Women and the Discourses of Science*, ed. Mary Jacobus, Evelyn Fox Keller, and Sally Shuttleworth, pp. 113–38. New York: Routledge.

Tsalicoglou, Fotini

1995   A new disease in Greek society: AIDS and the representation of "otherness." *Journal of Modern Greek Studies* 13, no. 1:83–97.

Tseperi, Popi, and Elizabeth Mestheneos

1994   Paradoxes in the costs of family planning in Greece. *Planned Parenthood in Europe* 23, no. 1:14.

Tsing, Anna Lowenhaupt

1990   Monster stories: Women charged with perinatal endangerment. In *Uncertain Terms: Negotiating Gender in America*, ed. Anna Lowenhaupt Tsing and Faye Ginsburg, pp. 282–99. Boston: Beacon Press.

Tsoucalas, Constantine

1991   "Enlightened" concepts in the "dark": Power and freedom, politics and society. *Journal of Modern Greek Studies* 9, no. 1:1–22.

Tzannatos, Zafiris

1989   Women's wages and equal pay in Greece. *Journal of Modern Greek Studies* 7, no. 1:155–69.

Vaiou, Dina

1992   Gender divisions in urban space: Beyond the rigidity of dualist classifications. *Antipode* 24, no. 4:247–62.

Valaoras, Vasilios, and Dimitri Trichopoulos

1970   Abortion in Greece. In *Abortion in a Changing World*. Vol. 1, ed. Robert E. Hall, pp. 284–90. New York: Columbia University Press.

Van Eeuwijk, Brigit Obrist, and Susan Mlangwa

1997   Competing ideologies: Adolescence, knowledge, and silences in Dar es Salaam. In *Power, Reproduction, and Gender: The Intergenerational Transfer of Knowledge*, ed. Wendy Harcourt, pp. 35–57. London: Zed Books.

Vance, Carole S.

1984   Pleasure and danger: Toward a politics of sexuality. In *Pleasure and Danger: Exploring Female Sexuality*, ed. Carole S. Vance, pp. 1–27. Boston: Routledge and Kegan Paul.

Vidali, Maria

1999   Living in a policy vacuum: The plight of Albanian immigrants in Greece. *Central Europe Review* 1, no. 21.

Visakowitz, Susan

2001   Impossible ethics: The connections between ontology, ethics, and the experiencing of womanhood. M.A. thesis, John W. Draper Program in Humanities and Social Thought, New York University.

Ware, Timothy

1963   *The Orthodox Church*. New York: Penguin Books.

Weeks, Jeffrey
 1995   *Invented Moralities: Sexual Values in an Age of Uncertainty.*
           New York: Columbia University Press.

Whitbeck, Caroline
 1990   Love, knowledge, and transformation. In *Hypatia Reborn: Es-
           says in Feminist Philosophy*, ed. Azizah Y. al-Hibri and Mar-
           garet A. Simons, pp. 204–25. Bloomington: Indiana University
           Press.

Williams, Raymond
 1977   *Marxism and Literature.* Oxford: Oxford University Press.

Yanagisako, Sylvia, and Jane Collier
 1987   Toward a unified analysis of gender and kinship. In *Gender and
           Kinship: Essays toward a Unified Analysis*, ed. Jane Collier and
           Sylvia Yanagisako, pp. 14–50. Stanford: Stanford University
           Press.

Yanagisako, Sylvia, and Carol Delaney
 1995   Naturalizing power. In *Naturalizing Power: Essays in Feminist
           Cultural Analysis*, ed. Sylvia Yanagisako and Carol Delaney,
           pp. 1–22. New York: Routledge.

Zinovieff, Sofka
 1991   Hunters and hunted: Kamaki and the ambiguities of sexual pre-
           dation in a Greek town. In *Contested Identities: Gender and
           Kinship in Modern Greece*, ed. Peter Loizos and Evthymios Pa-
           pataxiarchis, pp. 203–20. Princeton: Princeton University Press.

Index

abortion: as birth control method, 54–55, 143; criminalization of, 52–54, 271n23; decline in numbers of, 136; as demographic problem, 163, 196–97; within ethic of choice, 181, 182–83, 198; within ethic of service, 34, 51–52, 55–56, 58–60, 143–44, 199; within ethic of well-being, 35–36, 137–38, 199; family planning alternatives to, 102–3, 119, 126; feminist campaign to legalize, 180–84, 183 fig.; fertility decline linked to, 163, 185, 283nn41,42; hidden aspect of, 58–59, 147; *ikonomía* notion of, 61–62; for incestuous pregnancy, 145–46, 147; medical dangers of, 136–38, 140; method of, in Greece, 283–84n42; Orthodox church on, 60–61; parliamentary debate on, 184–89; pro-life movement against, 189–92, 191 fig.; as rationalized paradox, 121; resistance theory on, 122–23, 125–27; tradition-modernity clash on, 32, 140–41; ultrasound and, 246–47. *See also* legal abortion
abortion rate: compared to birthrate, 3, 173; compared to contraceptive methods, 106; compared to pregnancies, 163; before legalized abortion, 54, 112; in southern European countries, 272n28, 281n26; in United States, 112, 278n8

Abu-Lughod, Lila, 253
adoption, 194, 221–22, 289n6
advertising: for abortions, 53, 115; consumer-mother of, 241–46, 242 fig., 244 fig., 245 fig.; for contraceptive methods, 108, 133, 143, 194
After Nature (Strathern), 212
Aftónomi Kínisi Yinekón (Autonomous Women's Movement), 180, 181, 182, 183 fig.
Afxendiou, Georgia, 84
agency. *See* reproductive agency
aghápi (enduring love): in family planning context, 155; of heterosexual relationship, 149–50; of maternal relationship, 95–96
Agnew, Spiro, 272n32
agricultural communities. *See* rural communities
AIDS: cases of, in Greece, 132, 282nn30,31; and decline in abortions, 136, 283n39; misperceptions about, 282–83n32; prophylactic protection against, 133, 134–35
Albanians: birthrate of, 162; as refugees, 169, 176; as scapegoats, 176
Alexander, Katherine, 39, 52; abortion experiences of, 56–58, 271n26; background of, 271n24
Alexander the Great, 169, 171, 286n9
Allen, Peter, 272n31

Compositor:	Impressions Book and Journal Services, Inc.
Text:	10/13 Aldus
Display:	Aldus
Printer and Binder:	Malloy Lithographing, Inc.
Index:	Patricia Deminna